Obeah, Orisa, and Religious Identity in Trinidad
Volume II

Religious Cultures of African
and African Diaspora People

SERIES EDITORS

Jacob K. Olupona, *Harvard University*
Dianne M. Stewart, *Emory University*
and Terrence L. Johnson, *Georgetown University*

The book series examines the religious, cultural, and political expressions of African,
African American, and African Caribbean
traditions. Through transnational, cross-
cultural, and multidisciplinary approaches to
the study of religion, the series investigates
the epistemic boundaries of continental and
diasporic religious practices and thought
and explores the diverse and distinct ways
African-derived religions inform culture and
politics. The series aims to establish a forum
for imagining the centrality of Black religions
in the formation of the "New World."

DIANNE M. STEWART

Obeah,

VOLUME II
ORISA

Orisa

&

Religious
Identity
in   Trinidad

Africana Nations and the Power
of Black Sacred Imagination

DUKE UNIVERSITY PRESS—DURHAM AND LONDON—2022

Printed in the United States of America on acid-free paper ∞
Designed by Aimee C. Harrison
Typeset in Quadraat Pro and Avenir LT Std
by Westchester Publishing Services

Library of Congress Cataloging-in-Publication Data
Names: Stewart, Dianne M., author.
Title: Obeah, Orisa, and religious identity in Trinidad. Volume II,
Orisa : Africana nations and the power of black sacred imagination /
Dianne M. Stewart.
Other titles: Orisa : Africana nations and the power of black sacred
imagination | Religious cultures of African and African diaspora people.
Description: Durham : Duke University Press, 2022. | Series: Religious
cultures of African and African diaspora people | Includes bibliographical
references and index.
Identifiers: LCCN 2022020297 (print) | LCCN 2022020298 (ebook)
ISBN 9781478013921 (hardcover) | ISBN 9781478014867 (paperback)
ISBN 9781478022152 (ebook)
Subjects: LCSH: Orisha religion—Trinidad and Tobago—Trinidad—
History. | Religion and sociology—Trinidad and Tobago—Trinidad—
History. | Religions—African influences. | Black people—Trinidad and
Tobago—Trinidad—Religion—History. | Cults—Law and legislation—
Trinidad and Tobago—Trinidad—History. | Religion and law—Trinidad
and Tobago—Trinidad—History. | Postcolonialism—Trinidad and
Tobago—Trinidad. | Trinidad—Religion—African influences. | BISAC:
RELIGION / General | SOCIAL SCIENCE / Anthropology / Cultural & Social
Classification: LCC BL2532.S5 S749 2022 (print) | LCC BL2532.S5 (ebook) |
DDC 299.60972983—dc23/eng/20220729
LC record available at https://lccn.loc.gov/2022020297
LC ebook record available at https://lccn.loc.gov/2022020298

Cover art: Page from a Trinidad colonial slave register reprinted
by permission from National Archives (of the United Kingdom).
Photograph of procession reprinted by permission from the
Adefundara Foundation.

This book is freely available in an open access edition thanks to
TOME (Toward an Open Monograph Ecosystem)—a collaboration
of the Association of American Universities, the Association of
University Presses, and the Association of Research Libraries—
and the generous support of Emory University and the Andrew W.
Mellon Foundation. Learn more at the TOME website, available
at: openmonographs.org.

I dedicate this work to Dr. Josiah U. Young III,
my first mentor and most influential professor
of African and African diaspora religions.

&

To all omorisa in Trinidad and Tobago
for showing us how to become new evocations of ashé.

Contents

Abbreviations Used in Text

ACA	African Cultural Association
ATL	Afro Turf Limers
AUB	African Unity Brothers
BEW&CHRP	British Empire Workers and Citizens Home Rule Party
BP	Butler Party
BPM	Black Power Movement
CCCADI	Caribbean Cultural Center African Diaspora Institute
CMS	Church Missionary Society
EOE	Egbe Onisin Eledumare
EOIW	Egbe Orisa Ile Wa
HID	Harmony in Diversity
IESOM	Ile Eko Sango/Osun Mil'Osa
IRO	Inter-Religious Organization
IRSC	Inter-Religious Steering Committee
ISA	Industrialization Stabilization Act
KCAII	Kenny Cyrus Alkebulan Ile Ijuba
MNDSI	Ministry of National Diversity and Social Integration
NCOE	National Council of Orisa Elders of Trinidad and Tobago
NJAC	National Joint Action Committee
OOS	Opa Orisha Shango

OPO	Obeah Prohibition Ordinance
OWTU	Oilfield Workers' Trade Union
OYCO	Orisa Youths Cultural Organization
PDP	People's Democratic Party
POSG	*Port of Spain Gazette*
PNM	People's National Movement
SDMS	Sanatan Dharma Maha Saba
SJU	Saint James United
SLM	Southern Liberation Movement
SOA	Summary Offences Act
SPAO	Society of Peoples of African Origin
SPO	Shouters Prohibition Ordinance
T&T	Trinidad and Tobago
TIWU	Transport and Industrial Workers Union
TLP	Trinidad Labour Party
TWA	Trinidad Workingmen's Association
UMROBI	United Movement for the Reconstruction of Black Identity
UNC	United National Congress
UNIA	United Negro Improvement Association
WIRC	West India Royal Commission

Note on Orthography and Terminology

This volume uses concepts and words from the Yorùbá language of Nigeria and neighboring regions in West Africa. Diacritical marks are applied to Yoruba terms when referencing the phenomenon of Yorùbá-Òrìṣà religion and other phenomena on the African continent but not for generic references or for references to the Yoruba-Orisa religion in Trinidad and other parts of the African diaspora. I aimed to avoid the Anglicizing convention of forming plural nouns by adding "s" to a singular noun and used "Orisa" to represent the singular and plural forms as much as possible. At times, I do conform to the conventional pluralization of nouns such as Yoruba (pl. Yorubas). No such term appears in the Yorùbá language, and when I do use it, I do so for semantic simplicity because I am working in the English language. Consistent with volume I of this study, I adopt a semantic strategy of employing the capital "O" when referencing Africana conceptions of "Obeah" and the lowercase "o" when referencing the colonial invention of "obeah"—colonial imaginings, beliefs, discursive ideologies, and the like.

Conveying meanings is undoubtedly a slippery exercise because words fail to capture everything about a given phenomenon. I therefore introduce my own neologisms and strategies for approximating meanings of import to my conceptual analysis and explanatory frameworks. These terms include the stem concept of *"nation"* and many related words formed from this stem: *nationhood, nation-building, nationscapes, nationalism, multi-nation-al, inter-nation-al*, and so on. All such terms are printed in italics to underscore the point that I do not consider these terms to be English or Western terms. They might look similar to English terms such as nation, nationhood, nation-building, and the like, but they refer to identities and affiliations that cannot be reduced to race, ethnicity, the nation-state, and the identities it inspires. The first "a" in the terms *multi-nation-al* and *inter-nation-al* is pronounced as a long "a" as in the name "Tracey."

Other terms, such as *creactivity, numenym, motherland-ing, motherlanding,* and *motherness/motherness,* are explained in notes or the text itself. Because I draw from theorists whose works predate the interventions of Afropessimist and black nihilist scholars, I admit I use terminology that some critics will reject as impositions from a Western metaphysical and scholastic infrastructure. I do not contest such criticisms. However, I will have to wait for another project to sufficiently deploy Yoruba and other African indigenous concepts for phenomena, thoughts, and knowledge that best translate or render irrelevant Western English terms such as human, humanity, person, world, phenomenon, ontology, relation, and being. I only experiment with a few alternative concepts in this volume that can potentially anchor a more developed conceptual paradigm in subsequent scholarship.

In the last two chapters, when the discussion exhibits a more focused awareness of Afropessimist analytical interventions in black studies, I often place terms such as "world" and "worldmaking" under erasure using the strikethrough feature (~~world~~, ~~worldmaking~~) to signal that my use of these words emerges from religious studies frameworks (rather than philosophical theories) concerning the role of sacred poetics (religious ideas, practices, symbols, myths, and invisible powers, deities, and spirits) in orienting Africana communities as they navigate their environments. Similarly, mindful of the Afropessimist argument that blacks have no access to the human, when appropriate, I experiment with the terms "~~human~~," ~~humanity~~, and "~~human being~~." I implore the reader's sympathies for the semantic nuances these terms and their orthographic inscriptions are intended to capture and hope they contribute to a more profound appreciation of the peoples and phenomena under investigation once encountered in the volume.

Terms such as Iyalorisa (Iya) and Babalorisa (Baba) are priestly titles similar to Reverend and Imam. Their shortened forms can also serve as familial and social identifiers such as "mother" and "father" or "head" (leader). Exceptions to my orthographic preferences and terminology are made when citing sources that do not follow the conventions I use.

Preface

Obeah, Orisa, and Religious Identity in Trinidad is a collaborative study, the fruition of an idea that germinated in the plush accommodations of the Hotel Nacional de Cuba in Havana, Cuba, during the spring of 1994. Tracey Hucks and I were attending *El Segundo Encuentro Internacional Yoruba*, an international conference on Yoruba religion, and among the panelists was Iyalorisa Dr. Molly Ahye, an Orisa priestess from Trinidad and Tobago (T&T). We had read about Trinidad's Yoruba tradition of "Shango" in books by George Simpson and his mentor Melville Herskovits, who received a grant of $3,250 from the Carnegie Corporation to conduct research in Trinidad in 1939, but we had much to learn about the richness of Trinidad's Yoruba diaspora. We were determined to do so after meeting Molly Ahye.

Iya Molly lectured on the Yoruba-Orisa religion in Trinidad and Tobago. In addition to describing the ritual and ceremonial life of the Orisa community, she discussed Orisa devotees' struggle for religious freedom, a struggle they seemed to be winning—at least to a much greater degree than their counterparts in other regions of the African diaspora. By the end of our trip, we began to envision a womanist approach of "harmonizing and coordinating" our scholarly efforts to coproduce a volume on the Orisa religion in Trinidad and the role of women in the tradition's transformation during the latter decades of the twentieth century.[1] We were graduate students at the time and knew this book idea would be a future project for both of us.

We made our first research trip to Trinidad in December 1998 and over two decades conducted archival and field research that resulted in not one but two volumes, which we both expected and did not expect. Our two-volume project, as the title suggests, expanded beyond a focus on Orisa to incorporate a study of Obeah, an opaque repertoire of African spiritual systems that has been practiced throughout the Caribbean and regions of the Americas. In our first monographs, I wrote about Obeah and Tracey about Orisa; in this case, we switched subjects because Tracey was better suited to address the historical framing of Obeah in early colonial Trinidad. We determined too that I was better suited to explore how Orisa devotees intellectualize and make meaning out of their beliefs and spirituality. In this endeavor, I address our original aim for this project by engaging womanist and feminist discourses to examine institutional developments within the Orisa tradition and shifts in both internal and external narratives of Orisa presence and practice in post-1980s Trinidad. During this period Molly Ahye and other contemporary Orisa mothers held prominence as local and global leaders in this rapidly changing religious culture, and we discovered that a proper treatment of their contributions required me to flesh out other pertinent themes. Thus, volume II expanded into a study of the religious imagination and sacred poetics of African descendants—"Yaraba" nation-builders, Black Power sacred scientists, and women-mothers—in Trinidad who over a century and a half have held together "a moving continuity"[2] they have called "Ebo," "the Yaraba Dance," "Yaraba Work," "African Work," "Orisa Work," "Shango," "Ifa," and "Orisa."

While the project unfolded, we developed new perspectives as a result of our wider scholarly activities. We also offered direction to the field of black religious studies, especially through our 2013 article, "Africana Religious Studies: Toward a Transdisciplinary Agenda in an Emerging Field," which appeared in the inaugural issue of the Journal of Africana Religions. In that article we revisited the Herskovits/Frazier debate, its cultural and ideological context, and its impact on theoretical and methodological norms in the scholarship of academics trained in black religious studies/theology. We specifically explored roughly seventy-five years of knowledge production that, with few exceptions, had reduced black religion to black church studies and black Christian theology. Far too many works had missed opportunities to conceptualize black people's African religious heritage. The scholarship gave little attention to the "image of Africa" in the black religious imagination, limiting our understanding of the polyreligious and polycultural realities that indeed characterized the spiritual lives of enslaved Africans in the United States and elsewhere.[3] We concluded our article by providing some of the conceptual architecture and theoretical justifications for transdisciplinary Africana Religious Studies research as a way forward in twenty-first-century scholarship on African-descended peoples—their religions and cultures—in the Americas and the Caribbean.

While seeking to enrich Caribbean and Africana studies, we imagine this project as a contribution to a developing body of research in religious studies on the methodology we began to formulate in our 2013 article. Tracey approached the archives with the intention of examining Obeah as an assemblage of Africana sacred practices and cosmologies. Instead, what she unearthed in the archives on Trinidad was a colonial cult of obeah fixation operating as a lived religion.[4] Our most salient definition of religion in this project rests within the tradition of Charles H. Long. For Longians, religion is "orientation in the ultimate sense, that is, how one comes to terms with the ultimate significance of one's place in the world."[5] The colonial cult of obeah fixation "comes to terms" with its "place in the world" through imaginations and persecutions of Obeah/African religions. In the colonial imagination, obeah functions as *cultus* (derived from the Latin words to inhabit, habitation, toiling over something; variant stem of *colere*, meaning till—the Old English word for station, fixed point).

With this etymology in mind, *cultus* encompasses the concept of inhabiting a fixed point. Tracey discovered a singular and fixed approach to Obeah in the colonial archives that reduced it to an imaginary terrorizing supernatural blackness. African Obeah was virtually eclipsed by colonial obeah, a set of beliefs, rites, practices, and meanings mapped onto an imaginary enfleshed terror—the black body. Within this fixed orientation, ridding colonial Trinidad of obeah became of vital (and violent) significance to its civic, social, and public tapestry. Such devotion is what bound members of the colonial cult of obeah fixation one to another. Volume I courageously interprets the cult's lived religion by taking up the topic of obeah and African religious repression. Thus, refracted through a chronological account of African religious repression (volume I, authored by Tracey E. Hucks) and struggles for religious freedom (volume II, authored by Dianne M. Stewart), our study of Trinidad attends to the problem of religious identity as an outgrowth of colonial "racecraft":[6] it excavates the authentic religious identity of colonial whites and offers a textured theoretical interpretation of Africana religion as a healing modality that has provided blacks with authenticating narratives, identities, and modes of belonging. Bridging phenomenology of religion, indigenous hermeneutics,[7] and black affect theory, our interpretation pioneers an affective turn in Africana Religious Studies and underscores haunting insights of Afropessimist and black nihilist conversations that never lose sight of the black "death-bound-subject."[8]

Equally significant, our volumes contribute to the wider fields of religion and Africana/black studies in several respects. First, through explorations of colonial obeah, African Obeah, and Orisa, they excavate the phenomenon of relationality to expand the definitional and theoretical terrain for conceptualizing religion as sites of black care *and* black harm. An analytic of relationality has considerable implications for the broader study of religion.[9] It provides a lens for investigating contacts, interactions, and exchanges among and across seen and unseen persons/entities. Whether within the context of religious traditions or within social structures broadly speaking, relationality is an indispensable guiding category for assessing intimacies that reveal and conceal individuals' and groups' authentic religion. Our collaborative study demonstrates that although orientation is the first step in the creation of a religious ethos, it is relationality that sustains a religious ethos and actually gives rise to religion, whether that religion is established through intimate care, intimate terrorism, or something else. Orientation determines positionings and suggests locative awareness, while relationality operationalizes the perceptions and affects that substantiate them. Considering the singularity of whites' collective soul-life, we take seriously William James's designation of religion as "the feelings, acts and experiences of individual[s] . . . so far as they apprehend themselves to stand *in relation to* what-ever they may consider divine."[10] This understanding of religion accords with our privileging of affect and its mobilizing power in the making of religion. Interpreting colonial affects, however, led us to conclude that what white colonists considered divine was the image of themselves tethered to the mutilated black body; and the black body was a divine mirror of the white soul—the sacred fetish whites needed and created to live, breathe, and have their being. Sadly, as innovative as James was in theorizing religion, he was terribly shortsighted in his impoverished understanding of African religions. Our study both invalidates James's shortsightedness and embraces his privileging of affects, experiences, and relationality which help us to interrogate dimensions of religiosity that James himself could not perceive, namely *white racecraft as lived religion*.[11]

Second and relatedly, in its investigation of the white colonial imagination our study offers a new theoretical interpretation of lived religion. Third, using indigenous hermeneutics, it theorizes *nationhood* in the Americas and the Caribbean as an autonomous Africana index of identity. Fourth, it contributes to Africana Religious Studies a foundational methodological imperative and method of applying indigenous hermeneutics within comparative assessments of African and African diasporic cultures/religions. Fifth, it elevates the Africana concept of *work* as a religious studies category for ritual practice and spiritual intervention. Sixth, it advances a mode of theological reflection that privileges religious imagination and cultural values rather than systematic approaches to doctrine. Seventh, its analysis of white colonial responses to African heritage religions and its interrogation of the religious nature of antiblackness establish a new point of departure for theorizing white libidinal power. Eighth, it connects threads of continuity among African and African diasporic womanisms and feminisms through the non-gendered Africana concept of *motherness* and establishes an arena within Africana/black studies for further comparisons of womanist and black feminist intellectual lineages.

Book-length studies on Trinidadian Obeah and Orisa are still quite sparse, but to our knowledge, anthropologists and other social scientists have produced them. To help balance the growing number of important ethnographies that focus on Orisa ceremonies and rituals, and to expose the religious dimensions of white colonial power, we emphasize what religious studies scholars are trained to examine: the symbols, originary narratives (myths), performances, practices, rituals, and experiences that orient religious persons as they confront limits and shape possibilities for themselves. As scholars in the humanities—a trained historian of religion and a theologian—we treat interiority perhaps as much as we do the exterior worlds of the figures and personalities the reader will meet throughout each volume. Privileging their sacred poetics and self-narrations whenever possible, we offer what we believe is a new way to think about black religion, black religious imagination, black love, and religious belonging in the African diaspora.

Bringing this project to completion involved numerous field trips to Trinidad between 1998 and 2013 and one continuous year of ethnographic fieldwork (2000–2001), during which we visited Orisa shrines across the nation; frequented rituals, ceremonies, and educational workshops; and conducted more than forty interviews and two oral histories. Our research also involved combing through disparate sets of archives in Trinidad, Nigeria, Cuba, Jamaica, France, England, and the United States. Most of these trips were undertaken to conduct archival research at the National Archives of Trinidad and Tobago; Heritage Library of Trinidad and Tobago; University of the West Indies, Mona, Jamaica; University of the West Indies, St. Augustine, Trinidad; Bibliothèque Nationale de France; Bibliothèque du Saulchoir; British Library; National Archives in Kew Gardens; Lambeth Palace Library; School of Oriental and African Studies, University of London; Northwestern University Archives; and the Schomburg Center for Research in Black Culture. We also gained access to Hansard Reports, Bills, and Acts of Parliament from the Parliament of the Republic of Trinidad and Tobago, as well as unpublished correspondence, minutes, devotional literature, and educational materials at various Orisa shrines in Trinidad. Nonetheless, although we believe both volumes reflect our careful historical and ethnographic work on Obeah and Orisa, they are not intended to be comprehensive histories or ethnographies of these traditions. Rather, they bear witness to the dynamic endurance of African heritage religions among Trinidad's pluralistic black diasporas, identifying Africa as the epistemic source of an enduring spiritual legacy and potent religious orientation across three centuries. This theoretical move propitiously anticipates productive scholarly frameworks in the future of Obeah and Orisa studies. But it also demands a sea change in how scholars analyze global antiblackness and account for the foundational pillars of religions in the Americas and the Caribbean.

Dianne M. Stewart and Tracey E. Hucks

Acknowledgments

Numerous persons assisted, inspired, and supported me throughout my journey with this book. I must begin by acknowledging my collaborator, Dr. Tracey E. Hucks, who had to convince me that committing to this joint two-volume project should take priority over my immediate plans. After writing my first book on Africana religions in Jamaica, I was prepared to return to Jamaica to do more research on African heritage religions there before pursuing a project on Trinidad. So, I initially refused Tracey's invitation to travel with her to Trinidad to follow up on what we had learned from Iya Dr. Molly Ahye about her country's Yoruba-Orisa religion and other Africana religions. I soon realized that Tracey's idea was an excellent one for both of our research agendas, given Trinidad's rich multicultural African heritage. But even more, I experienced the power and rewards of Orisa devotional life in Trinidad and was welcomed with authentic generosity everywhere I traveled.

Those in T&T, the United States, England, and France who directed us to the best resources and made access to indispensable source materials possible are too many to name here. I extend my deepest appreciation to everyone who answered questions, forwarded email inquiries to the appropriate authorities, gave permission to reproduce images, and made digital maps and other materials accessible. Among this group, I especially want to acknowledge Nisha Harding of Ile Eniyan Wa; Embau Moheni, former member of Parliament, Republic of Trinidad and Tobago; Jacqueline Edwards at Guardian Media Limited; the staff at the Central Statistical Office of Trinidad and Tobago; Lisa Lum Kong and Dianne Gittens, then at the Judiciary of the Republic of Trinidad and Tobago; Celina Griffith at the National Archives of Trinidad and Tobago; and the library staff at the Special Collections of the

Alma Jordan Library at the University of the West Indies, the Northwestern University Archives, the Schomburg Center for Research in Black Culture, and the Archives of Traditional Music at Indiana University.

Others escorted Tracey and me to important shrines, invited us to feasts and key events, introduced us to influential mothers and fathers in the tradition, and allowed us into their sacred spaces for interviews, "participant engagement" (Hucks), and deep hanging out. The late Mighty Composer led us to Iyalode Sangowunmi Olakiitan Osunfunmilayo (long known as Iya Sangowunmi aka J. Patricia McLeod), and for that introduction I am eternally grateful. Burton Sankeralli, T&T's supreme organic intellectual, was a powerful source of encyclopedic information about the nation's history, politics, cultures, and peoples, especially its omorisa. Burton, thank you for sharing your infectious adoration for your natal home with me in so many formats—unpublished manuscripts, late-night conversations, tours around Port of Spain, and debriefings after ceremonies and public Orisa events. You exposed me to the vast *nationscapes* of Orisa presence in Trinidad, and you became my favorite interlocutor ever. I am profoundly grateful for your friendship and scholarly devotion.

Several influential omorisa whose narratives and experiences enrich this volume have made their momentous transition to the realm of the ancestors. *Modupe* Iya Melvina Rodney, Iya Dr. Molly Ahye, Baba Sam Phills, Iya Amoye (Valerie Leechee), Chief Ifakorede Oyayemi Aworeni (Mother Joan), and Baba Clarence Ford. I mean it when I say I went *back to school* at the shrines of Sister Sylvestine De Gonzalez, the late Jeffrey Biddeau, Iya Rodney, Iya Amoye, Oloye Ogundare Ife Olakela Massetungi (long known by his former title, Oludari), and Iya Sangowunmi. Oloye Massetungi and Iya Sangowunmi were gracious enough to sit with Tracey and me for numerous hours to educate us about their life journeys and sojourn into African sacred sciences, especially the Yoruba-Orisa tradition. I must acknowledge also the late great Mr. Isaac McLeod. Throughout my entire life, I have only called two men "daddy": my biological father and Mr. McLeod. His love, acceptance, and kindness were as warm and pure as my father's, and Tracey felt exactly the same. Mr. McLeod will always be "daddy" to us.

Other key holders of historical, political, and cultural memory in Trinidad who also sat for interviews and conversations deserve tremendous praise, especially Black Power activist and photographer Apoesho Mutope, Gerard King, Professor Rawle Gibbons and Dean Funso Aiyejina at the University of the West Indies, Iya Eintou Springer (then at the Heritage Library), Rev. Barbara Burke (former member of Parliament, Republic of Trinidad and

Tobago), ANR Robinson (the late prime minister and president of Trinidad and Tobago), Baba Aku Kontar, educator and film producer Joseph Valley, and vocalist Gary Cordner. Thank you, Gary, for sharing how the Vodou you witnessed while stationed in rural Haiti was a powerful family tradition filled with beauty, simplicity, prayer, libation, devotion, and hope. I am much obliged to all the photographers, especially Maria Nunes, Edison Boodoosingh, and Apoesho Mutope, who kindly gave me permission to reprint their images. Thanks to your impactful documentary work, we can tell the story of African religious cultures in Trinidad both verbally and visually.

I am grateful, too, to many others who initiated me into T&T's "liming" tradition, invited me to discussions at Tapia House, exposed me to bake and shark at Maracas Beach, and T&T's majestic caves—especially Afra Raymond, Burton Sankeralli, Peter Joseph, and Turunesh Raymond. Thank you for the delicious cuisine, laughter, dancing, and occasions to delight in your artistry. Perhaps the most enduring memory I have of those times is my first encounter with "the engine room," one of the most arresting historical iterations of what I call "the aesthetic of black militancy" ensconced within African diaspora cultural conventions and livites. The "engine rooms" of Carnival calypso bands—the sections known as "the irons"—epitomize an Ogun aesthetic. Afra, you first exposed Tracey and me to this distinct Afro-Trinidadian offering to the black condition. The explosive, ethos-altering sonic expressions musical blacksmiths create when striking the metal pipes in their pulsating ensembles compel a style of dance that is a prelude to some action or event of revolutionary significance. This awareness, which came to me in the flight and fugitivity of dance under the power of the irons, remains salient and generative even today.

The following persons were particularly helpful at critical junctures during the research and writing of this book. African American studies and US history librarian Erica Bruchko, at Emory University's Robert W. Woodruff Library, went to great lengths to track down documents that were difficult to locate. Spanish, Portuguese, and Latin American studies librarian Phil MacLeod, also at Emory's Woodruff Library, helped me gather sources and access digital archives over many years of research. He even gave me locally published booklets on Orisa tradition that he had acquired in Trinidad while attending a professional conference. Erica, Phil, and the entire staff at Woodruff Library have unfailingly found answers to my most daunting research challenges, and I treasure their expertise, initiative, and follow-through. Elaine Penagos handled all image permissions for this volume and reproduced tables and a graph when the original sources were not clear enough for processing. I am honored to have the opportunity to serve as her doctoral adviser and to join my former graduate school classmates, Michelle Gonzalez Maldonado and the late and dearly missed Luis Léon, who prepared her remarkably well at the undergraduate and master's levels, respectively, for the pathbreaking scholarship she is already producing. Dr. Shenila Lallani, my freshman advisee at the time, served as a research assistant for me throughout her undergraduate years at Emory. She was such a gift to me in all the wonderful ways she supported this project, including sending her younger brother Shoeb Lallani my way to take her place once she graduated. Shoeb picked up marvelously where his sister left off without skipping a beat. J. Rubén Díaz Vásquez also assisted me with research needed to complete this project. I immensely valued the maturity and intellectual habits each of them exhibited, and I thank them for bringing their best selves to their work. I equally treasure exchanges with students who enrolled in my graduate and undergraduate courses over the years. Conversations with numerous students have expanded my scholarly explorations and exposed me to additional interlocutors of tremendous value to my research.

My colleagues, department chairs, staff, and deans over the years encouraged me throughout the various stages of research and writing. Laurie Patton, Gary Laderman, and María Carrión in the Department of Religion and Mark Sanders, the late Rudolph Byrd, Leslie Harris, Andra Gillespie, and Carol Anderson in the Department of African American Studies made resources available to me and offered venues for me to present early versions of chapter sections from this volume. The staff in both departments have done everything in their power to help me focus on materials needed to complete this book. I am particularly grateful for Toni Avery's faithfulness, efficiency, and attentiveness in my home department of Religion and La Shanda Perryman's resourcefulness and reliability in the African American Studies Department. Originally from Trinidad, the late Jackie Wallace transcribed more than seventy hours of audiotapes. I was fortunate to find an Emory staff member of her caliber who was fluent in Trinidadian patois and could transcribe in hours what would have taken me days to do. Deans Carla Freeman, Michael Elliott, and Lisa Tedesco contributed subvention funds to help with securing permissions. Dean Elliott deserves special acknowledgment for making resources available through TOME, which supports the open-access digital publication of this two-volume project. Generous support from the American Academy of Religion (two Collaborative Research Assistance Grants) and Emory's Bill and Carol Fox Center for the Humanities also allowed me to conduct international research and write significant sections of this volume.

Rosanne Adderley, Kenneth Bilby, and J. Lorand Matory graciously accepted Tracey's and my invitation to review our manuscripts; in addition to their invaluable comments and suggestions, which helped us to sharpen our original arguments and highlight better the connections between both volumes, their rigorous yet encouraging feedback helped shape our vision of the project's limits and possibilities. Ras Michael Brown helped me to connect the dots that join primary source materials and historical scholarship to my arguments about African *nations* and cultures as moving continuities. Two anonymous reviewers also offered detailed feedback that enhanced the quality of our project, and Baba Ḳọlá Abímbọlá's scholarship and insights were indispensable to many topics treated in this volume. Modupe! Kola for your clarity and precision concerning Yorùbá sacred orature, ritual, and language and for the appendices you generously prepared.

Miriam Angress and her team of interns at Duke University Press, especially Roshan Panjwani, were nothing less than remarkable in assisting me with the editing process. This book has been incubating for a long time; no matter how much I tried to stay within my word limit, the word count would creep back up and gravely exceed it. Only the superior editing skills of Miriam Angress, Susan Whitlock, Ulrike Guthrie, and Shelli Gustafson could quell my anxieties about how to cut and what to cut to preserve the integrity of the scholarship. I give thanks for your talents and congeniality. It was a joy to work with each of you. My coeditors of the Religious Cultures of African and African Diaspora People series, Jacob Olupona and Terrence Johnson, had words of encouragement and celebration at each milestone throughout the process. Thank you both for your collegiality and friendship.

Dr. James H. Cone and Dr. Charles H. Long are two of our field's most towering intellectual ancestors: Where would I be without your mentorship and scholarly interventions? Whenever I reflect on how you each touched my soul, I am left with your unadulterated love for black people—past, present, and future. This is what remains most enduring and inspiring for me. Rest in peace my cherished and beloved teachers.

My family has been a constant source of support, championing me for the duration. Above all, my parents Roydel Stewart and Ruby Burrowes Stewart set everything in motion that brought me to where I am today as a scholar. Thank you for showing up for me every day of my life.

And to the ancestors and the omorisa in Trinidad, thank you for waiting!

Introduction
to Volume II

This text completes a two-volume collaborative project on *Obeah, Orisa, and Religious Identity in Trinidad*. Continuing where Tracey E. Hucks concluded her discussion of African Obeah and colonial obeah in volume I, this volume's treatment of Orisa explores the appearance of Yoruba religious cultures in Trinidad within two conflicting orders: (1) the intimate universe that organized Yoruba people-groups into a unified *nation*[1] and (2) the long horizon of colonial obeah. Whereas volume I contended with uncovering African understandings of the numinous in eighteenth- and nineteenth-century colonial records, volume II analyzes a range of source material to provide an intellectual forum for African voices—their narrations of spiritual cohesion and dynamism and their achievements in the struggle for religious freedom in Trinidad from the mid-nineteenth to the early twenty-first century (see figure I.1 and map I.1).

Emphasizing two critical periods in the history of Yoruba-Orisa religious formation in Trinidad—the settlement period (1840s–90s) and the expansion period (post-1960s), the volume attends to the shifting status, visibility, and intelligibility of the Yoruba-Orisa tradition within both "primordial public" and "civic public" arenas.[2] Benefiting from studies of continental Yorùbá religion and culture, I historicize Orisa beginnings in Trinidad by considering the

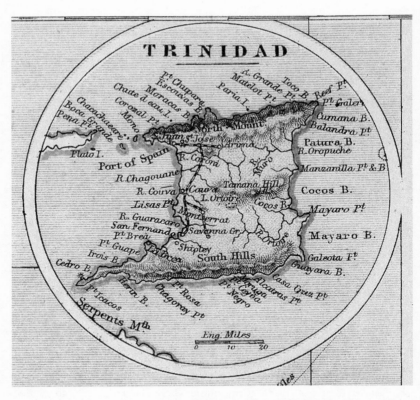

FIGURE I.1 Luscombe, S. 2021. Map of Trinidad, 1892 [online], britishempire.co.uk
/timeline/19century.htm [Accessed 1/21/2021]

cultural conventions that oriented custodians of a dynamic religious heritage.
In the early twentieth century this African religious heritage carried different
designations—the "Yaraba Dance," "Ebo," "Orisa Work," "African Work," and,
most commonly, "Shango." Its devotees garnered no sympathy from the Euro-
Christian establishment during the colonial period and remained stigmatized
on the margins of society, even in the minds of many black Christians.

By the height of Trinidad's Black Power Movement (BPM) in 1970, some
Christians of African descent would rethink their estimation of Shango.
Awakened by a powerful ethos of black consciousness and decolonial politics,
they severed ties with Catholic, Anglican, and other ecclesial institutions they
began to associate with an antiblack colonial regime. They looked to Trinidad's
African religious heritage for spiritual inspiration and reorientation. However, Obeah was too controversial and inaccessible as an organized religion to

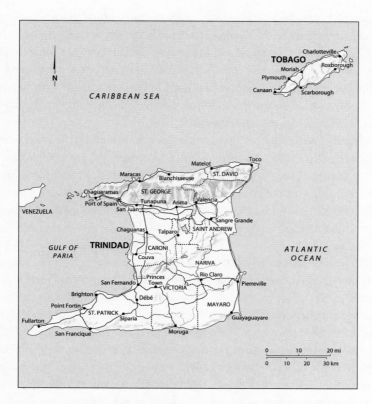

MAP I.1 Map of Trinidad and Tobago, 1969. (Prepared by Bill Nelson.)

address the quest for African spiritual authenticity that some BPM advocates led. Instead, the Yoruba-Orisa religion came to represent Trinidad's originary source of African spirituality—a religious heritage that has endured.

In volume I, Tracey Hucks untangled the mythical and historical narratives that once collapsed categories of "enslaved" and "liberated" and "preemancipation" and "postemancipation" in popular accounts of African Trinidadian experience. This volume revisits these social locations and temporalities in conversation with archival and ethnographic sources. It also adds to the late Baba Sam Phill's experiential and inherited knowledge of Yoruba "beginnings" that frames the introduction to volume I. Presuming that first-generation Yoruba custodians of the Orisa religion in Trinidad did not arrive as blank slates ready to be filled with Western Christian cultural material, I take seriously African indigenous hermeneutics and African continental sources of Trinidadian Yoruba-Orisa religious and cultural production from the mid-nineteenth to the twenty-first century and deconstruct the supremacy of syncretism frameworks in theorizing Orisa religiosity. Despite the scarcity of reliable sources, transdisciplinary methods allow me to recover overlooked indigenous perspectives. They illuminate enduring yet flexible Yoruba orientational structures that have provided continuity to Trinidad's Orisa heritage across time and memory.

I identify five motifs that are essential for understanding the inner workings of the Orisa tradition in Trinidad: (1) sovereignty, (2) nationhood, (3) kinship/family, (4) social belonging, and (5) motherness. I conclude volume II with thoughts on the appearance of these themes across wider Africana religious and cultural traditions in the Caribbean and the Americas, making the case that African religions in these regions partake in a shared Africana spiritual heritage.

This volume also engages the conflation of the sociocultural identifiers Yoruba and African in the post–Black Power period for many Afro-Trinidadians invested in the project of "African" spiritual recovery. Initially a Yoruba Trinidadian nation phenomenon, the Orisa tradition became after 1970 an African Trinidadian phenomenon (of Yoruba heritage). Orisa replaced Obeah as the principal religious repertoire of African heritage and identity. To be precise, different constituents—"older heads,"[3] Pan-Africanists, black nationalists, Afrocentrists, and so on—emphasized distinct aspects of this religiocultural inheritance, whether Nigerian Yorùbá, Anago, African, Trinidadian, or combinations of these. Consequently, a productive tension has existed between Orisa shrines that deliberately incorporate christianisms, hinduisms, and other external religious elements within their practice and those that eliminate them. The former are quite satisfied with the expertise inherited from Yoruba Trinidadians since the nineteenth century. The latter seek additional sources of instruction and authority from Nigerian Yorùbá religious experts. At times, these different approaches have led to contestation over theological beliefs and ritual protocols.

I assess this tension as generative because old and new custodians of the Yoruba-Orisa religion needed one another's knowledges, strategies, and resources to take steps toward arresting the legacies of violence and persecution that African heritage religions have endured in Trinidad since the slave period. However, I deliberately illuminate the innovations introduced into Orisa in the aftermath of Black Power, especially given that, until recently, established scholarly portraits of Orisa communities in Trinidad featured Yoruba-Orisa lineages founded on pre-1960s cultural and theological norms.[4]

Today, after four decades of cooperative efforts across ideological camps and spiritual families, Trinidadian Orisa is arguably the most civically engaged and legally protected African religion in the Western Hemisphere. To understand how the Orisa community overcame colonial obeah and colonial imaginations, I had to explore the emergence of what I term *Africana religious nationalism* among post–Black Power Orisa shrines.

I frame my theorization of colonial terror and the Orisa community's struggle for religious freedom and national inclusion through my training as a theologian with primary commitments in this project to the undertheorized domains of Africana religious imagination and sacred poetics. Luis León coined the term "sacred poetics" to capture how "religious actors . . . manage the often harsh and potentially overwhelming conditions they confront—the battle for survival and more, dignity, love, freedom—by deploying the most powerful weapons in their arsenal: signs, myths, rituals, narratives, and symbols."[5] Amplifying the contributions of phenomenologists of black religion, this volume offers an interpretation of *Africana sacred poetics* in Trinidad and other geographies of the African diaspora. In so doing, it underscores the important interventions a religious studies approach is poised to make in Trinidadian Obeah and Orisa studies, as well as the wider study of African heritage religions in the Caribbean and the Americas.

Chapter 1 shifts the discussion of African religions in Trinidad from volume I's treatment of Obeah to a focus on Orisa. Glossed as obeah in the colonial imagination, the African heritage religions dotting the Trinidadian landscape by the mid- to late nineteenth century continued to exist within an atmosphere of anonymity. By the early twentieth century, however, popular culture and the courts started to register at least one of those religions by name. Yoruba-Orisa spiritual repertoires had anchored alongside the ships that a half-century earlier began delivering thousands of liberated Yorubas to the shores of Trinidad. Following this *Extended Middle Passage* period, Yoruba-Orisa tradition, widely known as "Shango" for nearly the entire twentieth century, arguably became the most conspicuous, influential African heritage religion in postemancipation Trinidad.[6]

Methodologically blurring the lines between historical and ethnographic investigation, chapter 1 places nineteenth-century documents—newspaper accounts, missionary journals, and slave registers—in conversation with twentieth-century oral histories and ethnographies, both those original to my research and those accessed through archives. Most useful are the 1939 archived ethnographic fieldnotes and papers of Melville Herskovits, the first scholar to produce a book-length study of African-inspired religious and cultural traditions in Trinidad. Chapter 1 particularly considers how sovereignty and *nationhood* qualified Yoruba-Orisa ritual and cultural life before the era of independence and explores the Yoruba-Trinidadian diaspora as an archival site of West African religious and political history. The Orisa religion then is theorized as an institutional space for the simultaneous creation of diasporaed Yoruba culture and consciousness, the preservation of West African archives, and an extension of Trinidad's wider Africana spiritual heritage.[7]

Chapter 2 takes up the motifs of kinship and social belonging and brings theoretical substance to the volume's departure from standard social science studies of Yoruba-Orisa religion and other African heritage spiritual traditions in the diaspora. It analyzes aspects of Yoruba cosmology, theology, and ritual life phenomenologically to situate kinship as an orientational ethic and primal relational structure that furnishes commonsense Yoruba values. It draws on studies of both continental and Trinidadian Yoruba societies to reexamine the well-known personality of Ebenezer Elliott, aka "Pa Neezer" (1901–69). Chapter 2 offers an alternative exegesis of this celebrated Shango priest, Baptist, Obeah healer, and "lodge man" and posits an emic interpretation of Yoruba approaches to social belonging that reframes patterns and behaviors heretofore reductively conceptualized as syncretic.

Chapter 3 provides an overview of the Victorian aesthetic and spiritual mood that deemed African heritage religions deplorable and historicizes the expansion and transformation of the Shango cult into the Orisa religion during the period of black nationalist consciousness and Black Power mobilization among Trinidadian youths, beginning around 1968. Black Power staged the conditions for a new era of African religious cultures in Trinidad. Chapter 3 documents this transition, particularly how exchanges among religious, social, and political entities inspired new concepts of Africana *nationhood* and a black nationalist consciousness that borrowed from and brought into public view long-overlooked Yoruba-Orisa traditions of identity-making in Trinidad. The chapter examines the sacred significance of continental Africa for African Trinidadian religious and cultural thought, particularly authenticating accounts of African heritage that inspired the creation of new Yoruba-Orisa families formed through spiritual kinship and what I term *territorial poetics*. Chapter 3 closes by considering how the influential Black-Power-inspired Egbe Onisin Eledumare (EOE) community intellectualized its faith and practice for the past half-century.

Chapter 4 probes the last of volume II's central motifs, motherness, by exploring Yoruba-Orisa spiritual mothers' contributions to the tradition. Assessing their activism and accomplishments through an Africana feminist-womanist lens prioritizes the insights of African and African American thinkers whose explanatory frameworks extend to Caribbean contexts of African spiritual preservation and construction. Distance from the African continent did not signal a break with the long meta-tradition of mothering in Africa, with its matricentric consciousness and social ethics. Rather, Africa's "matriarchive"[8] diffused that heritage throughout the Americas and the Caribbean.

The mothers (iyalorisa) featured in chapter 4 epitomize this Africana cultural legacy of matricentricity in Trinidad and exemplify the labor and accomplishments of women-mothers whose status and leadership strengthened Orisa practice and public presence during the last quarter of the twentieth century. From the legal struggle for the civil right to religious freedom and protection during the 1980s to the founding of the National Council of Orisa Elders in the 1990s, and the representation of Trinidad's Yoruba-Orisa tradition on the global stage over the past four decades, Yoruba-Orisa mothers have helped open a third space of citizenship that blurs *nation-al* and national belonging. Their matricentric ministries continue to invigorate the tradition and expand its significance and influence within and beyond the Republic of Trinidad and Tobago. Chapter 4 also develops the discussion of black affective politics in theorizing "heritage love" as an *Africana affect* that mobilizes the black religious imagination and its *nationalist* expressions. Concentrating on a post–Black Power shrine with pan-Africanist leanings, the chapter analyzes Iyalode Sangowunmi's motherness innovations within Ile Eko Sango/Osun Mil'Osa and their import for the wider nation.

Chapter 5 synthesizes the volume's argument that Trinidad is a fertile diasporic context in which to theorize the nature, effects, and affects of black religion. It summarizes the modal operations of an Africana sacred poetics Obeah experts and Orisa devotees in Trinidad privileged across three centuries. Revisiting pivotal rituals, religious symbols, axiological principles, technologies of belonging, and originary narratives, the chapter frames my conviction that an Africana religious studies approach to research on African heritage religions in Trinidad yields resources for the following: (1) the continued theorization of and responses to what black nihilist philosopher Calvin Warren calls "ontological terror," (2) a phenomenological interpretation of black religion and its relational infrastructure as an "interruptive invention"[9] in conversation with the Longian tradition in black religious studies, (3) a new Africana womanist perspective analyzing the religious leadership and activism of Caribbean mothers who love the *African* Spirit, and (4) the next stage of comparative religions research in the development of Africana religious studies. The chapter calls for future studies that explore the religious dimensions of black abjection and diaspora analogues of the motifs that thematize this volume. It closes by analyzing one analogue (the black church) from one of the most undertheorized sites of the African diaspora (the United States).

Trinidad's unique multi-nation-al, multicultural, multiracial, multiethnic, and multireligious heritage has presented omorisa (orisa devotees) with platforms for advancing their activist and spiritual agendas that remain out of reach for their counterparts in the United States. The afterword comments on the distinct locations of omorisa in Trinidad and the United States who embrace Africana religious nationalism, underscoring the invaluable work that Orisa devotees in Trinidad have done to enhance their nation, their position within it, and their efficacy across the transatlantic Yoruba-Orisa nation.

Transitioning from volume I's concentration on the white colonial imagination, this volume addresses why and how the black religious imagination resides in the tension between primordial beginnings and black abjection. It makes no pretense of resolving that tension but depicts how, in the midst and "afterlife"[10] of colonial chaos, Africans in Trinidad have navigated that tension through praxes of nation-building—communal caretaking, uncooperative endurance, re-creation, and love.

I Believe
He Is a Yaraba,
a Tribe of Africans Here

ESTABLISHING A YORUBA-ORISA NATION
IN TRINIDAD

It is perhaps no wonder that during John Cooper's 1872 obeah case before Trinidad's Supreme Civil Court, an interpreter for the defendant mistakenly identified his cultural heritage as "Yaraba."[1] As Tracey Hucks explains in volume I, the appeal summary of Cooper's battle with the colonial justice system makes no mention of Yoruba deities or ritual terminology. Nor is anything mentioned about Cooper's native tongue; he is reported to have spoken "broken English and a little French."[2] However, the items in Cooper's possession on his arrest and his explanation of their spiritual and medicinal significance signaled his heirship to an African religious culture. Given the disproportionately high percentage of Yorubas to arrive in Trinidad between 1841 and 1861 under the liberated African resettlement program, Cooper, although a Rada, was assumed to be "Yaraba."[3]

With few exceptions, colonial observers were incapable of distinguishing Yoruba and other African heritage spiritual traditions from each other or from the range of antisocial practices and subterfuge they associated with "obeah." Cooper's arrest was the potential fate of any African descendant whose religious practices ran afoul of the Obeah Prohibition Ordinance (OPO) of 1868. Because Cooper resided in a colony that, between the mid-1800s and the early 1900s, increasingly censured displays of spiritual devotion and cultural traditions among African populations, neither he nor his interpreter would have anticipated Trinidad's eventual transition into a relatively hospitable home for a "tribe" of Yoruba-Orisa devotees during the last quarter of the twentieth century.[4]

In contrast to volume I, which analyzed Euro-colonial constructions of obeah, volume II focuses on Orisa, a Yoruba heritage religion that endured more than a century of proscription to eventually gain nearly a half-century of official recognition and inclusion in Trinidad and Tobago's (T&T) "civic public."[5] Phenomenological considerations of Yoruba-Orisa thought, spirituality, and politics encourage attentiveness to unexamined dimensions of the community's African cultural inheritance. Among the preoccupations shaping Trinidad's Yoruba-Orisa tradition are five prominent and interdependent motifs: nationhood,[6] sovereignty, kinship/family, social belonging, and motherness. These interactive cultural and spiritual structures orient custodians of Yoruba-Orisa religion and contribute foundational cultural ingredients to a legacy of Africana sacred poetics in Trinidad, revealing patterns of resilience and dynamism.

I access the meanings and orientations associated with what phenomenologists would term "prereflexive" Yoruba-Orisa norms and behaviors in this chapter's exploration of the co-constitutive motifs of nation and sovereignty.[7] The chapter reveals how the meanings and experiences associated with Yoruba-Orisa performances of nationhood and sovereignty during the community's settlement period challenge the conventional retrieval of "ethnicity" and "ethnonym" as satisfying translational terms for Africana nation traditions. Interrelated themes of kinship/family and social belonging do enter this discussion. However, they (along with motherness) are central to subsequent chapters, where shared ideas and practices of nationhood and sovereignty continue to warrant consideration.

To begin, we move from John Cooper's troubles with colonial religious repression to Paulina Samuel's experience of the same. Her case exposes continued social frictions surrounding Yoruba religious practice in Trinidad during the early twentieth century and illuminates the cultural and spiritual dynamics of nineteenth- and early twentieth-century Yoruba-Orisa religious formation.

John Cooper, a Rada expert, could not altogether escape colonial reduction of his religious inheritance to an invented "obeah" belief system. Presumably the same was true for Yoruba religious experts whose spiritual practices came under the state's surveillance. However, by the early twentieth century, the "Yaraba . . . tribe of Africans" in Trinidad had become known for something other than "obeah," at least officially. On July 10, 1919, the *Trinidad Guardian* published details of a court hearing concerning defendant Paulina Samuel, who was charged with "keeping a Shouters' meeting at Carenage on the 5th June last" (see figure 1.1). The complainant in the case reported, "There was a great noise at the defendant's house and he saw some people dancing, shouting and jumping . . . they were singing in the African language and were indulging in what was called the 'Yaraba dance.'"[8]

This mention of "Yaraba dance" was one of the first times a term other than "obeah" was invoked to label an African religion in Trinidad's public

Alleged Shouters' Meeting,

YARABA DANCE AT CARENAGE.

LICENSED TO BEAT A DRUM.

The Prosecution Fails.

Before the City Magistrate yesterday, Sergeant de Landro charged a woman named Paulina Samuel with keeping a shouters' meeting at Carenage on the 5th June last.

Inspector E. T. W. Car prosecuted and Mr. E. M'zumbo Lazare defended on a plea of not guilty.

Complainant said that he knew defend-

FIGURE 1.1 "Alleged Shouters Meeting," *The Trinidad Guardian*, July 10, 1919, p. 7. Perhaps the earliest newspaper account of Yoruba ("Yaraba") religious practice in Trinidad. Reprinted by permission from National Archives of Trinidad and Tobago.

records.[9] The newspaper's account indicates that the practice of a distinct religious culture was already known to outsiders. Although it is likely that others beyond the Yoruba were aware of the community's heritage ceremonies long before Samuel held her Yaraba dance in Carenage, available sources do not offer adequate information to substantiate this supposition. Hers is the first known instance in which the term "Yaraba" is connected to religious life in a public document.

Ten years later, the *Trinidad Guardian* ran a series of editorials discussing Yoruba (Shango) tradition. Writing under the pseudonym "Interested," the author of the first editorial, titled "A La D'Afrique," described a public "Shangoo" [sic] event in the St. Joseph district of Port of Spain: "Huge crowds gather nightly under a clear and serene sky to gaze upon a group of dark-skinned men and women garbed in motley coats. The tambours send forth their blatant sounds in the still air, accompanied by dancing and barbarous intonations of 'Way hee Way hee, Alla dee.' A rude tent lighted by candle lanterns offer [sic] an impromptu canopy to the actors. The spectators gaze on this scene in complete silence, and actually take delight in what they see."[10]

Four days later, Clarence from St. Joseph responded to Interested's description of "shangoo praises," asserting that, "the people who take part in this ancient dance of uncivilised days if asked their creed, all will profess to be Christians. They feign Christianity but are still firm upholders of this ancient dance." He asked, "Can nothing be done by the Authorities to rid the country of an uncivilised practice?"[11] The next day, "One of African Descent" responded to Clarence in a letter titled "'Shango' Is Not a Religion":

[Yesterday], an article appeared in your "Dear Sir" column, signed, "Clarence." That gentleman, perhaps, is not aware of the fact that it is not a matter for scornful comment, for one to be "closely related to Africans," or even to be one; and he might also be informed that that African dance termed "Shango" is not a religion, but an ancient tribal custom handed down to the present-day Africans of the community from their ancestors; just as are the festivals of that ancient Indian custom, termed locally "Hosea;" and that, except in his distorted imagination, there is no reason why "Shango" should be abolished.[12]

This unfolding polemic among three Trinidadian residents provides useful information about the status of Yoruba-Orisa religion and its custodians at a time before scholarly studies of the tradition were underway. That an "Interested" citizen had knowledge of and wrote with some detail about a "Shangoo" ceremony in St. Joseph suggests a common awareness that the Yoruba-Orisa religion had a following among local Africans. That the writer describes the audience participants as "huge crowds" indicates interest among diverse Yoruba and undoubtedly other African communities whose "gaze" of "silence" and "delight" speaks volumes. Their "silence," juxtaposed with the "tambours," "dancing," and "intonations" of the ritual "actors," is remarkable: "Interested" describes informed spectators who understand the ritual cues that demand silence at pivotal moments during the ceremony.

Shango was apparently a well-established spiritual and cultural tradition in some regions of Trinidad by the early twentieth century—but it was not necessarily well regarded. The disapproval Clarence expressed in his commentary reflects what many elder Orisa devotees testify was a common sentiment among Trinidad's Christian citizenry during the 1920s. Most revealing is the rebuttal "One of African Descent" recorded. Rarely do we gain firsthand access to the perspectives of African descendants on African religion in colonial Trinidad. The writer not only defends the Shango ceremony as a treasured heritage "custom" that in no way interferes with adherents' professed "religion" but also argues that—because permission was granted Trinidadians of Indian descent to celebrate their ancestral festivals, namely "Hosea"—the same courtesy was owed Trinidadians who inherited the Yoruba-Orisa tradition from their ancestors.

These remarks clearly indicate that Yoruba (and likely other liberated African settlers) and their descendants in Trinidad refused to view their spiritual rites and ceremonies through the eyes of the colonial establishment. As historian David Trotman explains, during the nineteenth century, "Yoruba vigorously resisted any attempts to participate in the construction of a 'new African slavery.'" Constituting a postemancipation liberated African community in Trinidad, "the Yoruba were not enslaved, and they knew it and therefore behaved as free persons." Trotman also notes, "Despite derogatory comments and racist characterisations, they insisted on their freedom and cultural independence. They refused to attend Christian church services or to send their children to Christian-run schools unless they were compensated for their time, and it was feared that any attempt to enforce this would 'lead to serious disturbances in those districts where their countrymen of older importations reside in greater numbers.'"[13]

Aware of the cultural diversity and multiple spiritual heritages that escorted European Christians, East Indian Hindus or Muslims, and West African Yoruba to different devotional spaces within the small British colony, some Yoruba-Orisa devotees capitalized on their location as bearers of one of the spiritual heritages that contributed to the colony's early twentieth-century ethos of religious pluralism. In their minds, the pluralism of the colony's immigration history secured a place for their religious customs to flourish in Trinidad.

Perhaps, too, distancing Orisa devotion from the term "religion" served rhetorical ends in a contest of social respectability. Or perhaps the term "religion" only demarcated a colonial ideological terrain, a bureaucratic structure, an elite experience, and a confessional engagement with the numinous. In any case, the Yoruba mapped a vast territory of meanings when they chose to label Orisa a "custom."[14] This territory has less to do with professed beliefs and more with how Yoruba-Orisa ritual process fortifies personal and communal capacity, binds family members to *nation* lineages, and fulfills social-ethical obligations across relational bonds.

When we focus on the voices and experiences of transgenerational Yoruba-Orisa devotees and associates such as the "One of African Descent," we encounter new material and a meaning system for theorizing Orisa religious consciousness and its implications for social life. Beginning with actual Yoruba/African persons often operating against the Western colonial project of signification but also creating their own identities forces a reckoning with the dissonances between academic categories such as "religion" and the self-naming and meanings those living out their inherited and innovated "customs" have issued over time.

In a few sentences, "One of African Descent" invites such a reckoning and challenges reigning narratives about the powerlessness and clandestine status that defined social existence for Yoruba-Orisa practitioners. As addressed in volume I, the remarks of "One of African Descent" are part of an African Trinidadian legacy of confronting the legislative process and challenging inaccurate, biased applications of jurisprudence surrounding the criminalization of Orisa and other African heritage religions. Given the campaigns that Orisa groups launched in Parliament to secure official recognition and civil rights following independence during the 1960s, this respondent's statement that "there is no reason why 'Shango' should be abolished" in Trinidad would have the last word.

But what about the first word on Orisa practice in Trinidad? Who uttered it, when, and where? The dearth of accessible primary source material documenting Trinidad's Yoruba-Orisa religious heritage poses one barrier after another. In his seminal article "Reflections on the Children of Shango: An

Essay on a History of Orisa Worship in Trinidad," Trotman maintains that for the period between 1783 and 1838 "references to African rituals are all very . . . vague and whatever distinctiveness that Yoruba ceremonies may have had seems to have escaped the eyes of the contemporary observers."[15] Sadly, until more sources come to light, this statement holds true for later periods too.

Highlighting the negligible numbers of Yoruba captives transported to Trinidad during the period of slavery, Trotman builds a case for the postemancipation genesis of Yoruba-Orisa religion in Trinidad. In my review of Trinidad's Colonial Slave Registers, housed at Britain's National Archives, nearly eight hundred pages of entries from 1813 and 1834 underscore Trotman's thesis. Of the extensive plantation lists documenting personal information of the enslaved population, only four entries recorded the "country" identities of enslaved Africans as "Nago"[16] and none as "Yoruba," "Yaraba," or any other variant.

In the 1813 Register of Trinidad Plantation Slaves, St. Magdelaine, a sugar plantation in South Naparima owned by Magdelaine Congnet, listed Pierre Gimmey, Magdelaine Gimmey, and Marthe Laurdat as "African Nago," the only three among the ninety-eight bondpersons enslaved on the estate. Entered in the register as having no profession, Pierre and Magdelaine were seventy-five and sixty-two years of age, respectively, and had two children listed: Silveste Gimmey, a "cooper," and Marie Gimmey, a "servant." Pierre and Magdelaine are described as having "country marks on the face," whereas their children are listed as having "no marks." In the context of slavery, one might suppose an eponymous relationship between the owner (Magdelaine) and her properties (Magdelaine the plantation and Magdelaine the slave), which could indicate extensive tenure at that location for this "Nago" elder. By 1813, Magdelaine Gimmey had spent at least twenty-six years in Trinidad—if not exclusively at the Magdelaine Plantation: her registered children were both "Creoles of this Island" born about 1787 (Silveste) and 1793 (Marie).

Sixty-three-year-old Marthe Laurdat is likewise registered as having no "employment" and is distinguished by "country marks on the face & arms." Her two sons, Antoine Laurdat (19) and Jean Louis Laurdat (30), are listed as "Creoles" born in Trinidad and Guadeloupe, respectively. Finally, Diligent Excelent appears in the 1813 Register as a five feet, four-and-a half inches tall, twenty-three-year-old "African Nago brickmaker" from Providence, a brick manufacture and provision plantation. He is listed as having "no marks."[17]

These entries among thousands are a good indication how small a proportion Yorubas were of the total enslaved population, an observation that aligns with Barry Higman's monumental study of enslaved African *nations* in Trinidad; it also supports Trotman's suggestion of the 1830s as the apt starting point for analyzing Yoruba-Orisa beginnings in Trinidad.[18] Trotman does not cite specific sources to justify his claims that "the religion had its optimum fidelity to Yorubaland practices" between 1830 and 1869 or that "many innocent Orisa specialists were harassed" by the police/courts through tyrannical applications of anti-Obeah and drum-regulating ordinances. Still, he pieces together a compelling narrative of the Yoruba-Orisa tradition's establishment during a time of relative autonomy (ca. 1830–69) and its eventual persecution with the "increasing use of coercion to make Trinidad culturally respectable as a tropical colony of . . . Victorian England (1870–90)."[19]

Along with Trotman's work, the ethnolinguistic and cultural ethnographic scholarship of Maureen Warner-Lewis offers helpful historical contextualization of the Yoruba-Orisa religion in Trinidad. Her research incorporates extensive primary source material and, like Trotman's, consults studies of African Atlantic affairs during the slave trade and Yorùbá imperial history to account more adequately for formative experiences of Yoruba descendants in Trinidad.[20] Both scholars furnish critical details about the intimate and wider social environments in which Yoruba-Orisa religion flourished in colonial Trinidad. From the crimes with which Yoruba were charged to the wares and produce they hawked; from their styles of dress to their protocols for paying respect, Trotman and Warner-Lewis compose a needed sketch of Yoruba descendants in Trinidad since the mid-nineteenth century.[21] Donald Wood's assessment that the enslaved populations of Trinidad "are enfolded in anonymity" would certainly extend to the religious cultures of the Yoruba and other liberated Africans were it not for the oral historical studies Warner-Lewis conducted with their descendants, which have yielded, to date, the most comprehensive record on the early appearance of a Yoruba-Orisa religious culture in Trinidad.[22]

Warner-Lewis's research provides the beginning of a historical portrait of the people-groups that laid claim to the Yoruba *nation*—a community with governing societies of initiated adepts and leaders trained to maintain social organization and sustain intimate relationships between the visible sphere and the sphere of unseen Powers.[23] The awareness that Orisa (deities), ancestors, and other spirits, though associated with the invisible domain, were no less members of the community at large imbued all ~~human~~ activities and experiences with "religion."[24] Societies of the Yoruba *nation* sponsored ceremonies and rituals designed to reinforce inherited West African customs that satisfied the predilection for structure and security, as well as for play and relaxation, while sacralizing the generative significance of maturation, marriage, death, ancestorhood, and other stages of life/the afterlife.

How did a Yoruba "*nation*" materialize within a nineteenth-century British colonial territory? Even before settlement in the Americas and the Caribbean, African captives found use for the European term "nation" to structure their lives as meaningfully as possible (see figures 1.2 and 1.3). Olabiyi Yai posits that African descendants in the diaspora "selected the term nation . . . not so much because the white folks used it to refer to themselves, but perhaps more significantly, because nation was perceived by them as the closest approximation, in translation, to concepts used in their respective African languages to refer to themselves in the Old World, Africa."[25]

In Trinidad, liberated pre-Yoruba[26] groups—already culturally heterogeneous—apparently were no different from other African groups that gravitated to the term *nation* to solidify Old and New World allegiances through conventional and at times unanticipated loyalties and fractures. Because, as John Thornton notes, "linguistic loyalty formed a first order of contact and companionship," language appeared to be the principal cultural adhesive, bonding even enslaved persons "whose relatives in Africa might have been at war with each other." The "Coromantee" *nation* is a case in point. Its membership surpassed the "little fishing village of Kormanti from which the *nation's* name derived," encompassing "Akan speakers from the [wider] Gold Coast."[27] In contrast, Peter Caron's research on Africans in eighteenth-century Louisiana underscores how religious, caste, and political frictions; in-group hostilities; betrayals; and other divisive experiences in Africa just as easily could prevent individuals of a shared African heritage from co-identifying in New World contexts.[28]

Through the thorny process, then, of establishing cohesion in a geography of dispersion that no one personally chose, identifiable *nations* did emerge in Trinidad and other Caribbean/American diasporas.[29] And although the most salient unifying element that brought those *nations* into existence was arguably language, including meta-speech communities allied by lingua francas, language was not the only adhesive. As Africana *nations* emerged in the Caribbean and the Americas, they established pillars of shared heritages that sustained their *nation* identities and customs. Religion or the spiritual family was one of the most effective and enduring among them.[30]

FIGURE 1.2 Entries from "Union Hall and Ben Accord Plantations in a Quarter called South Naparima Sugar Plantations owned by Henrietta Hall of which the said Henrietta Hall is in Possession" show "Country" (*Nation*) identities of enslaved Africans for the island of Trinidad. (Entries recorded in the *Colonial Slave Registry* 16 [1813]: 8.) Reprinted by permission from National Archives (of the United Kingdom), *ref.* T 71/501.

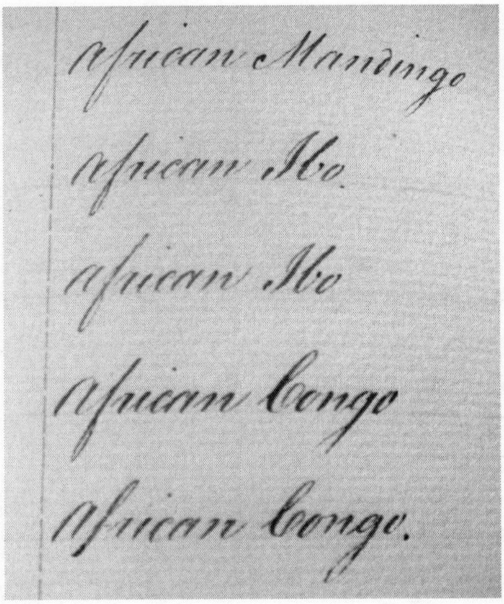
African Mandingo

African Ibo

African Ibo

African Congo

African Congo.

FIGURE 1.3 Entries from "The Return of Francois Sellier Famond for the Plantation called Champ Fleurs in the Quarter called Aricagua a Sugar Plantation." Column recording "Marks" (bodily scarification) of enslaved Africans in Trinidad. Adjacent column (left) records "Country" or *Nation* of origin. (Listed in *Colonial Slave Registry*, 16, [1813]: 1.) Reprinted by permission from National Archives (of the United Kingdom), *ref.* T 71/501.

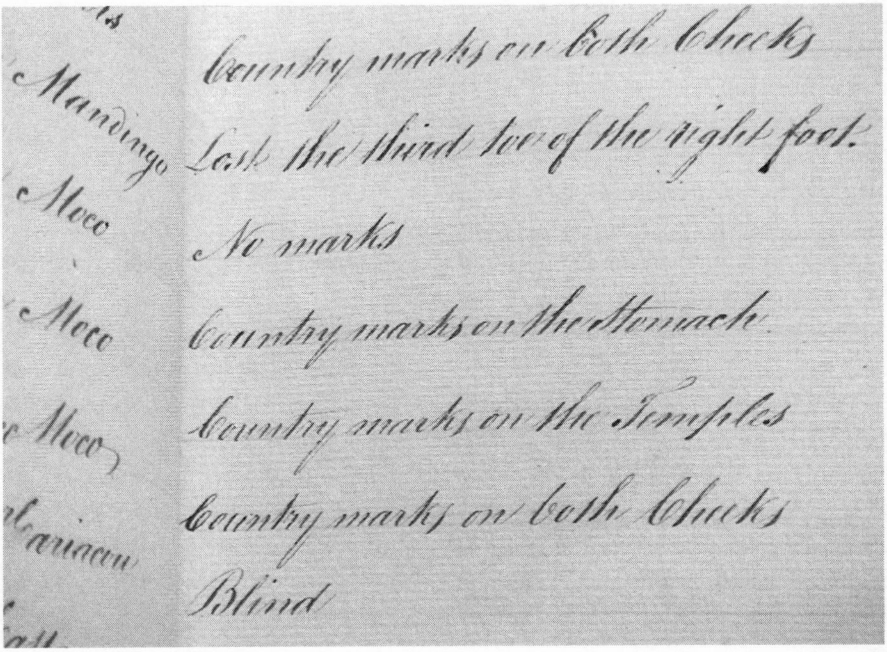
	Country marks on both Cheeks
Mandingo	Lost the third toe of the right foot.
Moco	No marks
Moco	Country marks on the Stomach.
Moco	Country marks on the Temples
	Country marks on both Cheeks
	Blind

Africana Nations: Rethinking Yoruba Ethnicity, Ethnonyms, and the Archive

The discussion thus far already challenges attempts to equate Africana *nation* identities and allegiances with the concepts of ethnicity and ethnonym. Across time, degrees of affiliative intimacies and organized differences among ensembles of related and interacting people-groups—under diversified social, political, economic, occupational, and ecological arrangements—shaped identity consciousness for many peoples of Africa. Moreover, Africana *nations* are also archives of traumatic episodes for individuals and groups whose diaspora*ed* condition compelled the sacrificing of treasured customs, the repurposing of less salient alliances, and the salvaging of worthful possibilities for convivial life from the violence of their captivity. As Alexander Byrd and James Sweet insist, the rise of *nations* in the New World is not solely a cause for marvel at African captives' ingenuity and bridge-building intelligence: it is equally a call for lament, because for every connection forged, many more were tragically severed. As *nations* asserted their multivalent identities, they absorbed both tangibly and intangibly the loss, devastation, grief, and despair individuals and societies experienced on *both* sides of the Atlantic caused by the centuries-long traffic in ~~human beings~~ and the political and military economies it produced.[31]

Heavily tempered by modern, static conceptions of race and a politically charged discursive history, twentieth-century US understandings of "ethnicity" are poor approximations of African *nation* configurations in Africa and the Caribbean/Americas.[32] Each of the Yoruba, Rada, and Mandingo *nations* in colonial Trinidad and other colonial diasporas already comprised ethnolinguistically and culturally diverse subgroups. Often those subgroups shared common cultural elements, but they also defined themselves by what they did *not* share. At the minimum, what we might think of as "ethnic" plurality and heterogeneity always inflect the Africana concept of the *nation/nationhood*. Each individual Africana *nation* was already a *plurination*.

Theorizing *nationhood* as an Africana formulation accomplishes the work anthropologist Michael Jackson contends should be performed by "knowledge wrought from . . . engagement with others." It "does justice to what was *socially* at stake for [diaspora*ed* Africans] in a particular time and in a particular place."[33] The *nation* was perhaps the most potent institution that enslaved and liberated Africans designed to ensure personal and social meaning-making in strange new worlds under disorienting geopolitical conditions, and there is value gained from contemplating its structures, symbols, and products.

This study of Yoruba-Orisa religion in Trinidad adds to the growing literature on the subject of Africana *nation-building* to diversify the lenses through which religion scholars can study African-descended communities in the Caribbean/Americas. Scholars such as Edison Carneiro, Beatriz Gois Dantas, J. Lorand Matory, Patrick Taylor, and Yvonne Daniel have observed across many African diasporic communities that the *nation* concept mobilized and made use of African heritage religious cultures (and at times even aboriginal and Asian heritage religions) to complicate identity affiliations among the manifold groups of Africans who found themselves captives in the New World.[34] Yoruba *nationhood* in Trinidad, and Africana *nation-building* generally, can thus be studied as a formulation that both precedes and exceeds concepts of race, ethnicity, and religion in the modern West: it is an identity-making process conferring cultural and "spiritual citizenship" through African heritage modalities in the Americas and the Caribbean.[35]

In Africana semantic contexts, then, the European term "nation" has been "creatively and idiosyncratically used by African" descendants across centuries to refer to constellations of allegiances that infer belonging, sovereignty, and spiritual family, including kinship with ancestors and invisible Powers.[36] In the slaveholding and colonial Caribbean/Americas, *nation* consciousness and spiritual practices of *nationhood* produced an affective environment that allowed members not only to share the ineffable experience of what black bards and vocalists have approximated with testimonies of *feeling black and blue* but also to uncooperatively "endure" what philosopher Calvin Warren describes as "the incessant violation of captivity." Captivity, Warren maintains, is "the experience in which 'a spirit, a soul, a psyche' is violated without end."[37] Through communication with *nation* deities, who visited their worshipping families by manifesting in the bodies of their devotees, *nation* members simultaneously condensed and expanded time and space, circumventing fictions and binaries of the colonial imaginary, and addressed, if not redressed, the otherness of their condition.[38] Although not untroubled by the power dynamics and conflicts that qualify the daily life of all institutions, these affective achievements have sustained African diaspora religious communities across centuries.

Moreover, *nation* consciousness and its material products archive something of critical importance not only to African diaspora religious studies but also to the current and future state of Africana studies scholarship. In refusing natal alienation and the inaccessibility of the past imposed by the Middle Passage and its afterlife, African diaspora *nations* have been knowledge repositories of the *trans-nation-al* formation of African people-groups and religious cultures. They warrant interrogation as "concepts and institutions that harbor ... potentials" for historicizing the disrupted religious and cultural heritages of African descendants exiled from their homelands through the transatlantic slave trade.[39] When we analyze the discursive traditions and material culture of the Yoruba-Orisa *nation* in Trinidad, for example, we can access not only new knowledge about *nation* formation within African diaspora religions but also the dynamics of sociopolitical and religious formation on the African continent. Orisa institutional life emerged in Trinidad among people-groups that, while remembering their sociopolitical and cultural identities, styled themselves members of the Yoruba *nation*.

Although references to Yoruba residents occurred periodically in newspapers, little was reported about their daily religious lives. Yet what we can glean from historical and ethnographic sources about nineteenth-century Trinidad also expands our knowledge of *nation-building* in West Africa where the Yorùbá affiliation as a *macro-nation* identity was simultaneously under construction. According to scholars such as J. D. Y. Peel and J. Lorand Matory, Yorùbá identity is the result of a mid- to late nineteenth-century process imagined and executed by both missionaries from liberated pre-Yorùbá subgroups in Sierra Leone and emancipated Brazilian, Cuban, and other returnees to pre-Yorùbá territories. The missionaries' religio-cultural and ideological agendas, particularly, paved the way for pre-Yorùbá *micro-nations* to become a solidified Yorùbá *macro-nation*.[40] Scholars agree that Hausa groups to the north of Ọ̀yọ́ first used the term "Yaraba" to refer to the Ọ̀yọ́ subgroup with which they interacted regularly. Peel believes the first recorded usage of the term "Yaruba" to designate a wider people-group than the Ọ̀yọ́ occurred in 1841 when Bishop Samuel Crowther, an indigenous pre-Yorùbá Church Missionary Society (CMS) missionary, and a German missionary colleague, James Schön, referred to both Ọ̀yọ́ and "non-Ọ̀yọ́ groups such as the Yagba" as subjects of the old "Yaruba kingdom."[41] The Yorùbá *macro-nation* identity spread and gained currency among pre-Yorùbá groups through the calculated efforts of the CMS, which, under the leadership of Crowther and other indigenous missionaries, played a significant role in solidifying linguistically related people-groups such as the Ìjẹ̀bú, Ẹ̀gbá, Ọ̀yọ́, Oñdó, and Èkìtì into the Yorùbá *nation*.

Also important is how pre-Yorùbá individuals such as Crowther used terms like "nation" and "country" during this period of shifting political and cultural identities. In 1836, Crowther located his hometown of Ìṣẹ́yìn in "Eyo Country,"[42] thereby attributing sovereignty and some degree of political independence to the region. He and other indigenous missionaries occasionally used the term "nation" to refer both to these smaller units of sociocultural and political affiliation and to the Pan-Yorùbá nation they were endeavoring to create.[43]

Cultural mixture among linguistically related pre-Yorùbá peoples caught up in the slave trade and situated in diaspora spaces such as Brazil, Cuba, Trinidad, and Sierra Leone eventually led to cultural fusion under varied nation nomenclatures, from Nago (Brazil/wider diaspora) to Lucumí (Cuba), to Aku (Sierra Leone), to Yoruba (Trinidad).[44] Ègbá, Ìjèbú, Oñdó, Èkìtì, Kétu, Òyó and other pre-Yorùbá captives became embedded in the dynamics of the transatlantic slave trade just as the unifying concept of a Yorùbá nation was emerging in West Africa. Thus, sources documenting this nation-building process are not limited to continental Africa but can be accessed in unexpected cultural materials of African descendants in the Caribbean and the Americas. Yorubas in nineteenth-century Trinidad, for example, proclaimed their sense of nationhood through melodies of heritages and homelands, unveiling a nation-building process that was underway simultaneously in newly consolidated West African territories that would become Yorùbáland.[45] Lines from one Yoruba-Trinidadian song archive this transatlantic phenomenon of Yoruba nation formation. References to both a shared micro and an emergent macro identity indicate that the Yorubas who composed this song either in a nascent Yorùbáland and transplanted it to Trinidad or composed it in Trinidad postsettlement, were among the latest generation of Yorubas to enter Trinidad:

> Subjects of the King of Ikoyi!
> This song identifies the origins of a people
> Subjects of the Archer!
> We women are hailing you with the greeting "Yoruba nation"[46]

In this verse, Ikoyi is first recognized as the sovereign political entity it was during the nineteenth century, which scholars often describe as an independent state that "acknowledged the leadership of" the aláàfin, or ruler of Òyó, and paid "annual homage and tributes in the Òyó kingdom."[47] Yorubas in Trinidad with ancestral connections to the region remembered Ikoyi as a political unit and continued to honor its distinct royal heritage even while claiming simultaneous allegiance to the "Yoruba nation." By addressing their ruler with the praise-name, Olófà or Archer, Ikoyi descendants preserved a connection to the cradle of their specific culture and political traditions. Yet the last line of the stanza conveys a reality of double belonging, when the independent political and cultural subjects of Ikoyi are equally affirmed as members of the Yoruba macro-nation. Here we see the dynamics of both micro and macro nation allegiances and identities unfolding for the Ikoyi members of the Yoruba nation in Trinidad and in Africa. Those who sang these lines in Trinidad were creating an archive and say as much with the line, "This song identifies the origins of a people." Other Yoruba-Trinidadian lyrics convey support for fellow nation members with no specific mention of micro groups, reflecting a process of sociocultural consolidation into a unified Yoruba nation:

> We are about to visit a descendant of our nation
> The Yoruba people have gathered
> Let's go now[48]

Yoruba and other African nation members often gathered at one another's homes. In practice, "private" yards and compounds were not reserved solely for genealogical family units; they were also nationscapes: arenas for sustaining and reinforcing nation traditions and kinship allegiances. Yoruba nationscapes fostered the institutions and customs that affirmed African conceptions of nation-al sovereignty and regulated group life. One such custom was institutionalized seniority, with roles reserved for a "'headman' or capitaine who was the spokesman for the group in its formal dealings with other Yoruba units and with the outer society." Under the capitaine's leadership, a public system for adjudicating conflicts and crimes prevailed, which reduced the need for Yoruba nation members to appear in civic courts.[49]

Nation-al sovereignty and sodality also intensified through the ritual re-purposing of African royal institutions and symbols, mutual aid (susu) associations, confraternities devoted to patron saints, and ancestral (egun-gun) masquerading societies.[50] Warner-Lewis writes that recreational and religious activities "brought together Yoruba from several scattered communities"—a point supported not only by the song cited earlier but also by a June 19, 1912, Port of Spain Gazette (POSG) announcement: "A band of Yaraba creoles, comprising some thirty-two, with their own band of music, travelled by first train yesterday en route for Irois Forest, where they proceed [sic] to take part in a wedding feast." Oral data indicate that such feasts involved marriage processions with percussionists and dancers/singers, including "shac-shac-shaking women" with "their busts stuffed to exaggeration as fertility symbols" and their melodies "rich with sexual references." As portraits from Warner-Lewis's Guinea's Other Suns convey, burial rites and ceremonies for the Orisa and ancestors were also highly ritualized, allowing for intimate engagement with the invisible realm:

[Wakes] held up to nine nights after death featured the singing of dirges that bewailed the loss of the beloved, others that defied death, and some that expressed a belief in the return of the ... ghost of the dead one. Apart from these functions, there were religious ceremonies to the orisha or deities. These ceremonies were hosted by families who had strong religious dedication and by individuals [with] training in the Yoruba priesthood. Ceremonies were held over a number of days to commemorate the annual festivals of the orisha, or for the purpose of special intercessions—for health, for success in financial undertakings, and litigation. Each orisha festival had its thanksgiving celebration two weeks later. Further religious rituals centered around religious initiations such as those to celebrate the first possession seizure by a devotee and the induction of a neophyte into priestly functions. Saraka were yet another religious form of expression. These were annual communal feasts sponsored by families and involving animal sacrifice, prayers and offerings to family ancestors, but not possession. Their purpose was to placate and honor ancestral dead as a means of ensuring material good fortune and psychic wholeness for the coming year. Saraka were also held for Emancipation Day anniversaries, and la bòn fêt took place at Easter.[51]

Warner-Lewis conducted most of her oral interviews in the late 1960s and early 1970s, which enabled her to glean details about the religious practices not only of her elder interlocutors but also of their parents and grandparents, first-generation Yoruba nation members in Trinidad.[52] More difficult to discern from her presentation of the data is how widespread such practices were, the diverse expressions they might have taken, or the pace at which they adopted catholicisms and hinduisms. Most of her analysis of Yoruba-Orisa religious thought during this early period, in fact, is influenced by one interlocutor, Titi (Lucy Charles).[53]

Puzzling as it might sound about a colony that officially invited so many Yoruba laborers to settle there after 1840, historians have not found any non-oral primary source references concerning the practice of "Shango" or the "Yaraba dance" before 1919; nor have I located any such references in England's Colonial Office records or from earlier editions of the Trinidad Guardian and other colonial newspapers. For example, the POSG covered obeah court cases and ran public notices of estate sales, auctions, and property demarcations involving persons with the surname "Yaraba" or streets and locales named "Yaraba."[54] Between 1907 and 1914 more than three dozen articles discussed obeah. Most contain details about obeah accusations, arrests, and trials in Trinidad, although some treat the subject of obeah and comparable phenomena in other Caribbean and South American colonies.[55]

In one article, a detailed account of "A Bush Doctor's Bath" suggests that the public's "unbending faith in the 'obeah' doctor" threatened to undermine the practice of the "honest" and "qualified Medical Man."[56] The December 15, 1907, edition of the POSG printed D. D.'s colorful verses about "de Creole an' Chinese, An . . . de ole Yaraba" under the headline "Cook at de Town Hall." Another POSG article described the June 24, 1910, Feast of St. John the Baptist in the parish of San Juan. During the day, devotees celebrated a "High Mass," culminating in "a procession when a statue of the 'Forerunner' was carried." The article also mentions two celebratory evening events: "a ball given at the Harmony Hall" through the hospitality of Mr. Toussaint Baptiste and "an African dance . . . held at Mrs. Flemming's residence."[57] We are left to speculate whether that "African dance" involved any ritual devotion to the Yoruba deity Shango.

Melville Herskovits was the first scholar to document the association between the Yoruba deity, Shango, and the Catholic saint, John the Baptist, among Trinidad's Yoruba-Orisa worshippers.[58] Although most scholars assume the phenomenological pairing of Yoruba deities with Catholic saints became a feature of Trinidadian Yoruba-Orisa religion during the nineteenth century, written sources have not factored into their discussions.[59] Oral tradition can provide reliable information, but no oral histories and other research that determine when Yoruba-Orisa devotees in Trinidad began to adopt Catholic saints into their theistic structure and translate aspects of their tradition through Catholic visual vocabulary have yet surfaced.

Historical ethnography and missionary diaries, however, do offer a partial view into the religious formation of omorisa since the mid-nineteenth century. Herskovits's extensive fieldnotes record useful information about Yoruba descendants in Trinidad and their participation in devotional communities at the time of his research in 1939. However, his focus on Yoruba-Orisa religious practices in Port of Spain clearly took a back seat to his documentation of wider African customs in the northeastern community of Toco. After three months in Toco, he was acquainted with many traditions, including bongo, bele, the "Shouters," Obeah, and Anansi. However, he learned he would have to travel to Port of Spain to encounter the "Shango people" who "form healing and dancing groups . . . and have African spirits."[60]

By September 1939, Herskovits had attended a few Shango ceremonies at one compound in Port of Spain. There, he and his fieldwork partner Frances Herskovits observed communal devotion to Yoruba and Dahomean theistic personalities, leaving Frances to speculate that "they must be descended from people who came from near the border between these two [civilizations]."[61] The Dahomean influence was particularly evident in the titles that devotees assumed on initiation: "A devotee takes the name of his god, adding the suffix—si to it to designate the relationship. Si in the language of Dahomey has the literal meaning of 'wife,' but by extension is applied to any worshipper of a god. In Trinidad the designation is employed in the same context as in Dahomey, Ogunsi, Oyasi, Shangosi, Yemanjasi becoming the names of those, whether men or women, . . . consecrated to these respective gods."[62]

Not lost on the Herskovitses was the fact that, although "these people, with their gods, mingle Yoruba and Dahomean deities . . . there is a Rada group with whom [they] have nothing to do."[63] This observation invites inquiries about intra-African exchanges across nation groups, shifting the scholarly gaze away from Yoruba-Orisa devotional practices that seemingly syncretize Euro-Catholic and African spiritual elements. We seldom see studies investigating the Orisa religion's intra-African multicultural elements, leading scholars to presume, as does Steven Glazier, that "Caribbean slaves had more than a passing interest in the religion of their masters." They were not simply being resourceful or hospitable when they adopted Catholic saints into their ritual practices. Rather, "they had an urgent need," Glazier insists, "to incorporate European gods (and the powers of those gods) into their own lives . . . [an] urgent need . . . perhaps at the root of perceived correspondences between Sango, Saint John, Saint Jerome, Saint Peter, and Saint Barbara."[64]

I think something else accounts for the "perceived correspondences" between Catholic saints and the Orisa in Trinidad and that inquiries into Catholic and indigenous African dimensions of Yoruba-Orisa ritual life can produce new knowledge if scholars denaturalize the association of Catholicism with a monolithic Euro-Western religious heritage. By placing historical ethnography and missionary archives in conversation, the ensuing analysis challenges unexamined assumptions about syncretism and African heritage religions in the African diaspora generally and within the Yoruba Trinidadian diaspora in particular. Yoruba-Orisa custodians, Trotman is correct, were not enslaved, but they were captives. To address their condition of captivity, they, with the support of their emancipated African-descended neighbors, mobilized ritual, political, and cultural memories of nation-al sovereignty and social belonging that privileged fusions of Africana religious cultures.

Africana Elements of Yoruba *Nation-al* Sovereignty and the Salience of Shango

When the Yoruba assembled for religious ceremonies, especially annual *ebos* (feasts), they met in a place that distinguished them from custodians of other diasporic African heritage religions. Ceremonies were held not in a temple or shrine but in a *palais* (palace), and the palais structure itself offers another angle on Yoruba-identified groups' preoccupation with *nationhood*—with remembered religious and political institutions in pre-Yorùbáland. Situating the palais's legacy in Trinidad adds credibility to the claim that *nation-building* is an African-diasporic phenomenon and provides an answer to the mystery of Orisa religious beginnings in Trinidad.

Trotman posits that Trinidad's "heterogeneous and numerically small slave population [20,656] for the short-lived slave society [1783–1838] did not bequeath a sufficiently cohesive religious culture to which subaltern [Yoruba] newcomers were forced to assimilate."[65] Missionary documents that comment on postemancipation Afro-Creole ceremonies, however, turn our attention toward the connections that likely emerged among formerly enslaved African descendants and liberated Yorubas between the 1840s and the 1890s. When forging Yoruba-Orisa religious cultures in Trinidad, liberated Yorubas seemed to take their cues not primarily from Euro-colonial institutional patterns but from their ex-enslaved, Afro-Creole neighbors.

To further explore such linkages, we can ask why the Yoruba shrines and rituals were housed in a palace. In "Wither Sango? An Inquiry into Sango's 'Authenticity' and Prominence in the Caribbean," Glazier questions why "words for buildings, [*palais, tapia,* and *chapelle*] continue to be referred to in the French, while leadership titles [*ìyá* and *mọgbà*] are expressed in African terms."[66] Glazier pauses at this point because his discussion of Orisa beginnings in Trinidad remains ensnared within an ossified narrative that positions a merger of African deities and Euro-Catholic saints at the center of the tradition. Perhaps we must look instead to fundamental yet largely neglected aspects of Afro-Creole Catholic ceremonies to explain why French terms became salient within the Orisa ritual vocabulary. Yoruba settlers in Trinidad were *not* the original architects of the Orisa palais: the palais structure in the Yoruba-Orisa *nationscape* was initially a borrowed space.

At least since 1838, and before Yoruba-identified people-groups thronged to Trinidad, the palais had an institutional legacy in the ceremonial life of Afro-Catholic communities, housing their spiritual, cultural, and political expressions of sovereignty. Despite Britain's colonial possession of Trinidad in 1797, Trinidad's unique pan-colonial heritage and multicultural composition during the eighteenth and nineteenth centuries meant that these Afro-Catholic communities were composed of French-Creole speakers whose linguistic culture did not feel the intrusion of Anglicization and the English tongue before the 1890s.[67] During the massive transportation of liberated Yorubas to Trinidad from the 1840s to the 1860s, the Afro-Creole term for any royal residence would have been palais—and Afro-Creoles apparently were the only Trinidadians at the time holding "palais" ceremonies.

In his diary, chronicling several years of missionary work in Trinidad (October 1882–January 1885), Dominican priest Marie-Bertrand Cothonay describes an annual Emancipation Day celebration ritual performed by ex-enslaved persons in Carenage (in 1882) that involved building a "palais." Nowhere near matched in English sources, this French account offers rare insight into the religiocultural universe of a people whose traditions were typically buried beneath the generic indictment of the colonial signifier "obeah":

> I have told you that our blacks of Trinidad and those of Carénage in particular, are former slaves or sons of slaves. Upon emancipation, which took place the 1st of August (1838), they resolved to celebrate every year, that very day, a solemn holiday, in perpetual remembrance. That holiday would begin in the morning with a high mass, with . . . musical participation, blessed bread, procession, etc, which prolonged itself [across] three days, during which there was feasting, dances and orgies . . . , all souvenirs of African life. The incumbent parish priest, initially well liked by his parishioners, had finally obtained, after much patience and many struggles, the suppression of this holiday of the devil. Since six years prior, it was no longer celebrated in Carénage. . . . Last year [1882], unbeknownst to him, the former slaves gathered . . . to take up the old traditions. They raised up therefore a bamboo hut, covered in palm leaves . . . and bestowed upon it the pompous name of palais. A negro was named king. . . . The 1st of August arrived, and the parishioners . . . piously attended the customary mass. At night, the good priest heard again the beating of the horrible African drum. . . . During three days and three nights, Carénage was sullied by bachanalias the like of which it had never seen, doubtless to compensate for those that had been suppressed in the preceding years. The following Sunday, the priest railed, but . . . impassive parishioners! . . . In these sorts of holidays, the king, usually elected by popular acclaim, is the one who gathers the necessary funds, makes invitations, presents the blessed

bread, etc. . . . and opens the dance. The king of this year was called Peter. . . . He is approaching fifty and has not yet received confirmation; he has attended preparatory instruction, and is counting on being admitted to the sacrament. Doubtless, he believes that the priest is ignorant of his participation in the holiday of the devil, or . . . would not dare to reject a great character such as himself. But he is mistaken. One evening, at my request, the priest had him come to the parsonage, in the company of an accomplice, himself a former king. I hoped to be able to manage the affair amicably with the two principal parties, to obtain from them the abandonment of projects. . . . But, the conversation had but begun, when the priest interjected himself, with impertinent reproaches that compromised all of the success of my designs. Our poor Negro kings retired, irritated, and absolutely refused to promise that which we asked of them, *viz.*, to demolish the *palais*, if they wished to take part in the confirmation.[68]

Cothonay's identification of these African parishioners with a slave past is credible; his larger *Journal* shows he was very aware of the distinctions between ex-enslaved and liberated Africans. On one occasion he describes having just met an Angolan nobleman who still spoke his original language. Cothonay explains how the young prince was captured by slave traders, sold to the Portuguese, and eventually rescued by the British naval squadron; he also references a good number of other blacks who were brought to Trinidad under the same conditions as the prince.[69]

Cothonay's account suggests that the palais structure surfaced in tandem with Emancipation Day ceremonies among ex-enslaved African descendants in Trinidad. Studies of African diaspora *nations* document analogous regal productions at pageants and festive occasions, especially Emancipation Day anniversaries, in regions as disparate as Brazil, Jamaica, the northeastern United States, and St. Lucia.[70] Every king or queen needs a "palace"—a theater of royal operations where political, cultural, and religious customs are tightly braided and reinforced in sacrosanct rituals. Although the movement of African descendants across slaveholding territories in the Western Hemisphere might have influenced the wide appeal such sovereignty rituals had among disparate Africana communities, the unbearable weight of chattel enslavement could itself make sovereignty a principal preoccupation of social life among any bondperson. It is reasonable then to consider sovereignty rituals as parallel developments among diasporaed Africans and their descendants across regions of the Western Hemisphere that benefited from cross-fertilization through the intradiasporic movement of African people and the new elements they introduced to the communities they joined.[71]

We can plausibly imagine that such communities in Trinidad attached spiritual significance to some, if not all, sovereignty rituals in a designated space—the palais—where a communally elected "king" oversaw the sharing of "blessed bread" during a ceremony marked by drumming and dancing. Though we do not know whether ancestors or African deities were invoked during sovereignty ceremonies, we can infer that the palais edifice liberated Yorubas encountered in the postemancipation period did provide a "sufficiently cohesive" Africana *nationscape* conducive to welcoming the "subaltern newcomers'"[72] Òrìṣà into Trinidad, especially the royal deity, *Kábíyèsí Ṣàngó.*[73]

Although definitive sources indicating when Yoruba-Orisa adherents began associating their worship spaces with the Creole term "palais" are unavailable, Trotman's point that internal migration caused the dissolution of many Yoruba-Orisa palais during the cocoa and oil booms implies an active palais structure among Yoruba-Orisa devotees as early as the 1870s.[74] Oral data regarding liberated African groups in Trinidad describe how Yoruba newcomers usually "roofed" their homes and ritual palais "with . . . leaves of the carat palm," the same *Sabal mauritiiformis* or *Sabal glaucescens* palm species that Cothonay identifies.[75] Most compelling are accounts of nineteenth-century liberated Africans' ritual practices and built environment. They match patterns that Cothonay attributes to Afro-Creole residents and confirm that liberated Yorubas participated in annual celebrations, including Afro-Creole Emancipation Day festivities:

> Animal sacrifice and possession were the spiritual cores of . . . [religious] ceremonies, which lasted from three days to a week. Such ceremonies involved much communal organization [regarding] fundraising, provision of food; accommodation of guests, and building of bamboo-framed, palm-covered tents, *chapelles* for housing sacred insignia such as flags, swords, food, and sacrificial vessels and consecrated musical instruments. These rites were held at particular times of the year, for instance to celebrate Emancipation and the New Year. And with the eventual syncretism of orisha with Catholic saints, the rites were increasingly [synchronized] with special dates in the Catholic Church calendar: an ebo would often be preceded by a mass.[76]

These details seem to corroborate those of a "half religious, half civil" palais celebration that Cothonay attended in San Fernando in 1885. It was hosted by the brotherhood of St. Dominique, and participants (presumably

Afro-Creole) displayed banners and flags for their patron saint. Cothonay notes there was nothing palatial about the palais's design. Rather, it captured the irony of such subaltern demonstrations of *nationhood* in a colony "divided into castes as strongly marked as those of Hindostan,"[77] with African descendants stationed at the bottom:

> Their procession was deployed ... on the flanks of the Papuré hill; the women [recited] the rosary, the men sang the litanies of the saints, the children, English canticles. I closed out the ceremony with a panegyric of saint Dominique in English. After the mass the civil holiday took place; the *King* of the Society appeared with his diadem in gilded paper and his vestments festooned in faux gold. [The *Queen* was present] in her most magnificent ensemble; her function is to distribute the blessed bread; [and preside] with the king at the feast. ... Each one contributes, one with the chicken, one with the rice, one with the cassava, etc. This common meal takes place in the house one calls the *Palais*. To give you an idea, imagine twenty or so posts three meters high approximately on which a roof of palm leaves rests; no doors, no windows, for flooring, the earth. Such is the *Palais* of Their Majesties.
>
> The king and the queen are elected each year. They have the right to choose a vice-king and a vice-queen. There is also a governor.[78]

Cothonay's narrative and Warner-Lewis's findings suggest that Afro-Creole communities did establish the palais sovereignty customs that Yoruba indentured laborers came to adopt in their confraternal *nation* activities and then adapted to their devotional obligations to the Orisa. This may shed light on another question: Why was the Yoruba ritual called "Shango" in Trinidad? Glazier alleges that "the term 'Sango was ... introduced ... by [several] American anthropologists: Melville J. Herskovits, Frances Henry, William Bascom, and George Eaton Simpson," each of whom "dealt with informants who saw themselves primarily as followers of Sango. While many of their interlocutors' public rituals were open to other members of the *orisa* pantheon, their personal (house) altars were dedicated solely to Sango."[79] Yet Glazier fails to account for the term's popular designation of Orisa devotion in Trinidad before Herskovits—the first of this scholarly quartet to travel to Trinidad—conducted and published his research between 1939 and 1947.[80]

In keeping with the antecedent Afro-Creole Emancipation Day custom of electing a *roi* of the palais to represent a sovereign *nation's* release from the tyranny of slavery, I suggest that the Yoruba *nation*, exiled from home, would have elected Ṣàngó as "*king of the palace*." Of all the Orisa deities worshipped in

Trinidad, Ṣàngó was distinguished as the patron deity of the Ọ̀yọ́ Empire—a metonym for the royal heritage of the "Yoruba" people—who repeatedly manifested in Ọ̀yọ́'s long lineage of monarchs. That male Orisa leaders traditionally assumed the title of "mogba" in Trinidad is additional evidence of the Yoruba nation's preoccupation with Ọ̀yọ́ sovereignty rituals grounded in the cult of Ṣàngó because mọ́gbà were senior priests of Ṣàngó who served the royal shrine at Kòso, a capital city of the Ọ̀yọ́ Empire.

Yorùbá-identified exiles did not enter Trinidad as enslaved persons, but their displacement from their homelands concluded an involuntary journey that commenced with the same trauma of captivity, branding, and commodification that the postenslaved Afro-Creole population endured.[81] Oral narratives indicate that many such Yorùbá-identified exiles experienced the indentured labor program as a deceptive scheme concocted by colonial officials and landowning classes to keep them in bondage.[82] By the time Yorùbá exiles began pouring into Trinidad in the 1840s, both groups (the Yorùbá and the Afro-Creole) knew something about enslavement and sovereignty, which might explain why many Yoruba exiles "lived in close relationships with Creole blacks."[83]

Holidays presented ideal occasions for exchanging customs and cementing bonds across diverse communities of African descent, and the Afro-Creole Emancipation Day holiday conceivably allowed some Yorubas to ritualize their yearning for home. For example, Trinidad's repertoire of Yoruba songs includes "Yé! Ekún ara wa la mí sun," a dirge typically performed on August 1, the anniversary of emancipation. Its appearance in Melville and Frances Herskovits's 1939 field recordings indicates that, at some point in their exchanges with Afro-Creole residents, Yoruba newcomers had composed commemorative rituals for this Afro-Creole holiday. The fact that the song title "Yé! Ekún ara wa la mí sun" is a refrain from the Odù Ogbèatẹ̀ of the Ifá corpus suggests that first-generation Yoruba laborers composed such commemorative songs by adapting West African Yorùbá sacred literature.[84]

For "liberated" Yorubas who remarked on and danced through their suffering on a day intended for celebrating African freedom, commemoration amounted to mourning their exilic status in a distant land, as the verse "oku yoku rele o" (the other dead have gone home) indicates.[85] Thus the oral-cultural data suggesting first-generation Yoruba participation in Emancipation Day rituals and the wider orbit of Yoruba nation traditions may point to their desire to interact with the Afro-Creole institution of the palais and to replenish its African religious and political inheritance with rituals and protocols of their homelands. Teeming with the kind of political, religious, and material culture that palais ceremonies idealized, the cult of Shango offered first-generation Yorubas resources for bridging a sorely missed sovereign past with a sovereign spiritual present unreliant on independent state formation.[86]

Yoruba Trinidadian Sacred Orature and Historical Memory: Deconstructing Colonial Christian Fabrications of Sango in Africa and the Diaspora

The figure of Sango also constructs an important bridge between African and African diaspora cultures and histories. The complementary and competing legends of Sango that exist across West Africa and the African diaspora enable and demand a comparative Africana religions methodology to fully understand both African and African diaspora histories. The work of some Yorùbá experts in analyzing authoritative sacred and cultural texts from the Ifá corpus and the Ṣàngó pípè (oral praise poetry)[87]—research that debunks a popular Christian invention of Ṣàngó's beginnings—underscores my framing of the Caribbean and the wider Americas as repositories of African archives.

The myth goes that Ṣàngó was a shrewd, influential eleventh-century ruler of the old Ọ̀yọ́ Empire. Fourth in the line of Ọ̀yọ́ rulers, the once successful and admired Aláàfin Ìtíolú Olúfinràn's eventual political missteps and military failings led him to hang himself. After his suicide, his close associates, attempting to salvage his reputation, popularized the saying "ọba kò so" ("the king did not hang"), a phrase that, as Akínwùmí Iṣòlá points out, misconstrues, perhaps conveniently or maybe unintentionally, the Yorùbá phrase "obaa Kòso" or "the king of Kòso."[88]

Suicide has a long and formal history in Ọ̀yọ́-Yorùbá political ethics. An opprobrious aláàfin (ruler) or one whose reputation became irreparably sullied by negligence or character flaws was obliged to commit suicide. Recalcitrant leaders would be reminded of their duty through a powerful symbolic gesture. The Ọ̀yọ́ Mèsì, the aláàfin's paramount advisory board and disciplinary council, would present such rulers with an empty calabash—a portent of the "honorable" death they were expected to enact. An aláàfin's suicide was an official acknowledgment that they had failed to demonstrate good judgment and to execute the divine assignment of political governance.[89] As with other religious traditions, hagiographic accounts are undoubtedly present in Yoruba orature and narratives about the Orisa. Thus, the interpretation that loyalists publicly denied Ṣàngó's suicide to preserve a sanitized image of their beloved ruler is quite conceivable.

Yet Ìṣòlá traces this account of Ṣàngó's origins to a Yorùbá reading book, *Iwe Kika Ẹkẹrin Li Ede Yoruba*, a collection of stories intended for young students attending the Church Missionary Society School in Lagos during the early to mid-twentieth century. If the CMS and other Christian missionaries wished to sever the strong attachment of their pupils and other potential converts to the Orisa, especially to a prominent Orisa such as Ṣàngó, deliberately transcribing the words "obaa Kòso" as "ọba kò so" would allow them to reinvent the regal Orisa, connecting him to a tragic suicide. Although *Iwe Kika Ẹkẹrin Li Ede Yoruba* was the fourth reader in a five-part series published between 1909 and 1915, it incorporated substantial sections of Andrew Laniyonu Hethersett's (d. 1896) work on the "history of Ọyọ." Hethersett's material included the narrative of the historical Ṣàngó's suicide and his associates' denial of their monarch's shameful death[90]—a standard account in the Nigerian popular imagination today. Ìṣòlá became suspicious of this CMS narrative when conducting field research among religious experts in Nigeria. "Early in 1983," he explains,

> I was interviewing a *babalawo* (an Ifa priest), and as background to a question, I quickly retold the myth of Ṣango according to Hethersett. The old man stared at me, concern written all over his face. He finally asked: "Learned one, where did you pick up that story?" When I told him that I read it in a book his surprise increased. He did not know that a book could contain lies. I too was amazed to discover that what I had read and believed for so long could be untrue and so began the search for the true myth of Ṣango. The babalawo took me through all the *Odu* that relate to Ṣango in the Ifa divination poetry. Among the important *Odu: Otua Oriko* tells the story of Ṣango's initiation into the Ifa cult and the origins of his powers. *Ofun-eko* tells of dancing as the main profession of Ṣango. *Ọwọnrinyẹku* narrates how Ṣango seduced Ọya, Ogun's wife. *Ika Meji* documents many interesting episodes in Ṣango's life, and *Ogbetura* tells us how Ṣango's presence got to Ọyọ from Ile-Ifẹ.[91]

Akíntúndé Akínyẹmí's research corroborates the point that "the mythical Ṣàngó ... [was] in existence before the establishment of the institution of the Aláàfinate at Ọyọ."[92] However, because "every Aláàfin incarnates Ṣàngó on accession to the throne,"[93] it would not be surprising if Christian outsiders had muddled the lines between official sacred and cultural narratives about the Òrìṣà Ṣàngó and narratives about the deeds and histories of one or more aláàfin. Two similar accounts of Ṣàngó's suicide also existed around the time of Hethersett's story. One appeared in British army officer Alfred Burdon Ellis's *The Yoruba-Speaking Peoples of the Slave Coast of West Africa*, published in 1894; the other was the CMS missionary Samuel Johnson's *The History of the Yorubas*, written in 1899.[94]

Given the global popularity of Hethersett's Ṣàngó narrative, many Yorùbá people (and Yoruba religious devotees worldwide) today might wonder about Iṣola's and Akínyẹmí's conclusions. Yet Trinidadian and other diaspora sources substantiate their findings. Around the 1970s, Warner-Lewis identified references to Shango as "Ọbakoso (King of Koso)" among the 160 Yoruba songs/chants she recorded from elder Yoruba Trinidadians."[95] Three decades earlier, Herskovits encountered "Shango" devotees in Port of Spain whose sacred ensemble included the deity Aba Koso, a member of the "Thunder group" with his brothers Shango and Dada (see figure 1.4).[96] Frances (Mischel) Henry's extensive contact with Orisa leaders since the 1950s gave her access to a collection of practices and customs spanning much of the twentieth century; she too confirms that Aba Koso had been a standard member of Trinidad's Yoruba-Orisa divine community during her early fieldwork.[97]

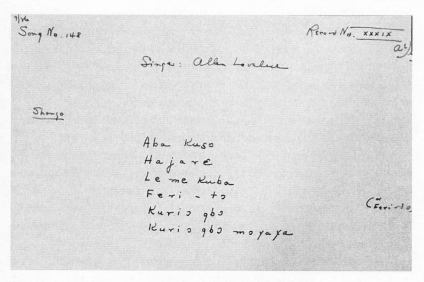

FIGURE 1.4 Lyrics of Yoruba-Orisa song about Shango/Aba Koso, handwritten by Melville Herskovits, performed by Allan Lovelace. Courtesy of the Melville J. and Frances S. Herskovits Papers, Schomburg Center for Research in Black Culture, New York Public Library. Reprinted by permission from John Corry.

A 1977 exchange between James Adeyinka Olawaiye, a native Yorùbá Nigerian, and Father Isaac, a prominent "Shango" leader from southern Trinidad, further indicates the significance of divine rulership to Yoruba descendants in Trinidad, personified through Sango/"Obakoso." It also challenges popular mythologies of Ṣàngó as the "king" who "did not hang." Recounting his doctoral field experiences in Trinidad, Olawaiye describes how

> Father Isaac invited me . . . to break bread with him. . . . During this social time together we discussed religious practices. He was eager to know more of Yoruba religious customs and concepts. For example, he asked me whether Obakoso was a town. I said, "No, but that Oyo is Sango's town and there is a gate there called Koso where several people, mostly women, went to meet Sango and plead with him not to hang himself. That place where Sango returned home to heaven is called "Obakoso" or "Koso" which means, "The Chief or King does not hang himself."[98]

Although Father Isaac understood the phrase "Obakoso" to be a single term rather than two words, what is significant is that he identified it not with suicide but with a place. Kọ́lá Abímbọ́lá explains that "the Ṣàngó temple is located in the Kòso neighborhood of Ọ̀yọ́ city."[99] Archaeologists describe Ọ̀yọ́-Ile and Kòso as "successive capital cities of old Oyo Empire,"[100] where the worship of Ṣàngó was associated with state protocols and regal installations. As Olawaiye states, Kòso was protected by a gate, as well as a wall that still stands today. At the same time, the fabricated Christian version of Ṣàngó's history had clearly influenced this Nigerian Yorùbá scholar.

In including this script in his dissertation, Olawaiye recorded a critical historical memory of significance to African and African diaspora studies. Reading this conversation alongside other oral data and secondary sources from Trinidad and Nigeria points to a generative and necessary methodological strategy for expanding the historical sources for research on continental African societies. The knowledge that Yoruba Trinidadian descendants, such as Father Isaac, inherited from their ancestors reveals a transgenerational, transatlantic memory of courtly traditions connected to civil religion and political governance in the old Ọ̀yọ́ Empire.

Meanwhile, Warner-Lewis and James Houk each cite one example of the deity Sango's association with some version of the phrase "king did not hang." But these interpretations must be interrogated within the wider record of scholarly research on Trinidad's Orisa Powers. Herskovits in 1939 and Mischel in 1956 left similar reports about "Shango" and "Aba Koso" as closely related, yet separate Orisa Powers: "Shango" was associated with

"St. John the Baptist" (Herskovits and Mischel), and "Aba Koso" was associated with "St. Anthony" (Herskovits) and "St. John the Baptist after beheading" (Mischel).[101] However, from 1930 to 1960, there are no references in the scholarship on Orisa deities linking Sango to hanging or suicide.

When Warner-Lewis collected data from Yoruba Trinidadian elders in 1968 and 1970, she recorded one verse from a chant, which she translated as "My king did not hang" (Mi ọba kò so); on three occasions she writes that "Shango's" titles and honorifics include "King of Koso" ("Ọbakoso") or "king of Koso town" ("Ọbakòsò"), designations that her primary interlocutor, Titi, learned from her grandfather Farode, a liberated Yoruba who settled in Trinidad when he was sixteen. Before political strife disrupted his life in old Ọ̀yọ́, Farode was training to become a babaláwo (Ifá priest). He died in 1948, purportedly at the ripe old age of 132, and passed on many Yoruba traditions to his granddaughter. "To Titi's knowledge," Warner-Lewis reported, "Shango is the ... 'thunder deity' whose other titles are Ọbakuso (king of Koso), Olubambi (the leader helps me give birth), Jakuta (the hurler of stones), St. John of the Cross, and Osogbo." In an endnote Warner-Lewis writes, "One Trinidad chant claims Shango died at a ward of Old Ọyọ city called Ajagban"; however, she makes no mention of suicide or self-hanging.[102] Thus with the exception of one chant, which Warner-Lewis likely misinterpreted in consultation with Nigerian translators,[103] up through the late 1970s, when Father Isaac conversed with Olawaiye, "Aba Koso" was understood in the available records to be either (1) a royal title for Sango, (2) a theistic personality closely related to Sango, or (3) a town ("Obakoso" or "Koso"). No account of suicide appears in the recorded narratives about Sango in Trinidad.

Among "typical prayers to Shango" that Houk includes in his study of Trinidadian Orisa (conducted between 1985 and 1992) is the verse "Baalẹ̀ ọba kòso, gba wa ṣégun ọ̀tá wa (Great King who did not hang, help me defeat the enemy)." Houk explains that the prayer was "from a collection of Yoruba prayers with English translations compiled by the post-Black Power Orisa Youths Cultural Organization" (OYCO), a "group of mostly young men" that "disseminates literature containing Yoruba prayers and information about African history and culture."[104] Thus, although this prayer might be "typical" today as a result of post-Black Power developments within the Yoruba-Orisa religion, it was apparently not traditional and was likely unknown to devotees of earlier generations like Titi (b. 1912).

Other curious details emerge when comparing late twentieth- and early twenty-first-century charts of Orisa Powers, their attributes, and Catholic counterparts with those described by Herskovits and Mischel. Not only is

Aba Koso not listed as an Orisa in Houk's or Keith McNeal's theistic charts but he is not mentioned at all. Instead of Aba Koso having a connection with St. Anthony or St. John the Baptist, "Dada" is associated with St. Anthony, and "Shango's" counterpart remains "St. John."[105] During the 1950s, Dada does not appear in Mischel's chart; he reappears later and replaces Aba Koso (in association with St. Anthony) in Houk's and McNeal's charts. However, the resonances between the grouping of the "thunder deities" and their associations ("Shango/St. John; Dada/The Cross; and Aba Koso/St. Anthony") in Herskovits's 1939 field research and Titi's ensemble of "Shango" Powers in Warner-Lewis's research are difficult to ignore. According to Titi, "Shango," the "thunder deity," is both "Aba Koso" *and* "St. John of the Cross (see table 1.1).

We may never know with certainty whether a connection exists between the fading of Aba Koso (the royal theistic personality) or Obakoso/Koso (the place/town) and the emergence of prayer verses such as "Baalẹ ọba kòso, gba wa ṣégun ọtá wa" (Great King who did not hang, help me defeat the enemy) in contemporary Yoruba-Orisa religious memory. However, Abímbọlá's translation of this prayer provides critical insights into Yoruba political and religious titles and their ascribed meanings in Trinidadian Yoruba-Orisa historical memory. Abímbọlá's preferred translation of the verse is "The Baálẹ (male leader) of Ṣàngo priests and priestesses, save us, give us victory over our enemies." Explaining that Kòso is "the neighborhood in Ọ̀yọ́ city . . . where Ṣango reigned as the Monarch of Ọ̀yọ́," Abímbọlá confirms nineteenth- and

TABLE 1.1
Groupings of Spiritual Powers

Orisa	Herskovits (1939)	Mischel (1956)	Houk (1985–1992)	McNeal (1997–2005)
Aba Koso	St. Anthony	St. John the Baptist (after beheading)	Unlisted	Unlisted
Dada	The Cross	Unlisted	St. Anthony	St. Anthony
Shango	St. John the Baptist	St. John the Baptist	St. John	St. John

early twentieth-century Trinidadian Yoruba-Orisa claims that "Ṣàngó himself is Ọba Kòso" (monarch of Koso). Furthermore, "Baálẹ̀ is a contraction of the sentence: 'Baba o ni ilẹ̀,' which literally means "Male elder owner of the ground." Abímbọ́lá clarifies, however, the following: "When we have the name of an Òrìṣà after the word 'Baálẹ̀' [in this context, Ọba Kòso aka Ṣàngó], this means that the 'leader' that is being referenced is the religious leader of that Òrìṣà's community. So, Baálẹ̀ Ọba Kòso is the political leader of Ṣàngó priests and priestesses in the city of Ọ̀yọ́. . . . Hence, Baálẹ̀ Ọba Kòso is an official religious position in the hierarchy of Ṣàngó priests and priestesses of the city of Ọ̀yọ́ (just like, say, the Archbishop of Canterbury is)."[106]

In the context of the wider historical legacy of Yoruba Trinidadian interpretations of the terms "Aba Koso" and "Obakoso/Oba Koso" examined earlier, Abímbọ́lá offers a reliable translation for the prayer that Houk documented.[107] Thus, encounters such as the one between Father Isaac and Olawaiye probably influenced the OYCO's translation. Since the era of Black Power, Orisa communities have expanded their repertoires of ritual prayers and songs and their translations of inherited Yoruba Trinidadian sacred orature into English through transnational exchanges with Nigerians, many of whom would be familiar with the popularized "ọba ko so" Christian narrative.

The Trinidadian oral data most closely connected with pre–Black Power elders and their grandparents support the conclusions that Yorùbá scholars such as Ìṣọlá and Akínyẹmí reach about the semantic contexts in which the phrases "ọba Kòso" and "ọba kò so" lent distinct narratives to Yoruba sacred orature, Christian missionary texts, and the collective memory of Sango worship. With the weight of popular interpretation signaling how deeply lodged the "ọba kò so" tradition is in Nigeria's collective Yorùbá imagination,[108] the Trinidadian emphasis on "Obakoso" (Oba Koso/Aba Koso) challenges the credibility of the more widely accepted "ọba kò so" tale. Unlike Olawaiye, who was raised in Nigeria during the mid-twentieth century, the liberated Yorubas who settled in postemancipation Trinidad would have been untainted by the "ọba kò so" legend that Hethersett advanced in Yorùbá-speaking regions of Nigeria during the late 1800s or by Ellis's and Johnson's versions from the same period.[109] The pre–Black Power Yoruba Trinidadian memory of "Obakoso" is particularly convincing when placed alongside Iṣola's and Akinyemi's scholarship and Abímbọ́lá's transcriptions and translations, which privilege overlooked Yorùbá vernacular experts, sacred literature, and oral culture.[110]

In addition to what the sources explored in this section reveal about the place of sovereignty in Yoruba/Africana nation formation during the nineteenth century, comparative analysis of source data from Trinidad and Nigeria demonstrates the import of research that, in historian Peter Caron's estimation, "stresses the value of wedding local histories in Africa and in the new world."[111] Studying the ritual legacies of African heritage religions in the Caribbean and the Americas changes how we view history, particularly African history and the sources for constructing it. The intangible cultures of the African diaspora archive corroborative information about how African continental history, culture, politics, and religion were unfolding during colonial periods of African settlement in the Caribbean/Americas. These archives can prove more historically reliable than continental sources, and they invite comparative approaches to *Africana* religious history.

Methodologically, the cultural memory and material culture of African-descended people in the colonial Caribbean/Americas expand what we understand to be archives of African(a) history and culture and justify new scholarly research inspired by Africana religious and historical studies frameworks. Africana frameworks should inform the research of diaspora specialists, as well as African experts. Conversely, African studies scholars have important reasons to incorporate diaspora sources, especially about periods in which African societies were enduring mass deportations as a result of the transatlantic slave trade. African history is archived in the Caribbean and the Americas among those very populations whose attachment to and disjuncture from Africa have been debated for nearly a century.[112]

Historical knowledge of Africa did not immediately disappear as diasporaed African populations became Afro-Caribbeans/Americans because cultural transmission occurred (as did cultural change) across time, despite *and because of* major social and historical transformations. Titi's and Father Isaac's accounts of Aba Koso and Obakoso during the 1970s substantiate this point, as does the Yoruba *nation's* ritual repurposing of the Afro-Creole palais and its symbols and relevant institutions of Ọ̀yọ́ civil religion.[113] Culture and cultural memory do not operate in toto as a structure of social life, defenseless against the dynamics of social change, and historical events do not disrupt all cultural processes. Cultural memory is a repository of historical and religious knowledge that remains authoritative in the training of religious experts; it certainly has been prevalent in traditions transmitted intergenerationally among Yoruba-Orisa cultural custodians since the late nineteenth century. The orienting power of Yoruba-Orisa cultural memory for African descendants in Trinidad attunes us to the effects of cultural processes on the archiving of historical knowledge and the construction of religious knowledge.

Yoruba-Orisa devotees' religious knowledge and sacred poetics also reflect heterogeneity and tension within Yoruba-Orisa subtraditions. Although discredited in this study, Glazier's theory that North American anthropologists universalized "Shango" as a designation for Yoruba-Orisa religious practice beginning in the 1940s and 1950s cautions us that "Shango" may not have been in use since the nineteenth century as an internal meta-designation for Trinidad's Yorùbá-identified cultic lineages. There is little evidence to support this common scholarly assumption, and the earliest available report identifying an instance of Yoruba ritual performance (in the 1919 *Guardian* Samuel court case summary) used the expression "Yaraba dance" rather than "Shango."

This terminology is reminiscent of African labels for key ritual ceremonies in other Caribbean countries, such as Carriacou's Big Drum Dance (also known as *Nation* Dance) and Jamaica's Myal Dance;[114] it also resonates with Olaudah Equiano's eighteenth-century note that in Kingston, Jamaica, "each different nation of Africa [would] meet and dance, after the manner of their own country."[115] The testimony that Paulina Samuel and others at her ceremony "were singing in the African language and . . . indulging in *what was called the Yaraba dance*"[116] might suggest that the label "Shango" initially gained currency at the same time other designations such as "Yaraba dance" were already widely known.[117] Equally revealing was the celebrated priest Pa Neezer's reaction when Frances Henry asked him to share his "extensive knowledge" of "Shango" with her while conducting fieldwork at his palais during the mid-1950s. "'It's not Shango,' he replied sternly 'It's the African work, the Orisha work.'"[118]

There may also be some merit in the distinction one of Herskovits's interlocutors drew between her inherited "Yoruba" rites and those of the "Shango group."[119] Although Toco offered no centers of Shango activity he could study in summer 1939, before departing Toco for Port of Spain, Herskovits interviewed and recorded Yoruba songs (August 24–25) from an "elderly woman," Margaret Buckley, and her son/drummer, Joe Alexander. Herskovits introduces the "proper Yarraba" elder in an August 23 field notebook entry as having "great contempt for the Shango people," a sentiment unrelated to any disapproval of *christianisms* absorbed into the religion because she readily "correlated" "perfectly good Yoruba gods' names . . . with Catholic saints very nicely."[120] Herskovits's representation of their subsequent conversations highlights the heterogeneity and contentions that have characterized micro-solidarities and divisions across Trinidad's Yoruba-Orisa religious communities and nation-al life. His description of Buckley's heritage and religious knowledge suggests that an array of labels captured the Yoruba-Orisa religious imagination at any given moment and draws us into early twentieth-century intimacies and conflicts that spanned Yoruba networks:

> She herself is from this island, but her father and mother, who came from Africa before the end of slavery, migrated here soon after emancipation. Her mother, she says, was Egba, and had three cuts on the face; her father was "Yoruba" and had six facial cuts. She sang for Ogun, Oshun, Egungun (which she knows is a society and who put a ribbon about the face when dancing here) Yemanja, Olorun, and others; when Fann [Frances Herskovits] asked her if she sang for Osa, she said "You mean Aussa. That is another nation. There are plenty of them in Grenada." . . . She said there are at present seven women and four men who are the head of the Yoruba group on this island, and that they get together to "play" and sacrifice at the New Year. . . . They meet for 7 days and kill a sheep. She has considerable contempt for the Shango group who, she says, do not know the proper way to do things, and also for Baptists and other sects. However, she realizes that her beliefs are dying.[121]

Herskovits apparently did not press Buckley to explain the features distinguishing what might have been two (or more) distinct palais associations devoted to Yoruba-Orisa worship. In *Trinidad Village* he frames Buckley's contribution as evidence of the Trinidadian negro's "historic residue rather than cultural reality" and classifies her perspective as "merely a gloss on Toco culture today, significant only as helping to indicate provenience."[122] According to Warner-Lewis, "the Yoruba-speaking subgroups recalled by Trinidad oral sources" did indeed include the Ègbá, Buckley's mother's subgroup, as well as Buckley's father's subgroup, the "Yaraba or Yooba or Yoruba . . . meaning, in indigenous, pre-European terms, the Oyo."[123]

This snapshot of one Yoruba descendant's personal genealogy and "dying" spiritual inheritance bespeaks the ritual variation evident across the palais *nationscapes* scattered throughout Trinidad, as well as the actual pre-Yorùbá *nation* identities that would have been claimed by liberated Africans similar to Buckley's parents. In addition to the divisions and peculiarities that omorisa brought with them from West Africa, distinctions between northerners and southerners or urban and rural dwellers, the adaptation of inherited customs to the local environment by descendants of Yoruba Trinidadians, and immigrant custodians of the tradition from neighboring Caribbean territories subjected Trinidad's Yoruba-Orisa religious culture to modifications over time.

Buckley's story suggests, too, that any historical study of African religiosity in Trinidad requires analysis of the country's multicultural, multi-nation-al, and multireligious heritage. This chapter's title—a reference to the nation heritage of an African descendant—is important to revisit here. The court interpreter at John Cooper's nineteenth-century appeal hearing was correct in associating the defendant with an "African tribe" in Trinidad. However, the nation that addressed him by his so-called tribal name, Hou Quervee (or Tuervee), was not Yoruba but one of the two identified Rada (Dahomean) enclaves in Belmont (Port of Spain) during the nineteenth century, which Andrew Carr first studied in the early 1950s. Cultural heritage, lineage, and local customs imposed boundaries and distinguished Trinidad's African communities, even within the same nation. Yet those boundaries contained portals of cultural access within and across nations that facilitated attachments and liaisons in Trinidad in much the same way they did among cultural/linguistic groups, societies, and wider polities in African continental contexts.

The distinct nation networks that defined Trinidad's African subcultures during the late nineteenth century did not preclude inter-nation-al cultural exchanges and affiliations. Each nation identity was already a polyvalent signifier.[124] The Port of Spain Gazette's mention of "Yaraba Creoles" and their social activities sheds light on the preservation of old and the making of new ensembles of African identity in Trinidad during the early twentieth century. The 1912 announcement might be taken at first as a conventional designation for African-descended persons of Yoruba heritage who were born in Trinidad. Early twentieth-century "Yaraba Creoles" were likely third- and fourth-generation Yoruba Trinidadians, because "Creole" was commonly used in slave registers and other colonial records to identify African- and Euro-descended persons born in the Caribbean. However, the label "Yaraba Creoles" captures the nuances of Yoruba identity formation in Trinidad.

It is tempting to address the experiences of African-descended communities in Caribbean and American colonial diasporas by emphasizing each group's distinct social, cultural, economic, and historical milieu. Complex experiences and allegiances of persons of African heritage are often eclipsed by labels that reduce their complexity to static groupings as continental "ethnics" or Creoles; negro/black or colored; slaves or liberated Africans. These designations can be useful and necessary, but as the label "Yaraba Creoles" suggests, they never exhaust the range of identity belongings and cultural locations that person's experience.

The details concerning the group of approximately thirty-two "Yaraba Creoles" highlight the range of circumstances that enable a culture to be taught and passed down transgenerationally, even in contexts of displacement. These persons of shared Yoruba heritage were said to be traveling together for a sociocultural purpose—to support the wedding ceremony of (presumably) fellow Yoruba-descended *nation* members "with their own band of music."[125] Yoruba culture was not some innate property of those born in Africa. It had been taught to successive generations through language,[126] customs, and quotidian activities involving artistic productions and performances, culinary traditions, aesthetic tastes, technological skills, games, sports, and other pastimes. Though "Yaraba Creoles'" cultural connection to the Yoruba heritage would not have been exclusive—they would have shared cultural practices and social attitudes with other Afro-Trinidadians across a spectrum of identities and even with other racial-ethnic communities in Trinidad—Yoruba culture was a fixture of early twentieth-century Afro-Trinidadian life, even after liberated Yoruba settlers were no longer alive to represent that culture.

Drawing on the range of stories and cultural practices encountered during her interviews with African descendants at the time of the Black Power movement (1968–70), Warner-Lewis showed that African *nation* legacies persisted in Trinidad during the latter decades of the twentieth century. Many of her interlocutors could speak Yoruba and other languages either ritually, proficiently, or fluently. Arthur Sampson, for example, claimed Yoruba paternal heritage and Congo maternal heritage. His maternal grandfather, Mowanda, died eighty-two years before Warner-Lewis first interviewed Sampson in 1968, yet he still remembered his grandfather's cultural heritage as "Congo Momboma" (a MuMboma from the town of Mboma/Boma). Sampson also "performed Congo drumming at weddings and wakes and learnt songs which," Warner-Lewis claimed, "he could reproduce in the 1970s with an authenticity of phrasing and . . . style that would impress native Congolese."[127]

Reinforced by *inter-nation-al* coupling and marriage,[128] liberated Africans and their descendants in Trinidad participated in polycultural[129] and pan-Africanized social experiences. The term *inter-nation-al* signifies that which distinguished diverse African *nation* identities while still gesturing toward the global nature of pan-African bonds and cultural belonging among African descendants.[130] Some sources explore the role that *nation* traditions and events played in facilitating *inter-nation-al* African relations in Trinidad across the centuries, explaining how the Yoruba-Orisa tradition would come to reflect *inter-nation-al* exchanges among Yorùbá and Dahomean peoples not only in

West Africa but also in Trinidad. For example, Carr describes a rare Rada "Gozen" ceremony, celebrated once or twice per century. The Gozen that took place around 1888 displayed "Yoruba drummers" and devotees whom Mah Nannie (aka Robert Antoine), the shrine founder, invited to participate in the ceremony.[131] Mah Nannie was John Cooper's brother. Yet Cooper, a chief priest at the shrine, did not live to see that particular Gozen, having died eleven years earlier. One imagines, however, that Cooper had ample occasions to fraternize with Yoruba priests or other adherents of the Orisa tradition during his seventeen-year sojourn in Trinidad.[132]

The research Melville Herskovits (1939), Charles Sydney Espinet (1945), and Andrew Carr (1952) conducted allows additional comparisons of Yoruba and Dahomean social and religious formation in nineteenth-century Nigeria, Dahomey, and Trinidad. When Herskovits reviewed a draft of Carr's pioneering article, "A Rada Community in Trinidad," his response to Carr tackled the issue of intercultural exchange among Radas and Yorubas in West Africa and Trinidad:

> It would be interesting to include the Yoruba (Shango) who are outside this ecological unit, but must have figured in the life of this community. (see p. 14, Yoruba participation in Gozen rite). Since founder of Rada community is a Whidah man, it is especially interesting to probe reason for this invitation, for historically we know that when the Abomeyans conquered Whidah and Popo, a large group of refugees from both these kingdoms were given asylum by the kings of Appa and Pokra, and they settled in Badagri [in Nigeria], which . . . is part Dahomean and part Yoruba in culture, i.e. there was intertribal acculturation of this . . . localised group as early as the first half of the 18th century.[133]

Espinet conjectured that the identifier Rada was "a contraction for the Dahomean Aradas tribe, . . . a hang-over in Trinidad of the importation of French slaves from Haiti, Martinique and other . . . islands to the north." He also characterized the Rada rites as encompassing "a double process of syncretism between Voodoo and Shango, on the one hand, and the African and Europo-Catholic religious beliefs and practices on the other."[134] More convincing grounds for synthesized pan-African elements that were possibly absorbed into Trinidad's Yoruba-Orisa structure is Espinet's treatment of Wêrê, a phenomenon of spirit manifestation during a phase of a trance experience that signals an incarnated deity's pending departure from a medium.

At the time of his 1945 study, Wêrê were associated with Duennes, a team of spirits "most often . . . described as 'unbaptised babies' . . . who die before being christened." The common belief held Duennes to be "mischievous 'little folks' who wear no clothes, live at the foot of wells, in caves and behind rocks in the forests, whose feet are 'wrong side' or 'before-behind' . . . to baffle those trying to follow their footprints."[135] Attentive to Herskovits's 1941–1942 encounter with an analogous "semi-possession . . . condition called *eré*" in the . . . Rio Grande do Sul Province of Brazil, Espinet hypothesized the Wêrê/Duenne structure was influenced by a comparable West African phenomenon of forest-dwelling "little people" in Dahomey, Yorùbáland, and, especially, Ghana where the Asante acknowledge a community of *moatia*—forest dwellers whose feet "point backwards."[136]

Nation heritage rituals and spiritual customs were bound to inspire *transnation-al* (pan-African) affinity and cultural exchanges among disparate *nation* groups. Newspaper articles and oral sources from the late nineteenth and early twentieth centuries indicate as much. When a smallpox epidemic swept the colony in 1871–72, the January 16, 1872, *Trinidad Chronicle* printed a rare account of a therapeutic rite performed to cure stricken patients at an independent Rada commune in the vicinity of the Rada devotees whom Carr studied in the 1950s. Whereas Mah Nannee's Rada rites were organized around principal devotion to the deity Dangbwe, this Rada commune's chief deity was Sakpata:

> The Radas, up Belmont Road, profess to know how to deal with it [smallpox] on African principles—saying it is a common disease in their country. They accompany their treatment with sacrifice, singing and dancing; the first followed up in a decidedly practical manner by a feast off the . . . fowls and kids previously slain in propitiation. The sacrifice is made in the morning, the feast about midday or afternoon then follow African songs and dancing down to night. At the feast, which is part of the religious ceremonial, they sit in a circle on the floor . . . a great bowl . . . in the centre, covered with a white cloth, holding the blood of animals sacrificed. Around the bowl are set a number of very large dishes . . . containing the meats of the sacrifice and various common vegetables. Each in turn . . . takes a very small portion out of each dish, and [heaps] these near the bowl, repeating . . . some words in Rada. This is held to be a peace offering to Mumbo Jumbo, or whatever the name of their particular jumby or deity. . . . At the holy dance they again sit in a circle, into which one gets up at a time, and goes through an amount of grave posturing to the sound of a tom-tom and singing.[137]

Without a doubt, the invisible power at the center of any Rada ritual against smallpox was the Dahomean earth deity Sakpata (Sagbata) whose Yoruba counterpart bore the name Shoponna.[138] Important here is the extent to which the *Chronicle's* editor, Thomas William Carr (an Englishman who happened to be Andrew Carr's paternal grandfather), featured an African (Rada) ritual as newsworthy information for the average citizen. The report arguably helped advertise the commune's services to those affected by the epidemic among the general public and likely attracted special attention from Trinidad's African community.[139] A detail from Andrew Carr's (1902–76) early life also suggests that Trinidad's diverse African *nations* could rise above petty disputes, disparaging stereotypes and even the occasional vicious rivalry that erupted among *nation* gangs.[140] The scholar recounts that he "frequently ac-companied" his Mandingo-Trinidadian grandmother (b. 1844) "to the [Rada] compound on ceremonial occasions" during his childhood and notes that "although she was not intimately connected with the rites, she was held in high regard by the community."[141]

Examined together, the scholarly sources presented in this section pro-vide a sketch of the polycultural *inter-nation-al* ethos in which Yoruba-Orisa religious traditions appeared during the late nineteenth and early twentieth centuries. Various subtraditions took shape around inherited Yoruba kinship structures that were not impervious to neighboring influences. In the Port of Spain area, where Rada and Yoruba-Orisa shrines received the earliest scholarly attention, research indicates that *vodunisms* had penetrated the Yoruba-Orisa ritual vocabulary in some communes by the 1930s, if not at the time of their initial formation. These vodunisms, documented by the Her-skovitses, could have traveled with first-generation Yoruba-Trinidadians from the regions of pre-Yorùbáland close to the Dahomean border, from displaced Ouida/Whydah and other Aja-speaking peoples living in pre-Yorùbáland (Badagry/Badagri), or from pre-Yorùbás living in Dahomey at the time of capture.[142] We cannot rule out, however, the possibility that Yoruba new-comers adopted vodunisms from enslaved Saint-Domingue Africans and other Afro-Caribbean practitioners of West African Vodun who relocated to Trinidad with their owners after the Cédula of 1783.[143] Finally, the vodunisms apparent in at least one shrine in Port of Spain might have resulted from interactions between that particular "Shango" (Yoruba-Orisa) group and Rada shrines in the area.[144] A combination of these factors also might have been at work, though the long history of interaction between Dahomey and pre-Yorùbáland deserves careful treatment that is beyond the scope of this volume as the backdrop to "Rada" and "Yaraba" presence in Trinidad and across the Atlantic world.

Histories of Dahomey, pre-Yorùbáland, and their frontier zones throughout the eighteenth and nineteenth centuries, coupled with demographic data on liberated Africans in the Atlantic world, explain the appearance of Rada captives on liberated African rosters well after their sizable presence in the slave trade during the eighteenth century had slowed to a trickle in the nineteenth.[145] This wealth of material, assessed alongside other data, indicates that some liberated Africans who identified as Rada and others who identified as Yorùbá carried to Trinidad religious cultures that had already interfaced and transformed one another's ritual terrains in West Africa long before their exile and resettlement.[146] For example, among the twelve oral family histories that Warner-Lewis presents in *Guinea's Other Suns*, her interlocutor Lucy "Titi" Charles's maternal line showed exactly this kind of interfacing. Titi's grandmother, Ashade (Aṣàdé), a native of Ibadan in pre-Yorùbáland, "came [to Trinidad] from Ajase, the coastal area called Porto Novo in the present-day Republic of Benin." Warner-Lewis speculates Ashade might have been transferred from Ibadan to a staging post in Porto Novo, "a major Yoruba slave port," before crossing the Atlantic. However, because Ashade's mother was a trader, the possibility exists that she was conducting business close to the Porto Novo area when she and other family members were taken captive. Warner-Lewis draws extensively from Titi's lived religion[147] to sketch Yoruba-Orisa practice during the nineteenth and early twentieth centuries, including her "drazon" litanies. Drazon is a "Fon [Dahomean] term for 'vigil' to designate the night of prayers before the dawn start of the five- to seven-day *orisha* ceremony."[148]

Rosanne Adderley's study of liberated Africans underscores the significance of such pre-Trinidadian sociocultural and political entanglements involving Yorùbá and Dahomean captives in West Africa, on slave vessels, and in other "imperial spatial formations" of the Middle Passage.[149] Her analysis of the international antislave trade British-Spanish court records from Havana, Cuba, where 10,391 freed captives—roughly one-tenth of the entire liberated African population—were processed reveals the following:

> In some cases from the Havana sample, Fon slaves from Dahomey who were classified as Mina Popo or Arara arrived on vessels that also carried Yoruba slaves from the territory east of Dahomey that has become modern Nigeria. Such mixing of ethnic groups reflected not only the movements of slave traders but also some degree of intercourse between such groups

within Africa long before their experience of shared community aboard foreign slave ships. A handful of marginal notations in the Havana registers provide evidence of such interaction. The slaver *Fila* carried a mostly Yoruba cargo but also brought two men designated as Mina Popo who were likely of Ewe or Fon ethnicity. Immediately following these Mina Popo slaves in the *Fila* list there appear three Yoruba males set apart with the following comment: "This man Number [386] and the two previous [boys], although they are Lucumí [Yorùbá], understand only the language of Mina, to which nation they went when they were very young."

Adderley also discusses the wide range of subgroups attached to *nation* identifiers such as Congo, Mandingo, and Lucumí, which the liberated Africans themselves must have given to authorities. "Lucumí eyó" (Oyo), "Lucumí eva," and "Lucumí ota" appear in the records identifying Yorubas who passed through Havana. These data complicate narratives of Yoruba-Rada exchanges in nineteenth- and early twentieth-century Trinidad and indicate the complex relations that situated Yoruba, Rada, and other liberated Africans within concentric and interfacing affiliative units.[150]

This chapter's analysis of Africana *nationhood* raises additional conceptual questions about standard approaches to studying the phenomenon of African *nations* in the Caribbean/Americas. Although historians have gone to great lengths to complicate our understanding of Africana *nations* as a distinct phenomenon in the shaping of African diaspora societies, the absence of adequate Western translational terms to convey the technologies and products of *nation* consciousness and affiliation causes many to substitute the conventional concepts of ethnicity or ethnonym for *nation* in their works. An example of why this trend should prove vexing to scholars is Alexander Byrd's analysis of the extensive range of people-groups to which eighteenth-century African Atlantic writer and abolitionist Olaudah Equiano applied the terms *country* and *nation*; many of these applications violate the manner in which ethnic groupings and distinctions are conceived today. At other times, Equiano used *country* and *nation* to convey "more subtle" and "more restrained" "boundaries and differences" than those of his European counterparts when they distinguished between nations such as "England and France" or even "England and Scotland."[151]

Byrd also identifies shifts in Equiano's use of the terms *country* and *nation* that align with his exilic diasporic experiences outside Africa and signal how and why the semantic boundaries of these designations were reconfigured in the wider African Atlantic world. Moreover, Byrd's contextualization of the term "Eboe" (Igbo), which was unfamiliar, loosely known, infrequently embraced, and differentially employed across the Biafran interior during and well after the eighteenth century, helps clarify why, for some Africans, their *nation* identities linked them exclusively to small towns and villages.[152] Byrd invites scholars to move beyond narrowly "describ[ing] being [of a certain *nation*] as possessing certain traits, performing certain actions, and practicing certain behaviors" so as to "interrogate the process or (processes) of becoming [a *nation* member]."[153]

Historians' concessions to the limitations of language can result in flattened treatments of *nations* as differentiated ethnic groups or ethnonyms, thus belying their own multidimensional portrayals of *nations* through painstaking research.[154] Douglas Chambers analyzes African *nations* as the products of African ethnogenesis in Africa and the African diaspora, explaining hermeneutical nuances in the term "ethnicity" that are useful for capturing the significance of Africana *nation* formation in the Caribbean/Americas. He locates a new analytical starting point for Africana *nation* studies in the concept of the "ethnie." "An ethnie," he writes, "is a named human population with myths of common ancestry, shared historical memories, one or more elements of common culture, a link with a homeland and a sense of solidarity among at least some of its members."[155] Chambers marshals compelling evidence to support this approach, which I agree is critical for understanding some valences of Africana *nationhood*.[156] However, as Chambers observes, Africana *nations* were "'doing things'"[157]—constructing intimate social environments and sacred universes that mattered to them in their situations of captivity and exile. They were also teaching subsequent generations cultural norms and traditions—in the case of this study, teaching them how to be Yoruba while living in Trinidad. To appreciate the Africana contexts in which diverse *nations* emerged, scholars will have to explore the relationship among *nation* loyalties in African *and* African diasporic locales/translocales. Yet to answer the question of what Africana *nationhood* was, we must also study what Africana *nations* did.

Building on Olatunji Ojo's conclusion that "during the nineteenth and twentieth centuries Yoruba cultural experts and their works traversed the Americas reinforcing the orisa basis of Yoruba-Atlantic nations,"[158] in this chapter, I endeavored to understand some of the things the Yoruba *nation* was *doing* in Trinidad, especially through its sacred poetics: its repurposed ensembles of Orisa religious thought and practice. I also tried to manage some of the translational slippages that the concept of ethnicity imposes on Africana *nation* studies first by acknowledging that the *nation* is in itself an irreducible phenomenon. To reinforce this understanding, I avoided substituting loaded terms such as "ethnicity" or "ethnonym" for the concept of *nation*.

At the same time, this chapter and this volume are no less haunted than historical studies of Africana *nations* by Byrd's inescapable warning that "neglecting the history and substance of slaves' consciousness of the nation, the details of when, how, where, and whether Africans and their descendants nurtured and articulated a certain ethnic or national consciousness, cannot help but produce an analytically flat and relatively ahistorical understanding of what it meant to be Igbo, or Nago, or Coromantee, or Congo, in particular times and in certain places across the Atlantic world."[159] This chapter tries to provide a small aperture to the kinds of investigations Byrd recommends. However, it has done so with attention to modalities of the sacred that link, for example, sovereignty to *nationhood* in the Yoruba-Orisa religious and social imagination. It unpacks how *nation-al* religious structures have accommodated the multitextured elements and differently accented cultural, spiritual, and political knowledges that have informed Africana *nation* consciousness wherever such loyalties emerged in the African diaspora.

It would not be far off the mark to consider Africana *nationhood* not only as a mode of access to sociable interactions with others of the same or related heritages in the diaspora but also as a psychic and social passport authorizing claims to (1) related heritages in Africa and/or shared identities during the Middle Passage, (2) sovereign Powers, (3) spiritual families in the invisible realm, and (4) *inter-nation-al* exchanges with ambient *nations*. Archival and historical ethnographic sources support this formulation. And although techniques of *nationhood* and sovereignty in the Orisa religious culture coproduced Yoruba persons who answered to alternative governing Powers beyond British colonial regimes,[160] practices of family and kinship were just as crucial to *nation-al* integrity and security. Chapter 2 analyzes kinship/family as the core structure that binds the Yoruba-Orisa *nation* together and explains why conventional theories of syncretism have obscured just how central the ethic and logic of kinship are to every dimension of Yoruba-Orisa religious consciousness and culture in Trinidad.

I Had a Family That Belonged to All Kinds of Things

YORUBA-ORISA KINSHIP PRINCIPLES AND
THE POETICS OF SOCIAL PRESTIGE

If Sango presented the most salient symbols of sovereignty for a nascent Yoruba *nation* in Trinidad, he did not do so alone. We know that, in at least some devotional communities, his Orisa "brothers" Dada and Aba Koso or other Orisa family members accompanied him.[1] They arrived to appease devotees' requests for support and to receive their gifts. Reportedly, Orisa adherents in Trinidad worship and engage a community of Powers numbering more than sixty. Of this group, close to twenty are from the Catholic tradition, including personalities such as St. Peter, St. Barbara, and St. Michael; five are from South Asian and Amerindian cultural heritages, and one carries the appellation Wong Ka and hails from a Chinese tradition.[2]

Inspired in part by this panoply of apparent interreligious theistic entities, anthropologists have argued or implied for decades that syncretism is a defining feature of Yoruba-Orisa religion in Trinidad, as well as of other African heritage religions of the Caribbean and the Americas. The polemics inherent in the conventional cultural anthropological stance toward theology collapse in the discursive environment of African diaspora religious ethnography. There, the discourse of syncretism operates as theological reflection.

Syncretism, like faith, is—using John Jackson's term—"thickened knowledge."[3] But the revelation that precedes syncretism is never self-evident in studies of Afro-Caribbean religions. Given that all religions have "syncretic" processes and elements, the emphasis on syncretism in African diaspora traditions seems calculated to disrupt the notion that "pure" African beliefs and ritual practices were "preserved" across Afro-diasporic landscapes. The syncretism conceptual framework is now, unfortunately, a fait accompli in African-Caribbean and African American religious studies. However, I bracket the assumption of syncretism in order to access core principles that shape Yoruba-Orisa sacred poetics. Adopting a phenomenological approach, I sympathize with the affective experiences of religious devotees—with what black captives have experienced in their "second creation" of commodification and how their social meaning-making and sense of belonging are realized in part through affective modes of caring, loving, and healing.[4] Through "informed empathy" and indigenous hermeneutics, I attempt to "bring out what religious acts [and emotions] mean to [religious] actors."[5] My analysis approaches some of the most salient transgenerational values of Yoruba-Orisa devotees and describes theoethical tenets of the tradition and the logics that inform those tenets. I am thus able to challenge what I call the "theology of syncretism" to argue that Yoruba cultural norms and spiritual logics have long provided orientation for Orisa devotees in Trinidad. Moreover, Yoruba norms and logics have even deeper roots in a centuries-long arc of Niger-Congo cultural patterns that have influenced the religious and cultural worlds of people-groups across "roughly half of Africa's surface"[6] (see map 2.1). This is why we might think of them not solely as Yoruba logics and norms but also as Africana logics and norms.

How do historical factors, socioeconomic arrangements, and local cultural and environmental dynamics affect the tenets and practices explored here? This is a worthwhile inquiry that other published studies have certainly addressed. They provide conventional temporal approaches to theorizing cultural resilience and change. However, local, historical, and cultural studies will never access all that can be known about a community's heritage and legacy. The scope of such studies might be too narrow to consider culture as a *moving continuity* and to trace broader orientational patterns in a given culture (religion) or across a set of related cultures (religions).

Wyatt MacGaffey assigns himself this latter task in "The Cultural Tradition of the African Forest," distilling the theoretical foundations and material

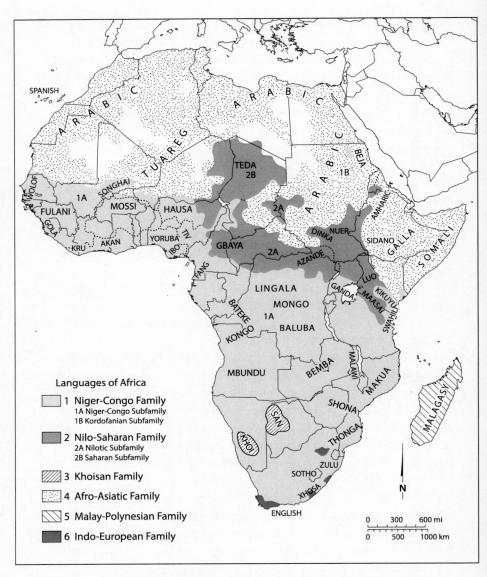

MAP 2.1 Map of six major linguistic families in Africa, including Niger-Congo language group. (Map prepared by Bill Nelson.)

expressions of a cosmological outlook that penetrates numerous Niger-Congo societies. Comparing artistic, religious, and medicinal cultural productions from dozens of West and Central African people-groups (including the Yorùbá), he finds that "all these forms are governed by the ambiguities of the container and the contained, the seen and the unseen, the transient and the eternal." He considers the phenomena in question to be "integrated not just by similarities but by the recurrence . . . of conceptual and practical oppositions derived from a particular cosmology. Knowledge of that cosmology," MacGaffey insists, "justifies the intuition shared by generations of scholars that a particular tradition gives the forest areas of West and Central Africa an organic cultural integrity" affirmed by the fusion of "orisas, vodou, and minkisi in the Americas." The interfacing of these spiritual traditions "testifies to their affinity as understood by transplanted Africans innovating in a new environment."[7]

Inspired by MacGaffey's methodology, I survey enduring cultural/spiritual principles that flow from ancient Niger-Congo cultural orientations across a longue durée of African history and that transcend the many differentiating features of diverse historic and contemporary Yoruba-Orisa communities in Trinidad (and beyond). Such principles disrupt conventional understandings of temporality and constructions of history. Still, because I assume that "Africans [have] the capacity and cultural mechanisms to establish ideals and ethical norms that endure over time,"[8] this chapter leans in the direction of conceptual argumentation rather than historical and ethnographic narration. It examines the motifs of family and kinship as orienting structures of Yoruba-Orisa sacred poetics. Because orthographic techniques are not privileged among African cultural mechanisms for communicating and teaching indigenous religious knowledge, accessing Yoruba religious ideas (in this case) and their historical or transhistorical contexts requires decoding songs and chants, narratives, dances, dreams, sacred objects, and symbols, including adopted symbols that acquire different significations in other religious traditions.

The logic, ethos, and ethic of kinship/family and social belonging are the driving impetus of Orisa religious imagination and practice in Trinidad, and the cosmic-social imperative to nurture and sustain family and kinship is the most enduring and authoritative precept of the common life and spirituality that Yoruba-Orisa devotees share. Their traditions—including Orisa devotion—were fostered primarily within genealogical family lineages well into the twentieth century. Even after Orisa leaders began to adopt spiritual children into their lineages, Professor Rawle Gibbons discovered through a nationwide poll of Orisa adherents in the late 1990s that attentiveness to the family principle was central. Reflecting on the regional meetings he held with Orisa shrines, Gibbons recalls that one "concrete consensus was that we needed to have a family day when everybody could get together and celebrate ourselves and all the rest of it [the Orisa heritage]."[9]

In Yoruba and other Niger-Congo African cultures, the kinship principle is a powerful rationale justifying how and why persons create meaning through social experience. It is the axiological framework that places limits and expectations on individuals as social actors within an economy of obligations. Such obligations are concrete and tacit, binding persons to roles and responsibilities that traverse the boundaries of visible and invisible existence. Because individuals are social creatures who must acquire social intelligence to survive, every culture across the globe has some notion of kinship or family, among other mechanisms for organizing within social groups. Yet not every religious culture privileges kinship and familial relations as a commonsense standard for navigating the social and cosmic environment. This chapter reflects on the spiritual/familial components of nature—a terrain of cosmic-social reality and relationality. However, it does not attempt to reify idealized conceptions of hospitable living among Yoruba people and Orisa religious practitioners; instead, it inventories the ingredients of an idea so powerful in its theoretical and practical effects that the spiritual and social operations of Orisa religious culture would lose all coherence without it.

Kinship arrangements encompass not only families but also ensembles of relationships, networks, and group affiliations, and the familial social unit is arguably the most intimate and affectively salient expression of kinship ties.[10] Although often coupled in this discussion, kinship and family are not interchangeable. Thus I examine both family and kinship motifs in authoritative sources of Yoruba sacred orature-literature and theology.

Despite local micronation heritages distinguishing pre-Yorùbá peoples, internecine wars that displaced and repopulated emergent Yorùbá territories between the 1790s and the early 1890s resulted in the circulation and cross-fertilization of local theological beliefs and religious traditions. As Olatunji Ojo explains, "The integration of local Orisa complexes into regional religious symbols began as Yoruba warfare created greater population mixture, new cities and interethnic marriages." After the collapse of the Ọ̀yọ́ Empire in the early 1830s,

> refugees, soldiers and traders traveled across ethno-political borders carrying their cultural artifacts, including Orisa. . . . Political disruptions

and population flow reconfigured the geography of orisa worship. As people moved to safety, they took along their ritual practices, thereby exporting these to places where they had been unknown. Hence, orisa began to evolve into pan-Yoruba symbols with a network of religious rituals and movement of priests across existing ethnic boundaries. A byproduct of population networking in the Yoruba homeland was the alignment of ritual performances and the evolution of a "unified" Orisa religion.[11]

From the moment of exile beyond their homelands to the moment of arrival in Trinidad, multicultural pre-Yorùbá peoples and micronations repeatedly experienced environments characterized by religio-cultural interfacing. Many would become knowledgeable about, if not affiliated with, previously exotic Orisa cults, sacred orature, and spiritual geographies.[12]

I also examine distinct local traditions of particular Yoruba diasporas that uphold the spiritual foundation for Yoruba kinship/family norms and customs. Attentiveness to indigenous reasoning and categories challenges the discursive dominance of syncretic theories in Yoruba-Orisa studies. Hence, this chapter posits the categories of kinship, family, and social belonging as grounded ones that (1) gloss the Yoruba-Orisa religion as an enduring, meaning-making African spiritual vernacular in Trinidad, (2) discredit the theology of syncretism and its resultant truisms concerning the Yoruba-Orisa religious phenomenon, and (3) require fresh theoretical frameworks for examining this religious complex in Trinidad today. To begin the task, we must first investigate the significance of kinship/family in Yoruba-Orisa sacred orature-literature and devotional life.

Sacred Narratives and Orisa Families

Sacred narratives guiding Yoruba-Orisa practice in Trinidad present the very deities/Orisa as a kinship group constituted by familial units that populate a vibrant invisible realm of interactive Powers. These invisible family networks are held together through relationships of consanguinity, affinity, and adoption; experiences of procreation, engagement, marriage, separation, widowhood, and divorce affect the Orisa's temperaments, destinies, choices, and influence.[13] Familial relatedness is a requirement for all theistic and cosmic operations, a truism conveyed through Yoruba sacred orature-literature. As the renowned professor and priest of Yorùbá tradition Wándé Abímbọ́lá explains,

> The verses of Ifá tell us that in those ancient times some animals and birds understood and spoke the languages of human beings and some humans

also spoke and understood the languages of birds and animals. To the ancient African mind, animals, plants, and humans were part of one large family. In those ancient times, whenever human beings were celebrating important festivals, they invited animals and birds. Some trees had the ability to change themselves into human or animal form, and they too were cordially invited to human events.[14]

This conception of family subtends the elaborate, fluid relational poetics and spiritual collectivity that characterize the Yorùbá cosmological outlook.[15]

One place to begin exploring the family motif is in the relationship that Yoruba-Orisa devotees forge with the Powers they know so well and experience as family members who demonstrate fidelity to their children, parents, in-laws, and other relatives. Relational terms indicate how devotees are expected to situate themselves vis-à-vis the divine community.[16] For example, Orisa devotees are typically called *omorisa* (child of the Orisa), and all devotees become spouses of their patron Orisa during the initiation process and are spiritually married to the Orisa.

The Orisa are Powers with extraordinary capabilities and qualities that distinguish them from their devotees. However, as family members, they are united within a moral ecology of mutuality, symmetry, and reciprocity that honors eldership and acquired wisdom. Underscoring this moral ecology are the sacred and social meanings that the concept of family invokes. For example, Yoruba theologies of belonging attribute respiratory power to Èmí, the breath of life that vivifies each person and sustains all creation. Èmí is also said to be Olódùmarè's *daughter*. Her relationship to the High God establishes a theological conceptualization of family, a divine blueprint for relational living. Èmí's role and function in the universe's diverse life systems reveal how family obligations are encoded within the universe's fundamental animating principle: breath.

In this framework, the notion that personal existence is contingent on the activating presence of Olódùmarè's daughter suggests that ~~human~~, animal, plant, mineral, and divine families breathe and vivify the universe together. They conspire (literally *conspirare*, "to breathe together" in Latin) in the project of cultivating relational and hospitable communal environments for all custodians of the universe. That this divine energy/generativity sustains ~~humans~~ and other forms of life reinforces an understanding of sociality as a sacred obligation of caring for Olódùmarè's daughter while caring for oneself and others. To carry Olódùmarè's daughter within—to breathe from her energy and animating qualities, physically and spiritually, as a condition for existence—

prepares omorisa to receive the energies and presences of the divine family that reside literally inside their bodies within ritual environments. A poem from the Odù Èjì *Ogbè* underscores Èmí's cosmic and social significance in Yoruba religious thought and culture:

> The whole head of an albino, gray hair;
> The hunchback carries the baggage of Òrìṣà without the possibility of
> setting it down;
> A strange and faraway place is where s/he has brought these strange
> ways.
> These were the names of the Babaláwo/Ìyánífá
> Who divined for Òrúnmìlà,
> On the day he was going to pay the dowry to marry Èmí, the daughter
> of Olódùmarè.
> Èmí, the daughter of Olódùmarè;
> An offspring who spreads a thin and fragile mat but whose Orí can
> weather the storm.
> Òrúnmìlà was asked to perform sacrifices,
> He did.
> Òrúnmìlà was asked to give a portion of the sacrifice to Èṣù,
> He did.
> Òrúnmìlà asks:
> "Isn't it the case that as long as Èmí is not lost there is wealth?"
> Yes, there is wealth!
> "Isn't it the case that as long as Èmí is not lost there is a spouse?"
> Yes, there is a spouse!
> "Isn't it the case that as long as Èmí is not lost there are children?"
> Yes, there are children!
> "Isn't it the case that as long as Èmí is not lost all the good things of
> life will come?"
> Yes, all the good things of life will come![17]

In addition to sourcing the universe's primordial and perpetual sacred breath, Èmí receives affirmation in this passage as the foundation of the Yoruba people's most prized social goods—kinship, family, and generativity. Family is a structure of relational life that crosses boundaries and binds the invisible and visible communities. It is the most intimate structure to which persons are oriented as they journey through the life cycle and assume visible and invisible states of existence. Examining the preponderance of narratives in continental and diaspora Yoruba-Orisa orature that reinforce the sacred and social significance of family bonds is beyond the scope of this chapter. However, even a sampling of narratives conveys the point here made. In Trinidad, Sango is commonly believed to have two brothers, Dada and Aba Koso (Obakosa), who also manifest during Orisa ceremonies.[18] In many West African and diasporic contexts, Ọya is one of Ṣàngó's wives. Ṣàngó is also said to be the son of Ọrănyàn.[19] Countless Odù narratives depict Ọrúnmìlà sending his "children" on all sorts of errands, and Ọ̀rúnmìlà's parents (Òrokò and Alájèrù) are named in sacred orature.[20] Even Ọbàtálá/Òrìṣà-nlá is associated with the birthplace of his maternal lineage. "At Ifọ́n, where one tradition says that [Òrìṣà-nlá's] mother was born, he is known as Olúfọ́n," writes E. Bọ́lájí Ìdòwú.[21]

Gary Edwards and John Mason also describe the multiple maternal, paternal, and sibling relationships that structure the community of Orisa in many diaspora traditions, some of which correspond with continental Yorùbá narratives. Ọ̀ṣọ́ọ̀sì and Ògún are said to be "blood brothers." Yẹmọja personifies the essence of motherhood for cosmos and creation and is understood to "have given birth to: Dàda (newborn babies), Ṣàngó (thunder and lightning), Ògún (iron), Olókun (bottom of the ocean), Ọlọ́sà (lagoons), Ọya (winds), Ọ̀ṣun (river), Ọbà (river), Òrìṣà Oko (agriculture), Òkè (hills), Babalúaiyé (earth's wrath), Ọrun (sun), Ọṣùpá (moon), Ọ̀ṣọ́ọ̀sì (hunters), and Ajé Ṣàlúgà (wealth and luck)."[22] As impressive as her lineage is, Yemoja is not the only Orisa to mother multiple children: in Brazil, Oya is commonly addressed as Iansan/Yansan, the mother of nine children.

Undoubtedly, myriad narrative versions of the Yorùbá deities' kinship connections entered Trinidad with the thousands of Yorubas who settled there in the nineteenth century. A poem published in Warner-Lewis's volume *Trinidad Yoruba* features a more obscure deity, Ọ̀gẹ́rẹ́, and in just two short lines conveys the centrality of familial relationships: "Ogere entered the earth with his horse, / Both he and his older sister." Warner-Lewis comments further that "the names of the *orisha* may be preceded by familial titles such as 'Papa' . . . or 'Mama.'"[23] In her 2011 meditations on the deity Esu, Trinidadian iyalode, Sangowunmi Patricia McLeod, describes him as follows: "Esu Odara the son of Osun was born on this earthly plain when Olodumare sent Irunmole to settle the earth and build the shrines." In the meditation titled "Esu Wielder of Protocol," Iyalode Sangowunmi reaffirms Esu's power as an extension of his mother's power and influence: "Esu powerful son of Osun, / who sits in a neutral place and knows / the protocol of the universe / teach us how to be humble, / teach us the correct and reverent postures to access the cosmos."[24]

Genealogical and social details about Orisa kinship bonds are ubiquitous across the manifold lineages of pan-Yoruba orature in Africa and the African diaspora, and in Yoruba cosmology the deities are assumed to have families *even if family members are unnamed*. Although understood as avenues to deep and efficacious knowledge that can resolve the problems ~~humans~~ create and encounter, narratives about the Orisa also convey to devotees that these Powers wrestle with the same set of challenges ~~humans~~ confront. Stories of the Orisa illustrate their constant struggles to sustain ideal conditions for sociality, health, good fortune, and wellness within family lineages and wider social networks, both in the invisible domain and with animals, plants, and other entities. As they succumb to jealousy, despair, fear, anxiety, arrogance, greed, and anger, these struggles highlight the Orisas' personal failings and challenge them to demonstrate noble qualities of sacrifice/selflessness, hospitality, forgiveness, generosity, and so on.

Examples from the Cuban Pataki narratives underscore this point. Ochun is said to have given birth to Osetura (Esu) among others, but Ochun loses custody of her children to fellow Orisa who assume roles as adoptive parents after she falls on hard times. She does not regain custody of her children until she secures a stable marriage with the rich and handsome river deity Aje-Shaluga.[25] By other accounts, Ochun has been known in Cuba as the "caretaker of [Aganjú's] children" and the "keeper of his secrets."[26] In another narrative, Obatala must choose among three suitors for his beautiful and beloved daughter's hand in marriage.

The standard portrayals of the Orisa as a divine community established first and foremost through family relationships convey the primacy of intimate bonds and the expectation that family members are responsible for one another. So important is situating the Orisa within sacred genealogies that when cultic devotion to one Power supersedes that of another with similar characteristics, communities can seek to relate both Powers through the ties of kinship, as Bọ́lájí Ìdòwú shows is the case of the two sky divinities, Ṣàngó and Jàkŭta: "There has been an earlier Yoruba solar divinity, to whom lightning and thunder have been attributed. His name is Jàkŭta, which means 'One who fights with stones,' or 'One who hurls stones.' In most of Yorubaland today, people are not quite sure whether to say that it was Jàkŭta who was the father of Ṣàngó or to put it the other way round."[27]

Stories and poems of Ifá, Ẹ̀rìndínlógún, and other orature-literature reveal that Yoruba people understand familial experience as primordial, numinous, and archetypal, encompassing all of creation, and that they conceptualize personhood relationally: to be a person is to be a member of a social and cosmic family and a holder of lineage rights and obligations.[28] It is no surprise then that among the material Tracey Hucks explores from British surgeon Robert Clarke's account of his encounters with liberated Africans in 1840s Sierra Leone are details suggesting that the Akoos (Yorùbá) adhere to a sophisticated relational theology. In a rare description of liberated Yorùbá religious beliefs, Clarke writes, "It [Jffeh or Ife] was the first place that God made, and where he put the first man and woman; it is also the place of departed spirits, for whose accommodation a market place has been erected, called Ouga Attehah, or the market of the dead,—where the dead buy and sell. In this place, the surviving relatives of a person lately deceased, may obtain an interview with the departed."[29] Familial relationships are not to be severed, even between the living and the departed, and the premium Yorùbás place on relational life situates the market geo-spiritually as a crossroads where visible and invisible family members meet, exchange, and perhaps reinforce their roles and their responsibilities to one another, their lineages, and wider kin networks.

Unquestionably, for the Yoruba, familial bonds are embedded within the structure of the universe, and a precept of inseparable kinship characterizes the relational Orí-àṣẹ (Soul-force) in all creation.[30] Yoruba orature-literature idealizes and even sacralizes family values of provision and nurturance, responsible and loving parenting, dutiful and loyal care for aging parents, representing one's family and lineage honorably and reverentially, and hospitality toward others external to the family or kin group. Kinship then should not be theorized as solely a mode of relationality and sociality. Instead, it functions across multiple valences as a core principle of Yoruba culture and sacred poetics.

Whereas anthropologists have published prodigious studies on kinship in Africa and other global regions, scholars of religion have not been nearly as prolific in addressing the subject. Kinship and family studies seem apropos for social-scientific analysis, whether researching social organization or cultural mechanisms. However, this study demonstrates that kinship is no less relevant to the field of religion, including definitional and theoretical scholarship.

All in the Family: Kinship, Seniority, and Belonging
in Yoruba-Orisa Tradition and Culture

Scholars have long theorized about the frequency and facility with which Trinidadian Yorubas attached themselves to or developed parallel structures mimicking wider institutions of the colonial order. Not surprisingly, the emphasis in Yoruba-Orisa diaspora studies on eclecticism and syncretism has, to date, monopolized the conversation. However, by attending to the social dynamics of Yoruba-Orisa sacred poetics, a different understanding emerges. Scholars such as Wándé Abímbọ́lá and Kọ́lá Abímbọ́lá have argued that one of the organizing principles of the Yoruba tradition is its "elasticity": its ability to engage and accommodate new circumstances and foreign elements from the outside world.[31] This facet of Yoruba-Orisa thought and practice is striking evidence that old-world Yorùbá social values have shaped how Yoruba Trinidadians position themselves vis-à-vis alternative *structures of belonging*, whether Kongo, Dahomean/Rada, Catholic, Baptist, Hindu, or Masonic. From their Catholic congregations to their lodges, or from their indigenous banks to their mutual aid societies, Yoruba and other *nations* in Trinidad approached maturation and social existence through old-world epistemological assumptions and norms about kinship, education, and knowledge, as well as leadership, influence, and power.

David Scott's reconceptualization of slavery and colonialism as arenas in which Africans were creative and assertive actors is instructive here because "our postcolonial present," and I would add colonial sources themselves, demand "a story more attuned to the productive ways in which power has shaped the conditions of possible action [and] the cognitive and institutional conditions in which the New World slave [and liberated African] acted."[32] Scott's approach encourages scholars to perceive how first-generation Yorubas and their descendants in colonial Trinidad have accessed and produced the power required to construct community, to enjoy status and leisure, and to relax and even thrive in concert with invisible kinship forces. The aura of the sacred and the authority of divine sanction made explicit in institutions such as the Catholic or Protestant Church and, more specifically, the "cult of the saints" would not be lost on Yoruba Trinidadians who valued the infinite knowledge of the Orisa and its comprehensive applications in the visible realm. Furthermore, initiation into smaller or wider circles of knowledge and influence was something the Yoruba person was socialized to desire and accomplish. The transition to Trinidad did not dampen this aspirational sensibility; seniority as a standard measure of social status and personal authority coupled with a *consciousness of belonging*[33] became a firm foundation on which to reestablish, from the chaos of a disturbed cosmos, the boundaries of community and the principles of sociality.

In Yoruba projects of social reconstruction, colonial institutions were not off-limits. Indeed, the influence and status official rituals conferred on candidates made colonial, as well as indigenous, institutions appealing arenas of instruction, initiation, rebirth, title holding, and leadership for displaced and colonized Yoruba *nationals*. Internal cultural agency and external structural power coalesced and collided as Yoruba exiles annexed colonial structures for purposes of their own, even as they complied with the constraints those same structures imposed.[34]

The biography of renowned Orisa leader Ebenezer Elliott, aka Pa Neezer, is one place to start this discussion. For many, the name "Pa Neezer" is a metonym for Yoruba-Orisa priestly expertise. Enhancing his reputation as a powerful Orisa priest is his relationship with his maternal grandmother, the honorable Orisa ancestor-priestess Ma Diamond, a native African who mentored him in the tradition.[35] Frances Henry's memoir of her ethnographic encounters with Pa Neezer, beginning in the 1950s, demystifies surviving narratives about him in Trinidad's popular Yoruba-Orisa lore. Opposite the memoir's acknowledgments page is a black-and-white image of a stout middle-aged Pa Neezer taken around 1945. His "Lodge Master's" decorative belt, apron, and matching medallions supported by an elaborate satin ribbon—symbols of his elite membership—cast in sharp relief his semiformal dark suit and tie. Perhaps only initiated eyes can discern whether his accouterments disclose an affiliation with the Oddfellows or the Mechanics.[36] The image supports Henry's account of Pa Neezer as not just the "Shango King," whom many in Trinidad dubbed an "Obeah man," but also a Baptist and a lodge man.[37]

Henry speculates that the structure of the lodges as "secret societies" appealed to Pa Neezer's Yoruba/African sensibilities:

> Pa also found a compatibility in Lodge membership because of his knowledge of African secret societies. I suspect he knew a great deal about their structure, forms and specific behaviour although these were not maintained in the merging of Orisha and Christianity. . . . Lodge membership satisfied his need to help people which is also evident in his bush doctoring but he was also powerfully attracted to the secret and ritualistic nature of these societies. They mirrored his attraction to and participation in Orisha religion which, in his time was largely secret and whose worship is replete with ritual and symbol most of which is African derived.[38]

Pa Neezer's simultaneous membership in multiple societies with the authority to confer titles and ranks might be understood as the natural consequence of engaging the social world through a Yoruba (and even a wider Niger-Congo) consciousness about *seniority* and *social belonging*.

TABLE 2.1

Microsocieties in the Nineteenth and Early Twentieth Centuries in Yorùbáland

Political Associations	Religious Associations
Ògbóni Secret Society	Òrìṣà associations
Warrior associations	
Hunters' Guild	
Age-Group associations	
Women's Political associations	

Occupation & Mutual Help Associations	Convivial Associations
Occupational associations	Ẹgbẹ́ associations
Aro	
Èsusú	

Yoruba social organization is defined by at least two principles: the privileging of seniority and an insider/outsider consciousness. Structured within the varied guilds, associations, and institutions that usher the Yoruba person from infancy to the doorstep of eldership are criteria for belonging and enjoying the privileges/responsibilities of membership and insiderness. These microsocieties were abundant across the diverse regions of what became Yorùbáland during the nineteenth and early twentieth centuries and, as Yorùbá sociologist Nathaniel Fadipẹ grouped them, encompassed the arenas shown in table 2.1.[39] Group activities and cultural proficiency guarantee the status of insiderness to novices and candidates undergoing authorizing rituals that confer a new status of belonging to a microsociety. These rites of passage often entail mystical experiences and spiritual instruction that are transformative for the novice. They change the newcomer from an outsider to an insider.[40]

During the mid-twentieth century, Peter Lloyd studied Yorùbá craft associations (occupational guilds) and their social, economic, and political functions. He was able to gain access to the minutes of a carpenters' union meeting, which offered a view into the craft associations' multifaceted objectives and ethical imperatives:

In 1945 the literate secretary of the Iwo Carpenters' Union wrote in his minute-book the following aims of his guild: "Reasons for having a meeting: 1. To know one another outside one's work and to love one another. 2. To make arrangements on our work and to be of unanimous voice. 3. To make merriment with each other in joy and to sympathize with those in sorrow. 4. To meet every eight days to make a true judgment on the work that comes to our company. 5. To keep the laws of our work, not to quarrel and not to fall into using bad medicine due to trouble over getting another man's work. 6. To contribute money to help when we have strangers or when we have a case in our work."[41]

It should not surprise us that the union's aims include the ethical principles of family care and responsibility, as well as hospitality toward strangers, because occupational guilds were structured across lineage relationships. Lloyd's comment that historically "the structure of these organizations was the lineage structure, the lineage meeting was the craft meeting; the craft head was the compound head, the oldest man in the lineage"[42] would have rung true for the nineteenth-century Yoruba elders who mentored Pa Neezer and other contemporary leaders of the Orisa tradition. If Yorùbá lineage structures were threatened by the mid-twentieth century when Lloyd conducted his research, the guilds remained intact, linked by the members' shared professional focus and advancing the family and kinship values they inherited. Augustine Agwuele outlines generic features of the kinship structures that would have been most familiar to Pa Neezer's ancestors when they settled in Trinidad:

> Precolonial Yoruba cities were made up of a series of patrilocal residences referred to as *agboile* (compound[s]). The compound was compartmentalized to hold several families and consisted of three stratified classes of people: (a) members of the patrilineal sib (*idile*) who resided in the compound and were known as children of the house (*omo-ile*); these included males and females who traced their descent to a common agnatic antecedent; (b) the wives of the male sib members; and (c) tenants, that is, outsiders (*alejo*) who were not biologically related to the sib members.

Protocols that regulated intimacy and distance between members of the compound were rigidly enforced to sustain a stratified social order that privileged seniority. Thus, Agwuele further explains,

> Within the compound . . . all the members were conscious of their place (*ipo*) and their obligations (*ojuse*). Like the individual compounds and their

residents, all the *agboile* that constituted the Yoruba *nation* were stratified and formalized into one big institution. Understanding the family structure and its organization is necessary for comprehending the kinship practices that evolved within it; the structure of the family, the compound, and the *nation* was seen reproduced at each layer and in the overall structure of the Yoruba society and politics.[43]

Agwuele joins a substantial list of Yorùbá studies scholars whose research identifies eldership or seniority as a long-standing organizing principle of social life. During the 1940s and 1950s, William Schwab studied the traditional Oṣogbo Yorùbá kinship system and explained how, in matters of political governance, "members of higher ranking lineages are accorded superior social position. . . . Thus, members of a chief's patrilineage are not merely granted special privileges by the chief, but it is their right, inherent in lineage membership, to avail themselves of the chief's political powers and economic prerogatives."[44] Writing during the 1970s, Fadipẹ claims that "the principle of seniority applies in all walks of life and in practically all activities in which men and women are brought together. The custom cuts through the distinctions of wealth, of rank, and of sex."[45] Yorùbá feminist sociologist Oyèrónkẹ́ Oyěwùmí adds that "seniority is the primary social categorization that is immediately apparent in the Yoruba language,"[46] a claim substantiated by Agwuele's observation that precolonial Yorùbá had "no personal terms for sibling." Instead, "[ẹ̀gbọ́n] (senior sibling) and àbúrò (junior sibling) were used as terms of reference for males or females on the paternal or maternal side."[47]

In describing the privileges and responsibilities that accompany senior status, Oyěwùmí shows that the structures of language, lineage, marriage, and religion reinforce customary standards for determining, rewarding, and holding responsible those occupying positions of seniority in Yorùbá institutions.[48] Implicit within the Yorùbá principle of seniority and its normative expressions across all societal domains that regulate ~~human~~ interaction is the valuing of social belonging and prestige as achievements enjoyed in stages throughout the life cycle. Both achievements are explicit measures of success because each rite of passage and life phase culminates in the individual undergoing a process to gain relative prestige through membership, insider positioning, or a formal title, each conveying social belonging within a status group.

The status of a typical spouse (usually a bride) within her marital partner's lineages exemplifies how seniority and belonging intersect to give the entering family member incremental access to insider status based on the duration of belonging. According to Oyěwùmí, the family lineage:

is best understood as an organization operating on a first-come-first-served basis. A "priority of claim" was established for each newcomer, whether s/he entered the lineage through birth or through marriage.... [The rank of a spouse] was independent of the rank of her conjugal partner.... If an old member [*oko* or owner/insider] married an *aya* ["nonowner/outsider in relation to the *ilé* as a physical space and the symbol of lineage"] after his own offspring had married, she (the father's *aya*) ranked lower than all the offspring's *aya*, because they preceded her in the lineage.[49]

As shown by the example of marriage, birth, and lineage, individuals acquire senior status by *belonging* to a unit, which could include marriage, family/lineage, age-grade initiation groups, priesthoods, and skilled labor and artisan guilds. Yoruba (and other African descendants) in Trinidad either instituted these kinds of social units or brought their principles of seniority and social belonging to their selected affiliations with cognate units in the colonial church and society. When they assumed leadership titles and formed confraternities within their Catholic congregations, for example, they exhibited a politics of respectability that had a two-pronged effect: it permitted access to social privileges within the wider civic public but did so based on their own *nation* values derived from a shared primordial public.[50]

Yoruba affiliations with colonial establishments were not necessarily maneuvers of dissemblance. Belonging to colonial structures that paralleled their own was a culturally sanctioned performance that accorded with specific Yoruba values concerning social prestige and privilege. In addition, some Yorubas' involvement with Catholicism might well have been motivated by a desire for respectability and acceptance by their Afro-Creole Catholic neighbors and associates.[51] Yoruba newcomers to Trinidad in the mid- to late nineteenth century met Afro-Creoles who had established Catholic identities—they engaged in confraternal processions and Emancipation Day practices of attending high mass before launching palais sovereignty celebrations that incorporated Catholic symbols such as blessed bread. As a result, some arriving Yorubas were likely empowered to conceive of their participation in Catholicism beyond the confines of colonial white constructions of Catholic piety. They witnessed and experienced firsthand African Catholic traditions unfolding around them and could locate familiar niches of cultural negotiation in a religious structure open to Africana cultural penetration.

Marie-Bertrand Cothonay's journal entry about the 1882 Afro-Creole Emancipation Day palais ceremony in Carenage concretizes theories of Afro-Creole autonomy and self-authorization in the face of oppositional white clerical power. His presentation of a historical instance in which he and the parish priest unsuccessfully attempted to disrupt an indigenous Afro-Creole custom by threatening to exclude Pierre, the "king" of the palais (and the preceding monarch), from confirmation in the Catholic Church indicates that even during the latter decades of the nineteenth century, when African traditions were increasingly censured and imagined as disruptions of cultural respectability, some African communities in Trinidad refused to adopt Euro-colonial norms at the expense of African norms. Indeed, they went so far as to restage the central liturgical event of the Catholic mass, appropriating to themselves the authority to perform the church's most sacred rite of communion. Twice Cothonay mentions the "blessed bread" that "the king . . . presents" and the queen "distribute[s]."[52] That the Orisa palais remains an operative institution in Trinidad today is evidence that Yorubas, too, chose African-derived norms over Euro-colonial norms in many arenas, even as they formed attachments to Catholic and other colonial structures.

Yoruba Trinidadians' strategies of belonging disabuse us of reductionist frameworks that simplify the factors underlying ~~human~~ social behavior. A concatenation of complex motivations drive individual decisions in any cultural context. We cannot always adjudicate what those are by assessing the degree of intimacy or distance that exploited groups permit between themselves and imposing regulatory structures.[53] Moreover, decolonial studies suggest that colonized and oppressed persons have always entered into complicated negotiations with imperial structures that both capitalize on and compromise the extent of their power and creative capacity. Rigid theories juxtaposing culture and agency with structure and constraint overlook that these terms are "slippery" and "contested."[54]

Sharon Hays writes about how social scientists use categories of culture and agency, often talking past one another through unidimensional and static definitions that mask how structures make room for creativity. "Social life is fundamentally structured," she maintains, "but social structures do make possible a whole range of choices in everyday life. Certain structural configurations of resources and constraints make it more or less possible for people to make larger or smaller 'creative' moves. Some portions of culture are easier to change than others (more open to reflective monitoring, less embedded in everyday practices), just as some elements of relational location are easier to change than others." By analyzing the role of seniority, insider/outsider consciousness, and belonging in Yoruba-Orisa cultural and social life, I am attempting to turn our attention away from syncretism arguments. Instead, as Hays suggests, I address "the question of under what cultural and relational conditions, and *through what cultural and relational processes*, structurally transformative [*creactivity*] occurs"[55] for Yoruba-Orisa custodians.

The historical, cultural, and philosophical roots of nineteenth- and early twentieth-century Yoruba Trinidadian affinities for microsocieties lie in continental Yorùbá social norms of seniority and prestige. These norms constitute a mode of power that confers social recognition and produces a desire for it. They define an essential aspect of personhood itself as an achievement. Seniority and social prestige then are not solely *values* that assign positive meaning and purpose to ~~human~~ existence and maturation: they are *valued* attainments toward which any respectable Yoruba person must aspire.

From the way the ọpẹlẹ divination chain and ikin (sacred palm nuts) are read when cast for clients in search of answers in the Ifá corpus (senior Odù take precedence over junior Odù)[56] to the manner in which twins (ìbejì) are distinguished by age at birth (the second to be born holds elder status), seniority is a normative principle of life and social organization. In the words of Bólájí Ìdòwú, "The young must respect the elder because of their seniority as well as because of their riper and richer experience from which the young should profit."[57] This aspect of the Yorùbá world-sense, and its counterpart consciousness of social belonging, profoundly affected the cultural orientation and attitudes of Yoruba descendants in Trinidad, who not only erected internal primordial structures of belonging but also chose to affiliate with cognate colonial religious and civic structures of belonging. Carving out a space for themselves on the margins of a racially and religiously stratified British colony intensified Yoruba settlers' desire for seniority, multiple belonging, and prestige and qualified how individuals and communities positioned themselves in social institutions during the nineteenth and early twentieth centuries.[58]

When the second scholarly study of Trinidadian Orisa was underway, the data Frances Mischel (aka Henry) collected for her dissertation, "A Shango Religious Group and the Problem of Prestige in Trinidadian Society," documented an emphasis in Orisa devotees' social consciousness that aligns with this argument about seniority and social belonging. Mischel and her then-spouse Walter had conducted research on the "Shango cult" in the summer of 1956 and discovered that social prestige was a collective preoccupation within the community at large. Although Mischel relied on the conventional category "syncretism,"[59] her analytical focus on prestige was an early indication in the scholarly literature that so-called syncretic elements of Orisa religious practice might actually signify deeply embedded spiritual norms and cultural patterns prescribing Yoruba social behavior.

Mischel employed standard social-science lenses to interrogate how social stratification affected the preoccupation with prestige among the "Shango" communities she studied. Her data indicate that Yoruba spiritual/cultural norms and social values concerning seniority, insiderness, and belonging remained at the core of twentieth-century Yoruba-Orisa social consciousness:

> The intense concern with in the vernacular "not being a nobody" and "becoming somebody big" . . . "being respected" . . . "able to stand up proud" . . . "having people look up when you pass by." . . . These kinds of concerns about being big and important, i.e., being esteemed and gaining recognition, having power, etc., with which our informants seemed so intensely involved, corresponded, in large part, with our own impressions about aspects of personal interactions and group behavior and structure in the Shango group itself. Our data suggested that recognition striving characterized large segments of the Shango group.[60]

My work draws from the contributions of scholars such as Mischel and posits we can deepen our knowledge of Yoruba-Orisa sacred poetics by attempting to understand not solely devotees' theological and ritual infrastructures but also their Yorùbá cultural heritage. The continental Yorùbá cultural mechanisms that allowed individuals to experience belonging, prestige, and insiderness during the nineteenth and early twentieth centuries have gone unrecognized in most studies of Yoruba religion in the African diaspora. Yet those mechanisms remain operative and continue to influence the creativity and elasticity of Yoruba religious cultures in Trinidad and in the wider Caribbean and the Americas.

Familial Logics and the Management and Use of Symbols

If the tendency in Yoruba-Orisa religious culture to engage the world/the other with openness and accommodation stems in part from deep-seated norms concerning seniority and social belonging, it also arises from familial logics that theories of syncretism fail to explain. In addition to seniority and belonging, these logics draw on the cultural ethic of hospitality toward kin, neighbors, and visitors that promotes conviviality, cooperation, solidarity, and meaningful exchange.

At first blush, when considering the incorporation of Catholic saints (and other Christian elements) into Yoruba-Orisa devotion, the logic of opting for the classificatory possibilities that the syncretic construct evokes seems quite reasonable. Syncretism is a seductive trope with a veneer of truth about global cross-cultural encounters. However, most scholars—not only ethnographers—apply this preferred trope indiscriminately in African diaspora religious studies. For example, Bridget Brereton's chapter "The Souls of Black Folk" historicizes the spiritual and cultural experiences of Africans in Trinidad during the late nineteenth century, and she adduces compelling primary sources from this period to construct her overall history. Yet when Brereton turns to exploring the "Shango" tradition in detail, she frames her one-paragraph analysis within a comparative conversation about the "syncretism" evident in wider African diaspora religions.

Surprisingly, Brereton cites only the 1960s and 1970s research and theoretical interpretations of George Simpson, David Trotman, and J. D. Elder to undergird her interpretation of a nineteenth-century phenomenon. Nowhere does she acknowledge the obvious lack of contemporary sources that could deliver a reliable portrait. When she discusses the Spiritual Baptists in the subsequent paragraph, and other cultural and social traditions for the remaining fourteen pages of the chapter, Brereton buttresses her discussion by returning to sources published during the 1880s. Yet, it is impossible to ignore the silence of the archive when piecing together a history of Yoruba-Orisa devotion in nineteenth-century Trinidad. In the absence of archival evidence, Brereton offers an anachronistic analysis of Shango as a static syncretic religion across time. Furthermore, her grouping of Shango with other African heritage diaspora religions simplifies complicated lineages of religious formation in diverse diaspora landscapes.

Brereton's assertions cannot be validated or invalidated. In the absence of sources, we clearly cannot say with certainty that "at least sixteen Yoruba deities were identified with saints" or that "nearly all the objects on the altar and on the upper half of the walls of the [Shango] chapelle were Catholic symbols" during the nineteenth century, as implied by her framing of data gathered during the mid- to late twentieth century.[61] Brereton's unwarranted historicization of syncretism during the early period of Yoruba-Orisa formation in Trinidad exemplifies a peculiar academic theology of syncretism, one that upholds it as an infallible lens for interpreting diasporic African heritage religions. In Africana religious studies, syncretism often becomes a dead signifier gesturing toward taxonomic and typological preoccupations in scholarly agendas. It obscures the internal dynamics of an engaged religious consciousness and forecloses indigenous hermeneutics.

Several other scholars offer different, more useful approaches. Rejecting syncretism as an explanatory framework, Baba Rudolph Eastman prefers to view the *christianisms* in the Yoruba-Orisa tradition as an expression of "symbolic dualism":

> They relied upon their knowledge of symbolism, the dual strategies of concealment and revelation, using them effectively in their customs such as kaiso, masquerade, and spirituality.... They used the structure of Roman Catholicism as its forms lent themselves easily to the dynamism of symbolic dualism and the African cultural pragmatism.... The Roman Catholic icons were consciously adopted and stamped for their representative value, using the visual art as a channel of communication and interpretation to convey meanings only known to the performer/ practitioner.... The external form [of the Catholic icons] was only used as a catalyst in creating the mental focus for ritual action and at no time used to assimilate or replace the Vodun or Orisa. The divinity remained the symbol of worship.... Just as the verbal form makes use of metaphors and the masquerade symbolises through masking and costumes, it is through ritual behaviour that meaning can be addressed, and only the knowledgeable performer can regulate access to that knowledge. This reality of symbolic dualism is unmistakable in the Western diaspora as the main elements of the Orisa system of thought and its Africanness still figure prominently in worship.[62]

With Eastman's perspective in mind, scrutiny of the historical encounter between Yoruba-Orisa and Catholicism suggests an alternative theoretical apparatus and interpretive faculty at work in Orisa devotees' collective negotiations with the wider universe of unseen forces and their material representations. Whether Catholic saints were incorporated into the Yoruba-Orisa religion during the nineteenth century or the early twentieth century, I understand this collocation as an outgrowth of the fundamental orienting religious and social principles discussed throughout this chapter. The cosmic and social salience of *family bonds, seniority, prestige, insiderness,* and *belonging* signals the extent to which relative privilege and responsibility are distributed to all members of the visible and invisible realms. Thus, Yoruba orature-literature reinforces a cultural *ethic of hospitality toward kin, neighbors, and visitors.* This ethical imperative regulates relational life among seen and unseen members of Yoruba communities. (For example, the Orisa must be fed their favorite foods or snacks, adorned in identifying vestments, and armed with distinctive implements when they visit their children in ceremonial settings.)

The Yoruba ethic of hospitality also arguably elicits a *familial logic of managing and using symbols* when Orisa devotees encounter religious resources from other faith traditions. Eastman's symbolic duality theory clarifies that symbols can reside simultaneously in multiple thought systems. Moreover, Eastman's attention to how symbols conceal and reveal addresses a Yoruba epistemological sensibility about the role of mystery in the cosmos and creation.

Marcus Harvey's phenomenological study of Yorùbá religious culture explores this epistemology and provides a conceptual foundation for theorizing Orisa approaches to other religio-cultural materials. Constructing his argument from a careful analysis of Yorùbá sacred literature, orature, ceremonies, and rituals, he frames the following theory of knowledge and spirituality:

> Yorùbá epistemology suggests that one of the vital functions of human knowledge is to sharpen our awareness of matter as a fundamentally irreducible reality whose deepest meanings always frustrate and elude the powers of human reason. . . . As a theoretical . . . principle of the internal logic of Yorùbá epistemology, the motif of mystery forces us to conceptualize . . . knowledge not as a tool with which to ultimately control reality but rather as a tool that enables us to create and develop meanings and resilient connections to the spiritual realm that allow us to live more productive lives.[63]

In their use of concealing/revealing symbols from the Catholic, Hindu, and Spiritual Baptist traditions, Orisa devotees thus manage and use an array of guises that convey something but not everything about the Orisa.

George Brandon's research on Santería in West Africa, Cuba, and the United States underscores this point. He proposes a theory of *antisyncretism*, culminating in a nuanced analysis of the concealing work that Catholic statues and adorned altars in Santería ceremonies display. What we *see* is not all there is. Yoruba theological imperatives account for why devotees would display ornate Catholic statues and lithographs of saints on or above their altars, and an imperative to syncretize religions is *not* one of them. Rather, Catholic objects are given high visibility to distract the observer's gaze from particularly sacred environments that are abodes of the Orisa. The Catholic saints conceal and shield other (Orisa) family members from exposure.

Commenting on the Lucumí/Santería altars he studied, Brandon concludes that all the Catholic "visual symbolism is but decoration . . . an accommodation to external circumstances and an extension of the symbolism of sources of power that remain hidden and invisible."[64] That power source—a family of sacred stones, bathed and fed by sacrificial herbs and consecrated animal blood—enjoys a seclusion arranged by the strategic placement of ritual objects on and around the altar. Brandon insists that "what is concealed" by elaborate Catholic decorations "is not only the ashe but also those elements of Santeria which are least compatible with either official or folk Catholicism yet represent the union and condensation of the whole array of powers encompassed within the Yoruba cosmological system. The stones," which are standard in continental Yorùbá shrines, "serve, then, as a powerful symbolic link to the African past."[65]

Something similar occurs in the Trinidadian Orisa palais, which incorporates a separate concealing structure, the *chapelle*, where ritual objects, an altar, and some Orisa stools (metonymic material representations and dwellings of the Orisa) are housed. Within the *chapelle*, the traditional elevated placement of lithographs and statues and the low placement of Orisa sacred tools and objects, including "thunder stones," are likely done to deceive uninformed observers into misperceiving what is central and what is marginal.[66] As in Cuba and other regions where Yoruba heritage religions are practiced, "the most powerful stones are those brought from Africa."[67] Felipe García Villamil, a master drummer and Lucumí priest of African descent, offers additional insight into the arrangement of Yoruba sacred stones and Catholic statues in Cuban devotional settings. When queried about his position on "the rejection of the Catholic saints by santeros in the United States," Villamil defended not so much the saints as he did the poetic intention and purpose behind his ancestors' adoption of them. "Our ancestors used the statues to be able to manifest the power of *their things—the stones were below those statues.* Even if they were Catholic figures and at the time may have had no spirituality, our ancestors gave them a spirituality by using them the way they did."[68]

The juxtaposition of Orisa and Catholic ritual objects in a divided spatial arrangement also situates the Powers near their assigned invisible abodes: the saints reside in heaven, and the Orisa (most of them) reside in the earth's crust. These abodes far above and far below the plane of ~~human~~ existence are sacred loci of power, knowledge, and mystery. At every level of participation and belonging to Orisa devotional families, members confront the limits of knowledge and extraordinary power. They learn that mystery and discretion are essential in the ritual acquisition and application of knowledge and power—and the incorporation of Catholic saints amplifies this desired ritual environment.

Devotees operating from their own epistemological center and out of their core commitments to the invisible Mothers and Fathers therefore find suitable locations for St. Raphael, Shiva, or any new Power they adopt. Yet the

symbols do not manage them; *they* manage the symbols, as well as the resonances and juxtapositions the symbols imply.[69] When an Orisa devotee says,
"Ogun is Saint Michael," our task is to access the intended metaphorical and
metonymic significations in the equation. These invented affiliations among
Yoruba Orisa, Catholic saints, and Hindu deities spark a semiotic valence
because the symbols retrieve a meaning-making principle that inheres across
cosmic and social phenomena, placing kinship and relationality at the center
of Yoruba-Orisa theology, hermeneutics, ritual life, and power relations. In
explaining the reasoning behind such affiliative statements for the typical
devotee during the latter twentieth century, Ìdòwú captures the prominence
of kinship ties for omorisa globally, and Nigerian adherents specifically:

> It happened some time ago that when the arch-priest of a principal divinity
> in Ilé-Ifẹ̀ was asked the question, "May I see the emblem of Òrìṣà-nlá?"
> he turned to his assistant and said in a matter-of-fact way, "This is one
> of our sons; he wishes *to see our father*." The emblems themselves are usu-
> ally referred to loosely as òrìṣà. As a rule, the Yoruba does not go into the
> analytical trouble of saying, "These are the 'emblems' or 'images' of my
> òrìṣà." He only says in a sweeping way, "This is my òrìṣà," although if the
> question is put to him whether the emblems were in reality the òrìṣà, his
> prompt answer will be "No, these are only images—*ère*—of the òrìṣà."[70]

Whether adopted for symbolic or concrete purposes, two principles of
familial logic undergird the Orisa tradition's adoption of Catholic, Spiritual
Baptist, Hindu, and other Powers and elements: (1) family relations as a condition for existence and personal/social meaning and (2) recognition of the
self in the other and the other in the self. Across the centuries, nurturing, sustaining, protecting, and enhancing the family and nation have constituted an
ultimate concern for Yoruba descendants in Trinidad, and they have deemed
the Orisa religion a primary arena for addressing this concern. Not unlike
approaches to comparative religions that recognize family resemblances
among diverse religious traditions, Orisa devotees exercise the powers of recognition when they adopt new members (who resemble old family members)
into the invisible Orisa kinship structure.[71]

Because the expansion of the family was typically a social good among
Yorubas, adoption of Catholic saints and Hindu gods into their religious
structure was common: it extended hospitality to the other and expanded
the family without altering its structure or the relational ethic that stabilizes
and sustains it. Additionally, assigning the Orisa multiple identities, some
derived from Catholic saints and Hindu deities, must have several explana-

tions, one of which is permitting two or more entities to occupy one body simultaneously, to be present and absent at the same time, just as symbols at once conceal and reveal. Ethnomusicologist Steven Friedson's analysis of the Ewe Vodu also rings true for the Yoruba-Orisa: "The gods are not a single transcendent entity analogous to a Western projection of personhood with a bounded identity and delimited personality, but always a multiplicity of effect."[72]

The extent to which devotees engage other spiritual heritages and cultural resources positions them to relate to the sacred Other in the most intimate and enigmatic settings, including feeding and bathing the Orisa, receiving the ashé of the Orisa inside the body during initiations (desunu), becoming the Orisa during manifestation rituals, speaking for the Orisa in divination sessions, and so on. These ways of relating to the sacred Other are not disconnected from Orisa devotees' appreciation of other religious cultures nor from their tendency to call old gods by new names[73] that are symbolically and metaphorically potent to them.

Building on Friedson's insights, it is important to remember that the Orisa often have multiple Yoruba appellations, which are widely recorded in Yoruba orature-literature, chants, and prayers. Such diverse sets of names and honorifics signal multifaceted and protean aspects of identity, including aspiration, destiny, and character traits. They convey devotees' attempts to acknowledge how the Orisa manifest in their ~~world~~ as "a multiplicity of effect," a density of evocations worthy of ~~human~~ contemplation. But Yoruba names also partake in a spiritual ecology that renders all life both potent and vulnerable. Thus, calling the Powers by foreign names enciphers the Orisa's authentic, sacred names and advances a Yoruba ethics of discretion and protection.[74] From this vantage point, we can see how the addition of Catholic saint names to a complex personalization system clarifies the tacit cultural reasoning and devotional poetics behind Yoruba-Orisa naming customs in Trinidad and the wider African diaspora.

Yoruba-Orisa: A Moving Continuity of Kinship in the Family and Nation

Bearing in mind the ~~humanity~~ of first-generation Yoruba settlers in Trinidad entails reflection on the transportability of culture. On what basis did they name their children; choose life partners; establish rules of etiquette and decorum; expect privacy and discretion; negotiate social tensions; treat illnesses; develop fishing, hunting, market, and culinary traditions; demonstrate courage and vulnerability; celebrate important events; comprehend nature; evaluate a worthy life; and sacralize death?

Kevin Roberts appropriately concludes that "Yoruba in the Caribbean succeeded in establishing a New World identity that was based more on their native culture than the pressures of enslavement might lead one to realize."[75] The continental families and societies from which they came provided foundational resources to express and transmit ~~humanity~~ even as they experienced displacement and exposure to new stimuli and cultural traditions in Trinidad. Cultural continuity, creativity, and rupture disobey a neat correspondence with the historical frames that scholars construct to capture the ethos of any given period in the African and African diaspora experience. As Yoruba Trinidadians designed their *nation-al* institutions across several centuries, they implicitly drew from a Yoruba cultural heritage to interpret phenomena and assign meaning to the symbols and relationships that governed their religious and public life. Whether they were enslaved or liberated "their native culture" transcended "the pressures" of their involuntary presence in the New World.

Although sources that provide an extensive portrait of Yoruba and other African communities' religious and social life in nineteenth- and early twentieth-century Trinidad are sparse, they allow some insight into family values and culture-bearing institutions. From Cothonay's journal we learn that confraternities were pivotal spaces of social belonging for African men during the late nineteenth century. In San Fernando's Saint-Dominic'-Village, for example, Cothonay reports that "nearly all men belong to a confraternity." His portrayal of the brotherhood's 1885 "patron ceremony . . . in which the whole village [took] part," suggests that such events would have been opportune occasions for liberated Yorubas/Africans to participate in established Afro-Creole customs, because the varied African *nations* and communities did not settle exclusively in segregated enclaves by the late nineteenth century.

If men officially hosted the brotherhoods, they were not simply homosocial male spaces; they were familial and village social spaces of intergenerational cooperation and teaching. "Each one contributes," Cothonay writes, "one with the chicken, one with the rice, one with the cassava, etc." to a "common meal." We derive a strong sense of how all family members played their roles in the confraternities' "half religious, half civil" public rites; for among the St. Dominic' confraternal families, "the *women* would recite the rosary, the *men* sang the litanies of the saints, the *children*, English canticles."[76] The impact of Anglicization on a custom previously steeped in French-Creole Afro-Catholic traditions should not be overlooked. Adults were scarcely equipped with English-language skills in 1885; thus, the children's presence and participation were more than ancillary. Children sang in a language they were probably teaching their parents and grandparents to speak at home. The brotherhood's dramatic display of royal governance—the presiding king, queen, vice-king, vice-queen, and governor elaborately adorned by rank and extending blessings to the assembled society—indicates that novel traditions, such as the singing of English canticles, had not decentered the decades-long postemancipation Africana *nation-al* sovereignty celebrations.[77]

Through *nation* institutions, from Orisa devotion to familial storytelling, Yoruba ways of life were taught transgenerationally. Resonant with my argument in chapter 1 about early twentieth-century Yaraba Creoles of Trinidad having been taught to be Yaraba by their ancestors, Villamil (b. 1931) shared, during the late twentieth century, a similar view about his own training in Cuba: "I'm a person who's here and who does things the way he was taught to. And who taught me? People of *nación*, a Lucumí—or a Yoruba."[78] Moreover, the available sources also indicate that the "Yoruba ideology of kinship, emphasis on extended kin, and centrality of family . . . fit well with the traditions of most other West and West-Central African cultures."[79] The array of Afro-Creole social institutions and ceremonies that Yoruba newcomers encountered in nineteenth-century Trinidad offered familiar conventions that they often supported and adapted to suit their particular customs and ways of life. Hence, as this and the previous chapter have shown, Yoruba values and spiritual traditions could be taught and transmitted via *inter-nation-al* and pan-Africanized social mixing.[80]

Discussions of African cultural durability and dynamism in the diaspora suffer at times from conceptually static correlations of specific bodies with their "native" cultural geographies. African culture is treated as something innate (not taught) that those born in Africa possess. Once continental Africans find themselves enslaved or indentured in the Caribbean and the Americas, they either retain their innate possession, through enduring mechanisms such as religion, music, and dance, or they lose it. But cultures and the peoples who invent them do not operate this way: they are both abiding and yielding—resilient in the flow of time, under dynamic pressures of life and death. They are shifting continuities.[81]

A chief aim of this study is to emphasize how familial and kinship networks serve as sources of cultural and religious transmission, at times even *because of* cultural change and creativity. Considered collectively, archival and ethnographic data include prosaic evidence that Yoruba parents and elders have socialized younger generations to engage the world through inherited cultural norms (e.g., seniority) and structures (e.g., initiation and multiple belonging). The Yoruba presence in Trinidad, in particular, has conveyed across time the power of culture as a carrier of values, desires, judgments, meaning, memory, rationality, reality, and much more. When we view the dispersed locations that received enslaved and indentured African laborers primarily as landscapes of African-European syncretic cultural remaking, we neglect questions and archival/ethnographic clues concerning Africana cultural transmission that this text seeks to engage.

Unlike syncretism, the concepts of kinship, family, *nation*, and belonging allow access to understudied cosmological, ethical, and social conventions that orient omorisa in their commitment to a common life and religious heritage, with resonances across wider social and religious Africana worlds. The rituals and cultural habits that shaped the various Yoruba-Orisa microtraditions were sustained initially within biological lineages, eventually expanding to incorporate spiritual lineages forged among "Orisa workers" with no genealogical ties.[82] Comparable spiritual lineages were not unknown in pre-Yorùbá continental lineage structures. According to Yai, in precolonial Yorùbá and Dahomean societies, devotees to a particular deity constituted a spiritual kinship group often while maintaining plurination-al allegiances.[83] Moreover, the nineteenth-century archives of CMS activities in modern-day Nigeria provide evidence of genealogical and spiritual kinship networks involving households, families, lineages, and devotional communities. Peel explains, "Cult members [spoke] of their fellowship in terms of their together being the 'children' of their *orisa*. In many cases this arose from their regard for that deity as their protector from birth or even before it." For example, on October 6, 1850, the Anglican missionary Thomas King recorded in his journal a "fervent declaration of a woman at the yearly festival of Kesi, her township in Abeokuta." She testified publicly, "'By Sango I was begotten and by Lakijena I was brought forth, and them will I ever serve.'" Thus, "cult attachments were connected with lineage in several ways," including as means of ensuring fertility and reproduction. Cult relationships were also "expressed in kinship idioms, and they were largely passed on through family ties."[84]

The family dynamics at play in the Yoruba-Orisa heritage and culture ensure that a network of spiritual care and holistic provision remains accessible to family members, especially those in crisis. "'Shango here is dancin' and curin' people,'" proclaimed Emil Paul, a sixty-five-year-old fisherman from Toco whom Herskovits interviewed in 1939.[85] In the Yoruba-Orisa tradition, the consanguineal, affinal, and spiritual family does indeed dance and cure people. Families are the source of spiritual-social care and healing as visible and invisible members work together to facilitate the redistribution of ashé toward the sustenance of health and longevity. James Sweet explores how "ideologies of lineage . . . could be built around healing communities" among West African Gbe-speaking societies. His historical research on a West African healer also underscores the salience of family/kinship/lineage connections for West Africans long after they crossed the Atlantic Ocean. "A person was a person," writes Sweet, "only insofar as he or she was a member of a kinship group, and the kin group was defined by the number and quality of people in its ranks."[86] Stephen Ogbonmwan also characterizes the African family as "a system whereby . . . everybody is linked with all the other members, living or dead, through a complex network of spiritual relationship into a kind of mystical body. Consequently," Ogbonmwan continues, "it is not just *being* that the African values; *being-with-others* or *being rooted in kinship* is an equally important existential characteristic of the African."[87] Large lineages with strong and extensive kinship bonds indeed amounted to tangible social currency in many African societies. As Sweet indicates, "Wealth, power and prestige were measured primarily in people, not land or money," and "to be alienated from the collective wealth, power, and protection of the natal lineage group was tantamount to social death, a virtual erasure of one's personhood."[88]

Writing in the 1850s, politician, planter, and medical practitioner Sir Louis de Verteuil characterized liberated Yorubas in similar terms—as a "family," sustained by a communal ethic of reciprocity and collective responsibility: "They are . . . guided, in a marked degree, by the sense of association; and the principle of combination for the common weal has been fully sustained wherever they have settled in any numbers; in fact, the whole *Yarraba* family in the colony may be said to form a sort of social league for mutual support and protection."[89] Orisa religious culture, with its sacred and ritual families, contributed significantly to the "*Yarraba* family's" strong "sense of association" and "mutual support" from the mid-nineteenth to the mid-twentieth century.

Just about a century after the last ship delivered displaced Yorùbá laborers to the shores of Trinidad, the Orisa religious culture would undergo dramatic changes. Explosive political transformations, including independence from British colonial rule and the Black Power struggle, ensured that Yoruba devotees' engagement with the civic public would involve new arenas and political agendas. In this era, the Yoruba *nation* and its familial networks proliferated beyond anything the earliest descendants of liberated Yorubas could have conceived while living under tyrannical anti-Obeah laws. The catalyst for such growth was a wave of black consciousness-inspired political activism, which reached its zenith in 1970. During this time, some Black Power activists turned to the Yoruba-Orisa *nation* for sacred solutions to their social predicament and its wider cultural and political manifestations. Trinidad's Yoruba-Orisa heritage inspired new iterations of what I call Africana religious *nationalism* that challenged long-standing conventions within the tradition.

Modifications in Orisa's structure and ritual life during the latter twentieth century must be viewed, however, within a wider historical and cultural account of Yoruba-Orisa foundations in Trinidad, which this present chapter has attempted to provide. By placing the analytic of syncretism under scrutiny and drawing liberally from indigenous hermeneutics, I offered an explanatory framework for theorizing the appearance and formation of Yoruba-Orisa religion in Trinidad for the past century and a half. Yet beyond identifying Yoruba cultural values still at work in Trinidad's Orisa communities today, this chapter apprises scholars of a necessary analytical and conceptual decolonial turn in Africana religious studies that situates *relationality* at the heart of religious thought, meaning and devotion. What seems warranted moving forward are substantive investigations of the semiology (sign language), structures, and habitations of relationality in the religious cultures of African-descended people.

"We Smashed
Those Statues or
Painted Them Black"

3

ORISA TRADITIONS AND AFRICANA RELIGIOUS
NATIONALISM SINCE THE ERA OF BLACK POWER

Published in 2008, Lise Winer's *Dictionary of the English / Creole of Trinidad and Tobago* lists three definitions for the term "African":

1n   A person born in Africa, enslaved or free. . . .

2n   A person of African descent: black, Negro. Now used to emphasize pride in the overall common origin of much of the *creole*
population. . . .

3n   A participant in SHANGO/ORISHA religious ceremonies (fr origin
of practice and participants in Africa)—Trinidadians who are associated with *shango* cult centers refer to themselves as "Yoruba
people," "the Yoruba nation," "*orisha* people," or "African people."
Some of them believe they are descended from Yoruba stock. They
distinguish themselves from the Radas and other groups of Afro-
Trinidadians. Neither in Nigeria nor in Trinidad are the members
of the *shango* cult limited to a particular family or lineage.[1]

Winer cites material from 1825 to 1997 to support her multiple definitions of "African"; the term encompasses macro, micro, and blended identities issuing from Trinidad and Tobago's (T&T) African *nation* communities during the eighteenth and nineteenth centuries. However, among the various *nation* groupings, Winer indicates that the "Yoruba nation"—the sponsor of "SHANGO/ORISHA religious ceremonies"—became a metonym for "African" identity during the Black Power era.[2] And it is to this Yoruba *nation*, the most visible representation of African heritage in the postindependence period, that a number of Black Power advocates turn today to "emphasize pride in the overall common origin of much of the *creole* population."

Although *nation-al* and *inter-nation-al* affiliations were becoming absorbed into a more generic African or Afro-Creole group identity by the mid-twentieth century,[3] Winer's third definition of "African" reminds us that many Yoruba descendants continued to fulfill obligations to social and spiritual kin whom their parents and grandparents taught them to honor, thus maintaining links with departed "Yaraba" *nation* members.

The late 1960s unveiled a new period of *nation-building* among Yoruba and other African descendants in Trinidad, just as Trinidad and Tobago was unfolding its own project of nation-building. Yoruba-Orisa devotion became the source for new iterations of *nationhood*, which this chapter elucidates as Africana religious *nationalism*. Repurposing the Yoruba-Orisa *nation* to account for their varied needs as African Trinidadian citizens of a newly independent nation-state, newcomers expanded the *nation's* genealogical family structure to encompass spiritual lineages of Orisa devotees. One of the most striking results of such growth has been the collective and successful effort to expose and thwart the colonial control of African religious representation.

After the rise of Black Power in Trinidad, old and new custodians of the Yoruba-Orisa tradition often worked cooperatively to invalidate colonial constructions of their spiritual heritage and other African religious cultures. These accomplishments remain unmatched in the African diaspora. The first half of this chapter provides a concise overview of pivotal events leading up to these developments, from the labor movement to the Black Power movement (BPM). Then follows a close examination of the phenomenon of Africana religious *nationalism* as expressed in the sacred poetics of Egbe Onisin Eledumare (EOE), the first and most strident Orisa-inspired spiritual organization/shrine with an explicit commitment to the politics of Black Power.

Why place EOE at the center of this analysis? First, although studies of contemporary Trinidadian Orisa communities mostly cite EOE as the quintessence of Black Power's impact on the Orisa tradition overall, this chapter offers a substantive treatment of its theology and religious culture. My research challenges a tendency in the literature to reduce EOE's agenda to reductive understandings of "identity" or "authenticity" politics. Identity politics, as understood today, has its origins and most potent historical appearance in the white colonial imaginations and institutions responsible for Trinidad's racial arrangement. Using the frameworks of phenomenologists of religion, my reading of EOE's presence and impact highlights instead the *politics of affect* in connection with the multivalent symbol of Africa as mobilizing technologies for EOE's identification with and repurposing of Yoruba-Orisa sacred poetics in postindependence Trinidad.[4]

Second, EOE is the institutional result and embodiment of African descendants' struggle to surmount colonial constructions of African spirituality and culture by asserting their right to religious freedom and civic inclusion. We know from the testimonies of Orisa elders that social and legal persecution of Orisa devotees was arguably as strong in the early to mid-twentieth century as it was in the nineteenth century. Orisa elders remember the hundreds of Paulina Samuels who confronted systemic abuses during the first half of the twentieth century and whose fidelity to African Powers under siege would embolden a future generation to derive the most potent sources of Black Power from those same *African Powers*. This chapter outlines those systemic abuses and their implications for new developments in the Yoruba-Orisa tradition since the 1970s.

Yoruba-Orisa and the Ethos of
African Religious Persecution before Black Power

Ask any Yoruba-Orisa elder about the status of their tradition across most of the twentieth century and a picture of legal suppression and cultural derision materializes. Yoruba-Orisa custodians were trapped. Although they were not identified directly as sponsors of illegal activity, Yoruba-Orisa devotees and custodians of other African heritage religions regularly confronted the penal system under the 1868 Obeah Prohibition Ordinance (OPO) and the 1917 Shouters Prohibition Ordinance (SPO), which were not repealed until 2000 and 1951, respectively.[5]

How many and which particular *nation-al* and pan-Africanized religious cultures endured the insufferable penalties meted out to "obeah" offenders eludes scholars. Obeah and other cases brought against African religious practitioners were prosecuted at the lowest levels of the judicial system in resident magistrates' courts and police or petty sessions courts. Unless a defendant appealed the court's ruling, these courts did not file official trial transcripts.[6] John Cooper's and Mah Nannie's court cases (1871 and 1886, respectively) are accessible in more than newspaper reports precisely because they appealed the lower court's rulings, resulting in the preservation of their appeal documents and other relevant court records in the British Colonial Office archives.

Nonetheless, even in the absence of countless trial transcripts across centuries of African presence in Trinidad, "there are indications that some of those prosecuted for obeah were engaged in Orisha Worship." Diana Paton discusses several twentieth-century cases, including those of Francis Caradose (1902) and Albertha Isidore (1940), where items associated with the defendants offer evidence of Orisa devotion:

> Francis Caradose, an African, was charged with obeah. His house was marked by a bamboo flagstaff, underneath which "three old cutlasses planted in a triangular position were found." Caradose had another arrangement of three cutlasses under a kerosene oil pan, and sang "a jargon song in his own tongue" to an image found in a neighbour's garden. Nearly forty years later Albertha Isidore was charged under the obeah laws. The evidence against her included the presence in her house of a bowl containing stones, feathers and seeds, another with oil and a wick, a crucifix, a statue, an old Bible, an axe, wooden hatchets, and swords. Neither of these defendants mentioned [the religion of] Shango in their defence, but the presence of cutlasses, axes and swords arranged in ritual ways strongly suggests that they were participants in Orisha Worship. Swords and cutlasses are symbolically associated with Ogun and St. Michael.[7]

Axes, too, were associated with the deity Sango, and bowls with stones and feathers would have been commonplace in Yoruba-Orisa shrines.

In the twentieth century, with the ratification of the Shouters Prohibition Ordinance, which officials brutally enforced at will until its repeal more than three decades later, circumstances changed.[8] Under this law, we know exactly which religious culture was targeted because the SPO was the only statute in Trinidad's history to have outlawed an identifiable African religious tradition by name (see figures 3.1 and 3.2).[9]

Paton's survey of the *Port of Spain Gazette* and *The Trinidad Guardian* uncovered twenty-nine and three cases, respectively, in which five hundred persons were prosecuted under the SPO between 1917 and 1939, "many more than [those prosecuted] under the obeah and related laws" between 1890 and

TRINIDAD AND TOBAGO.

No. 27—1917.

I ASSENT,

[L.S.]

J. B. CHANCELLOR,
Governor.

28th November, 1917.

AN ORDINANCE to render illegal indulgence in the practices of the body known as the Shouters.

[*28th November, 1917.*]

BE it enacted by the Governor of Trinidad and Tobago with the advice and consent of the Legislative Council thereof as follows:—

1. This Ordinance may be cited as the Shouters' Prohibition Ordinance, 1917.

2.—(1.) A "Shouters' meeting" means a meeting or gathering of two or more persons, whether indoors or in the open air, at which the customs and practices of the body known as Shouters (hereafter in this Ordinance referred to as "the Shouters") are indulged in. The decision of any Magistrate in any case brought under this Ordinance as to whether the customs and practices are those of the Shouters shall be final, whether the persons indulging in

---

such customs or practices call themselves Shouters or by any other name.

(2.) A "Shouters' house" means any house or building or room in any house or building which is used for the purpose of holding Shouters' meetings, or any house or building or room in any house or building which is used for the purpose of initiating any person into the ceremonies of the Shouters. The decision of any Magistrate in any case brought under this Ordinance as to whether a house or building or room in any house or building is a Shouters' house shall be final.

(3.) The word "manager" includes any person having control over or charge of any estate or land whatsoever in the Colony.

3. It shall be an offence against this Ordinance for any person to hold or to take part in or to attend any Shouters' meeting or for any Shouters' meeting to be held in any part of this Colony indoors or in the open air at any time of the day or night.

4. It shall be an offence against this Ordinance to erect or to maintain any Shouters' house or to shut up any person in any Shouters' house for the purpose of initiating such person into the ceremonies of the Shouters.

5.—(1.) If it shall come to the knowledge of the owner or manager of any estate or land in the Colony that a Shouters' house is being erected or maintained or that Shouters' meetings are being held on the estate or land over which such owner or manager has control, he shall forthwith notify the non-commissioned officer in charge of the Constabulary station nearest to such house, estate or land of the erection or maintenance of such Shouters' house or of the locality or place at which such Shouters' meetings are being held.

(2.) The manager or owner of any estate or land in the Colony who fails so to notify such non-commissioned officer as aforesaid, or who knowingly permits the erection or maintenance of any Shouters' house or the holding of Shouters' meetings on any estate or land over which he has control, shall be guilty of an offence against this Ordinance.

---

6. It shall be an offence against this Ordinance for any person at or in the vicinity of any Shouters' meeting to commit or cause to be committed or to induce or to persuade to be committed any act of indecency.

7.—(1.) It shall be lawful for any party of members of the Constabulary Force, of whom one shall be a commissioned or non-commissioned officer, without a warrant to enter at any time of the day or night any house, estate, land or place in or on which such commissioned or non-commissioned officer may have good ground to believe or suspect that a Shouters' meeting is being held or where he may have good ground to believe or suspect that any person or persons is or are being kept for the purpose of initiation into the ceremonies of the Shouters and to take the names and addresses of all persons present at such Shouters' meeting or Shouters' house.

(2.) It shall also be lawful for any member of the Constabulary Force to demand the names and addresses of any persons taking part in any meeting in the open air which he has good reason to believe is a Shouters' meeting.

(3.) Any person refusing to give his name and address to any member of the Constabulary Force when asked to do so under the authority of this section shall be liable to be arrested and to be detained at a Constabulary station until his identity can be established.

8. Any person guilty of an offence against this Ordinance shall be liable on summary conviction before a Magistrate to a fine not exceeding £50 and in default of payment thereof to imprisonment with or without hard labour for a term not exceeding six months.

Passed in Council this Sixteenth day of November, in the year of Our Lord one thousand nine hundred and seventeen.

HARRY L. KNAGGS,
Clerk of the Council.

FIGURE 3.1 AND FIGURE 3.2 Trinidad and Tobago Shouters Prohibition Ordinance (SPO) of 1917. Under the SPO, Spiritual Baptists and Yoruba devotees were arrested and prosecuted for illegal activities such as initiations, ceremonies, and erecting and maintaining worship structures. Reprinted by permission from Law Library, Judiciary of the Republic of Trinidad and Tobago.

1939.[10] Intended to censure persons affiliated with the Spiritual Baptist religion, the SPO characterized that African-Christian practice as a public offense. The tradition's expressive religiosity and sonic rituals unnerved the establishment and disturbed the aesthetic sensibilities of the colonial ruling classes and those among the wider population who aligned themselves with Eurocentric Christian devotion.

This African-Christian religious culture was a bona fide Atlantic institution, with roots stretching in one direction back to immigrant enclaves of American Negro Loyalist soldiers who fought with Britain against the United States during the War of 1812,[11] and in another direction across neighboring Caribbean countries, such as St. Vincent and Grenada.[12] These American and Caribbean nations, in particular, have sustained localized iterations of the Spiritual Baptist religious complex, in some cases under the appellations "Converted," "Travelin'," and "Seekin'." As Christian as their African custodians considered them, none of these religious expressions constituted "proper religion" in the colonial imagination. In the end, the established Euro-Christian denominations mapped an exclusive terrain of cultural respectability for all African religious practitioners during most of the twentieth century. Those identified as custodians of both Yoruba-Orisa and Spiritual Baptist traditions bore the disgrace of belonging to a caste bereft of moral decency and social legitimacy.

Orisa devotee Paulina Samuel's 1919 court case offers a suitable example of how citizens and civil authorities used the 1917 SPO to criminalize and control the activities of Yoruba-Orisa devotees. Much of this strategy is captured in the headline and subhead of *The Trinidad Guardian* article about her trial: "Alleged Shouters' Meeting: Yaraba Dance at Carenage, Licensed to Beat a Drum." First, although the unidentified claimant described the activities at Samuel's house as Yoruba devotional practices, Samuel was charged with "keeping a Shouters' meeting"; the ease with which she was charged conveys the perilous position that Orisa devotees occupied as members of an African religious community. Second, we know that Samuel anticipated resistance in the social climate of her day, by virtue of having "obtained a license to beat a drum." However, this license apparently only lasted "until 10 o'clock in the night" because in addition to being troubled by the fact that Samuel and her guests were keeping a "Yaraba dance," the complainant also "objected to the beating [of the drum] after [the 10 o'clock] hour."

The article does not disclose why Samuel was charged under the SPO. During cross-examination, Emmanuel M'Zumbo Lazare—Trinidad's first black solicitor and first convener and vice president of Trinidad's Pan-African

Association—elicited facts that further distinguished Samuel's ceremony from a Shouters' meeting; for example, "the parties in defendant's house were using a little drum, and shouters, as a rule were never in the habit of beating drums." Samuel's case was dismissed because "there was not sufficient evidence to prove that defendant kept a shouters' meeting." Notably, however, "His Worship said that . . . if she was charged with disturbing the peace he would have dealt very severely with her."[13]

It is no small matter that Lazare succeeded in having the case dismissed by distinguishing between the ritual practices of two African religions that many outsiders loved to collapse under one umbrella of heathenism.[14] Ironically, the foundation for this legal strategy exists in the complainant's narration of what he observed at Samuel's ceremony on June 5, 1919. So-called Shouters did not sing "in the African language" or indulge "in the 'Yaraba dance,'" as Samuel's gathering did. "Shouters" maintained a robust ritual process distinct from other African nation rituals. And if proximity and social survival dictated a healthy exchange between the two traditions across the twentieth century, this cross-fertilization and mutual participation did not eliminate the discrete roots of each spiritual legacy in Trinidad, which generate distinguishable institutional iterations even today.

The cases discussed here suggest the ubiquity of the 1868 OPO and the 1917 SPO in the policing and persecution of African religious devotees, including those devoted to Orisa worship. Thus, nineteenth-century "obeah" and twentieth-century "Shouters," as constructed in colonial jurisprudence, were what I term *numenyms* ("numen" + "pseudonym"). Numenyms are discursive colonial inventions designed to execute an imperial or, specifically in this era of colonial rule, a Victorian Christian ideological agenda. As explored in volume I, numenyms subtend an antiblack/African libidinal economy.[15] But beyond this, they import a sense of the extraordinary, the numinous, to the discursive power of deceptive labels used to stereotype and demonize African religious practices and sources of power. The currency that these numenyms have in shaping African people's own negative perceptions of African religious cultures thus goes beyond the political, economic, social, and cultural. Keeping with Yoruba epistemology and conceptualizations of the sensorium—namely the Orí, as one's mind, seat of the soul, and personal deity—what is *sensed* through one's Orí can very well be associated with divine revelation because numenyms retrain the senses to perceive abnormally.

Volume I's discussion of the colonial cult of obeah fixation and Governor Picton's war against Obeah discloses that the success of colonial numenyms is owed to their ascriptive and punitive operations not only at the sociocultural level but also within the affective register. Through a violation and manipulation of African religious consciousness, colonial numenyms such as "obeah" and "Shouters" construct African indigenous thought systems, sacred medicines, and devotional practices as the archetype—the original heritable expression—of malevolent spiritual power. They thereby conjure in the sensing minds/bodies of African descendants a condition of perpetual angst and even paranoia over the expected torment that African heritage religious cultures are purported to cause individuals and communities.[16]

With the codification of numenyms what gets eclipsed are African descendants' self-designations for their religious cultures as well as their protestations of colonial numenyms. For example, during his 1918 court trial "Teacher Bailey," a Spiritual Baptist, levied a powerful display of insider rejection of the "Shouter" label. Bailey testified as follows: "My father is 58 years old, my mother 49, and from the time I was born, 27 years ago, that is the religion I found my mother and father following—*not shouting*, but *praying* in the name of the Lord." Holding his cross uplifted, Bailey continued, "I am prepared to go to jail every time, and to carry on these meetings, I will always do so. Christ was persecuted for religion, and if I go to jail for religion, it does not matter."[17]

Whether created through appropriations of indigenous African terms (Obeah, Vodou) or through troubled translational Western categories (juju— from the French word *joujou*, or plaything, witchcraft, magic, idolatry, fetishism, paganism, heathenism, etc.), numenyms anonymize the African religious cultures they are purported to typify. They have long exploited and distorted Africana theories of misfortune and imbalance, supplying the ideological and theological content for an enduring *colonial belief system* fixated on devils, demons, and dark magic. Obeah, like Christianity, Islam, Hinduism, or any other religion of ~~human~~/human design, could at its worst destroy, control, and harm—but at its best it healed, liberated, protected, neutralized, and empowered. The moral logic that grounds Obeah culture construes healing and harming or destroying and creating as generative energies and intentions that qualify the range of options and outcomes ~~humans~~ inhabit and produce from moment to moment. Eradicating or "cooling" the slave owner and overturning the slavocracy's ethos of social death via Obeah technologies of weaponry and warfare provided one means of delivering social medicine to enslaved populations trapped by such forces.

Obeah and other African spiritual systems introduce a moral ecology regulated by situational and communitarian ethics. Even if some charlatans and corrupt Obeah/African spiritual practitioners received due sanction when arrested and prosecuted, many more legitimate, prosocial doctors and priests, such as John Cooper and Mah Nannie, faced the antipathy of unjust criminal courts simply because they served their communities as spiritual experts and health consultants. For centuries, numenyms such as "obeah," "witchcraft," and "magic" have capitalized on an existing commonsense caution that African descendants have tended to exhibit about the ubiquity of evil and its spiritual-material causes and effects in the cosmic-social environment. The imposed numenymic colonial belief system (or *Numenysm*) often turns a pragmatic caution into paranoia and even hysteria, thereby annulling all sophisticated and nuanced interrogations of African spiritual practices that would lead African-descended people to distinguish between sanctioned rituals and religious practices and unsanctioned behaviors stemming from antisocial intentions.

The career of the "obeah" numenym in Trinidad and the wider Anglophone Caribbean begins much earlier than the passing of the 1868 OPO (as discussed in volume I). And although actual members of the Spiritual Baptist tradition suffered brutal arrests and penalties under the SPO, this twentieth-century numenymic law doubled as yet another obstacle to religious freedom for custodians of Yoruba-Orisa devotional life. The SPO and the OPO functioned similarly in misidentifying and mischaracterizing Orisa religious culture and religious experts as did earlier anti-obeah statutes with respect to untold numbers of African heritage religions and Africana *nations*, including many whose names and identities are still unknown.

Elders of the Orisa tradition readily recall the persecution they experienced within the wider society, particularly under the "stigma" of colonial numenyms (see figures 3.3 and 3.4). When asked whether most Yoruba-Orisa devotees attended church during his adolescence in the 1930s, Baba Sam Phills presented a picture of exclusion and social caste that enveloped all uncloseted practitioners:

The Orisa people who tell you they went to church—(we had a few that would go)—they could not have gone to church and taken part in any sacrament or anything of the kind. Once you were . . . known as an Orisa—at that time, the stigmatic name . . . was "Shango"—you were a "Shango man." Even the yard boy work was hard for a Shango man [to secure]. It is a known fact that if you were a Shango man you couldn't go to clean Mr. so and so yard or get a job. Your children then had limited scope. In school,

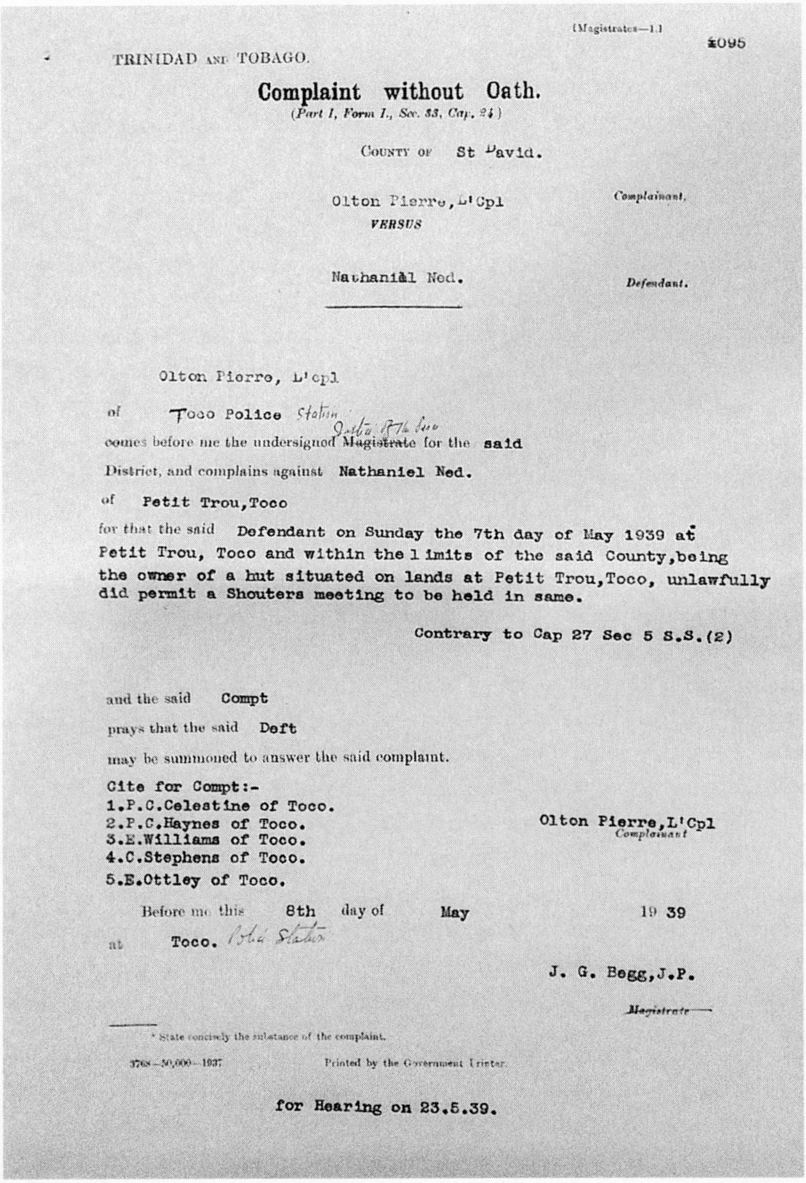

(Magistrates—1.)

£095

TRINIDAD AND TOBAGO.

Complaint without Oath.

(Part I, Form I., Sec. 33, Cap. 24)

COUNTY OF St David.

Olton Pierre, L'Cpl — *Complainant.*

VERSUS

Nathanial Ned. — *Defendant.*

Olton Pierre, L'cpl

of Toco Police Station

comes before me the undersigned ~~Magistrate~~ Justice of the Peace for the said

District, and complains against Nathaniel Ned.

of Petit Trou, Toco

for that the said* Defendant on Sunday the 7th day of May 1939 at Petit Trou, Toco and within the limits of the said County, being the owner of a hut situated on lands at Petit Trou, Toco, unlawfully did permit a Shouters meeting to be held in same.

Contrary to Cap 27 Sec 5 S.S.(2)

and the said Compt

prays that the said Deft

may be summoned to answer the said complaint.

Cite for Compt:-

1. P.C.Celestine of Toco.
2. P.C.Haynes of Toco.
3. E.Williams of Toco.
4. C.Stephens of Toco.
5. E.Ottley of Toco.

Olton Pierre, L'Cpl
Complainant

Before me this 8th day of May 1939

at Toco. Police Station

J. G. Begg, J.P.

Magistrate

* State concisely the substance of the complaint.

3768—50,000—1937 Printed by the Government Printer.

for Hearing on 23.5.39.

FIGURE 3.3 Official criminal complaint against Nathaniel Ned for "unlawfully" holding a "shouters meeting." Courtesy of the Melville J. and Frances S. Herskovits Papers, Schomburg Center for Research in Black Culture, New York Public Library. Reprinted by permission from John Corry.

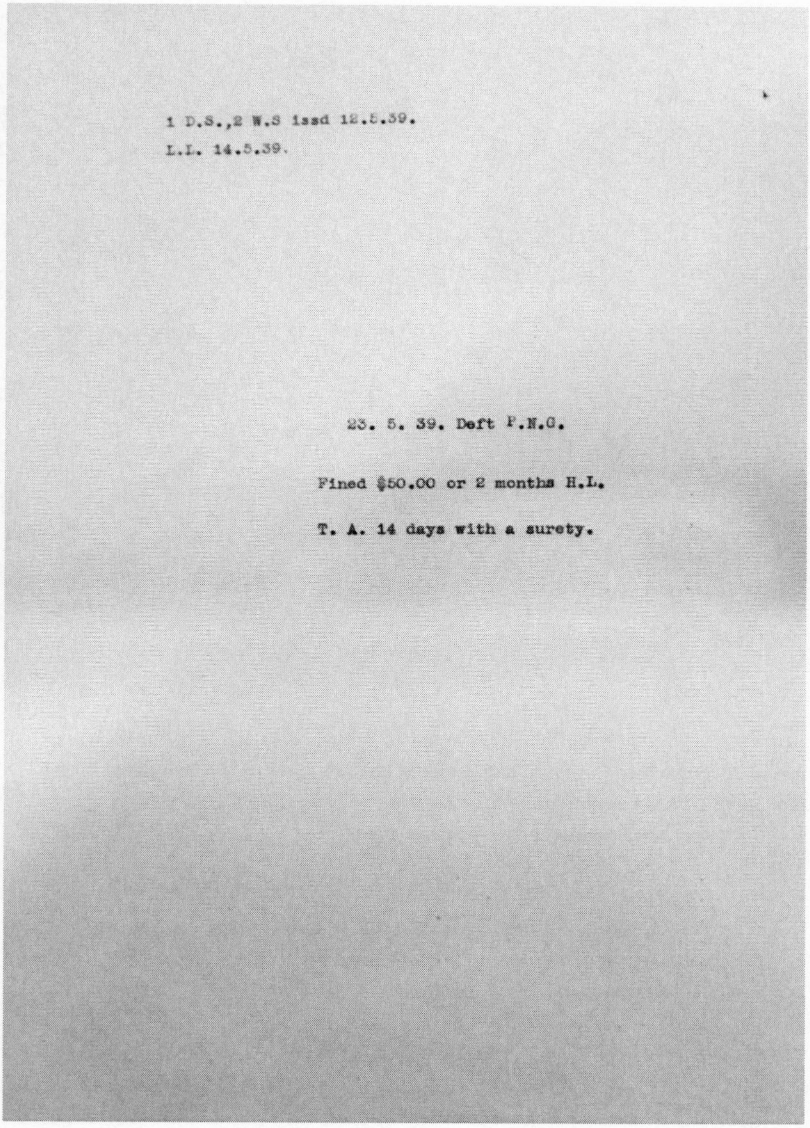

1 D.S.,2 W.S issd 12.5.39.
L.L. 14.5.39.

23. 5. 39. Deft P.N.G.

Fined $50.00 or 2 months H.L.

T. A. 14 days with a surety.

FIGURE 3.4 Nathaniel Ned's penalty for "unlawfully" holding a "shouters meeting."
Courtesy of the Melville J. and Frances S. Herskovits Papers, Schomburg Center for
Research in Black Culture, New York Public Library. Reprinted by permission from
John Corry.

FIGURE 3.5 Photograph of black churchgoers, c. 1914, Port of Spain. Yoruba-Orisa devotees were denied the social respectability that members of the Anglican Church and other Christian denominations commanded during this era. Reprinted by permission from National Archives of Trinidad and Tobago.

even down to the students would shun them: their father is a Shango, and they work obeah. Stigma! That stigma . . . remained . . . for a long period of time until recently. So, stigma has been the real upstanding curse against all Shango people.[18]

Beyond the scandal of membership in an illicit tradition was the burden of honoring one's religious commitments while under constant surveillance, the threat of imprisonment, and the obligation to pay heavy fines for conditional freedom in a climate of increasing fidelity to Eurocentric religious norms (see figure 3.5).[19] Baba Sam recalls, however, that the Orisa community devised tactics to circumvent the conundrum of religious repression. Manipulating the natural world and built environment to create practical ritual landscapes, devotees skillfully nailed vulnerable architectural veneers onto a sturdy institution:

In the thirties, a feast was a strange thing. We built a bamboo tent; covered it with coconut leaves; bar round the sides of the coconut leaves. But it could not have been anything that was permanent. The police would always make a raid. And in that time, we had no electricity and all of these things. We would get flambeaus; we would put kerosene in a bottle; and we would put a wick. And that supplied the light, plus what candles you could get to put on the ground. And so, from these humble beginnings came the Orisa people.[20]

Although Baba Sam seated himself behind consecrated bata drums at various Orisa feasts as early as twelve years old, he also remembers that the colonial establishment and its socializing institutions—church, school, and some family lineages—compelled compliance with Christian norms. "They beat Christianity into you!" he exclaimed, while reflecting on the instruction he imbibed at school and around his paternal family's dining table. Describing his patrifamilial culture, Baba Sam confessed, "My father family were the bourgeoisie type of black. . . . They were so clean and pure. They were puritan black that you couldn't go to sit at the table to have breakfast unless you had your tie and your thing on [implying formal attire] . . . and you had to be able to say that prayer for the meal with feeling."[21]

Baba Sam's narrative intersects those of other elder omorisa of his generation. During the 1920s and 1930s, children received cultural messages of disapproval and social taboos concerning Yoruba-Orisa religion.[22] Their formal education in colonial schools established expectations for respectable cultural behavior, and Orisa and Spiritual Baptist traditions were considered retrogressive, pointing backward to an African past that had no place in civil society. Alexander Kennedy's assessment of the wide social cleavage between African and European descendants during the late 1830s would have been no different one hundred years later. Writing to a minister in Glasgow's Greyfriars Church, Kennedy, the founder of Trinidad's first Presbyterian congregation (1838), remarked, "With a few honourable exceptions, the black and coloured population are notoriously ignorant and unblushingly immoral. On the other hand, the more wealthy and influential members of the community, principally from Europe and America, are the devotees of etiquette and fashion."[23] Indisputably, cultural, religious, and class status codependently reinforced the colony's heritage of racial stratification, and each of these factors would have an impact on African movements for social and political change in Trinidad throughout most of the twentieth century.

Antecedents to the Black Power Movement:
Trade Unions and Pan-Africanism

In the aftermath of slavery, Trinidadian social relations revolved around a three-tiered system dividing (1) white aristocrats from (2) free coloreds and a handful of free blacks and (3) those African descendants who had been enslaved and were made to serve as apprentices between 1834 and 1838. The liberated Africans who settled in Trinidad after the 1830s would find themselves struggling on the bottom social rung with ex-enslaved populations. East Indians too would eventually take a collective position somewhere at the bottom. However, Bridget Brereton contends that although "their economic or 'class' position, at least in the nineteenth century, would have categorised them with the third tier, the differences between them and the descendants of the ex-slaves were too great. . . . Indians constituted a fourth distinct tier in the social structure."[24]

In response to this unsettling social hierarchy and its material consequences for those on the bottom, the twentieth century brought the rise of the labor movement and mobilization against class exploitation. Between the 1840s and World War I, Trinidad had absorbed not only liberated Africans into its population but also approximately 144,000 East Indians, 1,300 Portuguese Madeirans, and 2,500 Chinese.[25] Despite the overwhelming presence of African and Asian descendants, white racial privilege reserved the best facilities, opportunities, institutional accouterments, and social comforts for phenotypic European descendants. As Trinidad's dying sugar-based economy shifted to accommodate the cocoa (late 1870s to 1920s) and oil (1920s) booms, the white proprietors, many of whom feasted on prosperous bequests from the days of plantation slavery, were well positioned to profit from the cheap labor that the African and Indian populations provided. This structural supremacy was not the least bit shaken by unionization efforts in the 1930s, despite a mass movement that mobilized thousands of African- and Indian-descended laborers to fight for more equitable working conditions and compensation.

Nevertheless, the struggle to achieve workers' rights played a role in hastening the pace toward national sovereignty. Although the Trinidad Free Labourers Society had first organized in 1844, the conditions allowing labor movements to achieve sustained political transformation in Trinidad only manifested in the twentieth century. Populist leaders such as the French-Creole Arthur A. Cipriani, former World War I commander of the British West India Regiment, protested the crown colony governance system and advocated for greater political autonomy, beginning with universal (male) suffrage. Siding with the "'unwashed and unsoaped barefooted man,'" Cipriani assumed the presidency of the Trinidad Workingmen's Association (TWA) in 1923 and used this platform to win a Legislative Council seat in 1925.[26]

As crown colony rule slowly ceded to increasing egalitarian political representation during the mid-1920s, the added pressures of labor unrest and social agitation, the depressed sugar market, and economic instability throughout the Caribbean led to new political experiments. During the 1930s, the TWA splintered into three groups, among them the British Empire Workers and Citizens Home Rule Party (BEW & CHRP) headed by Turbal Uriah "Buzz" Butler (1897–1977). Butler, an ex-soldier turned oil worker and organic homiletician of Moravian and Spiritual Baptist persuasions, held too powerful a sway over a wide mass of the laboring classes (including fellow Spiritual Baptists) to be left to his own devices.[27] Thus, with the SPO firmly in place for more than two decades, it is not surprising that Butler—who was imprisoned at the time for his militant unionizing efforts—included "Freedom of 'Workers' Religious Worship"[28] among the six demands he forwarded by petition to Lord Moyne, chairman of the 1938 West India Royal Commission (WIRC) dispatched by Britain to investigate the socioeconomic state of its regional colonies in the wake of widespread riots and strikes.

Because of Butler's radicalizing effect on labor, colonial authorities surveilled and repeatedly imprisoned him for his influential role in the 1937 oil workers' strike and subsequent labor campaigns during the late 1930s and early 1940s.[29] Despite these measures, Butler's pioneering efforts could not be undermined. The labor movement soon saw incremental changes, beginning with government recognition of trade unions, the founding of the Trinidad and Tobago Trades Union Council, and regulations for collective bargaining established by the Trade Disputes (Arbitration and Inquiry) Ordinance in 1938. The Trade Disputes and Protection of Property Ordinance guaranteed additional rights in 1943.[30]

By the September 1956 general elections, thanks to the ongoing labor struggles, two political parties had gained prominence in T&T: the People's National Movement (PNM), led by Dr. Eric Williams, and the People's Democratic Party (PDP), led by Bhadase Sagan Maraj. The PNM represented mainly the African community, whereas the PDP represented the East Indian, especially Hindu, community. Other parties such as the Trinidad Labour Party (TLP) and the Butler Party (BP) contested for seats as well. At the end of the day, the PNM outpaced its opponents, winning 39 percent of the popular vote and thirteen seats in the Legislative Council. T&T finally severed ties with imperial Britain in 1962.[31]

Formal independence, however, like the limited labor gains won during the 1930s and 1940s, could not undo the unbridled power of the white aristocrats who had inherited land, industry, and wealth from their estate-holding and slaveholding ancestors. The established distribution of social rewards remained stacked in favor of whites at the expense of Africans and Indians. Even destitute Portuguese immigrants from Madeira, small groups of Chinese indentured laborers, and Syrian settlers had earned more stable upwardly mobile opportunities during the nineteenth and twentieth centuries than their neighbors of African descent. The Trinidad and Tobago Union of Shop Assistants and Clerks' specific inclusion of "all Syrian Pedlars" among the operations targeted by its "Boycott against Victimization" campaign offers some indication of how aligned fair-skinned immigrants had become with the colonial economy by the late 1930s (see figure 3.6).

Comparing Trinidadian social relations with race relations in the United States during the mid-twentieth century, Black Power activist Teddy Belgrave explains how segregation customs created physical and social distance between whites and blacks in Trinidad right up through the time of its Black Power Movement: "The telephone company had an entrance on Frederick Street, the main headquarters, and one on Henry Street. . . . On Frederick Street, the white or off-white expatriates—that's their entrance. On Henry Street, the opposite. It's where the black workers came through. . . . That was many years ago now, but that was segregation."[32] Raffique Shah, an army lieutenant who would play a leading role in the social unrest of the Black Power era, also remembers those years as a period of economic depression intensified by color stratification: "Unemployment in the nation was high, and there were people close to us [enlisted soldiers] who were unemployed. We went to the banks, and similar institutions and saw the selected few who enjoyed jobs there. White control of the economy was very visible to us."[33] These two testimonies do not exaggerate. In 1970, the University of the West Indies's Institute of Social and Economic Research (ISER) published a study revealing that African descendants held only 4 percent of the executive positions in T&T businesses with more than one hundred employees. By contrast, European descendants held 69 percent of such positions, and persons of mixed heritage held 10 percent. East Indian and Chinese descendants held a meager 9 and 8 percent of executive positions, respectively; however, Chinese executives were well represented relative to their numerically small national population, which had peaked at 8,361 in 1960. When the study was conducted in 1969, Chinese persons constituted less than 1 percent of the total population.[34]

Trade Unionists, Fellow Workers of Trinidad and Tobago

Boycott Against Victimisation

Gabriel & Co., of 17, Henry St. and 23, Frederick St. Port-of-Spain have dismissed two girls because they joined a Trade Union.

The answer of the Working Class to this highhanded action of Gabriel must be.

NOT TO BUY FROM GABRIEL & CO.
Not to buy from all Syrian Pedlars
Not to buy from Whaby and Co. of San Fernando an Associate of Gabriel and Co.

Boycott all Customers and Supporters of Gabriel & Co.

Gabriel & Co. Must realise that they cannot deprive any one the right of freely organising.
Support this Boycott strongly, Employers must be taught a lesson.

Raise your United Voices and demand with the Union. Gabriel & Co. must re-employ these girls  **Now**

Issued by the Trinidad and Tobago Union of Shop Assistants and Clerks   Head Office, 70, Oxford St.—Tel. 1326
General Secretary, QUINTIN O'CONNOR.

Fraser & Argyle St.

FIGURE 3.6 Trinidad and Tobago Union of Shop Assistants and Clerks poster, ca. 1939, soliciting support for boycott against Syrian merchants. Courtesy of the Melville J. and Frances S. Herskovits Papers, Schomburg Center for Research in Black Culture, New York Public Library. Reprinted by permission from John Corry.

In effect, Trinidad had a race-relations social dilemma—and those on the frontlines of popular resistance to racist imperialism knew it. George Weekes's 1967 President General's address to the Oilfield Workers' Trade Union (OWTU) discloses how this dilemma sat in the nation's conscience:

> The Afro-Americans in the U.S.A., are struggling to the death for bread and freedom, therefore it is necessary for us—the blacks in Trinidad and Tobago to understand that the liberation of oppressed peoples of the world depends on the liberation of black people in the U.S.A. I hope the delegates are as happy as I am to know that Trinidad and Tobago has contributed a noble and famous son to the liberation struggle of the Afro-Americans in the person of Stokeley [sic] Carmichael. He has given them the slogan that has electrified the world "BLACK POWER."[35]

If the labor and independence movements were two strands of activism that helped make Trinidad an influential locus of Black Power organizing within the Caribbean region, a third strand was the country's long history as a symbol of Pan-Africanism in the African diaspora. Trinidad produced two of the Pan-African movement's earliest global intellectual architects and activists in Henry Sylvester Williams (1869–1911) and George Padmore (born Malcom Ivan Meredith Nurse, 1903–1959). After seeking educational opportunities at Fisk and Howard Universities in North America during the early 1890s, Williams moved to England to complete his legal training. While a student there in his late twenties, he preceded Cipriani by more than a decade in denouncing crown colony rule as "a heartless system" and "a synonym for racial contempt." During those student years, he organized fellow Trinidadians to lobby for their rights and took their grievances to members of Parliament in 1899, becoming the first person of African descent to address the House of Commons. Two years prior, Williams had founded the African Association (later called the Pan-African Association), and in 1900, his African Association sponsored the first organized Pan-African Conference in Westminster.[36]

Williams's pioneering work fueled several pan-African agendas in Africa, the United States, and the Caribbean, including Trinidad's satellite branch of the Pan-African Association, which won the loyalty of James Hubert Alphonse Nurse in 1901, just two years before his son Malcolm was born. Forty-four years later, Malcolm Nurse, aka George Padmore, would organize the sixth Pan-African Congress in Manchester, England, after spending decades at the helm of anticolonial efforts that reverberated across related movements and organizations in Africa and the Caribbean. In addition to his achievements as a theoretician of Pan-Africanism and a mentor to many global black leaders, Padmore founded the International African Service Bureau and the *International African Opinion*, a modest but influential journal that connected and informed activists of African descent globally.

Historian Leslie James notes that C. L. R. James (1901–1989), another celebrated Trinidadian Pan-Africanist, attributed "his own political methodology" to the influence of Padmore, whom he had known since childhood. James then trained another generation: "from his home, James advised young people who would then go out and apply their ideological training to their own activism."[37] Among them were young radicals of Afro-Caribbean/American heritage. Some, such as Orlando Patterson of Jamaica and Walter Rodney of Guyana, would later have influential careers as prominent intellectuals and advocates for Black Power.[38]

During the first half of the twentieth century, Padmore, James, and (Sylvester) Williams were critical nodes in the circulation of pan-African ideas via conferences, published journals and books, study groups, and a network of organizations that mobilized activists across Africa, the Caribbean, and the Americas. And there were many other African Caribbeans, including less memorialized African Trinidadians, studying and living in Europe in the late nineteenth and early twentieth centuries who reinforced the ethos of Pan-Africanism within the region itself. For instance, F. Eugene Michael Hercules (1888–1943), though born in Venezuela, was raised in Trinidad. While enrolled at Queens Royal College in Port of Spain, he founded the Young Men's Coloured Association, and in 1907, at the age of nineteen, he founded the Port-of-Spain Coloured Association. Hercules eventually worked transnationally, promoting a pan-African agenda that received a wide hearing among African descendants both in the metropole and the colonies. As secretary of the London-based Society of Peoples of African Origin (SPAO) he toured the British Caribbean and American colonies in 1919, exponentially increasing its membership.

According to Tony Martin, when Hercules lectured in Trinidad, he "spoke to packed audiences at the Princes Building in Port-of-Spain and at other venues in other towns," where "many people joined his Society of Peoples of African Origin. . . . Trinidad at the time was in the grip of strikes and unrest," writes Martin. "Anti-colonialist and anti-white feeling were running high, and the authorities were alarmed at the enthusiastic local response to Hercules's call for race pride, freedom and self-reliance."[39] At the same time, the speeches and pan-Africanist philosophy of Marcus Garvey circulated widely among strikers, especially in the 1919 and 1920 dockworkers' strikes and related activities of the TWA. By the mid-1920s, Trinidad was home to the most branches of Garvey's United Negro Improvement Association (UNIA) in the Anglophone Caribbean. In the wider Caribbean, only Cuba boasted more branches than the thirty affiliated offices dotting Trinidad's landscape; Jamaica's eleven branches could hardly compete.[40]

A half-century later, "guided by notions of black nationalism and wedded to an anti-imperialist sense of autonomous Caribbean development,"[41] Black Power advocates and sympathizers of the 1960s and 1970s constituted a new vanguard of Trinidad's own pan-Africanist leaders. The ideology of Black Power, in Trinidad and beyond, would come to express—as had Pan-Africanism before it—the ardent convictions of grassroots communities, students, and intellectuals through political campaign networks, the dissemination of literature, and the embrace of social theories from Marxist to Afrocentric perspectives.[42]

The 1960s brought transnational change to postcolonial Trinidad as activists took inspiration from radical political events engulfing black and brown populations in Cuba, Guyana, Jamaica, Canada, and the United States.[43] And although the word "Shango" failed to appear among the titles of Black Power organizations on the rise, Black Power enthusiasm nevertheless swept up Yoruba-Orisa devotees in a mood and moment that arguably began in 1967, ended during the mid-1980s for political elements of the movement, but continues today for several Orisa lineages and a growing contingent of individual devotees across the country.[44]

At the onset of this dramatic and disorienting era, the spotlight was on the new prime minister and impatient purveyors of youth and labor movements for black empowerment and wider redistribution of the country's wealth, land, and resources among African and Indian inhabitants. In the years leading up to the disturbances of the 1970s, Eric Williams had navigated his way to the top of the political ladder in an ethos of racial-ethnic tensions between T&T's two majority African and Indian populations. To do so, he had to traverse a decolonial era that faithfully married electoral politics to identity politics. "There can be no Mother India for those who came from India. . . . There can be no Mother Africa for those of African origin," Williams pronounced in his nation-building rhetoric. "The only mother we recognize is Mother Trinidad and Tobago, and Mother cannot discriminate between her children."[45]

But Williams had much more to contend with than instilling national allegiance across disparate racial-ethnic enclaves in T&T. Unemployment had accelerated considerably between the mid-1950s and the late 1960s, reaching 15 percent in 1968, and labor unions, especially in the oil and sugar industries, had launched hundreds of strikes. Between 1960 and 1964 official figures place the number of strikes at 230, "involving 74,574 workers and the loss of 803,899 man days."[46] The consistent wave of strikes presented opportunities for large clusters of African oil workers and Indian sugar laborers to unite under one banner. Rather than confront the wider political implications of labor consolidation across ethnic and other divisions, Williams resorted to alienating measures. James Millette identifies the 1965 Industrialization Stabilization Act (ISA) as the "first overtly hostile piece of anti-worker legislation" that severed the already weakened bond "between the PNM and a substantial segment of the organized labour movement."[47] Thus, adds Scott MacDonald, "the leadership of the Afro-Creole trade unions . . . found black power as the vehicle of power to challenge the ISA and what was regarded as a corrupt and declining PNM government."[48]

The political ironies and unavoidable dissonances of protesting a nation under colonial rule and then leading one in its aftermath distanced Prime Minister Eric Williams of 1970 from the aspiring prime minister Eric Williams of 1961, whom one American envoy described as having a "chip on his shoulder and smoldering resentment in his heart against colonialism which, of course, means the whites."[49] This Eric Williams never showed up during what would come to be known as the "February Revolution" of 1970. His delayed rhetorical embrace of demonstrators' "insistence on black dignity, the manifestation of black consciousness, and the demand for black economic power" arrived a month too late, failing to impress radicalized youths that he was anything other than a protector of the status quo. Williams even went as far as declaring, "If this is Black power then I am for Black Power."[50] These belated comments before the nation, however, would not allow the prime minister to clean himself with his tongue like a cat.[51]

By this time, organizations had proliferated across a spectrum of political leanings within Black Power circles that campaigned around labor, class, race, and cultural rights. In addition to the OWTU, groups of different abilities and localities, such as the Transport and Industrial Workers Union (TIWU), United Movement for the Reconstruction of Black Identity (UM-ROBI), African Cultural Association (ACA), Afro Turf Limers (ATL), African Unity Brothers (AUB), Southern Liberation Movement (SLM), Tapia House, and the National Joint Action Committee (NJAC)—a student-led "federation of organizations"—worked their various channels to champion the causes of their constituents under the banner of Black Power.[52] These and other Black Power initiatives attracted supporters in diverse venues and absorbed personalities that pursued complementary and contentious agendas.

Black Power strategies ranged from intellectual theorizing to militant tactics, including the deployment of Molotov cocktails for defensive purposes and the destruction of property connected with symbols of colonial power. Eventually, elements within the military put the final punctuation mark on extreme expressions of Black Power dissidence in 1970 with a ten-day mutiny at the Teteron National Defense Force Base. Although the mutiny was principally motivated by institutional failings of the Trinidad and Tobago Defense Force and, by extension, other government ministries, the chief lieutenants involved operated under the consensus that "the army, so long as we were a part of it, must never be used against the people of the country." According to Raffique Shah, "On April 21, 1970, when Eric Williams declared his state of emergency and moved to crush the Black Power uprising, we countered by seizing control of the military."[53]

What some have called Trinidad's "aborted" or "unfinished"[54] revolution with its "insistence on black dignity" seemed to reach the palais as swiftly as it reached the prime minister, the president, and the Parliament. Columnist Lennox Grant's description of "the 1970 revolution" as "relatively godless"[55] spoke to its disenchantment with mainstream Christianity but neglected to capture the role African gods played for some in the movement. The sway of Black Power consciousness among Afro-Trinidadians eventually brought custodians of Yoruba-Orisa religion into the center of activities as they performed public libations to invite ancestral and Orisa support for planned protests.[56]

Orisa Powers in the Era of Black Power

Even before the dust of the 1970 demonstrations rose, from the left–right march of determined feet pacing the roads of town and country, the movement had needed music, and that music had issued from the Yoruba-Orisa drumming and chanting traditions of Afro-Trinidad. The Orisa religion's music also created the ideal aesthetic environment for spirit manifestations that Black Power youths never predicted.

John King, an officer of the ACA who was in his late teens and early twenties during the height of the movement, describes the ethos and activities that summoned the Orisa to the ACA's Black Power gatherings and events in the district of St. James:

We had an organization—African Cultural Association. . . . It started in the housing scheme. And we were under the leadership of a brother called Mansa Musa. We used to keep weekly meetings at a park in the Village, and we had the first big cultural explosion. Some people call it the first Kwanzaa, ... this celebration where we had drums, music, arts on display.... In 1968, globally, there was a kind of wind of change blowing around the place. A lot of things didn't relate to us in particular, and we were pushing an African agenda.... We needed to have an upliftment for our people.... And we started to wear African clothes ... and then we started to play drums at certain fêtes, and that is when the problem started. We were playing drums and singing the African chants. (We started to learn one or two African chants, before we began going to the palais.) And just now manifestation came.[57]

King explains that the first time they experienced an unexpected spiritual visitor, a local resident of St. James and a trained dancer with international experience, Dunstan Dottin, heard the Orisa drumbeats and "came up the road to calm the waters because we really didn't know what was going on. We were looking at things differently because we were into ourselves." But being into "ourselves" inevitably involved being into the Orisa Powers:

We got introduced to this Orisa priest, Leader Boisey in Tunapuna. So, we went up there, had some feasts, did all the work, planted all the flags, cleared up the place.... Well, the next thing you know, people started hearing about these boys wearing African clothes at some palais up in the back of Tunapuna. So, crowds started to come: Who are these fellas? What is really going on? Well, that was a bacchanal! That feast lasted from Sunday till the next Sunday ... in August of 1970. So, from there, our grouping used to go to feasts and play drums down in Marabella, down by [Iya Melvina] Rodney, Isaac "Sheppy" Lindsay in Fyzabad, Mother Gerard in Tacarigua, others in Petit Valley, Carenage, Diego Martin. You had a lot of palais, a lot of feasts![58]

King and other young advocates of "African culture" were learning firsthand that Black Power *was* Orisa Power. The cultural and spiritual satisfaction they experienced through aesthetic and ritualistic involvement with the Orisa palais sustained them from one feast to the next, even if they found other norms regulating priestly authority and control less appealing.[59] The youths' presence at Orisa feasts extended the palais's *nation-al* purpose. It was now an arena where colonial Yoruba Trinidadian *nation* politics met postcolonial Afro-Trinidadian black *nationalist* politics. Both constituents knew cognitively and somatically that spirituality and politics were like conjoined Ibeji, fused at the ori.[60]

However, not all aspects of the Yoruba Trinidadian tradition were equally attractive. Its well-established politics of social belonging—a double-edged politics of respectability—would not survive the scrutiny of the newcomers' politics of decolonization. Social belonging for these young black *nationalists* encompassed not only ideas of authentic citizenship within the independent nation of T&T but also spiritual citizenship within an African religious *nation*.[61] Thus, the youths entered the palais thirsty for a libation they could ingest, and their understanding of Black Power left no room for swallowing the bread and wine of Christian communion, whether literally or figuratively. They were done with all aspects of Christian dogma and devotion. As King recalled, "We realized that the Christian faith didn't have anything for us . . . we couldn't be Christians. We came from this great tradition. Christianity is a religion that they formulated somewhere in the third or fourth century. Who was responsible for that? We weren't responsible for that. That wasn't a part of us. And Christianity and Islam were responsible for enslaving black people. So how could we follow a tradition that enslaved our people?"

This posture of distance from Christianity, King explains, clashed with the kinship practices of adoption and inclusion they encountered in the authority figures at the palais:

> They used the "hail Mary, mother of God," a lot. We rebelled against that, and we actually told them that this doesn't relate to us. Calling the spirits—"Ogun is Saint Michael" and "this one is Saint Anne." We said we don't need to equate our manifestations with the Christian names. We are not Christians. Well, they had a problem with that. As far as they were concerned, they were Christians . . . even though they called what they were doing "Shango." . . . We used to make carvings and give them to put in their places so they wouldn't have these pictures of the white Jesus that don't represent us . . . and they would put the carvings inside, even by Iya Rodney . . . and we gave a lot of carvings to Boisey, and he kept them in the shrine.[62]

Oloye Ogundare Ife Olakela Massetungi (formerly Oludari), a pan-Africanist founding member of the well-known Egbe Onisin Eledumare Orisa shrine, recalls similar encounters with long-standing palais elders during this period: "Several of us, sometimes not coordinated, went to several Orisa palais and challenged the elders about their pictures. This Power you have manifesting here—this is a African Power? What is that saint doing there?"[63]

Whatever else might be attributed to the BPM in Trinidad, the experiences of King, Massetungi, and others like them underscore that the movement was the catalyst for a small exodus of Afro-Trinidadians out the cathedral doors that separated the saved from the sinner on Sunday mornings. Where did they go? Recollections from those active during the period reveal that some took refuge in secular, aesthetic, and political venues to express or retire their spirituality. Others gave a distant spiritual nod to the Yoruba-Orisa religion. But a critical mass became initiated and active members of Orisa shrines across the country.

Some schooled in Orisa social thought and ritual practice applied the symbols of their tradition to interpret the signs of the times. If the late Iyalorisa Louisa Catherine Toussaint's perspective tells us anything, it suggests that Orisa devotees, like many other Trinidadians, followed and formed opinions about the political events of the independence era. Massetungi recalls, for instance, how Toussaint (his spiritual mother) read Eric Williams's diplomatic gestures toward an empire on the decline through a Yoruba-Orisa figurative lexicon:

> She said when Trinidad and Tobago was about to become independent and the then prime minister, Eric Williams, sent a steelpan to England, to the queen, her interpretation of it was the steelpan was representing steel cutting steel—the chains of colonialism. . . . And so, she felt that really the primary Orisa here [in Trinidad] was Ogun. I suspect several things would have colored her vision because, no matter who your Orisa was, once you came under her, you had to train under Ogun because, as far as she was concerned, the African was in a state of war, and when you in war you need to know Ogun.[64]

The Yoruba-Orisa tradition was no fleeting fad or quixotic innovation. Just as Iya Louisa could apply its logics and symbols to the macropolitics operative at the time, so too, soon, would some within the ranks of the younger generations. Orisa was Trinidad's most resourceful system of meaning, with the power to undo and replace a colonial semiosis in the collective psyche and "soul-life" of the wider African-descended population.[65] It provided those in quest of African cosmologies and revelatory sources a desired "field of tropes, styles, and sensibilities" that addressed the emptiness of Christian revelation as they had come to experience it.[66]

Whereas middle-class Pan-Africanists of a previous era, at best, took up the cause of publicly defending Shango/Yaraba devotees against colonial encroachment on their right to religious freedom, middle-class Trinidadians of the Black Power era, persuaded by the *power* of Orisa, went as far as actually becoming Yoruba-Orisa practitioners. They wanted to look into the faces of Yoruba gods and their caretakers and visit with all their kin.[67] On the verge of participating in Trinidad's emerging nation-statehood, they were preparing to join an old *nation* and its Yoruba-Orisa families, as they endeavored to sustain their nascent ideology of a new black *nationalist* politics.

It was a substantive matter to locate new sources for cultural and spiritual construction in an informal African heritage institution historically cast aside for being out of step with the march of modernity. But it was in many ways a logical outgrowth of the Black Power consciousness that first mobilized advocates to satirize and denounce the colonial structures in place. In partnership with St. James United (SJU), King and his ACA comrades seemingly led the charge when they brought out 1001 *White Devils*, their first in a series of infamous Carnival bands between 1970 and the mid-1980s (see figures 3.7 and 3.8).

Since colonial times, Carnival had been a historically significant public stage for African political theater.[68] The colony's legal proscriptions (1880s) of African participation in the annual revelries only served to expose the Carnival space as a critical arena for hidden transcripts to read themselves aloud, and 1970 was no different.[69] That year, Carnival provided many Black Power advocates such as King their most public platform to protest the unconscionable global reach of white supremacy. Examining his one remaining photo of the event, now archived in an unpretentious black frame on his living room wall, King noted with great pride and a hint of nostalgia how "Junior Green played the pope, while Gail and others played the Ku Klux Klan."

The name of the band, King explained, materialized after "I read Chancellor Williams's book where he titled one chapter 'White Devils from the West.'"[70] *The Destruction of Black Civilization: Great Issues of a Race from 4500 B.C. to 2000 A.D.* (authored by an African American sociologist) and similar texts that graced the libraries of King and other young black *nationalists* also inspired a new awareness of Western imperialism's accumulated violations. Such pan-Africanist texts allowed them to connect their experiences of Euro-colonialism with global black suffering under systems of segregation and apartheid that deified whiteness and the global reach of white political, economic, and cultural sovereignty. Thus, Khafra Kambon's description of the Carnival band's effect is especially apt: "The St. James village drummers had not so much played 1001 WHITE DEVILS—the Ku Klux Klan, Enoch Powell, Vorster etc.—as they had performed a public ritual of exorcism."[71]

Meeting of the people

PAGE 2

Violence in WI cricket

PAGE 8

Third Anniversary of the February Revolution

PAGES 6 & 7

GUERRILLA

WITH

THE PEN

PAGES 10, 11, 12.

Many are perhaps not astonished at the findings of this

"The mark of the beast"

IN 1970, they brought "1001 White Devils" into the streets. In 1971, it was "The Great White Hope", and in 1972 "Europe to America".

This year, St. James United, famed for their original Jouvert presentations, are bringing "The Mark of the Beast".

The band is intended to represent the history of white western "society", from the days of the cave man through to modern-day hippies.

Some of the feature characters will be "the missionaires who paved the way for the subversion of world cultures and religion", the Klu Klux Klan, "the unofficial arm of Imperial America's attempt to keep down African resistance", and the Bwana European Game Hunters, glorified in the movies.

And, of course, there will be a "devil" complete with horns and tail.

The African Cultural Association Drummers will provide music for the band, which is expected to be 300 strong. Band Fee is 75 cents and further details may be had from the organizers at 18 Ranjit Kumar Street, St. James.

SEE PAGES 6 and 7

FIGURE 3.7 "Third Anniversary of the February Revolution" chronicles four years of mas bands launched by the African Cultural Association/ St. James United. (Printed in *Tapia* 3, no. 8, [1973]: 1.) Reprinted by permission from the Caribbean Newspapers, Digital Library of the Caribbean, George A. Smathers Libraries, University of Florida, Gainesville.

FIGURE 3.8 St. James United/African Cultural Association mas players march in their *1001 White Devils* Carnival band during Trinidad and Tobago's 1970 national Carnival celebrations. (Photographer unknown. Courtesy of Gerard King, personal collection.)

The secret to any empire's dominance lies in its capacity to invade and violate with impunity the bodies and psyches of its colonized victims—to penetrate and reorder their very sensorium such that their tastes, desires, and sensibilities adjust and become attuned to those of the ruling class. Even in the absence of a majority-white governing presence, during the 1970s black Trinidadians still experienced colonial violation as it lingered and comingled with political "independence." They wrestled with the coloniality of power beyond structures of social ordering and knowing. King and his comrades were coming to understand and resist how the coloniality of power seduces the senses in service to imperial lust and logics, equipping the (former) colonizer with hegemonic control that appears most totalizing and insidious at the level of affect.[72]

The national Carnival was the perfect place to exorcise such spirits of white supremacy and dramatize black resistance to overt and subtle effects of Euro-imperialism. Baptized in a global black *nationalist* consciousness that linked the Klan and the pope to Trinidad's retention of color caste and economic apartheid, 1001 *White Devils* marshaled artistic and aesthetic weapons to dislodge the colonizer's tastes, desires, and sensibilities from black Trinidadians' shared psyche. Parading in the poetry of disguises that revealed more than they concealed, the ACA made a statement that day that anticipated a later, more constructive move in the direction of the Orisa palais.

Just a few weeks after Carnival, the controversial arrest of nine leading demonstrators on February 27, 1970, further revealed how Black Power advocates and their sympathizers were denouncing institutional sites of Euro-colonial power in Trinidad, including the Christian Church. Among the barrage of summary offenses that the state machinery leveled, the most effective charge against the nine defendants, all of them members of NJAC, was the desecration and destruction of the Cathedral of the Immaculate Conception, a prominent Catholic church, on Independence Square. Current collective memory historicizes the activism most symbolic of the movement's spiritual dimensions—the destruction of Catholic icons or splashing of black paint over Catholic statues—as Black Power's genesis within the public sphere. Yet some witnesses and actors during the period contest this narration of the BPM's inaugural commentary on Christianity.

Press coverage of events cast the spotlight on the year 1970, especially the fifty-six days between February 26 and April 21 during which massive demonstrations by and detentions of Black Power advocates captured the attention of the new nation.[73] Apoesho Mutope, NJAC member and official photographer, followed events with both feet and lens and provides a different perspective based on his firsthand knowledge. He marched in demonstrations, suffered political imprisonment along with other Black Power leaders at Nelson Island, and survived with memories and memorabilia that narrate a historical account of the events.[74] "The story that had circulated," Mutope explains, "was that, when the demonstrators went into the Catholic cathedral, they took black paint and painted all the white statues black," but "that never happened!"

> What happened was that the demonstration was shortly after Carnival. It was in the Lenten period. At that time (and I understand it still happens to some extent), what they did in some of the Roman Catholic churches was to drape the statues with either black or purple cloth as part of the whole Lenten activities, because it was supposed to be a period of mourning and so on. So, when the demonstrators went in, a number of the statues were

actually draped with cloth. Now, subsequent to that demonstration that day, very early the next morning, the police rounded up about nine of the persons they identified as being the ringleaders of that demonstration. And they were charged with summary offences. . . . The most serious was desecration of the Roman Catholic cathedral. The demonstrators went into the church, but the desecration that authorities were claiming never took place.

Mutope challenges all reigning narratives suggesting willful intent on the part of demonstration organizers to desecrate any church, noting instead that some of the "brothers" not only marched inside the Cathedral of the Immaculate Conception but also sat down with several priests there to discuss their grievances.[75] Mutope further maintains that the logical sequence of events itself exposes the desecration rumor as a fabrication: "Now, they set out to demonstrate against the Canadian interests, to march and identify all the different interests.[76] Nobody was walking with black paint. . . . Is it that you think that they stopped then, and found a hardware store, and bought paint and went back there? If you examine the logistics of it, it doesn't make sense."

Mutope does indicate that, "subsequently, it [the desecration and painting of Christian statues] could easily have happened in any church after February 26th because of the mood that evolved in the wake of the arrests." In fact, "as a result of what grew out of that, there were instances of attacks on certain religious institutions . . . during the period of demonstrations."[77] The April 7, 1970, issue of the *Express* printed a photograph of one such attack with the following caption: "Crucifix smeared with black paint by Black Power demonstrators recently in San Fernando." Although the date of the "desecration" remains unrecorded, it likely occurred on the prior evening—the same day a young black man and NJAC member from the grassroots population, Basil Davis, was shot dead by police in the vicinity of Woodford Square in Port of Spain (see figure 3.9). Davis's death on April 6 took on meta-significance for the wider population of Black Power advocates and sympathizers three days later, when a crowd, estimated in size from thirty thousand to one hundred thousand persons, joined the funeral procession and lined the streets in mourning from Port of Spain to San Juan where Davis was buried in Barataria Cemetery.

Whose clenched fist(s) darkened the white porcelain crucifix with such a heavy splash of jet-black paint and protest we may never know. However, the iconoclastic gesture registered the collective antipathy toward Christianity uniting many Black Power sympathizers and denounced the imperialist role of the Catholic Church in the historic global capitalist ventures of slavery

FIGURE 3.9 This iconoclastic protestation likely occurred in response to the police killing of grassroots NJAC member Basil Davis on April 6, 1970. Caption reads, "Crucifix with black paint by Black Power demonstrators in San Fernando," *Express*, April 7, 1970. Reprinted by permission from National Archives of Trinidad and Tobago.

and colonialism. In such an environment, black consciousness and spiritual movement toward symbols of Africa superseded class divisions to grip the hearts and souls of more than a few African Trinidadians. According to Mutope, "It was a case of African people being drawn to a point of power, a point of force that had never existed before in the country. In the past, people had congregated because of political allegiances, because of working class interests—like in the thirties with Butler—but this was the first time that they were being brought together as black people."[78] Even blacks in the military had experienced cultural humiliation and repression in their professional training and work environments. "A soldier could speak of De Gaulle or Churchill as being great," recalls Shah, "but no mention must be made of Nelson Mandela or Julius Nyerere as being heroes. He could not wear an African carving on a chain, but he could wear a crucifix or something pornographic."[79] Thus, in rejecting Afro-Trinidad's captivity to Christianity and Eurocentric cultural conventions of respectability, the BPM conscienticized participants to reevaluate their cultural roots and reconnect to their African heritage.[80]

While Carnival and subsequent protests yielded political space for deconstructive performance, the palais—notwithstanding its hospitality toward external religious symbols—established an entelechial environment where Black Power advocates could actualize new spiritual and cultural commitments with revolutionary potential for Trinidadians of African descent. The Orisa religious culture came into play because it possessed the most accessible structural apparatus to reorient those seeking tangible affiliations with African sources of spiritual and cultural instruction. This focused attention, if even demonstrated by limited elements within the movement, such as the ACA, turned the page on a new chapter in the history of African religions in Trinidad. Yet, if journalism is "the first rough draft of history," the Orisa did not figure prominently in that draft.[81] Trinidad's mainstream press neglected the cascade of events linking Black Power and the Orisa tradition. Of the dozens of articles that made front-page news and the dozens more that filled the inside pages of the Express, Guardian, and the Evening News during crucial months of Black Power demonstrations (February–April), few make mention of "Shango," even in periodic features about African history and cultural heritage.[82]

Even more telling of the Yoruba-Orisa tradition's invisibility in civic life at this moment of social unrest was the Inter-Religious Steering Committee's (IRSC) full-page message to "Our Brothers, Our Sisters, Our Fellow-Citizens of Trinidad & Tobago" in the April 23, 1970, edition of the Express. Penned just "a few hours after the declaration of the state of emergency" by representative Christian, Hindu, and Muslim leaders, the message pleaded for peace and unity while promising programs in support of "the needy members of our community" and imploring citizens "to pray earnestly to God in your churches, your temples, your mosques, and most of all your homes and families." At a time when the nation's source of social unrest sent some Trinidadians in search of solutions to the consecrated stools of Orisa deities, the IRSC did not think of inviting custodians of a tradition on the brink of its own revolution "to pray earnestly to God" in the palais (see figure 3.10).

But what remained out of view in the press's rough draft of history was the way the BPM created the context for the perfect cocktail of socially influential personalities and agendas to tilt the nation's view of the Orisa tradition and its adherents in a more positive direction. Emerging from a history of stigmatization and repression, "Shango" finally mounted the public stage to assume the role it alone could play in the social ~~world~~ of Trinidad's postcolonial African descendants.[83] This era of resistance was momentous for the privilege it afforded political-spiritual activists to escort Orisa out of the forests of seclusion and clandestine operation where elders had been compelled to retreat for safety and survival during the nineteenth and much of the twentieth centuries. Orisa's "coming out" could be observed, at times, at the heart of public protest where its custodians partnered with or doubled as Spiritual Baptists to bring ritual reinforcement and spiritual sanction to the movement for black social justice. Mutope recalls,

> Because of the black identity of the Orisa and the Spiritual Baptists and so on, a number of them were taking part in the demonstrations. You had two months of demonstrations throughout the country. And . . . sometimes when we assembled at Woodford Square . . . you would find some of the Baptist people coming up to give some prayers before the march would start. Some Orisa people would come up and . . . do a little libation because of all that was being drawn into the movement.[84]

These assemblies activated the "weak ties" between elder omorisa and younger disciples of black *nationalism*. Black *nationalist* interests, in fact, transformed some of those weak ties into strong ties when some advocates who were not Yoruba descendants claimed solidarity with the Yoruba *nation*'s religious heritage in Africa and legacy in Trinidad.[85] Their affiliation with the Yoruba-Orisa tradition expanded the meaning of *nationhood* among African descendants beyond consanguineous relations. In the era of Black Power, an ideological and spiritual pan-Africanist heritage was enough to secure any

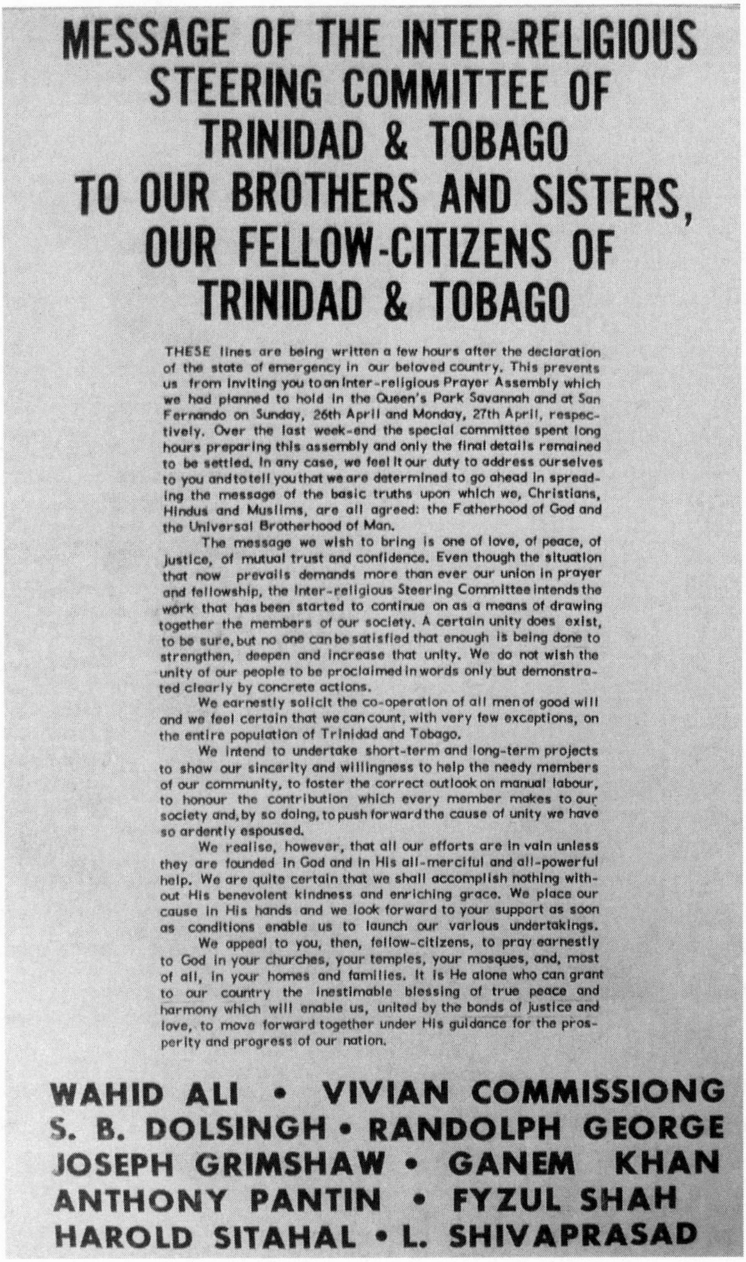

MESSAGE OF THE INTER-RELIGIOUS STEERING COMMITTEE OF TRINIDAD & TOBAGO TO OUR BROTHERS AND SISTERS, OUR FELLOW-CITIZENS OF TRINIDAD & TOBAGO

THESE lines are being written a few hours after the declaration of the state of emergency in our beloved country. This prevents us from inviting you to an Inter-religious Prayer Assembly which we had planned to hold in the Queen's Park Savannah and at San Fernando on Sunday, 26th April and Monday, 27th April, respectively. Over the last week-end the special committee spent long hours preparing this assembly and only the final details remained to be settled. In any case, we feel it our duty to address ourselves to you and to tell you that we are determined to go ahead in spreading the message of the basic truths upon which we, Christians, Hindus and Muslims, are all agreed: the Fatherhood of God and the Universal Brotherhood of Man.

The message we wish to bring is one of love, of peace, of justice, of mutual trust and confidence. Even though the situation that now prevails demands more than ever our union in prayer and fellowship, the Inter-religious Steering Committee intends the work that has been started to continue on as a means of drawing together the members of our society. A certain unity does exist, to be sure, but no one can be satisfied that enough is being done to strengthen, deepen and increase that unity. We do not wish the unity of our people to be proclaimed in words only but demonstrated clearly by concrete actions.

We earnestly solicit the co-operation of all men of good will and we feel certain that we can count, with very few exceptions, on the entire population of Trinidad and Tobago.

We intend to undertake short-term and long-term projects to show our sincerity and willingness to help the needy members of our community, to foster the correct outlook on manual labour, to honour the contribution which every member makes to our society and, by so doing, to push forward the cause of unity we have so ardently espoused.

We realise, however, that all our efforts are in vain unless they are founded in God and in His all-merciful and all-powerful help. We are quite certain that we shall accomplish nothing without His benevolent kindness and enriching grace. We place our cause in His hands and we look forward to your support as soon as conditions enable us to launch our various undertakings.

We appeal to you, then, fellow-citizens, to pray earnestly to God in your churches, your temples, your mosques, and, most of all, in your homes and families. It is He alone who can grant to our country the inestimable blessing of true peace and harmony which will enable us, united by the bonds of justice and love, to move forward together under His guidance for the prosperity and progress of our nation.

WAHID ALI • VIVIAN COMMISSIONG
S. B. DOLSINGH • RANDOLPH GEORGE
JOSEPH GRIMSHAW • GANEM KHAN
ANTHONY PANTIN • FYZUL SHAH
HAROLD SITAHAL • L. SHIVAPRASAD

FIGURE 3.10 The Inter-Religious Steering Committee appeal to citizens of Trinidad and Tobago just hours after the government's announcement of a state of emergency. While imploring those of varied faiths to pray for peace in their houses of worship—Christian, Hindu, Muslim—the appeal's omission of Yoruba-Orisa devotees and the Orisa palais evidences the tradition's unmistakable position beyond the purview of respectable religions during the 1970s. *Express*, April 23, 1970. Reprinted by permission from National Archives of Trinidad and Tobago.

African descendant's place within Trinidad's Yoruba-Orisa lineage and would inspire the founding of new Orisa families.

Memorializing the collective mood of the young post-Christians seeking adoption within these spiritual kinships, Iyalorisa Eintou Pearl Springer's untitled poem escorts audiences into the recesses of black consciousness as it enveloped many of her comrades and her during the 1970s.

> In Time
> We smashed
> Those statues
> Or painted them
> Black
> Black like we
> In vengeance wreaked
> On a God
> With seaming bias,
> Against our colour,
> Maybe because,
> He came from the same culture
> As our oppressors.
>
> Black power
> Urging we
> Like Boukman,
> To give allegiance
> To a God
> Of vengeance
> Possessed
> Of one cheek,
> That will not turn
> That will not turn.[86]

Some went beyond destruction and renovation to sculpt new statues of Yoruba deities and erect new palais to house them. The political moment precipitated an expanding Orisa religious lineage whose understanding and performance of *nationhood* were bound to change. Genealogical Yoruba *nationhood* had decreasing relevance for later generations of filial and spiritual Yoruba descendants. These descendants were not Yoruba settlers, and despite the range of spiritual, cultural, and political meanings that the "Yoruba" identity possessed for affiliated omorisa, they were also *Trinis*, citizens of a newly independent nation. Identity construction in their context required a postcolonializing strategy of pan-African *nationhood*.[87] For emerging spiritual leaders such as Olakela Massetungi, a generative correspondence existed between a particular Yoruba-Orisa heritage and wider African heritages from which African Trinidadians could draw resources for their spiritual and cultural rebirth. Egbe Onisin Eledumare, the Orisa shrine organization Massetungi cofounded, became a center of belonging that facilitated this rebirth.

Although reliable figures do not exist for the number of Orisa devotees in Trinidad during the 1970s, approximately thirteen thousand people identified as Orisa in Trinidad and Tobago's 2011 population census. Given the significant rate of dual membership linking the Orisa and Spiritual Baptist traditions, adding just half of the 5.7 percent of self-identified Spiritual Baptists to the pool raises the number of Orisa devotees and affiliates to twenty-five thousand.[88] Among this number, it is not easy to determine how many devotees adhered to a theology and devotional life shaped by the philosophy and politics of Black Power, black *nationalism*, Pan-Africanism, or neo-Africanism. However, Castor's contemporary research on devotees' privileging of Ifa traditions in their daily lives suggests that number is increasing in the twenty-first century, especially as elders who incorporate Catholic and other spiritual elements into their practice of Orisa age and pass on.[89] Since its inception, EOE has rejected all Yoruba-Orisa conventions with perceived connections to Euro-Christian symbols and theology while repurposing and embodying the tradition's enduring orienting principles. The project of *nation-building* has been foremost among EOE's preoccupations, a project of Africana religious *nationalism* that addresses the opacity and multiple belongings of African descendants not only in T&T (their home nation-state) but also in the wider African diaspora.[90]

Egbe Onisin Eledumare: "Black Power in the Open"

Founded just a year after the 1001 *White Devils* mas players performed their anticolonial endorsement of black empowerment in Carnival streets and nine Black Power advocates were arrested, EOE surfaced as the most enduring Orisa institution with pan-Africanist commitments in the Black Power and post–Black Power eras. Reflecting on his ile's thirty-year legacy in a 2001 interview, Massetungi reaffirmed EOE's central mission while gently mocking his critics: "I remember when we held our Second International Congress. There was a newspaper article headline, 'Black Power in the Open,' because basically people was starting to say because of our approach, they say, 'Oludari and them is Black Power in disguise.' I say, 'what Black Power in disguise,' I say, 'we is Black Power in the open'; that was my speech!"[91]

Massetungi's riposte underlines that EOE was unabashedly undisguised and uncensored from its earliest days of operation: it "grew out of the need for African people to reassert their identity and to address the social imbalances in the present society." EOE's identity as a spiritual community emerged through a repertoire of organizations and a series of shifts in those organizations' social emphases: "We had coming out of that [EOE] several pan-African organizations forming themselves into what became the African Advancement Association which later evolved into Egbe Ilosiwaju Ile Alkebulan.... That organization was a Garveyite organization.... However, a small core of that organization recognized that the African person is a total person—that African spirituality is included in the character of the African, and therefore we decided to form what we called a spiritual foundation."[92]

The group aligned itself with Iyalorisa Louisa Catherine Toussaint, a descendant of the Ojo family and "founding member of the Ethiopian Orthodox Church" in Trinidad, while still "a very strong practitioner of Yoruba Sacred Science tradition." Toussaint was versed in Yoruba ritual prayers and songs, and Massetungi trained under her leadership for nearly twenty years after his initiation into the Yoruba-Orisa tradition in 1971.

The EOE advocated a different vision for Trinidad's African descendants than did NJAC, whose use of social, symbolic, and ~~ontological~~ "blackness" invited African and Indian descendants to partner in the liberation struggle. EOE also took a different turn from the Garveyite organizations from which it sprang. Those organizations refused to endorse one religion over any other. By contrast, Massetungi and his comrades grounded their activism in Yoruba-Orisa ritual and other African legacies. Refining EOE's mission to include the provision of spiritual services, they launched on Trinidadian soil what Tracey Hucks has termed "black religious nationalism":

> When we looked at the African person we saw that spirituality was part and parcel of the character called African. Therefore, we decided to form a spiritual foundation. That's the first thing we called our thing, the spiritual foundation. We had a meeting . . . in Morvant and this was probably early 1972 or '71, but '71 [is when] we count the beginning of the organization. . . . And following that meeting [about] the spiritual foundation, a few of us still remained with the organization. But we remained as a spiritual entity because, as pan-Africanists, some of them were saying—and as Garveyites, they were saying—that Garvey did not choose a spirituality in

his time ... and so, they would not endorse one above the other. But what was happening was, while the claim was to be a nonspiritual organization ... several people were marrying, having naming ceremonies and these are spiritual rites; so ... whenever they needed a ceremony or anything we did it and we are still functioning there.[93]

A home for post–Black Power Orisa *nation-building* in Trinidad, EOE "intends to reestablish the sacredness of the African Yoruba paradigm." The qualifier "African" here distinguishes a perceived "Yoruba paradigm" in Nigeria (Africa) from those in the Americas and the Caribbean—Cuba, Brazil, the United States, and especially Trinidad. The EOE's embrace of Trinidadian Yoruba *nationhood* involved the postcolonializing program of "reincorporating the essence of Ifa sacred science into the present paradigm of Orisa practice in [T&T]." Its leaders structured EOE's entire institutional framework to engineer this very project. Alluding to the fissures between elder devotees (many with genealogical familial ties to Yoruba cultural heritages) and newcomers (typically affiliated via spiritual adoption within Orisa ritual families), Massetungi explains EOE's didactic mission toward the wider Orisa community:

> For historical reasons and circumstances, those who walked before have had to take the path that they have taken. Some of us who have moved outside the flow of that flow, therefore would have been seen as upstarts, in presenting to the elders and the custodians, the essence of the sacred science as it is on the continent. In fact, the elders have a legitimate claim to say that, whatever we develop here is also legitimate, and we don't say that it is illegitimate. What we do say is that, if you are practicing a sacred science tradition that has a home, ... that has a foundation, and from which you emerged, in order to properly reengineer what was originally created, you have to understand the original. And therefore, we have advised all of our elders to return to the basis of the sacred science tradition, so that now if you want by choice to reengineer and adopt Saint Anne, or Saint John, or Jesus, or Mary or La Divina Pastora, or Hanuman, you could do so, but understand your base, and then, don't call it Orisa sacred science. Call it Orisa sacred science II, if you want.[94]

Yet EOE's mission goes beyond the particular focus on Yoruba-Orisa heritage to encompass what it deems "African sacred sciences." In this sense, EOE is not solely an iteration of black religious *nationalism* but also an expression of *Africana religious nationalism*:

We say that we recognize the unity and diversity of the various African sacred sciences. Whether you call it Kemetic, Kongo, Zulu . . . we look at the common things in it, and if I see a good Kongo ritual, then I'm going to use it. I'm not going to say no I'm not going to mix it with Yoruba. We accept *African* sacred science, and that's why we always say, African slash Yoruba sacred science. So, we don't try to make people feel it's all pure Yoruba. . . . The vision here, of Egbe Onisin Eledumare, . . . is to place in its correct perspective . . . the heart of African sacred science . . . throughout the Caribbean.[95]

The roster of visitors to EOE confirms this principle and practice: Massetungi has collaborated with and accessed resources from African spiritual leaders and cultures as diverse as the Queen Mothers of Ghana, Kemetic theology, and Rada (Dahomean) rites.[96] Nevertheless, EOE also invests tremendous energy in developing its Yoruba-Orisa repertoire of in-house rites and public rituals.

Like other global lineages of Yoruba-Orisa religion, EOE upholds a theology and ritual life that accord with its local collective realities and experiences. Although the organization has sought instruction from Nigerian and other African religious authorities, its members also benefit from a long legacy of ancestral expertise in Trinidad and the wider diaspora. Most important, they operate from the premise that the Orisa Powers never abandoned diasporaed Yorubas but have spoken to them and have authorized their self-recovery in Trinidad and other diaspora spaces. Thus, to speak of this creative theological and ritual dialogue between Orisa Powers and their EOE devotees is to capture at once the repurposing of kinship, *nationhood*, sovereignty, and social belonging that accounts for the allegiances EOE has to the present and the past, the ancestors and the unborn, the Yoruba *nation/* family, and the Trinidadian nation-state/citizenry. Most radically reworked and expanded since the days of nineteenth-century Yoruba *nation* formation have been EOE's *nation* ideas and *nationalist* allegiances.

ENTERING THE WATERS OF OLOKUN

Given EOE's robust ritual calendar and social service agenda ranging from highly publicized events, like the festival for the Orisa Olokun (*Ase Odun Olokun*), to a spiritual care ministry for incarcerated young men, the organization's *nationalism* defies the separatism one might readily associate with twentieth- and twenty-first-century black nationalist religions in the United States. Remaining faithful to its earliest mandate of institutionalizing "Black

Power in the open," EOE seeks to incorporate and transform the entire Trinidadian nation. Indeed, by holding a significant part of its three-day Olokun festival at Trinidad's Banwari Heritage Site, the locus of the oldest fossil remains in the Caribbean region (dating back nearly seven thousand years), EOE pays homage to the Warao, another nation whose members are understood to be descendants of the earliest indigenous custodians of the territory that is now the Republic of Trinidad and Tobago.

Similar to other diaspora Olokun and Yemaya[97] festivals, EOE's *Ase Odun Olokun* performs the work of collective memory, solidifying among participants a sense of peoplehood with attention to the tragic events of the Middle Passage (the ancestral past) and a view toward environmental justice and caretaking (the present and unborn future).[98] As the Orisa who governs the deep ocean waters, Olokun is associated with the captive Africans who died and were buried within her watery womb-tomb during the Middle Passage.[99] Hence diasporaed Yorubas apprehend the Atlantic Ocean's numinosity as linking sacred time and historical time for African spiritual descendants in the New World. Through public rituals, EOE memorializes the tragic loss of sovereignty of unknown ancestors, as well as the coincidental historical trajectory of the Warao, while simultaneously celebrating the undefeatable sovereignty of the earth and affirming a collective commitment to respect and sustain a balanced, cooperative relationship with the natural environment— with Olokun (see figure 3.11).

A foundational pillar of EOE's ritual legacy in Trinidad, the *Ase Odun Olokun* attracts significant participation from other Orisa shrines and even the wider population, perhaps owing to its ability to cross boundaries of time, memory, and cultural heritage. In the October 6, 2016, *Trinidad and Tobago Guardian Online*, EOE published its customary open invitation to the festival, reminding the nation of the needed values and virtues the festival teaches all who participate and abide by its universally appealing precepts:

> Olokun is the Orisa god of the ocean and the theme of this year's Olokun Festival is Retrieving Our Memory, which is apt as Olokun is also custodian of planetary memory. The Olokun Ocean Festival is the ceremony in which man's indispensable link and connectivity to the force of the ocean is celebrated. Olokun is the deity of . . . marshes and wetlands, and is protector of the African diaspora. . . . The Festival is an environmental festival which acknowledges our oceans and seas as sources of food, life-giving water, raw materials, medicine, recreation, transport and communications for millions of the planet's inhabitants. . . . Many Old World

FIGURE 3.11 Omorisa from EOE carrying offerings to the sea at Grand Chemin, Moruga in Salibia, Trinidad, during the October 2013 *Ase Odun Olokun* (Olokun Festival). (Courtesy of Edison Boodoosingh, photographer.)

societies recognise the importance of the seas and oceans, and special propitiatory rites were performed each year to encourage the co-operation of the living force called sea or ocean. The Orisa community continues to believe that communion with the ocean is necessary for our survival. . . . Offerings of fruits, silver coins, dried foods, honey, and other items will be accepted.[100]

ENTERING THE NATIONAL CARNIVAL SPACE

In addition to festivals and ceremonies for individual Orisa powers, EOE has found other expressive arenas for its *plurination-al* agendas. Against the wishes of fellow members of the National Council of Orisa Elders (NCOE), Massetungi's band, *401 Meets 2001*, was one of two Orisa mas-playing groups planned for the February 2001 Carnival.[101] The bone of contention concerned respectability politics. Many Orisa elders of NCOE viewed the prospect of unveiling the Orisa in T&T's annual Carnival celebration as the ultimate iconoclastic act. Parading Orisa effigies alongside scantily clad mas players in an atmosphere of decadence and bacchanal would desecrate the Orisa Powers and the entire religious tradition. However, Massetungi, an elected NCOE member himself, insisted, "We are . . . going into the Carnival to re-sanctify it whereas others might be staying on the outside. . . . We would not do any-thing to do damage to the integrity of the faith. . . . We're following the will of the Orisa and we doing what has to be done."[102]

Massetungi refused to reduce the Carnival phenomenon to its more con-spicuous, superficial elements of wanton indulgences. The EOE's participa-tion, he contended, would bring into focus the generative Africana spiritual heritage that breathed life and substance into T&T's Carnival from its earliest iterations during the slave period to its present-day expressions. Accom-panied by its steel band and traditional Orisa drumming, EOE exhibited a range of Orisa masquerades, including the lesser-known Aganju, along with the popular Powers of Oya, Yemanja, Osun, Esu, Ogun, Orunmila, and Sango.[103]

The purposeful practice of commemorating ancestral customs and re-membering Yoruba and other custodians of African heritage religions who were mas players in earlier eras saturated the rituals and activities of all involved before and during the events. In the months leading up to the 2001 Carnival, Massetungi and his collaborators found themselves energized by the ancestors as they manufactured elaborate costumes and displays, at times offering their sweat as a libation to the same earthen spaces where deceased adherents of African spiritual traditions had labored to produce Carnival displays of their own:

> While we were at the mas camp I began to learn that what we were doing was nothing new. The mas camp where we were was . . . of a black Indian group too . . . and several elders from the community came and told us that that area where we had the mas camp is a historical area in Trinidad. And they said that there were at least six Yoruba who used to bring bands in that area of Port of Spain. Now, we became very close to the Rada com-munity in Trinidad over the past few years. And we went to them just to tell them . . . and they said, well, "We brought mas before . . . on two occasions . . . one year with drums only and the next year . . . with drum and steel band." And . . . they show us the songs they sing. But their songs is hard for us to sing. . . . So, we had one song that we learned from them, "*kojo billy, kojo billy, kojo billy, go ah go lie lie, kojo billy, kojo billy, ah go lie lie.*" So, we decided now that we going to take that song, and wherever we going to a main stage, in tribute to them, I'll call libation and call their ancestors. . . . Using that song did two things. In other words, the contemporaries of the Rada elders we are talking about ('cause one just died the other day [Sed-ley Cadet Johnson Antoine], the . . . head of the Rada community), the

contemporary of those elders actually, well, he was actually older than some of the members on the Council [NCOE], so they would have known him [see figures 3.12 and 3.13]. And they [Yoruba-Orisa elders] ought to have known the history. Some of them lived in the [Belmont] area [of the Rada compound] and some of them [the Yoruba-Orisa elders] were actually close to the Rada elders. So, I said, well if we have this song and they ask anything, I would say, those who went before me sang this song, and I am only singing after what they sing; and those who went before me did this, and you should know that because you were very close to them.[104]

The EOE band members embraced what they learned along the way about their ancestors' contributions to Carnival. They also strategically borrowed ancestral innovations for their unfolding rituals to remind dissenting Orisa elders of the wider African religious elements that were part of T&T's Carnival heritage. Collective singing, chanting, praying, drumming, and spiritual dancing brought EOE participants closer to Rada ancestors. The Rada-Dahomean religious culture shared more than just a boundary with neighboring Yorubas, not only in Africa but also in Trinidad, as the Herskovitses observed during their fieldwork in the 1930s.[105] Massetungi's Africana religious nationalism had ample room for this kind of inter-nation-al connection. Showcasing it within the Carnival venue where various stakeholders derived new meanings from Orisa/African spiritual traditions was one way of fulfilling EOE's commitment to the principles of "African sacred science" and making its wisdom available beyond the practicing community.

The national Carnival was also an ideal stage on which to shift the Republic of Trinidad and Tobago's disposition toward a novel appreciation for the Orisa's sacred significance to Carnival conventions perceived as "secular."[106] Just as Olokun opens pathways to balanced coexistence with the ocean and other aquatic habitations, Ogun, the Orisa of blacksmithing, technology, and war gave Carnival its steel pan and percussive irons. Moreover, Ogun's spirit permeates the "engine rooms" of all Carnival bands, piping sonic steam and vibrations into their booming musical ensembles. The band 401 Meets 2001 proclaimed that these and other resonances between Orisa culture and Carnival culture should be owned and celebrated as aspects of a sacred–secular African lifeway. It comes as no surprise, then, that Ifa sanctioned the band's Carnival mission. "Nothing is done without the blessing of Ifa," one EOE member testified. "When [we are] in doubt about what to do [we] do divination. This [participation in Carnival] was authorised by higher forces than ourselves."[107]

FIGURE 3.12 (*beside*) AND
FIGURE 3.13 (*opposite*) Memorial
program for Sedley Cadet Johnson
Antoine (grandson of Mah Nannie).
Antoine's family ties are extensive in
Canada where relatives there held a
funeral Mass on April 17, 2001.
(Photos by author.)

IN LOVING MEMORY OF
Hubono - An African
High Priest
(fourth in line since 1868)

Sedley Cadet Johnson Antoine
Rada Community/Tribe

APRIL. 30th, 1918   APRIL 09th, 2001

Fare thee well father / friend of the
soil
One who has brought us treasured
moments
Through sweet and toil

It seemed like only yesterday
We thought that you'd be always
here to stay

But we were so wrong it seems to
me now
You are so far away

Now that the time has come for us
to part
We dread this moment with all our
hearts
But the memories we share will
linger on
Through unborn generations

You are not defeated in death
Lest we forget - lest we forget
With saddened hearts we watch you
go a far

A man of quiet words, an African
Priest
Who would take his rightful place
On this earth or anywhere in space

Fare thee we'll Father / Friend
In whom we're well pleased
For the contribution you have made
By your short journey here on earth.

BLESSED ARE THEY THAT MOURN
FOR THEY SHALL BE COMFORTED

St.Matt. Vs.5

Order Of Service

Reception of the Body at Church
Processional Hymn - Blessed Assurance
Eulogy

Sympathy on the
Behalf of Fraternal Groups
Yoruba Community
Pan African Community
West African Rada Community

For EOE, Carnival functioned as pilgrimage as much as ritual theater—
from the cascade of mas-making ceremonial rites preceding the public procession to the catharsis of shared engagement in nation-al and inter-nation-al
spiritual customs on the eventful day itself.[108] Three decades earlier, a group
of Black Power radicals launched their 1001 White Devils Carnival band and
often found themselves overtaken by unfamiliar Orisa Powers. Now, EOE, a
spiritual family born from that same movement and mood, proudly paraded
down those same Carnival streets with a forty-person entourage that replaced
the pope and the devil with Queen Oyeku Meji and Esu (see figure 3.14).[109]
With these and other reversals on display, they shined a light not on corrupt colonial agents and institutions but on their familiar Orisa energies—governing
Powers that rule dissimilarly to colonizers of the past and postindependence
leaders of the present. The shift from a deconstructive Black Power agenda
of the 1970s to a constructive Africana religious nationalism in the twenty-first
century signaled yet another era in the nation's history and perhaps even a
new chapter in the Orisa community's public life.

FIGURE 3.14 Queen Oyeku Meji, the central installation of EOE's Carnival band 401 *Meets 2001*. (Courtesy of EOE.)

A Nation within and beyond a Nation

W. E. B. Du Bois and E. Franklin Frazier's theorizations of the nineteenth- and early twentieth-century negro church as a *nation* within the American nation-state explore some characteristics that also typify Africana spiritual territories of *nation-building* beyond the United States.[110] The EOE offers analogous structures for comparison. This particular Orisa family adheres to a deliberately organized Yoruba/African Trinidadian way of life and a system of governance to regulate cosmic-social relations and religious obligations. The EOE operationalizes cooperative economics, a formal leadership structure, educational curricula, and healing arts all under the roof of an active spiritual center sponsoring religious ceremonies for *nation-al* and national public edification (see figure 3.15). Within this framework of social organization, EOE rites and customs bind members into familial relationship with one another, other Trinidadian Orisa families, known and unknown African ancestors, Orisa devotees in other diaspora locations, and numinous Orisa Powers (see figures 3.16 and 3.17).

If EOE's institutionalization of Africana religious *nationalism* shares many elements with the negro church under North American slavery and segregation, its parallels with black *nationalist* religious communities such as the

FIGURE 3.15 EOE teaches Yoruba language to members. This EOE chalkboard displays common Yorùbá greetings, August 28, 2013. (Photo by author.)

FIGURE 3.16 EOE members preparing offering for 1999 Olokun Festival in Mayaro. (Courtesy of EOE.)

FIGURE 3.17 Oludari Olakela Massetungi leading EOE members in prayer during 1999 Olokun Festival in Mayaro. (Courtesy of EOE.)

Nation of Islam, founded in Detroit, Michigan, in 1930, and Oyotunji African Village, a North American Yoruba *nation* founded in Sheldon, South Carolina, in 1970, are even more striking. However, EOE's religious *nationalism* departs from North American sibling traditions in one major respect: its disposition toward the nation-state. At the borders of Oyotunji Village, which marks its black religious *nationalism* through separatist strategies of sovereignty, visitors immediately confront an edict declaring Oyotunji an independent territory, equipped with it own *nation* flag, and distinct from the nation-state that European colonists constructed and codified as the United States of America.[111] The EOE also claims a degree of sovereignty in mounting its *nation* flags throughout its territory, as did the nineteenth-century Afro-Creole communities that first performed sovereignty rituals in their Trinidadian *palais* innovations (see figure 3.18). But at EOE, the winds of Oya blow on the national flag of T&T as they do on the flags of the Orisa and the EOE *nation* (see figures 3.19 and 3.20).[112]

Oyotunji Village's approach to *nation-building* accents the historicity of racial ascription and racial stratification customs in North America that placed black citizenship in jeopardy after Emancipation and well after most Americans of African descent had become practicing Christians in the late nineteenth century. Racial blackness prevented authentic inclusion within the nation-state and access to the rights and privileges accorded to white American citizens.[113] Yet in post–Black Power T&T, African descendants shared majority status with South Asian descendants, annulling black racial otherness in social relations. The question of inclusion and authentic citizenship for the Yoruba-Orisa *nation* revolved around the legitimacy and respectability of the religion being practiced, rather than the racial makeup of its practitioners.

Electoral politics offers another glimpse into the sociopolitical realities that have steered black/Africana religious *nationalism* along different trajectories in the two diaspora regions. For example, the *Nation* of Islam's separatist politics have long instructed its members against participating in any US electoral process, whereas EOE would see no reason to entertain this kind of separatist political agenda.[114] Indeed, during a visit to the shrine in November 2000, Tracey and I learned that the Orisa are invested in national electoral politics as much as EOE members. Although no formal ritual dancing was underway, members were twirling their bodies in brightly colored uniforms in perfect and imperfect postures. Devotees took turns balancing as best they could under the guiding hand of their leader, who prepared them for later ritual moments and the responsibilities associated with "falling

FIGURE 3.18 Oludari Olakela Massetungi pointing to EOE's *nation* flag, August 20, 2013. (Photo by author.)

under the Powers." Suddenly, without any warning, Ogun materialized in a young medium-built female devotee to deliver a forty-five-minute discourse on why it was important to vote in the upcoming December 2000 elections.[115]

The season was ripe for political debate, and through the muzzled linguistic codes and guttural sounds the Powers commonly use to communicate with their interpreters, Ogun was clear: this was not a time for indifference or apathy but for decisive reflection and involvement in the political process. The Yoruba-Orisa community had secured more civil rights and endorsements under the United National Congress (UNC) administration of Basdeo

FIGURE 3.19 AND FIGURE 3.20 EOE's *nation* flag, Orisa flags, and national flag of Trinidad and Tobago, August 20, 2013. (Photos by author.)

Panday, T&T's first prime minister of South Asian descent. Although Ogun did not indicate how members should vote, the point was that members should not default on this particular duty of citizenship. On December 11, the UNC party won the general elections, extending Panday's leadership for another term.[116]

Yoruba, African, and Trinidadian, EOE's Africana religious *nationalism* allows its members to claim allegiance to multiple "nations." Especially revealing of EOE's focus on reconstructing T&T's national consciousness is its deliberate decision to invoke the sovereignty of T&T's indigenous inhabitants through one of the country's oldest names: *Iëre*. In EOE's renaming, the country becomes Ile (Yoruba for land/earth) Iëre (Arawak for "land of the hummingbird"):[117] EOE thus redesignates the nation-state as Ile-Iëre to bridge Yoruba and indigenous Arawak concepts and give "recognition to the First Nations People" who named the island Iëre well before European colonizers arrived.[118]

Through the ballot and blessings of the Orisa, EOE members continue the long tradition of Yoruba-Orisa *nation* formation by practicing "Black Power in the open." Their politics and spiritual sensibilities allow them to blur even further the already porous lines between race, heritage, ancestry, lineage, family, religion, *nation*, and nation-state and to remove the territorial geopolitical boundaries separating Yoruba-Orisa *nations* across the transatlantic world. Their performance of Africana religious *nationalism* illuminates how these unfixed markers of identity naturally collide and collapse, exposing and exploiting their slippery and ascribed social meanings while also exploring their psychic meanings for omorisa and other African descendants.[119]

Critical elements of Africana identity-making are eclipsed by theories of "imagined communities" in contemporary treatments of nations, diasporas, and the identities they innovate.[120] First, unlike many nation-states and diaspora societies, EOE self-consciously engages in a process of identity-making, of re-creation. Massetungi is aware of how he is retrieving resources toward a specific end. In interviews and EOE's ritual ceremonies, he candidly discloses the symbiosis that characterizes his approach to Trinidad's specific Yoruba heritage and its broader African heritage in constructing an EOE way of life. This deliberate project of identity construction does not make Massetungi and other EOE members immune to unselfconscious ideological and static appropriations of African symbols and traditions; but far too much weight has been placed on the ideological underpinnings of EOE and other similar religious movements, rather than their religious reorientations of *nationhood*.

Black Religion as the Capacity to
Re-Create Commodified Creation

Another dimension of EOE's identity-making likewise departs from the "imagined communities" thesis, one that epitomizes Charles Long's and James Noel's insights into the very nature of black religion in the African diaspora.[121] "Black religion and black people," Noel maintains, "appeared simultaneously in modernity . . . as what Long calls the 'empirical Other' in the consciousness of those who constructed themselves as 'white' through this perception. They also made their appearance through their perception of being apprehended by what Rudol[f] [Otto] refers to as the 'Holy [sic] Other.'"[122]

The coappearance of black people and black religion that Noel describes is the first cause stipulating African-descended peoples' second re-creation and re-created (in)habitations. In other words, the coappearance confirms that blacks' involuntary presence in the New World prompts their sacred reinvention of "being apprehended by" the "Wholly Other."[123] Before their brutal sacrifice at the altar of Modernity, before the screams and moans in the tomb-wombs of slave ships, other spaces, dimensions, temporalities, and affects had organized their original habitations. Thus, for blacks, an original or first creation is ever present in their collective mythical consciousness symbolizing *beginnings* and a primordial habitation prior to the disruption of capture and deportation from Africa and even prior to the master–slave relationship.[124]

Dispersal, however, was destructively constructive, characterized by the commodification of creation and what Calvin Warren terms a "violent transubstantiation."[125] The Middle Passage and racial enslavement constituted a temporality whose signature event was the twofold Euro-colonial desecration of the first creation and successive fashioning of the second creation. To deal with the trauma of desecration and re-creation, black religion appeared as a mechanism of critique and renunciation for reinventing the second creation. By nature, black religion then is an ordering of symbols whose opacity gives rise to thoughts, articulations, meanings, actions, and orientations beyond decipherable registers that allow for the transparency of knowledge. Through emanations of black religious consciousness, a third creative moment unfolds, allowing African descendants to invent themselves anew and disclose their unintelligibility within the scripts of Western ontology. Their invention as *new evocations of ashé is a continuous improvisation* that eludes those who, through the logics of racecraft, desecrated their own first creation and invented themselves to be white.[126]

The impetus for the fashioning of a new creation in black religious consciousness stems from the fact that peoples from disparate regions of Africa, reduced to "'cargo' that bled," were *made black*, violently *created black*, by others during the formation of the Atlantic world.[127] Thus, as Warren insists, "Being lost integrity with the Trans-Atlantic Slave Trade; at that moment in history, it finally became possible for an aggressive metaphysics to exercise obscene power—the ability to turn a 'human' into a 'thing.' The captive is fractured on both the Ontological and ontic levels."[128] The untenability of this re-created otherness has been inescapable for its victims, compelling the simultaneous appearance of black religion—the power to re-invent the black community through processes of dehistoricization internal to and beyond the community or, as Frantz Fanon felicitously phrases it, through "introducing invention into existence."[129]

Expanding the contributions of Long, Noel, and Fanon, I borrow Janice Fernheimer's concept of "interruptive invention" to further elucidate the nature and achievements of black religion. Although she introduces it as a framework for rhetorical analysis, "interruptive invention" has purchase for this discussion because it

> describes and articulates the very acts that many groups, especially those who are not part of the dominant discourse, engage in when they attempt to interact with and change what appear to be impervious, hegemonic norms in the common ground they seek to reform. Even when the stated goals of a particular interruption are not fully achieved (in that they are not fully accepted or recognized by the group with whom the interrupters are engaged), they still do important rhetorical work by creating the space for dialogue to continue (often in spite of disagreement).[130]

Extending decolonial interventions in religious studies, Africana/black studies, and the emerging field of "black study," I theorize black religion phenomenologically as the *interruptive invention of belonging* that cultivates desired habitations of kinship in contexts of captivity. Although this kind of interruptive invention creates the potential to "change" an antiblack/African world "which appear[s] to be impervious," black religion's primary achievement is the creation of black belonging and sociality determined by black and/or African norms. Belonging to a *nation* and belonging to a family that for custodians of African heritage religions includes invisible Powers, flora and fauna, and rivers and mountains is an opaque mode of inhabitation that the world of antiblackness/Africanness can neither penetrate nor vanquish. Nevertheless, diasporaed African modes of belonging are often mistranslated as assertions of "humanity," "human being," or national "citizenship" in normative post-Enlightenment discourses. For example, Long makes room for my definition when he argues that black religion has the potential to create "a new form of humanity" or "a new historical consciousness and thus a new historical community."[131] Unlike many in the Afropessimist school of thought, which his broader scholarship anticipates, Long sees redemptive possibilities in the human—but only in a "new form" once the human has been refashioned through the silence of the symbols and myths of black religion. In the context of this study of Yoruba-Orisa religion, I discovered that the symbols and myths (i.e., sacred poetics) that orient omorisa are not statements about how *human* they are or how they should be viewed and treated as *human beings*. Rather, Yoruba-Orisa sacred poetics are statements about belonging, and for this diaspora*ed* community, I argue that belonging manifests through new evocations of ashé. I prefer this terminology because no precise word exists in Yorùbá language for the modern Western concepts of the human and human being. The Yorùbá term ènìyàn is often translated reductively as ~~human~~ or ~~human being,~~ which can imply it signifies an ~~ontologically~~ discrete form of life. However, ènìyàn is more expansive than often presumed because it includes chimpanzees and some spiritual entities. It is true ~~human beings~~ are ènìyàn, but not exclusively. Furthermore, conceptualizing black persons and black belonging as "ashé" attunes us to the inventive power pervading and intimately linking ~~humans,~~ chimpanzees, all materiality, and indeed all unseen entities. Everything, even the wind, is a vessel of ashé. Ashé is a primordial poetics of relation.[132]

Yoruba religious thought and other African thought systems arguably have more productive conceptual resources to address the problem of the human in black experience than the languages of Western Enlightenment. Mobilized by those resources and their legacies in the African diaspora, and compelled as well by gratuitous suffering, diaspora*ed* Africans have always turned to old- and new-world Africana sacred symbols and spiritual resources to exit the ontological trap of colonial blackness and to perform the sacred poetics of establishing re-created origins and new modes of belonging. They accessed the power to re-invent and belong through historical knowledge of and affective desire for Africa, the place that, despite its disfiguration in the enlightened Western mind, represented African persons' authenticity. In addition to symbols of historical valence, diaspora*ed* Africans relied on myths and reconfigured intimacies between spiritual and material presences to fashion their second re-creation, including the salvific wit and resilience of Brar Anansi, Brer Rabbit, High John the Conqueror, the suffering Jesus on the cross who "never said a mumblin' word" to his persecutors, and the Rastafari "I-n-I" proclamation that sacralizes blacks under the sovereignty and will of Jah.[133]

That same re-creative power resurfaced when newly emancipated US African descendants needed legitimate or additional names. To take one example, the famous educator and institution builder Booker T. Washington (1856–1915) emerged from slavery a young child with no surname. When faced with school enrollment at the age of nine, he adopted his stepfather's first name, "Washington," as his surname:[134]

> From the time when I could remember anything, I had been called simply "Booker." Before going to school it had never occurred to me that it was needful or appropriate to have an additional name. When I heard the school-roll called, I noticed that all of the children had at least two names, and some of them indulged in what seemed to me the extravagance of having three. I was in deep perplexity, because I knew that the teacher would demand of me at least two names and I only had one. By the time the occasion came for the enrolling of my name, an idea occurred to me which I thought would make me equal to the situation; and so, when the teacher asked me what my full name was, I calmly told him "Booker Washington," as if I had been called by that name all my life.[135]

Reginald Hildebrand's contention that "selecting a religious affiliation was just as significant as selecting a surname" for nineteenth-century African Americans acknowledges the co-constitutive power of religious, personal, and social identity for diasporaed African descendants across time.[136] The issue of *which* surnames or religious affiliations African descendants chose to identify themselves—Washington, Mohammad, Semaj, X, Massetungi, Adefunmi; or African Methodist, Muslim, Hebrew, Rastafari, Yoruba—is not the immediate point of this discussion.[137] At issue is how the second creation, the invention of black "empirical Others" by people who "needed to be white," has required diasporaed African descendants to adopt re-creative strategies for communal remaking.[138] Long explains, "The oppressed must deal with the fictive truth of their status as expressed by the oppressors, that is, their second creation, and the discovery of their own autonomy and truth—their first creation. The locus for this structure is the mythic consciousness which dehistoricizes the relationship for the sake of creating a new form of humanity—a form that is no longer based on the master-slave dialectic."[139]

Sylvia Wynter echoes these ideas in her critique of the West's invention and reinvention of "Man." By "overrepresenting their conception of the human," Wynter contends, "all other modes of being human would have to be seen . . . as the lack of the West's ontologically absolute self-description." She insists that the "interlinked nature of . . . the Coloniality of Being/Power/Truth/Freedom" means "one cannot 'unsettle' the 'coloniality of power' without a redescription of the human outside the terms of our present descriptive statement of the human, Man and its overrepresentation."[140] Wynter's decoupling of the human from Man gestures toward the "new form of humanity" that Long believes is possible through black mythic consciousness and the operations of black religion. However, the tension between the task of "redescription" and the denied opportunities to actually redescribe leaves me apprehensive about both Wynter's and Long's assessment that black projects of invention can potentially salvage the human. Long actually acknowledges the tension as the source of the revolutionary nature of black mythic consciousness. "When slaves, ex-slaves, or colonized persons become aware of the autonomy and independence of their consciousness," he maintains, "they find that, because of the economic, political, and linguistic hegemony of the master, there is no space for the legitimate expression for such a human form. The desire for an authentic place for the expression of this reality is the source of the revolutionary tendencies in these religions."[141]

Thus, black religion must be apprehended first as African descendants' ineluctable quest and capacity to re-create commodified creation through a dehistoricizing process that approximates "first creation." Undoubtedly, the first creation is imagined within black religious consciousness.[142] However, and more importantly, it is also an awareness unvexed by burdensome ascriptive race-making anxieties of the repeating Western project—what Renaldo Rosaldo describes as "imperialist nostalgia, the curious phenomenon of peoples longing for what they themselves have destroyed."[143] Unintelligible within Western philosophical discourses aimed at resolving subject/object dualisms, the first creation is a state of primordial collectivity—harmonious "concentrations of ashé," to use a Yoruba concept.[144] Although unreachable, the first creation is approached through memories and images of "an authentic place for the expression of this reality." That place is Africa.

From the earliest disembarkations to the present moment, Africa has been the most constant "historical reality" and "religious image" for the remaking of diasporaed African descendants. "One can trace almost every nationalistic movement among the blacks," Long observes, "and find Africa to be the dominating and guiding image. Even among religious groups not strongly nationalistic, the image of Africa or Ethiopia still has relevance."[145] Africa continues to be apparent in the manifold structures and institutions, moods, motivations, styles, patterns, and productions of black people within and outside formal religious institutions because black desire for a symbol of land, with historical significance, arises out of a condition of landlessness that has no resolution in an antiblack world. Africa is the symbolic and often subconscious destination where new creation meets first creation, a destination that Africana religious *nationalist* communities, such as Oyotunji Village and EOE, materialize or "territorialize" within their diaspora locations.[146] Like its sibling traditions in North America, Brazil (where the Candomblé *terreiro* also epitomizes African descendants' "revalorization of the land"), and other regions of the diaspora, EOE accomplishes this territorialization through strategies that use the *affective* power of the image of Africa to temper and even trump so-called identity politics.[147]

Since the rise of Black Power, EOE has boldly acknowledged and accepted this religious bequest. Its "vision" of this inherited assignment of fashioning a new creation, Massetungi declares, "is to allow people to know that the boundaries of African sacred science are limitless.... African sacred science is culture, is food; it's dress, it's dance, it's language, it's savings, it's politics, it's investment, it's land, it's sacred spaces and places."[148] Massetungi's approach continues a tradition of Africana theorization of African spirituality that never succumbed to the Western Enlightenment's division of religion and science. His configuration of "African sacred science" rescues the long tradition of Obeah doctoring from colonial criminalization. It acknowledges the relationship between mathematics, medicine, and music that Yvonne Daniel distills in her study of Cuban Yoruba, Haitian Vodou, and Brazilian Candomblé.[149] The EOE's commitment to the economics, politics, culture, and aesthetics of "African sacred science" is a micro-example of movements toward an "African Renaissance," conceptualized during the 1940s by the Senegalese scholar Cheik Anta Diop and popularized in the twenty-first century by the former president of South Africa, Thabo Mbeki.[150]

This chapter has argued that EOE's window into black religion and identity-making provides a clear view of Africana religious *nationalism* in the Caribbean and the sacred poetics it inspires. Theorizing EOE as a deep reflection of the phenomenon of black religion rounds out the research on the Yoruba-Orisa in Trinidad.[151] Through a comparative religions' analytic lens, this approach balances the interpretive sciences that anthropologists have brought to bear on their research questions and conclusions since Herskovits first studied the tradition in the 1930s. In 1983, Frances Henry was compelled to revise her prediction of Shango's (the Orisa religion's) cessation in the 1960s after confronting the "astonishing resurgence" of the tradition just a decade later.[152] The context of Black Power renders transparent the signs of the time that inspired a number of Afro-Trinidadians to search for spiritual healing within the "Shango" palais. Yet something more has lain behind the quest, and this powerful "more" remains beyond the reach of social science theorizing.

Keith McNeal discusses how a number of organic movements and communal initiatives aimed at studying and disseminating African culture and customs in Trinidad have been documented across the twentieth century. These efforts are archived in the popular knowledge of Trinidadians who are connected with or are custodians of African heritage religions and Africana cultural movements. Ethiopianism, Garveyism, and other pan-Africanist organizations; Afrocentric biblical hermeneutics; Yoruba translations of Christian prayers; and Yoruba dictionaries and language schools all found personages and platforms for expression and display throughout the twentieth century (see figures 3.21 and 3.22).[153]

These efforts disclose the religious phenomenon behind the quest to re-make colonial blackness. In the era of Black Power, Shango had to be revived because it was the most viable institutional means of making tangible the sacred "image of Africa," of accessing that "wholly other"[154] authority and power needed to re-create colonial blackness into sacred blackness (i.e., a new evocation of ashé). Nearly a half-century into this mission, EOE seems far removed from the days of empirical black otherness, forever focused on preparing and rendering its innovative "ebo" to African-descended peoples' new creation.

EOE's Dynamic "Plus 1" Yoruba Diaspora Theology

Theological and ritual innovation provides another avenue into the dynamic expression of Africana religious *nationalism* that EOE has made of itself. As a diasporaed Yoruba community, EOE renders intelligible the "plus 1" principle in Yoruba theology. Yoruba theism holds that in total, the Orisa number 400 + 1. However, "the 'plus 1' does not refer to any particular divinity," writes Yoruba philosopher, Kọ́lá Abímbọ́lá. "Rather it's a principle of elasticity by which the Yorùbá account for any newly deified Òrìṣà. . . . This 'plus 1' principle allows new beliefs, new thought systems, and new deities to be brought into the fold of Yorùbá culture."[155]

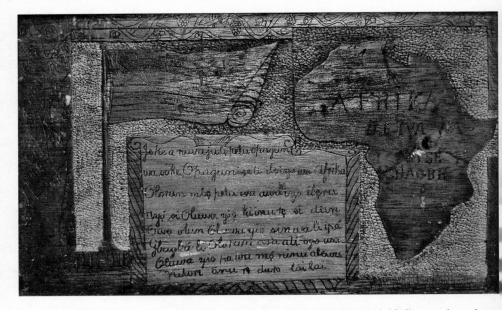

FIGURE 3.21 Wooden plaque with Christian "Lord's Prayer" translated into Trinidadian Yoruba and embellished by a flag of the Garvey movement (*left*) and an image of Africa with Yoruba script: "Afrika Ile Iya Wa Maṣe Gbagbe" or "Africa Our Motherland/the Land of Our Mothers Don't Ever Forget" (*right*) engraved by Joseph Joseph, aka Mr. Zampty (1885–1973). This carving displays symbols and cultural elements of African identities—Pan-African, Yoruba *nation*, and Afro-Trinidadian—that many African descendants embraced during the early twentieth century. (From the "Christian Prayers in Yoruba," Special Collections at Alma Jordan Library, University of the West Indies, St. Augustine, Trinidad and Tobago.)

FIGURE 3.22 African Trinidadians parade through the streets celebrating the abolition of slavery in the British Caribbean. This August First Emancipation Day Celebration photograph was included in a November 21–25, 2016, exhibition. Reprinted by permission from National Archives of Trinidad and Tobago, https://natt.gov.tt/sites/default/files/pdfs/Our_African_Legacy_Roots_and_Routes.pdf.

Theological elasticity explains the dynamism of Yorùbá people's sacred poetics. Although transatlantic Yoruba-Orisa communities share core beliefs and practices, individual spiritual communities constantly experiment with new symbols and materials or reinterpret inherited traditions to suit their particular sociocultural contexts. And although Abímbọ́lá references the incorporation of Catholic elements within Cuban and Brazilian Yoruba traditions as prime examples of how the plus 1 principle operates, chapter 2 of this volume theorizes elements of this theological flexibility as reflecting Yoruba ethics and kinship principles, rather than a syncretic impulse.[156] The Yoruba plus 1 principle is a conceptual shortcut to the end of my argument about the cosmological and ritual significance of kinship and family to Yoruba sacred poetics.

The EOE's structure and approach to sustaining its spiritual family epitomize the plus 1 principle. From its "Black Power in the open" philosophy to its honoring of the Warao indigenous people during the Olokun Festival and its *401 Meets 2001* Carnival band, EOE embraces a transatlantic tradition of Yoruba thought and practice. Key authority sources in EOE's innovations are the individual and collective wishes of the ancestors. Through dreams, visions, meditations, and divinations, the ancestors speak. Some of the most appealing Yoruba-Orisa innovations and recapitulations across the diaspora are devoted to ancestral veneration. Many such traditions are inspired by transgenerational interaction between the Yoruba heritage and other African ancestral heritages. The EOE's incorporation of Trinidad's ancestral Rada Carnival rituals is one example. However, even within expanding repertoires of Yoruba ideas and ceremonies, we see contemporary expressions of old-world traditions, most notably the reinstitutionalization of the Egungun masquerade at several Trinidadian shrines.[157]

Perhaps the most affectively unifying of such ancestrally based rituals are the Olokun and other oceanic festivals (Yemaya/Yemoja) that honor unknown African ancestors who died in captivity during the Middle Passage. From the shores of New York's Coney Island to the northeastern corner of Trinidad where the Matelot River takes its offerings to the Caribbean Sea, new-world Yoruba-Orisa devotees invest their oceanic rituals with desire and pathos, mourning and celebration. The annual Yemaya/Olokun ceremony at Coney Island in Brooklyn, New York, is an exemplary analogue to EOE's *Ase Odun Olokun*. Chandra Walke's remarks at the 2014 ceremony underscore the role of ritual in reinforcing vital links between the living and the dead and producing affective environments of *omni-nation-al* belonging:

Wherever you are in the world, we invite you to join this movement and "reclaim those bones in the Atlantic Ocean." On the 2nd Saturday in June, go to the water, bring flowers, light a candle, pray/commune in the way that speaks to your spirit and remember them. As we remember them, we drum, dance, pour libations, cast flowers in the ocean as offerings to Yemaya and Olokun, recite poetry, sing, share the stories [of] how we resisted, and celebrate the beauty and diversity of traditional African culture and spirituality. At 12 p.m. EST globally, we pour a communal libation connecting each of our ceremonies to the other.[158]

Vilashini Coopan explains how affect "flows through and across different subjects, objects, histories and places . . . invit[ing] us to . . . construct new histories of feeling that both recognize the force of violence and imagine a future beyond it."[159] EOE and similar Africana religious communities reckon with the violence of captivity and imagine a new future (and present) through an affective landscape/waterscape produced and intensified during public rituals such as the Olokun and Yemaya festivals, and even T&T's national Carnival.[160] With each reckoning, each negotiation, the plus 1 Yoruba theological framework is constantly under construction. It had to have influenced the youth organizations that played mas as 1001 White Devils during the 1970 Carnival. Blacks knew that white devils were legion, and at a historic moment when Yoruba logics seemed to prevail for those who felt it and knew it most, "1000 White Devils" would have been a deceptive designation. Only the plus 1 principle could have imparted the truth about whiteness—its globality, climate, and atemporality; its libidinal consumptive habits, its talent for infinite exponential growth and expansion, its spectral nature when at rest; and its swift and slow violence.[161] How clever, and how conceptually sophisticated the Black Power youths were in their accuracy and political poetics. Turning again to EOE, the clearest sign of its fidelity to the plus 1 principle is the name it too assigned its first Carnival band. More an announcement than a label, 401 Meets 2001 publicizes the plus 1 theological legacy that diaspora Orisa families have inaugurated since Yarabas began to establish their nations in the New World. Massetungi explains, "The band . . . was called 401 Meets 2001; and it was our attempt to bring the old-world paradigm together with the new-world paradigm and neutralize whatever negativity [was] impeding the African progress, and to open portals for liberation for the African and some of the elders."[162]

Egbe Onisin Eledumare's presence in Trinidad illustrates the dynamism of the Orisa heritage and culture through preservation and innovation. Its sacred poetics—rituals, symbols, narratives, performances, and affects—have mobilized black religious actors' quest for re-creation and belonging in the afterlives of slavery and colonialism.

The Yoruba-Orisa Nation: Past, Present, and Future

What happens when elders die with cherished secrets? Does the tradition they upheld with those secrets perish too? Do their descendants go in quest of new secrets? This chapter has shown that the search for Black Power in the late twentieth century led some African Trinidadians to the lips of Orisa elders; they yearned for sequestered secrets that fed African spiritual traditions for more than a century, even when those traditions had to remain under the radar. Aware of this transition period in the history of Orisa's presence in Trinidad, Baba Sam Phills characterizes the state of Orisa at the dawn of the twenty-first century as an orienting force that fosters the inner person and roots devotees in an African way of life:

> But all in all, I believe that Orisa is alive. It is a force and it is a way of life. The Orisa is the inner self of man, the spiritual aspect of man that has been hidden for many a year. And I believe that the time of revolution, of spiritual revolution, in all the different aspects that you will want is now coming to being whereby the black man, who normally would not have acknowledged his roots, who normally had become so orientated within the white world, and ha[s] lived in a world of make believe, is coming to believe that his world is real. His world is something that was there from creation.[163]

If Orisa was there from creation, so were mothers. Some practitioners of African heritage religions have embraced the view that the moment when an expectant mother's water breaks is a ritual libation, welcoming the ancestor who has reentered the family lineage to travel the visible realm once again.[164] When Yorùbá mothers gave birth in traditional settings, they often assumed the kúnlé posture of sacred greeting and obeisance to the ancestors, the Orisa, and Olodumare.[165] Massetungi, for instance, gives full credit to Iya (Mother) Louisa Toussaint's spiritual expertise as the ultimate authoritative source of EOE's emergence in 1971. Toussaint's and other spiritual mothers' practices of leadership and care are conversant with a legacy of Africana womanist-feminist theorizing that Caribbean thinkers have been slow to join, emphasizing instead other important topics such as gender and development, gender and popular culture, gender and sexuality, as well as gender and masculinity. The next chapter engages this womanist-feminist legacy to examine the sacred poetics and institutional presence of Orisa spiritual mothers in Trinidad and to track pivotal developments in the Orisa religion's changing status from a marginalized folk religion to a burgeoning civil religion. In so doing, it identifies *motherness* at the center of black affective terrains that attest to the re-creative power of black religious consciousness in an antiblack/African world.

You Had the Respected Mothers Who Had Power!

4

MOTHERNESS, HERITAGE LOVE, AND
WOMANIST ANAGRAMMARS OF CARE
IN THE YORUBA-ORISA TRADITION

One ought not to assume that men alone supplied the political and spiritual imagination for novel Yoruba-Orisa religious institutions in the post–Black Power era. Women in Trinidad had long exerted power and assumed leadership roles in Yoruba-Orisa *nationscapes* during the nineteenth and early twentieth centuries.[1] They were no less visible and vocal advocates of Black Power during the 1970s, as Iyalorisa Eintou Pearl Springer's feminist poetics illustrate (see figures 4.1 and 4.2).[2] Her lyrical archive of this critical stage of black consciousness among Trinidadian youths and the feminist politics that activist women embraced during the 1970s functions as an *eleke* of sorts linking the Black Power Movement to the expansion and institutionalization of the Yoruba-Orisa tradition since the 1980s.[3]

This claim is a literal one, because Springer is the spiritual daughter of the most prominent public face of Orisa heritage during the latter twentieth century, Iyalorisa Ijoye Elizabeth Melvina Rodney (1914–2009). Springer

FIGURE 4.1 Students march (1972) in support of soldiers convicted for involvement in ten-day mutiny at the Teteron National Defense Force Base in 1970. The visibility of adolescent girls in this demonstration of Black Power shows cross-gender solidarity and the prominence of female activism. *Front left*, Josanne Leonard. *Behind Josanne*, Debbie Kilgour (face mostly covered). *Third row (left)*, Onica Kimathi aka Cynthia Evelyn (in white dress) and Ayesha Mutope-Johnson. (Courtesy of Apoesho Mutope, photographer.)

FIGURE 4.2 Trinidad and Tobago male and female university students and grassroots activists participate in "March to Caroni." This March 12, 1970, national call for racial unity was organized by the National Joint Action Committee. (Courtesy of Embau Moheni, Deputy Political Leader, NJAC.)

recounts, "I was taken there by a friend of mine [Baba Rudolph Eastman] . . . who had been protected and hidden by the Orisa [community] in 1970 when the police were on the hunt for the leaders [of the Black Power demonstrations], and they had quite a lot of the leaders in the palais . . . and so on."[4]

Rodney could conceal Black Power advocates, such as Eastman, because she possessed institutional space and authority. In their 1999 study of Trinidadian Orisa, Rawle Gibbons and Funso Aiyejina found that women such as Iya Rodney were, in fact, the leaders of more than half of the eighty active Orisa shrines across the country.[5] Although some of these women leaders and visionaries are affectionately called "Sister," most are respectfully addressed by the spiritual title of "Mother."[6] The authority and deference accorded female spiritual experts in Orisa tradition are best conveyed through this unparalleled matricentric familial role.

This chapter focuses on *mothers* and *mothering* and, only by extension, on women and gender. It specifically identifies *motherness* as a tradition that simultaneously disrupts and qualifies black *otherness* in the modern world.[7] That is, motherness is a mode of attending to black captives and reorienting their sense of becoming and belonging in the midst of captivity. It is conceptually capacious, illuminating modes of loving and liberating that the term womanism, as a gendered concept, fails to capture in the Africana experience. Thus, in one sense, I *linguistically* distinguish it from womanism because it is a more apt term for the phenomena and affective states I address when exploring contributions of spiritual mothers to Yoruba-Orisa religious culture and consciousness. However, I also situate motherness *within* womanism because the substance of womanist theorizing has long accounted for this nongendered mode of Africana family and *nation-al* caretaking.

In *The Womanist Reader*, Layli Maparyan argues that, since its emergence in the 1980s, the tendency to identify womanism as a form of black feminism has been an understandable conceptual misstep. She goes to great lengths to elucidate womanism's close connection to black feminism but insists that the two social change perspectives are neither interchangeable nor collapsible: womanism and black feminism, Maparyan unequivocally asserts, are two distinct traditions.[8] Similarly, I contend that womanism is a misnomer for motherness, which needs to be named if we are to fully investigate and appraise its significance to Africana communities. Although African scholars have advanced terms such as "motherism," "matricentricity," and "mothernity,"[9] all of which encapsulate much of what I discuss in this chapter, I posit motherness as a term with the semantic scope to characterize critical expressions, feelings, and desires because it describes an affective modality.

Although motherness certainly has the power to inspire philosophical or political movements—it fosters, for example, a love politics—it is neither a movement, ideology, nor development. Acknowledging that motherness is not an "ism" sharpens our appreciation for its conceptual distinctiveness from similar and more prominent labels and our understanding of its particular utility for exploring African Caribbean religious imagination and sacred poetics. If the scholarly center of womanism is arguably North America and the scholarly center of motherism, mothernity, and matricentricity is Africa, a study of the institution of spiritual mothers in Trinidad identifies the Caribbean as an indispensable context for explicating a modality already inherent to womanism and motherism but not properly named until now. Motherness is a Caribbean contribution to Africana affect, spirituality, and thought with resonances throughout the wider African diaspora and Africa. African Trinidadian motherness, as explored throughout this chapter, is what black feminist scholar Christina Sharpe calls an "anagrammatical" site of black care in the African diaspora,[10] and it is no less so in Africa.

Going beyond ties to biological offspring in Yorùbá and other Africana religious cultures, motherness and motherhood extend to spiritual children and families. Consequently, the "mother" descriptor is an honorific, a social and spiritual rank, and a central kinship practice (to mother/mothering) that conveys communities' highest standards and expectations for relational life. Conceived this way, motherhood for Afro-Trinidadians takes its cues from Bantu and Niger-Congo religio-cultural orientations where a "mother" also accesses and represents sacred reality.[11] Yorùbá and other African societies of Niger-Congo heritage have complex views of motherhood that are cosmologically and socially derived. Thus, motherhood distinguishes a particular phenomenon—pregnancy and parturition—as a sacred environment thanks to the divine agency of the female parent and other deities/entities who usher, host, and deliver the unborn from invisible to visible existence.

Among the Yorùbá the Orí is a divine entity (one's personal Òrìṣà), but so too is the vagina, which carries the namesake of the Òrìṣà, Ìyámàpó, "the tutelary deity of craftswomen particularly of potters and dyers."[12] The very first stages of motherhood—pregnancy and delivery—emblematize cooperation between visible and invisible members of the family and cosmos. Similar to manifestation, motherhood is another context where entities are made corporeally present and visible through the corporeal materiality of other entities. This spirituo-bio-anatomical experience inspires the metaphorical and sacred significance of motherhood in Yorùbá cultural contexts, where "it is said that 'the power of the mothers is equal or superior to that of the gods . . . the mothers own and control the gods.'"[13]

African feminist scholars explain the value that Africana cultures place on motherhood as a social position, practice, and principle through concepts such as matricentricity, mothernity, and motherism, indicating the influence and authority mothers have within Africana kinship structures and collective consciousness. Scholars such as Ifi Amadiume, Oyèrónkẹ́ Oyěwùmí, Catherine Acholonu, and Mary Kolawole examine the prominent role of biological, social, and spiritual motherhood in the organization of precolonial African societies and the matricentric legacies issuing from this heritage even today.[14] For example, Amadiume, a Nigerian anthropologist of Igbo heritage, uses the term "matricentricity," and Oyěwùmí, a Yorùbá-Nigerian sociologist, the term "mothernity," to conceptualize the habitus that actual and symbolic motherhood (not equivalent to womanhood) creates in the psychic, social, and axiological orientations of many African families and societies. Both terms index motherhood as a social institution and an idealized symbol of love, care, provision, protection, solidarity, loyalty, and leadership.[15]

Under colonial slavery, African mothers in Trinidad and the wider African diaspora occupied prominent caregiving and authoritative roles, often in matrifocal families and matricentric kin networks. In addition, gendered geographies of labor curtailed the presence of residential fathers. During the late eighteenth and early nineteenth centuries, Trinidadian labor arrangements and mating patterns, as well as the physical distance between urban female domestics and larger communities of enslaved peers, reinforced African matricentric traditions.[16] As a result, transgenerational matricentric households became a norm. According to Maureen Warner-Lewis, "the mother- and grandmother-centered family unit" was not only "a prominent pattern in black Creole society" but also "explains the significance . . . of mothers and maternal grandmothers as transmitters of African language and culture."[17]

Some of Trinidad's maternal "transmitters of African . . . culture" were also religious leaders and spiritual adepts who bequeathed African religious epistemologies to their children as much as or more than their paternal counterparts.[18] Yet in the wider discourse on Yoruba-Orisa diaspora traditions, the male Ifa priest is often positioned as the embodiment of ultimate theological and ritual authority. I focus on motherness and women-mothers not to exclude male priests but to examine an understudied Orisa familial tradition and ethic with roots in continental Yorùbá and other societies of Niger-Congo/Bantu heritage—and in the end to include males in this framework. In their respective research, Francis Henry and James Houk feature three powerful male pillars of the Orisa tradition in Trinidad: Ebenezer Elliott (Pa Neezer), Baba Sam Phills, and Leader Jeffrey Biddeau. However, we should examine more closely the testimony of Baba Sam, who noted, "Well, while you will hear more about Pa Neezer (he was the most ambitious of the Yoruba pantheon in Trinidad as a man eh), we had the women that were powerful!"[19]

The subsequent discussion illumines the contributions of iyalorisa—women-mothers within the Yoruba-Orisa tradition—who have exercised significant authority and influence in and beyond their spiritual families since the era of Black Power. I theorize their matricentric modes of leadership, institution-building, activism, spiritual diplomacy, and theological innovation under the province of womanism because they reflect what Layli Maparyan calls the "logic of womanism," an "experiential, narrative, ecological, moral, emotional, communal, and mystical" logic that guides their reasoning, love ethic, and decision making. The womanist traditions of spiritual mothering and "homeland mothering" in Trinidad's Yoruba-Orisa community are important case studies for apprehending what womanist scholars have theorized as "forms of mothering-as-social-change-leadership," I would add, that are cultivated through motherness modes of caring and loving. Empowered by love, womanist mothering is imitable and therefore exceeds sex and gender. As Maparyan elucidates, "Each of these forms of mothering . . . is capable of being embodied by a person of any gender or sexual orientation, further detaching" the womanist "mother-as-activist model from biological constructions of motherhood."[20]

To access this imitable tradition, I examine motherness within Trinidad's Yoruba-Orisa heritage with a focus on the life and legacy of Iyalode Sangowunmi Olakiitan Osunfunmilayo. Emphasizing how the Yoruba-Orisa religion has nourished Trinidad's matricentric heritage and continues to inspire an ethic of kinship among Yoruba-Orisa mothers and their spiritual families, I continue to trace the important narrative themes of judicial and broader civic engagement, as well as Africana nationhood and religious nationalism of the Yoruba-Orisa community's pre- and postindependence history. The discussion thus broadens chapter 3's theorization of black religion and Africana affective terrains in conversation with diverse Africana/black feminist and womanist lineages.[21]

Iyalorisa Ijoye Elizabeth Melvina Rodney and the National Council of Orisa Elders: Seniority Making Way for Mothers to Rule

Although often undertheorized, matricentric values undoubtedly influenced the Yoruba-Orisa community's plans to organize Trinidad's existing shrines under one national body. The National Council of Orisa Elders (NCOE) came to symbolize a new and significant phase in the internal and public affairs of the Yoruba-Orisa religious community in Trinidad at the end of the twentieth century and early in the twenty-first century. Yoruba *nation* ideas had a residual impact on this attempt to fortify the Yoruba family through formal institutional affiliation and to strengthen genealogical and spiritual kinship bonds across disparate shrines, with an emphasis on bridging divides between northern and southern Orisa shrines.[22]

If the 1970s marked the explosion of black nationalist ideologies in Trinidad, the 1980s attached institutional power and public influence to that consciousness. This decade unveiled the civic realm as a new theater of operations for Orisa devotees who were staging the unprecedented appearance of African religious cultures in public arenas. Determined to keep the personal political, some of the new Orisa devotees aligned their activism with Trinidad's African *nations'* historical struggle for religious freedom within the judiciary and the Parliament and created the conditions for African religious cultures to have their days in court unlike any before. Although the perception of African religion as *numenymic* obeah had remained distorted within the new republic's collective memory, nothing less than a civil rights agenda of securing religious freedom brought institutional credibility and national recognition to the image of African religion as Orisa.[23]

By the 1980s, it appeared that the right combination of local and global events, such as the founding of the internationally constituted Orisa World Congress (1981), had finally created the conditions for the revaluation of the African religious heritage in Trinidad. The Yoruba-Orisa tradition was uniquely positioned to symbolize that heritage and profit from a legacy of struggle for religious freedom and the protection of African religions under the laws of Trinidad and Tobago. The signature event was the passing of the 1981 Act for the Incorporation of the Orisa Movement of Trinidad and Tobago, Egbe Orisa Ile Wa (EOIW), a Yoruba-Orisa group governed by Iya Melvina Rodney (see figures 4.3 and 4.4).

The purpose of this act was to provide protection and government sponsorship for Orisa shrines as adherents sought to standardize their devotional practices and organize their activities within formal institutional structures.[24]

Legal Supplement Part A to the "Trinidad and Tobago Gazette," Vol. 20, No. 258, 17th September, 1981

Fifth Session First Parliament Republic of Trinidad and Tobago

REPUBLIC OF TRINIDAD AND TOBAGO

Act No. 35 of 1981

An Act for the Incorporation of the Orisa Movement of Trinidad and Tobago. Egbe Orisa Ile Wa.

[Assented to 9th September, 1981]

Whereas there has been established in the Republic of Trinidad and Tobago a religious body known as the Orisa Movement of Trinidad and Tobago.

Legal Supplement Part A to the "Trinidad and Tobago Gazette", Vol. 30, No. 221, 29th August, 1991

Fifth Session Third Parliament Republic of Trinidad and Tobago

REPUBLIC OF TRINIDAD AND TOBAGO

Act No. 27 of 1991

[L.S.]

An Act for the incorporation of Opa Orisha (Shango) of Trinidad and Tobago

[Assented to 20th August, 1991]

Whereas there has been established in Trinidad and Tobago a religious body known as The Orisha Religion (Shango) of Trinidad and Tobago:

And whereas it is expedient that The Orisha Religion (Shango) of Trinidad and Tobago be incorporated as Opa Orisha (Shango) of Trinidad and Tobago:

FIGURE 4.3 AND FIGURE 4.4 Parliamentary publications of 1981 Act for the Incorporation of the Orisa Movement of Trinidad and Tobago Egbe Orisa Ile Wa (issued September 17, 1981) and 1991 Act for the Incorporation of Opa Orisha (Shango) of Trinidad and Tobago (issued August 29, 1991).

Under the auspices of the Ministry of Culture, the Orisa community was empowered to (1) develop archival materials (written, audio, and visual) to document the history and practice of the tradition; (2) devise an educational curriculum to teach the West African Yoruba language; and (3) invite indigenous Yorùbá devotees from Nigeria to discuss methods of healing and ritual life. This decriminalization of the Orisa religion protected practitioners against violent encounters and physical altercations.

After 1981, under the jurisdiction of a new republic, the government's focus shifted from eradication to inclusion and education, and the Orisa community worked to remake its image through individual and corporate endeavors of national significance. Through Iya Melvina Rodney's motherness and matricentric leadership, EOIW became the first representative Orisa community to play a pioneering role in the tradition's formative period of institutionalization. Ten years later, the Orisa organization, Opa Orisha

Shango (OOS), was incorporated and legally protected by the Act for the Incorporation of Opa Orisha (Shango) of Trinidad and Tobago. The OOS was coheaded by Iyalorisa Dr. Molly Ahye, another prominent Orisa mother with transnational visibility in the global Yoruba-Orisa community.

During this period, EOIW and OOS pursued similar goals that would benefit Orisa devotees nationwide and facilitate their reconnection to their Yorùbá Nigerian roots. Within the "Aims and objects" section of Act 35 of 1981, item 3b specifically states EOIW's intention "to expose members of the faith to the traditional practices of the religion as taught by experts of Africa."[25] Act 27 of 1991 registers a comparable mission for OOS in item 3a of the same heading: "to continue the Orisha Traditions and Practices as they are known in Trinidad and Tobago and are taught by approved experts of Africa and the African diaspora."[26] Legislative support for Orisa institutional development through national and transnational endeavors yielded tangible results in ensuing years, most significantly the founding of NCOE of Trinidad and Tobago.

Although NCOE's influence has declined under the weight of contemporary shifts in approaches to leadership and governance among omorisa in Trinidad, the events precipitating its establishment, as well as its activities and influence, extend the narratives of black consciousness into African consciousness, religious freedom into religious institutionalization, and matricentric household/palais leadership into matricentric Orisa *nation-al*/national leadership. The personality lending power and authority to the new umbrella institution was Iya Melvina Rodney, EOIW's mother-priestess. NCOE's vision and influence rested on Iya Rodney's credibility and experience, reflected in her extensive spiritual legacy in Trinidad and beyond. An orienting norm of that heritage had been the organizing principle of seniority. Iya Rodney's position as the highest-ranking leader-priest was established not because of her gender but because of her expert status as *mother*, enhanced and secured by her seniority relative to other mothers (iyas) and fathers (babas) in the Orisa tradition.

Authorized by the most senior Yoruba religious leader worldwide—Nigeria's Ọọni of Ifẹ—Iya Rodney's position of authority over Orisa affairs in Trinidad and Tobago was accepted within the global Yoruba-Orisa community. Reportedly based on her age and wisdom, Iyalorisa Melvina Rodney (in her eighties at the time) was the Ọọni's person of choice. She was a spiritual descendant of the legendary Orisa leader Elliot Ebenezer (Pa Neezer) and by extension his renowned predecessor (Ma Diamond), who reportedly was born in Africa. Rodney was also the spiritual mother of hundreds of devotees in Trinidad and North America, many of whom made pilgrimages to her home for spiritual guidance and renewal and for personal and communal ritual observances.

Just seven years after EOIW's incorporation, the spiritual head of the Yoruba religion, Qòni Okùnadé Şíjúwadé Olúbùşe II, did indeed honor the nation of Trinidad, and the Orisa community in particular, with an eight-day visit (July 31–August 8, 1988) concurring with Emancipation week.[27] The invitation was much more than a simple extension of hospitality. As the titular head of the Yoruba people, the Qòni's visit symbolized a new era in Orisa religious formation in Trinidad. His presence not only elevated the esteemed position of the religion among its adherents but also supplied the missing link between what some had come to dismiss as either a primitive or invented heritage in Trinidad.

The Qòni was well received among Orisa devotees, and reporters from Trinidad's two leading newspapers tracked his movements throughout the week as he graced prominent Orisa shrines, attended local Orisa feasts and cultural events, and participated in a nationally televised Orisa ceremony held in Port of Spain at the National Stadium on August 1, Emancipation Day. The recognition given to Trinidadian expressions of Yoruba religion transformed its public image, even if marginally, and imbued its members with confidence and commitment to formalize Orisa's legacy in T&T as a local African religion with global analogues across the Atlantic world. The Qòni himself was allegedly the first to voice the idea of organizing an institutional body to establish and nurture an efficient infrastructure of benefit to Orisa devotees of T&T. Of lasting significance, however, was the Qòni's selection of a woman as the spiritual head of Orisa practitioners throughout the nation (see figure 4.5).

After the Qòni's visit, initial attempts to found a national council of Orisa elders resulted in the formation of an umbrella organization of thirty-three registered Orisa shrines.[28] Its purpose, according to Gibbons, a chief spokesperson during the organization's formative years, was "to establish a group that would be tolerant of difference and nonetheless establish the necessary standards that were required by the people themselves and the kind of public profile that would give the tradition a sense of social respect without having necessarily to change itself."[29]

Governed by an official board of directors of six Orisa leaders, NCOE was incorporated in 1998. Iya Rodney, being at the apex of the governing structure, was responsible for selecting via spiritual divination the five additional board members who were (1) leaders of Orisa shrines, (2) the spiritual leaders of initiated children, (3) knowledgeable about the tradition, and (4) esteemed as having a "good solid social reputation" or "good standing in the society."[30]

Each of these five members—Sam Phills, Clarence Forde, Sylvestine De Gonzalez, Arthur Monseque, and Eudora Thomas—were distinguished Orisa elders who were expected to hold lifetime positions and to "demit office upon death or voluntarily or upon request by the Spiritual Elders only."[31] In addition to the leadership of these six elders, NCOE's membership structure included administrative personnel and a national body encompassing the heads of registered shrines.

NCOE's approach to leadership compelled the recognition of women's authority over policy and wider governance protocols during the Orisa tradition's period of postindependence institutionalization, establishing a precedent to recover should patriarchal conventions creep into the institution in the future. Women's efforts to organize a loosely affiliated yet decentralized Yoruba-Orisa community were painstaking and deliberate with regard to policy making and enforcement. Under Iya Rodney's leadership, NCOE operationalized governance procedures and standardized some conventions. Modifications were important as the Orisa tradition transitioned from a marginalized and misunderstood subculture to an official religion. As Gibbons notes, "Certainly when one is dealing with other bodies, be it the state, private sector or international organizations, rather than have two or three different voices talking, you need some standards in that respect. There ha[ve] to be broad areas of agreement, and that was what was intended in establishing the Council."[32]

The NCOE's substantial collection of correspondence and documents indicates the level of consideration it gave not only to administrative efficiency but also to standardizing ethical norms and protocols pertaining to ceremonial and ritual life. One of the first administrative tasks the board of directors tackled was documenting the number of operative shrines throughout the nation and making the wider Orisa community aware of the aims and objectives of the newly formed organization. It first established an official registration process, allowing shrines to become active members of NCOE for a fee of 100.00 TT dollars. The registration form recorded relevant information: the shrine's patron deity, its period of Ebo (which is considered to be the most sacrosanct ritual among Orisa devotees), other religious festivals observed, and community or educational activities.

The Council also established "General Rules and Regulations" for its leadership and wider membership: "Elders of the Orisa Council" were "expected to be role models for the community, particularly the youth and children," and "behavior inimical to the aspirations of the Orisa Community [could] elicit severe sanctions," notably:

Itinerary

TODAY

8:15 a.m. HRH The Ooni leaves residence for Office of Hon. Leader of the Opposition.
8:45 a.m. Courtesy call on Leader of Opposition.
9:30 a.m. The Ooni leaves to plant freedom landmark in Couva.
10-12 a.m. Tour of Trintoc.
12 a.m. to 1:30 p.m. Lunch at Trintoc.
1:45 a.m.- 2:15 p.m. Visit to Wild Fowl Trust.
2:30 p.m. The Ooni leaves Trintoc for Marabella to plant freedom landmark.
4-5 p.m. Meeting with members of the African community resident in Trinidad and Tobago or visit to the High Commission.
5:15 p.m. to 7 p.m. Free.
8 p.m. Nigerian Cultural show at Jean Pierre Complex.

TOMORROW

9 a.m. Tour of main shopping areas, including Central Market.
10-12 a.m. Meeting followed by lunch with selected members of business community.
3-4 p.m. Meeting with Mongbere and adherents of the Orisa faith at residence of HRH.
4:30- 6:30 p.m. Free for general public by appointment.
7:30 p.m. Dinner at Holiday Inn hosted by women of COAATT.

SUNDAY

8:45 a.m. Leaves Piarco for Tobago.
9:30 a.m. African worship
11:30-1 p.m. Meeting with Tobago House Assembly and lunch
1:15-3 p.m. Tour of Tobago and planting of freedom landmark.
3:15-4 p.m. Audience with Orisa adherents.
4:30-6:30 p.m. Cultural performance by local and Nigerian cultural groups.
8:45 p.m. Depart for Trinidad.

MONDAY

6 a.m. Breakfast with the Ooni at residence, members of organising committee and chiefs.
9:30 a.m. Press conference at residence.
10 a.m. Depart for airport.
10:45 a.m. Arrival at airport
11 a.m. Departure ceremonies
11:10 a.m. Airborne.

tumultuous as scores of children lined Antilles Road, dancing and singing African songs.

The keys to the borough were presented to the Ooni as we entered Point Fortin, greeted by dancers. Prayers were said in Amharic and Yoruba.

The party retired to Festival Square for the Emancipation Day Historic Pageant. For me, it was the most touching experience for the day. The centre court of the Square was filled with hundreds of youngsters, dancing and swirling in brilliantly-coloured costumes.

Strictly Afro-Trinidadian delicacies were served: kosai-akara (pigeon peas accra), yam casserole, green plantain foo foo, pastelle, kantu (sesame seed balls), gigere (bene) balls, cassava pone and tooloom.

Pressed for time, His Royal Highness and the royal party were forced to leave Point Fortin without witnessing what must have been a spectacle: the *Flambeau Tableau Procession.*

FIGURE 4.5 Page 2 of Peter Ray Blood's article, "The King and I," on Ọọni Okùnadé Ṣíjúwadé Olúbùṣe II's historic August 1–8, 1988, visit to Trinidad and Tobago captured the highlights of his reception and itinerary. Blood's article was originally published in the now defunct *Weekend Sun.* Courtesy of Trinidad and Tobago National Library and Information System Authority. Reprinted by permission from Peter Ray Blood. (Photographer unknown.)

- Criminality as determined by the legal system of Trinidad and Tobago
- Public intoxication or similar forms of immorality
- Abuse of office including neglect of duty and divulging the business of the Council
- Disrespect of/to other members, aggressive conduct toward other members
- Disrespect of other Orisa shrines
- Refusals to carry out directions of the Assembly Meeting where sanctions, excluding expulsion, were imposed.[33]

The ultimate authority to "reprimand any Shrine which does not support its programs for the . . . training [of] Elders, drummers, singers, ritual officers, marriage officers, etc.," also rested with the Council.[34]

Emphasis on respect and dignity has been the impetus behind the various reparations, rights, and public acknowledgment that NCOE has exacted from the national government with measurable success. For example, little time passed between NCOE's incorporation and its launching of a program designed to dismantle the disparaging narrative of Orisa presence in Trinidad and the discriminatory practices that restricted NCOE's influence over national culture and civic life. The Council immediately established a campaign to portray Yoruba-Orisa as a valid religious tradition deserving of the status, legal rights, and respect conferred on other recognized religious bodies in Trinidad and Tobago in public and private domains. Two years after its incorporation, NCOE issued two communiqués on May 24, 2000, on the subject of religious freedom and legitimization. One was directed toward omorisa but sent a clear message to an external audience as well. It specifically indicated NCOE's vigilance in challenging the exclusionary policies of the national government, stating,

> The Council of Orisa Elders of Trinidad and Tobago wishes to bring to the attention of all Orisa devotees, the gross disrespect still being perpetuated on Orisa people by the current census being taken by the Government of Trinidad and Tobago. There is still no listing of the Orisa faith in Trinidad and Tobago. We are still "Other." All Orisa people are advised not to sign under "other," in the area reserved for religion. That is to be crossed out and Orisa written in. It is time to insist that this ancient belief system of our ancestors and one of the oldest existing in the world be recognized. Declare yourself proudly as Orisa, and insist that you be given the recognition and respect that we deserve.[35]

The second communiqué addressed fraudulent "priests" and informed the public of NCOE's function as the official legitimizing structure of the Orisa tradition:

> The National Council of Orisa Elders wishes to state that there are umbrella bodies in Trinidad and Tobago which have shrines registered with them. These are Egbe Orisa Ile Wa, the organization headed by Iyalorisa Melvina Rodney . . . there is Opa Orisa Shango, headed by Babalorisa Clarence Forde and Iyalorisa Molly Ahye. There is also this National Council of Orisa Elders, an incorporated body that brings together both Egbe Orisa Ile Wa and Opa Orisa Shango. The members of the public are advised that not anyone declaring him or herself an Orisa Priest must be taken at their word. People are urged to make contact with any of these bodies or persons for verification. This is an ancient belief system. It is time that the disrespect and gullibility of people come to an end. The religion is properly documented and structured. Information is plentiful and available in libraries and bookshops and on the internet. Let us respect ourselves and this ancient sacred science.[36]

This statement characterized NCOE's public disposition in its campaign to both reclaim and demand a revaluation of the Orisa tradition in Trinidad at the close of a long century of Orisa/African religious persecution. Its posture toward an external public has been unapologetic, yet NCOE is simultaneously self-critical in advocating a particular consciousness and activism on the part of its internal public. It had disputed the incalculable injustice that Orisa practitioners have confronted over centuries of religious repression. However, at the dawn of the twenty-first century, NCOE privileged domestic and international self-definition and self-representation among all priorities facing the Orisa community. One of the most important victories on this front was NCOE's success in expanding demographic categories on the national census. Since 2011 it has included "Orisha" as an option under religious affiliation (see figure 4.6; tables 4.1 and 4.2).[37] Other achievements within the past forty years that complement the government's recognition of T&T's Orisa tradition in its decennial census are discussed later in the chapter as we explore the contributions of five additional Orisa mothers.

NCOE has conceded some governing power to a new generation of leadership since 2010. However, the community's monumental march toward religious recognition and liberty is unparalleled among custodians of African-heritage religions in the wider Caribbean, and arguably the entire

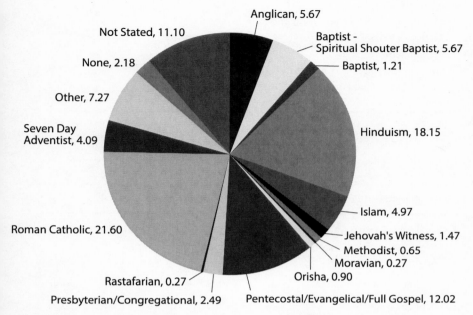

Anglican, 5.67
Baptist - Spiritual Shouter Baptist, 5.67
Baptist, 1.21
Not Stated, 11.10
None, 2.18
Other, 7.27
Seven Day Adventist, 4.09
Hinduism, 18.15
Roman Catholic, 21.60
Islam, 4.97
Jehovah's Witness, 1.47
Methodist, 0.65
Moravian, 0.27
Orisha, 0.90
Rastafarian, 0.27
Presbyterian/Congregational, 2.49
Pentecostal/Evangelical/Full Gospel, 12.02

FIGURE 4.6 Graph of Religious Composition. (Adapted by Elaine Penagos from "Trinidad and Tobago 2011 Population and Housing Census Demographic Report," pp. 130–31. Courtesy of Elaine Penagos.)

Americas. Omorisa in T&T constituted the first Yoruba religious diaspora that the Ọọni of Ifẹ visited. And through that unprecedented meeting between descendants of Trinidad's Yoruba nation and Ọọni Ṣijúwadé Olúbùṣe II, the scripting of a new chapter in Orisa religious history began under the matricentric leadership and priestly expertise of Iyalorisa Ijoye Elizabeth Melvina Rodney (figure 4.7).

The original composition of NCOE reflected the stature and significance of women, in their role as mothers and foundational figures, in the Orisa religion. Not only did a woman hold the title of chief spiritual elder but she also was joined on the Council by two other women and three men, comprising a gender-balanced power base at this initial stage of formalization. This balance of power was achieved by both deliberate design and fidelity to Yoruba cultural norms. Those who led the movement to found NCOE were determined to preserve women's influence during deliberations and resolutions of the core Orisa elders.[38] And they were equally committed to upholding the Yoruba principle of seniority that had long been honored

TABLE 4.1
T&T Population by Age Group and Religion,
Birth to 39 Years Old
Trinidad and Tobago
2011 Population and Housing Census Demographic Report, P
Non-Institutional Population by Age Group and Religion

	Both Sexes		
	AGE GROUP		
	All Ages	0–4	5–9	10–14
Municipality And Religion	(1)	(2)	(3)	(4)
TRINIDAD AND TOBAGO	1,322,546	94,033	91,140	87,673
Anglican	74,994	3,924	4,195	3,941
Baptist-Spiritual Shouter	75,002	6,280	6,050	5,681
Baptist-Other	15,951	1,431	1,316	1,266
Hinduism	240,100	13,556	13,586	13,629
Islam	65,705	4,547	4,207	3,732
Jehovah's Witness	19,450	1,264	1,284	1,390
Methodist	8,648	446	472	475
Moravian	3,526	217	183	181
Orisha	11,918	1,118	1,067	964
Pentecostal/Evangelical/Full Gospel	159,033	14,738	13,414	13,012
Presbyterian/Congregational	32,972	1,862	1,878	1,931
Rastafarian	3,615	263	238	196
Roman Catholic	285,671	19,128	19,224	19,144
Seventh Day Adventist	54,156	4,656	4,382	4,184
Other	96,166	8,145	7,735	7,271
None	28,842	2,409	1,673	1,351
Not Stated	146,798	10,046	10,236	9,328

	Both Sexes			
	AGE GROUP			
15–19	20–24	25–29	30–34	35–39
(5)	(6)	(7)	(8)	(9)
98,001	**113,771**	**123,008**	**105,161**	**92,183**
4,302	5,334	6,243	5,944	5,069
6,000	6,815	6,711	5,266	4,419
1,365	1,469	1,539	1,187	984
16,449	20,210	22,922	20,212	18,238
4,567	5,924	6,662	5,394	4,475
1,531	1,774	1,824	1,425	1,371
572	583	721	586	557
198	249	290	255	210
1,067	**1,081**	**1,080**	**911**	**782**
13,876	15,302	15,786	12,665	10,922
2,121	2,641	2,790	2,624	2,395
170	294	427	477	278
20,636	23,927	25,721	21,869	18,913
4,529	5,095	5,155	4,147	3,363
7,680	8,702	9,218	7,584	7,028
1,700	2,488	3,267	2,908	2,261
11,237	11,882	12,652	11,706	10,919

(continued)

Table 4.1 (continued)

Municipality And Religion	Both Sexes			
	AGE GROUP			
	All Ages	0–4	5–9	10–14
	(1)	(2)	(3)	(4)
TRINIDAD	**1,261,811**	**89,202**	**86,677**	**83,494**
Anglican	67,218	3,496	3,752	3,565
Baptist-Spiritual Shouter	68,589	5,786	5,568	5,208
Baptist-Other	15,563	1,401	1,289	1,237
Hinduism	239,692	13,530	13,563	13,607
Islam	65,360	4,509	4,181	3,709
Jehovah's Witness	18,464	1,186	1,219	1,311
Methodist	5,655	272	307	313
Moravian	757	39	33	35
Orisha	**10,993**	**1,029**	**987**	**883**
Pentecostal/Evangelical/Full Gospel	150,112	13,781	12,550	12,217
Presbyterian/Congregational	32,865	1,851	1,873	1,925
Rastafarian	3,381	250	215	187
Roman Catholic	281,641	18,848	18,976	18,901
Seventh Day Adventist	44,279	3,800	3,533	3,382
Other	90,847	7,628	7,300	6,851
None	25,567	2,220	1,497	1,201
Not Stated	140,828	9,576	9,833	8,962

		Both Sexes		
		AGE GROUP		
15–19	20–24	25–29	30–34	35–39
(5)	(6)	(7)	(8)	(9)
93,316	**108,760**	**117,659**	**100,491**	**88,128**
3,852	4,802	5,626	5,360	4,593
5,461	6,250	6,150	4,808	3,988
1,330	1,446	1,508	1,158	957
16,425	20,179	22,889	20,158	18,202
4,543	5,893	6,633	5,360	4,448
1,448	1,687	1,734	1,365	1,310
339	362	443	372	357
36	63	71	46	50
989	997	1,020	834	710
13,060	14,504	14,965	11,973	10,286
2,112	2,632	2,786	2,611	2,386
163	274	404	447	263
20,392	23,625	25,395	21,553	18,635
3,659	4,218	4,268	3,429	2,733
7,240	8,192	8,783	7,233	6,707
1,489	2,202	2,867	2,587	2,013
10,778	11,436	12,118	11,194	10,490

TABLE 4.2

T&T Population by Age Group and Religion,
40–80+ Years
Trinidad and Tobago
2011 Population and Housing Census Demographic Report
Non-Institutional Population by Age Group and Religion

			Both Sexes			
			AGE GROUP			
40–44	45–49	50–54	55–59	60–64	65–69	70–74
(10)	(11)	(12)	(13)	(14)	(15)	(16)
85,832	95,750	86,901	73,005	58,442	44,383	30,096
4,351	5,237	5,237	4,902	4,441	3,802	2,838
4,252	4,785	4,700	3,988	3,095	2,442	1,891
843	970	894	699	552	474	353
17,775	20,208	17,212	14,950	11,180	8,665	5,386
4,329	4,924	4,714	3,801	2,893	2,225	1,538
1,244	1,446	1,290	1,093	852	605	394
465	555	601	509	555	434	384
217	249	262	224	184	164	157
722	769	657	532	411	305	202
10,112	10,832	8,808	6,644	4,617	3,197	2,187
2,354	2,520	2,408	2,101	1,656	1,464	1,012
220	373	395	182	66	22	6
17,460	19,362	18,536	16,274	13,901	10,942	7,874
3,372	3,745	3,197	2,368	1,848	1,317	1,069
6,351	6,878	5,861	4,618	3,313	2,333	1,394
1,924	2,175	1,942	1,558	1,251	793	540
9,838	10,723	10,189	8,562	7,628	5,200	2,873

75–79	80+	
(17)	(18)	*Municipality And Religion*
20,559	**22,608**	TRINIDAD AND TOBAGO
2,316	2,918	Anglican
1,244	1,382	Baptist-Spiritual Shouter
258	351	Baptist-Other
3,167	2,755	Hinduism
903	871	Islam
302	363	Jehovah's Witness
324	410	Methodist
122	162	Moravian
123	**127**	**Orisha**
1,425	1,496	Pentecostal/Evangelical/Full Gospel
639	575	Presbyterian/Congregational
5	6	Rastafarian
5,708	7,051	Roman Catholic
740	989	Seventh Day Adventist
996	1,058	Other
314	288	None
1,973	1,807	Not Stated

(continued)

Table 4.2 (continued)

	Both Sexes					
		AGE GROUP				
40–44	45–49	50–54	55–59	60–64	65–69	70–74
(10)	(11)	(12)	(13)	(14)	(15)	(16)
82,010	**91,178**	**82,949**	**69,934**	**55,955**	**42,502**	**28,656**
3,873	4,624	4,682	4,420	3,980	3,415	2,515
3,887	4,314	4,265	3,660	2,793	2,240	1,746
816	945	859	673	541	461	343
17,748	20,174	17,179	14,926	11,166	8,651	5,379
4,306	4,895	4,696	3,788	2,883	2,221	1,531
1,161	1,367	1,236	1,043	822	574	376
299	343	406	343	396	306	280
41	48	49	46	43	46	44
649	710	601	496	385	288	191
9,546	10,227	8,337	6,341	4,421	3,068	2,066
2,340	2,519	2,401	2,098	1,655	1,460	1,006
200	345	365	168	61	22	6
17,213	19,043	18,240	16,004	13,689	10,768	7,778
2,722	3,044	2,603	1,967	1,515	1,083	889
6,030	6,482	5,538	4,345	3,134	2,190	1,302
1,703	1,889	1,692	1,394	1,119	703	467
9,474	10,210	9,799	8,222	7,351	5,006	2,737

75–79	80+	
(17)	(18)	Municipality And Religion
19,506	**21,396**	TRINIDAD
2,057	2,607	Anglican
1,178	1,285	Baptist-Spiritual Shouter
255	345	Baptist-Other
3,161	2,755	Hinduism
898	865	Islam
280	345	Jehovah's Witness
225	290	Methodist
30	39	Moravian
109	**113**	**Orisha**
1,353	1,417	Pentecostal/Evangelical/Full Gospel
637	573	Presbyterian/Congregational
3	6	Rastafarian
5,625	6,956	Roman Catholic
600	836	Seventh Day Adventist
911	981	Other
275	249	None
1,907	1,735	Not Stated

FIGURE 4.7 Iyalorisa Ijoye Elizabeth Melvina Rodney holding a double-headed axe, the principal emblem of her patron Orisa, Sango. (Photographer unknown. Courtesy of Esmond King, personal collection.)

in Trinidad: seniority not gender determines elevated privilege and status. Thus, in a diaspora setting where patriarchal leadership structures were normative in most Christian, Hindu, and Islamic communities across the nation, the Yoruba-Orisa religion has been a forerunner for gender parity at all levels of institutional representation and leadership. NCOE's progressive stance on gender and institutional power is noteworthy. However, the fact that female elders (Iya Melvina Rodney, Mother Eudora Thomas, and Sister Sylvestine De Gonzalez) occupied three of the highest positions within NCOE at its earliest stage is evidence of the Orisa community's commitment to its Yoruba heritage. Despite wider trends of patriarchal religious leadership structuring communal life for their compatriots, in privileging seniority over patriarchy and gender stratification, enduring cultural legacies of the Yoruba *nation* continued to define the Orisa religion during its period of formal institutionalization.[39]

Orisa Mothers and Legacy-Building at Home and Abroad

While Iya Rodney was officially overseeing the first historical wave of Orisa formalization in T&T, other Trinidadian mothers were making landmark domestic and international contributions.[40] Orisa mothers such as Iyalorisa Eintou Pearl Springer, Iyalorisa Molly Ahye, Otun Iyalode Awo Agbaye Ifakemi Aworeni (aka Iya Amoye and Valerie Lee Chee), Iyalode Ifakorede Oyayemi Aworeni (aka Mother Joan), and Chief Oregi Ajagbe Obagunle Iyalode San-gowunmi Olakiitan Osunfunmilayo (aka J. Patricia McLeod) have upheld their traditions through conservation and innovation with attention to micro and macro, *nation-al, inter-nation-al,* national, and international theaters of power, from the yard shrine to the Orisa World Congress.

IYALORISA EINTOU PEARL SPRINGER

T&T's Inter-Religious Organization (IRO) is an ecumenical constituency with long-standing representatives from the four major religious groups in Trinidad: Roman Catholicism, Anglicanism, Hinduism, and Islam. Since its inception in 1972, other religious groups, such as the Spiritual Baptists and Bahá'í, have entered the IRO, broadening its representation and diversifying its voice. Yet it had resisted inclusion of the Yoruba-Orisa community. It was the IRSC (a forerunner of the IRO) that in the April 23, 1970, *Express* neglected to include the Yoruba-Orisa community when it penned a passionate and prayerful interreligious plea for peace and unity during the height of social tensions in the Black Power Movement. For decades, the

IRO was one of NCOE's greatest obstacles, preventing its full access to public discourse and depriving it of opportunities to influence civic and national affairs.

In her capacity as NCOE's public relations officer, Iya Eintou Pearl Springer succeeded in having the Council represented in the IRO, which led to a wider public and national stage for Orisa participation in the shaping of civil society and in national conversations concerning the role of religion in public life. The IRO aids and advises the government on religious matters and is the institution the government approaches when seeking religious officials to lead prayers at parliamentary meetings, diplomatic events, and other auspicious occasions. Although the IRO remains an independent group, it receives government funds for its initiatives and has easy access to national and local politicians. Thus, gaining membership in the IRO was a noteworthy accomplishment.

The founding director of T&T's Heritage Library (1993), Springer was a masterful tactician with the perfect blend of skills and political savvy to secure NCOE's desired results. She initiated an application for IRO membership on behalf of NCOE in 1995, only to meet with six years of embittered exchanges and dismissal on the part of the organization. As she told it in 2002, "it's been a fight; it's been a fight." She continued,

> And in fact what I did a couple years ago, we linked with [the Sanatan Dharma] Maha Saba [SDMS], the most powerful Hindu organization, in a protest march in the streets. And we said, "If by so and so time, there was not an Orisa member on the IRO, Hindus and Orisha people will come together and form our own inter-religious organization." We sent several correspondences to the IRO requesting membership status and there are letters to the press backward and forward. . . . Listen, the IRO did not lobby the government for us to come on! We had to lobby against them because they were dominated and controlled by the Roman Catholic Church. So now, since 2001, Orisa has a full presence there with equal power. . . . We have picketed the Parliament with our drums you know, we've circled Woodford Square with our drums. . . . And it's just been a few of us.[41]

Today, the fruits of Springer's persistence in petitioning for NCOE's membership can be seen at IRO's executive level, where Baba Neal Ryan Rawlings recently served as the IRO secretary (2017–2018) on a leadership team of ten.

Esteemed leader of Opa Orisha (Shango), the late Iya Molly Ahye (1933–2018) had a visionary international presence at conferences, official meetings, and ceremonies governing and celebrating the global Orisha community in Africa, the Caribbean, Latin America, and North America. Moreover, she was at the negotiating table with officials to lobby for many of the legal rights and privileges the Orisa community has come to enjoy over the past thirty years, including the incorporation of her own Orisa organization.[42] Although more than a few Orisa mothers have traveled near and far for religious activities, Ahye's distinguished career as a performance artist with a PhD in dance from New York University placed her in a unique position to leverage her credentials within scholarly, artistic, and governmental circles as a representative and even defender of T&T's Orisa legacy.

At the inaugural international conference of Orisa devotees, held in 1980 at the Caribbean Cultural Center African Diaspora Institute (CCCADI) in New York City, Ahye and Springer were among the delegation from Trinidad and Tobago. Ahye and the center's founder Marta Vega were the engine behind the conference's conception and execution: their womanist genius and harmonizing/coordinating ethic inspired the eminent Nigerian scholar and Yorùbá priest Wándé Abímbọ́lá to convene Yoruba devotees across the globe under the auspices of the Orisa World Congress.[43] Ahye was one of the first Trinidadians to raise her voice at the Orisa World Congress in Nigeria, held just a year after the CCCADI conference in New York (see figure 4.8). She challenged the view that Yoruba-Orisa diaspora lineages had deviated from their original, authentic Nigerian ritual and theological sources. In response to a Nigerian priest who expressed his satisfaction with the return of diaspora omorisa "to Africa" to "correct a few points" regarding their local practice of the tradition, with one decisive and elegant statement Ahye introduced the central thesis I have advanced in the two preceding chapters—that the Yoruba-Orisa religion is *a moving continuity* wherever it is practiced in the world. "I would like to say," Ahye declared, "that we shouldn't be 'corrected.' We should leave to oursel[ves] the way we worship because I'm not sure that 'you' are correct or 'we' are correct." The critical purpose of such an international assembly was not "a matter of correction, but to exchange ideas."[44]

Omorisa Burton Sankeralli's postmortem tribute to Ahye describes the scope of her influence in Trinidad and within the transnational Yoruba-Orisa spiritual family:

FIGURE 4.8 Molly Ahye in a dancer's pose that gestures toward her cultural ambassadorship of her Orisa heritage and evidences her prowess as a professional performer. Dancing by the sea and under the sun, her bare feet seek contact with air and earth, natural spaces where Orisa energies are present and felt by those who pray with their feet. Ahye embodies not only T&T's "golden" dance heritage but also her nation's black Yoruba heritage. Her book, *Golden Heritage: The Dance in Trinidad and Tobago* (Petit Valley: Heritage Cultures Ltd, 1978), was published with this photograph as its cover image around the time she co-conceived the Caribbean Cultural Center African Diaspora Institute's first international conference of Orisa devotees.

Molly was (and is) a priestess in the Orisha Tradition and played a pivotal role in that critical period when the Tradition moved out of the shadows of persecution, harassment and stigmatization into the sphere of public visibility and acknowledgement. With the organization Opa Orisha Shango, she pioneered such efforts at national visibility. Here we may note the establishing of the Oshun Festival as a public nation-wide observance. This was also the first step in establishing the public calendar of Orisha festivals that we have today. Opa also endeavoured, perhaps for the first time, to, in effect, establish a comprehensive register of Orisha shrines. Molly was made the female head of Opa Orisha Shango and given the title Iya L'Orisha of Trinidad and Tobago. . . . Let it also be remembered the tremendous work Iya L'Orisha Ahye did across the world. And here for instance we may mention her research on the Tradition in Brazil. And I recently discovered she is well-known in Cuba.[45]

Ahye's national and *nation-al* legacy is comparable to that of the late indomitable Iyalorixá Stella de Oxóssi (Mãe Stella, born Maria Stella de Azevedo Santos) from Salvador, Bahia in Brazil. Each was recognized by her government with a prestigious national honor: the Hummingbird Medal (Ahye) and induction into the Bahia Academy of Letters (Mãe Stella). Both spiritual mothers were authors and cultural/sacred science ambassadors of Yoruba-Orisa religion through the healing arts of Africana dance and movement vocabularies as well as medicinal knowledge and spiritual care. Ahye, in particular, brought widespread awareness to her Trinidadian Yoruba-Orisa tradition through organized events across a number of performative theaters, including natural arenas. During Opa Orisha (Shango)'s first public Oshun Festival in August 1990, a journalist from a local television network attended the event and interviewed Ahye, providing a platform for her to teach the nation about how omorisa and Orisa relate to one another—how they wait for one another, show up to one another, and interact with one another—in the theater of the natural world. I quote her at length because she elucidates how seen and unseen presences communicate through the silence of the symbols of black religion. This kind of communication is a mode of religious apprehension that Charles Long argues extends possibilities for a new creation, and I would add a new poetics of relation.[46] After explaining how the inaugural festival came about. Ahye described the events as they unfolded:

> Osun is an Orisa that governs all sweet water expanses: rivers, lakes, lagoons, and so on. And you know the healing quality water has. . . . She is a great mother, and she has to do with the elements that work for nourishment,

as all mothers will nourish. She gives her children good graces. . . . Whatever they want of her, that is . . . for their well being, she will grant. And . . . she is known for assisting women who think themselves barren. As a mother, she knows the beauty in having a child . . . and she would want others to benefit from it. She is Orisa of riches. She's very powerful in the pantheon. . . .

Explaining the ritual protocols of the festival, Ahye continued:

Whenever you're going to do anything anywhere you've got to ask Mother Earth permission. So they did have some songs for Mother Earth and they're asking for permission to use the ground, to come to the ground with respect for the ground. Notice how they cleaned the ground before [the ritual began]. Well, that is the kind of respect that people should have for Mother Earth.

Ahye then described how the roughly sixty assembled omorisa arranged Osun's altar and supplicated her with drumming, song, and dance: "They took all their offerings to the river mouth, and they set up that table with all the offerings, no blood offerings, they were all offerings of perfumes and oils and candles and fruits and flowers and cake—whatever people had to bring and to offer. They did lay a beautiful table."

And Osun's response? Ahye interprets it as follows:

Rivers come down. Yes. But in this case what we saw was timing, a particular kind of timing. They were on the beach. They prayed, they sang, they danced, they did everything; the river never came down. They walked to the spot where they laid the offering. The river never came down. When the river came down was after they had laid everything. They lit their candles, they said their prayers, they planted the flag, they invited Osun to come. Osun came, as you saw, in this great mother [omorisa], and she blessed everybody; and she received her offering, and she brought beauty. Then I witnessed something: well, Yemanja manifested . . . it could have been Osun, but from what I saw, it looked to me like another great mother [omorisa] was receiving Yemanja, Mother of the Orisas. And as she went into the sea, right afterwards, the phenomenon occurred, and the river came down . . . the river took the offering, with quick speed, took it out to sea because people were wondering if this [offering] was going to stay there for fowls[?] to pick . . . and some were saying, "Well, I like this juicy thing; I would eat afterwards." They didn't get a chance. As soon as the water came down, it came with such hurry! It took not only the offering, but it took the table and all, because that whole piece of sand, and it was quite a big piece of sand . . . it just went into the sea.

When Osun accepted her offering through displays of sweet force (coming down and taking her offering under the waters, perhaps with the help of Yemanja), the omorisa who witnessed the event knew immediately that she was pleased and blessings would follow.[47] Here, Ahye decodes the sign languages of the Orisa and explores with her wider nation Osun's complexity and sublimity, while savoring the opportunity to engage the environment reverently, rewardingly, delightfully. I emphasize Ahye's powerful oratorical gifts because her extensive career in dance did not eclipse her penchant for theological reflection nor her efforts to convey truths about Orisa that many non-omorisa in Trinidad would not have known in the 1990s. Ahye's visionary leadership led to greater domestic and global respect for the Yoruba-Orisa religion. However, through organizing events like the Osun Festival, which now enjoys more than three decades of legacy building, Ahye's motherness and creactivity mobilized the formation of an Orisa nation-al public.[48]

OTUN IYALODE AWO AGBAYE IFAKEMI AWORENI/IYA AMOYE

During a 2013 interview, the now late Iya Amoye expressed great admiration for Iya Molly Ahye's invaluable contribution to the civil rights and privileges devotees enjoy today in Trinidad:

> Molly "opened us up to a lot of international connections, especially like the . . . Congress, and she gave a lot, she did a lot of research, and from what I have seen, being around Baba [Clarence] Forde, she was able to guide him a lot. I appreciate what she did, now. I admire the woman. I don't know her personally. I met her a few times, but I admire the work that she did.[49]

Although not well connected with Ahye, Iya Amoye, founder and leader of the Eniyan Wa shrine in Tableland (southern Trinidad), did align herself closely with Baba Clarence Forde, the male counterpart head of Opa Orisa Shango and one of the leading elder priests in NCOE before he passed away in 2011. When Tracey and I visited Iya Amoye, the retired secondary school teacher was far removed from the initial context in which I came to learn about her visionary leadership within the Orisa community. During the early 2000s, Iya Amoye broke barriers by reinstituting the (traditionally homosocial male)

Egungun masquerade in Trinidad.[50] When asked what motivated her to focus on Egungun, she placed herself within a longer lineage of Egungun tradition in Trinidad, which had been nurtured by the presence of global Yoruba practitioners and priests who were eager to share their expertise with earnest seekers of spiritual resources and newcomers to the Orisa religion during the early 1990s: "I found out in research that Egungun existed in certain areas in Trinidad before. And it was curious that when Egungun came back to us, it came back in a place called Gasparillo, south Trinidad. And then it came back in Princes Town with me. And these are the two locations that they said Egungun was powerful in those days [the nineteenth and early twentieth centuries]."[51]

Iya Amoye clarified that the "Egungun came back to" Gasparillo through the efforts of another spiritual mother in the early 1990s, Iya Aina Olomo. Iya Aina is today a distinguished African American priestess of Shango and Iyalawo (Mother of mysteries/Ifa priestess) who began her training with Yomi Yomi and Carol Robinson in the Bronx, New York, within the Assunta Serrano Ascension-Osa Unko lineage.[52] Iya Amoye sought knowledge from Iya Aina for three years before Iya Aina left Trinidad to return to the United States in 1995. Another Yoruba expert, a babalawo of Trinidadian heritage by way of New York, also influenced Iya Amoye's spiritual quest beginning in 1995. Yet, after two years she became disillusioned by his tutelage at Ile Orisha Shango because of what she and others discerned was none other than their "exploitation" through "the exorbitant sums of money that were being charged for initiations" and other services. By November 1997, Iya Amoye had left the group, along with those she had introduced to the community. It was then that others authorized "Sister Valerie" to assume leadership of what would become their new spiritual family. Describing the deliberations that elevated her to this new role (and title of "Mother Valerie"), she explained how she reluctantly became the leader of the Eniyan Wa Orisa shrine: "When we separated, they said . . . who's going to guide us now. And I said, well I don't know because I need guidance myself. And they said . . . we have decided to come with you, so therefore, you will be our mother."[53]

Between 1995 when Iya Aina departed Trinidad and the 1999 Sixth World Congress of Orisa Tradition and Culture where I first heard Iya Amoye speak about Egungun, Iya Amoye had many visions prompting her to embrace her central role in reestablishing Egungun masquerading traditions in Trinidad (see figures 4.9 and 4.10). She confessed before all Congress participants at the Holiday Inn in Port of Spain, and reminded me more than a decade later that she "kept getting these messages":

FIGURE 4.9 Ile Eniyan Wa's Egungun masquerades, Tableland, Trinidad, October 9, 2019. These *Eku* (energy bearing the ancestor) appear during *asingba oro* (memorial festivals for the departed). Iya Amoye's resurrection of this traditionally male-identified Yoruba institution disrupted gender-exclusive protocols associated with Egungun rituals and performances. (Courtesy of Nisha Harding.)

I kept seeing the face of Egungun. . . . I'd be looking at the television, and I'd close my eyes quickly, and I would see this face appear in front of me. I would open my eyes and the face is not there. But when I close the eyes, I would see the face. I would see the colors of the clothing. Until then I'd known nothing much about Egungun, but I started seeing it, and I was told, this is how the clothes should be made. . . . After three years, I said, I just better do it. I just better do it. And we started, and that is what happened.[54]

FIGURE 4.10 Ile Isokan Annual Ancestral Festival in Febeau Village, San Juan, Trinidad, February 3, 2019. (Courtesy of Maria Nunes, photographer.)

Her visions did not go unchallenged, however. Many in the conference room balked at the idea of a woman taking charge of the Egungun society. Yet the following day, Chief Adenibi S. Edubi Ifamuyiwa Ajamu from Oyotuni Village in South Carolina and Chief Bìsìríyù Adéyẹ̀lá Adélẹ́kàn from Nigeria had a change of mind. Apparently, the ancestors and the Orisa had conveyed to them that Iya Amoye's initiative was indeed legitimate and sanctioned. Iya Amoye explained further:

> [Chief Adélẹ́kàn] said, "Yesterday we doubted you. Today, we've come to congratulate you. We've come to tell you that what you're doing is authentic." Chief Adélẹ́kàn did divination when he went back to the hotel . . . and he said, "My daughter, you are of the lineage of so and so"—he called the lineage. He said, "Your ancestor was the chief advisor to the Ọ̀ọni of Ifẹ̀ in that time, and your lineage is the lineage of Egungun. Your lineage used to carry on Egungun in those times." . . . He said, "It used to be carried on by the men, but there came a time when there was no man willing or able to do it, and my daughter it has been passed to you." And that man told me my title, my function, he even told me what I was given to use. And

he said, "We apologize for yesterday." And by then I was in tears because, I said, "I *know* what I've been telling you. I wouldn't do this by guessing. There's this force that's driving me. It's something that I must do; it's something I was given. I'm not going to fool around with my tradition, so when I tell you that it is pure guidance, that's the only way I can explain it because I did not have a book to read from. I didn't have anyone to teach me before, so this, what I am doing here, is what I'm supposed to do."[55]

Chief Adélékàn then promised to oversee Iya Amoye's initiation at no charge but told her to be prepared to supply a large feast for the community. Over the years, the chief reminded Iya Amoye that the invitation still stood. He even offered to pay her airfare to Nigeria if it was prohibitive. Still, she never found the opportunity to travel to Nigeria before he transitioned in May 2008. Iya Amoye finally went to Ilé-Ifè with Baba Clarence Forde in 2009 and received the title of Otun Iyalode Awo Agbaye in honor of her contributions to the Yoruba community in Trinidad.

In addition to the reestablishment of Egungun, Iya Amoye made other significant contributions to the community. Her shrine's ritual calendar devotes nearly every month to the veneration of major Orisa and cosmic forces and to activities that fulfill the ethical mandates associated with them. In January, members of Eniyan Wa pay homage and leave offerings to Orisa at seven sacred sites across the country. During the second or third week in January, they customarily focus on Obaluaye (aka Babaluaye), holding a festival for him as instructed to do during her initiation to Ifa.[56] In February her spiritual family celebrates Oya. The new moon during the month of April signals the precise time to "go and feed Esu's children." In Iya Amoye's words, "Manifestation told us that the women must come together, bless the food and go and feed your Father's (Esu's) children. So, anyone who is on the street, without money that day, we have to offer food." May is reserved for the Gelede festival, a pan-Yoruba ritual celebration of invisible and visible Mothers and the cosmic-social powers they wield, performed in Nigeria and other regions of the Yoruba religious diaspora. In June the shrine honors the Warriors (Esu, Ogun, and Ososi), a tradition adopted from Cuban Yoruba-Orisa legacies and not known to be practiced in Nigeria. September, October, and November are dedicated, respectively, to Yemoja, Obatala, and Egungun.

Eniyan Wa members also gather every first Sunday for ancestor veneration rituals. Besides providing a place for devotional observances the shrine is the site of wedding ceremonies (at which Iya Amoye officiated before her passing); Ifa divination sessions; naming ceremonies; and Orisa initiations and burial rites, during which "Egungun has the very important function" of ensuring "the proper disposal of the dead."[57] At the time of our last interview (summer 2013), Iya Amoye had about a hundred spiritual children in Trinidad, Tobago, Barbados, and the United States. She had also constructed five round "huts" with thatched roofs to house these spiritual children during their initiations (see figures 4.11 and 4.12). These structures resembled the homes I had visited in rural areas of the Bas Congo region of Democratic Republic of Congo, regions of South Africa, and Oyotunji African Village in the United States. I had not observed any similar dwellings in Trinidad during my fieldwork, and thus it made sense the blueprints for the designs came about through precise spiritual visions and ancestral messages that

FIGURE 4.11
Sango's "Hut,"
Eniyan Wa, Table-
land, Trinidad,
August 18, 2013.
(Photo by author.)

FIGURE 4.12 Initiation "Huts"/Temples for the Orisa on the Grounds of Enyian Wa, Tableland Trinidad, August 18, 2013. (Photo by author.)

FIGURE 4.13 Otun Iyalode Awo Agbaye Ifakemi Aworeni (Amoye) delivering her historic sermon at the Law Courts of Trinidad and Tobago. (Courtesy of Ile Eniyan Wa.)

Iya Amoye received. The revelations were later confirmed by a man whose dream placed him under Iya Amoye's charge at her spiritual compound and prompted him to travel about an hour from Port of Spain to Princes Town to request her guidance as his spiritual mother. The man, who eventually became her spiritual son, told her, "I was at a place in the bush. There were trees all around; and then there were some little houses—round. There were about five of them. And they were covered in carat [palm thatch], and I was lying on the ground; and you were attending to me, and you had on white clothes." The visitor also informed her of a "manifestation in Port of Spain that said, 'Go to the woman in South, the woman with the carat houses and let her do this [the initiation] for you.'"

Ancestral/spiritual guidance might well account for an intention I perceived when I observed Eniyan Wa's built environment. I suspected the designs were chosen deliberately to produce an affective terrain inspired by the image of Africa, and I found them personally appealing in their evocation of African (homeland) spaces, symbols, and pathways to religious belonging.[58] Iya Amoye explained that the "huts house the vessels of the Orisa," many of them mother deities, including Yemoja, Olokun, Osun, Aje (female Orisa of wealth), and Oya. Obatala, Ifa, and Sango also have their specified locations among the shrine's five circular temples. A candidate for initiation "will spend the entire seven-day period" in the hut dedicated to their parent Orisa. "If someone is being initiated, let's say to Oya, we put that person in Oya's house."[59]

With such an active shrine, it is not surprising that Iya Amoye's priestly influence surpassed the boundaries of her own initiation houses and other sacred domains of import to the Yoruba-Orisa community. By invitation from a "female employee" of the Law Courts who had attended one of Eniyan Wa's Gelede celebrations, in 2004 she became the first omorisa to deliver the annual sermon for the Ceremonial Opening of the Law Courts of Trinidad and Tobago (see figure 4.13).

In educating the nation at large about fundamental aspects of Yoruba philosophy and cosmology and in demystifying the role of the Orisa in the maintenance of social justice and civil rights, Iya Amoye pointedly encouraged her audience to exercise personal and collective moral responsibility. She explained the many portals to justice in the Yoruba-Orisa tradition: "As original citizens of Heaven . . . we are required to live our lives in such a manner that when we make that transition, we leave a legacy of which our children can be proud. The fundamental requirement of the ~~human being~~ according to Ifa is the development of 'Iwa pele' or 'Good and Noble character.'"

She urged every citizen "as individuals, [to] ask Obatala to bless us with the gifts of humility and obedience to the Divine will . . . to help us to avoid staining our vision so that we will see clearly to make ethical decisions." Knowing, however, the history of legal and social persecution that Orisa devotees have struggled to surmount, she did not leave the podium without also insisting,

> We must . . . examine our laws, regulations and business practices to ensure that we are not discriminating against various ethnic or religious sectors and institutionalizing crime in our society. Our Ministers of Religion must desist from slandering and maligning other religions thereby instilling religious prejudice and intolerance among the population. As patrons, arbiters of justice, it is important that we seek to maintain the highest level of ethical behaviour—that which according to Ifa/Orisa is called Iwa Pele.[60]

As with many post–Black Power omorisa, resocializing the nation to respect T&T's African cultural and spiritual heritages was important to Iya Amoye. In multiple arenas, she "targeted [government] ministers" to protest the nation's "skewed curriculum" pertaining to African religion and culture. Her views on African studies curriculum reform influenced audiences even at regional UNESCO seminars during which she repeatedly "let them know that they are treating African religion incorrectly."[61]

Reporting on Eniyan Wa's fifteenth annual Egungun festival, Egbe Onisin Eledumare's web home page acknowledges the prominent role that Iya Amoye's Orisa family has played in institutionalizing Egungun and other Yoruba traditions in Trinidad while simultaneously linking the female-headed institution to Trinidad's Black Power Movement:

> Eniyan Wa an African spiritual organization led by Otun Iyalode Awo Agbaye Ifakemi Aworeni—Valerie Stephenson Lee Chee, has been functional in the Republic of Trinidad & Tobago for several years now and [has] highlighted and hosted Gelede Festivals, Egun and Egungun Festivals and activities. . . . The organization has added to the colour and diversity of Trinidad & Tobago African/Yoruba spiritual and sacred science manifestation and retentions of our African heritage. It can be listed . . . among those organizations that some scholars have identified as innovators of a "new" African sacred science narrative, that has in the main manifested itself as a direct consequence of the "Black Power Revolution of 1970."[62]

For nearly two decades, Iya (Mother) Amoye birthed and nurtured a spiritual community with a strong affinity for traditional Yoruba Trinidadian conceptions of family and kinship. Not only did the group's initial members confer on her the title of "Mother" when she agreed to serve as their leader but they also "wanted a [shrine] name that meant 'our family,' 'our kin group,' 'our clan.'"[63] According to Iya Amoye, the members "received guidance for the name of the organization. . . . We got two names. We divined on it. Eniyan Wa [Our People] came up. Again, several years later, Professor Babatúndé Lawal came here to do a feature address for us for Gelede . . . and he mentioned to us that the name Eniyan Wa is of special significance because it meant those ~~human beings~~ specially chosen to bring goodness to the earth."

Professor Lawal, in his address to the group, further confirmed "the influence of spirit guidance" in the selection of the organization's name and, more importantly, that Eniyan Wa had pursued its spiritual vocation in alignment with the will of the ancestors. Iya Amoye described a spiritual life path deeply influenced by an invisible presence and recurring revelation since her first encounters with Yoruba tradition. The same could be said for the shrine she mothered that she said "receive[s] a lot of guidance from the ancestors, and each time when it's put to the test, it proves true."[64]

If there are any living witnesses to Babaláwo Kóláwolé Oshitólá's position that "the wisdom of Ifá is not necessarily received only through the complex act of divination," they are the custodians of the Yoruba-Orisa diaspora traditions who, whether in Trinidad, Brazil, the United States, or elsewhere, constantly attest to the daily import of ancestral revelation. In alignment with the revelations of Ifa, the ancestors often provide priestly instructions and supply missing information pertinent to ritual and devotional life, not to mention personal and social concerns. Oshitólá explains that Ifa's wisdom "may also be revealed in dreams or heard while walking on the street, seen in visions, or felt in the body. The experience of divinity is not bound exclusively to ritual performance, but is rather an integral part of the everyday experience of the prepared initiate."[65] The mothers of Trinidadian Orisa tradition bear witness to this reality in every bone, fiber, and tissue of their being. They are "witnesses to the Unknown"—coded knowledges only partially translatable and often unintelligible to academics untrained in ancestral modes of communicating.[66] Trinidad's Yoruba-Orisa mothers share poignant stories of somatic and sensorial portals of access to Ifa's wisdom. Many of the events on their shrines' ritual calendars were initiated under the instruction of manifested Orisa or after receiving ancestral/divine messages conveyed through dreams. Thus, Eniyan Wa founded its Sango Festival only after "there was a manifestation of Sango that told me that, every year, I should keep a festival for him on the 24th of July."

When asked *how* the ancestors speak, Iya Amoye replied,

> Ancestors speak through spiritual communication. You'll be sitting and get a message . . . you will hear a voice inside of you saying something, and sooner or later you will see, if it doesn't happen today. Down the road, something will happen eventually, and you will say, "Oh-ho, that is what they were talking about." . . . In Trinidad, in the absence of the tradition where we do divination, this is the guidance we had to rely on, our ancestors had to rely on . . . we have it in several ways, but . . . it's very strong.[67]

Spiritual mothers often describe learning over time how to apprehend the messages they receive from the ancestors and other entities in the invisible domain. With experience, they cultivate capacities associated with each of the senses. Deeply seeing, hearing, smelling, touching, tasting, and knowing involve decoding signs and symbols in a register different from what Western rational understandings of sensory experience suggest. Thus, the spiritual mothers become fluent in ancestral languages and modes of communicating that teach, heal, and sustain persons and communities, both visible and invisible.

The ancestors also link the living African community with its muted and unremembered history, alerting present-day devotees that Yoruba spiritual work is a portal to an *inter-nation-al* pan-African heritage in Trinidad. "In 2004," Iya Amoye shared,

> We [the national Orisa community] had a Family Day at Lopinot, and when we were about to leave, there was this manifestation that told us that we should come on the site on a regular basis and pour libation because we were the only people that remember to come and give them water. And they told us that water was very important to keep the energies alive. . . . And then we were told . . . , "not only Yaraba. . . . All of us blood was shed here . . . Hausa, Igbo, Asante. So when you come here, remember all of us, not only Yaraba."[68]

"Not only Yaraba" is certainly correct with regard to the ancestral remembering of Trinidad's African *nations*, their histories, and indigenous hermeneutics. Within all the African heritage religions, revelation and history are mutually constitutive in ancestral memory and messaging. The agency to reveal information, to unveil history, and to make present and accessible what is invisible often rests with invisible family members—the ancestors, Orisa, and other spiritual powers.[69]

Conveying, for example, which materials should be included in the "special vessel" used in Gelede rituals (as the ancestors did to Eniyan Wa members) is as much the revelation of knowledge as it is the re-membering of history, of a community's moving cultural continuum that involves diverse ashé-endowed agents— ~~humans~~, plants, animals, and minerals—each a vessel onto itself.[70] ~~Humans~~ alone do not construct history in Yoruba and other Africana religious cultures. Each consecrated substance breathes with agency (ashé) and historical knowledge that reveal a web of relations among "copresent" mediums of life.[71]

Eniyan Wa's ancestrally inspired Gelede vessel is an active universe in which all its contents collaborate to promote sociality, healing, and balance. The vessel's identity and significance escape reductive categories that objectify its contents. Thus, as a "ritual participant," the Gelede vessel is simultaneously an archive of a people's transnational "Yaraba" heritage and religious history, legible and authoritative to Orisa devotees alongside (and at times correcting) other national or official scripts of history and heritage in T&T and the wider Caribbean.[72]

Lorgia García-Peña abstracts a compelling conceptual framework from this kind of Africana epistemic orientation and hermeneutics to analyze how spiritual sources of knowledge challenge official historical narratives in the Dominican experience. She theorizes "Dominican diasporic texts as *textos montados* (possessed texts) that . . . allow for the possibility of finding a more complete version of the truth through the embodied memory of silenced histories."[73] M. Jacqui Alexander also contributes to a conceptualization of history born of spiritual sources. Honoring her own experience with spirit communication, she describes the dissonance between the pursuit of knowledge via rational scholastic modes versus Africana spiritual modes. Her quest to recount the silenced history of Thisbe (whom Tracey Hucks discusses in volume 1, chapter 2) yielded pieces of Thisbe's unknown narrative in Mayombe (Bas Congo) and colonial Trinidad only after Alexander herself became a "texto montado" through whom Thisbe could tell her story, including her original name, Kitsimba.[74] Yoruba-Orisa religious culture performs this same work, bringing to life ancestral re-memberings of "silenced histories" that mothers such as Iya Amoye hear and understand.

One mother in particular both understood Trinidad's "silenced [Orisa] histories" and embodied them by the very nature of her family's legacy. The late Chief Ifakorede Oyayemi Aworeni Joan Cyrus (aka Mother Joan) inherited the leadership role in her shrine from her spiritual and genealogical grandfather, Kenny David Cyrus. Currently denominated the Kenny Cyrus Alkebulan Ile Ijuba (KCAII) and widely known as Ile Ijuba, the shrine is noteworthy for its uninterrupted existence since the late 1800s.[75] Under Mother Joan's leadership, KCAII offers a view into matricentric authority and spiritual diplomacy within an Orisa lineage that links the late nineteenth century to the early twenty-first century.

Mother Joan's ile was founded in 1897 after her grandfather Kenny Cyrus (b. 1870s) and his friends Ebenezer Elliot (aka Pa Neezer) and Francis Saunders bought land in the same vicinity in southern Trinidad. Each Yoruba-Orisa priest reportedly established a shrine on his respective compound—Cyrus in Enterprise, Elliott at Jerningham Junction, and Saunders in Longdenville— before the latter two purchased additional land in Moruga and subsequently moved their shrines. By the time Mother Joan was born in 1948, her grandfather's shrine had been in operation for a half-century. Although her mother "was not into this catching Power business at all," Mother Joan could not escape "falling under Oya" as a child, because she grew up in her grandfather's compound and received her first initiation at the age of eleven.

In a 2001 interview, Baba Sam Phills summarized how initiation always followed the kind of preliminary Orisa visitation the young Mother Joan had experienced:

> There was what we called desunu. . . . At that time in the early 30s, 40s, 50s, even 60s . . . if, while a drum was beating, a person got possessed and fell down . . . they had a term . . . loosely used for it. They say, "You fall under Tante Taiwo or Pa Neezer or Mr. Leonard," or whatever have you. That drum then was your calling. When that person fell down [under manifestation], you would take them into the chapelle or whatever have you, get water, get little thunder stones and all the different things. And there were people there versed in tradition; and they would do the desunéing of your head.[76]

"Papa Neezer was the first person to wash my head—desuné," Mother Joan recounted, and "Sheppy" (Isaac Lindsay) "was my spiritual father."[77]

"Sheppy" must be the same "Father Isaac," the "Shango leader" from San Fernando whom the Nigerian scholar, James Adeyinka Olawaiye, interviewed and exchanged ideas about "Obakoso" in 1977.[78] Mother Joan was only the third person I met in Trinidad who testified to a strong interpersonal connection with Pa Neezer, the other two being Iya Rodney, his spiritual daughter, and social anthropologist Frances Henry. Everyone knew *about* Pa Neezer, but not everyone *knew* "Papa" Neezer.[79] In fact, Mother Joan was connected to several of the towering male figures featured in this two-volume study: Mr. Francis (volume I, introduction),[80] Father Isaac (chapter 1) and Pa Neezer (chapter 2). Still, as a young woman, she felt no special calling to continue the Orisa traditions of her grandfather. She even told him she "didn't want to keep up the feasts with all that was involved." Her grandfather explained that "she didn't have to do all of that but just keep a little thanksgiving."

Instead, Mother Joan studied nursing and "thought all was well." Yet, she soon began to have dreams and visions, and when she visited palais, "the Orisas would speak to me," she recalled. Eventually, she suffered grave illnesses from which she could find no relief, even after bouncing from one hospital to the next. She eventually consulted her spiritual father, and when he asked her if she was "ready now [to hold feasts], I said 'yes,' and from that day on I stopped feeling sick. I always tell people I am not here because I wanted to open a shrine. I am here because I *had* to be here."

The ancestors and the Orisa have guided members of Ile Ijuba to shift their focus from internal to external activities, inspiring them to engage the broader community and address violence and social imbalance in the nation. A pivotal moment of discernment occurred in the year 2007, during the second visit of Awóreni Àdìsá Awóyẹmí (aka Mákọrànwálé), the Àràbà Agbáye of Ilé-Ifẹ̀. According to Mother Joan, "The Àràbà came to Trinidad and did a reading with all the notable heads of the various shrines and it was revealed that the Orisa community needed to appease some of the Orisa, especially Esu because the predominance of crime and murder was . . . based upon a spiritual crisis." Mother Joan wondered "whether other folks followed through," while making it clear that "Ile Ijuba did the appeasement as we were supposed to." Still, "for six months . . . there was a serious reduction of crime in the area."

Crime and the kind of bloodshed Ile Ijuba aims to diminish in society continued to inspire new public rituals in the shrine's communal outreach, although "now we don't stay at the shrine; we go out and try to teach the public about Orisa," Mother Joan explained. Teaching begins with ceremonies that assemble local community witnesses at rituals where the Orisa, through their spiritual children, reclaim dangerous streets and public zones. Ile Ijuba's ritualized mode of hallowing space disrupts infractions and imbalance within the visible–invisible realms and heals broken relationships.

The Orisa have instructed Ile Ijuba via manifestations, dreams, and visions to penetrate some of the most underresourced and violent areas in Trinidad with their drums, songs, prayers, and libations. In 2011, members of the shrine "received guidance" to make twenty-one stops in Laventille, including one spot "where they used to have a lot of killings." Rather than shun and chase them away when "Oya manifested," the community "came out and asked us to pour something on that spot because someone got killed on that spot." Two years later, the Orisa guided about thirty Ile Ijuba members to stop at a particular location, once again in Laventille, and sing for the ancestors. "People, including folks in the [steel] pan yard, watched and responded very well. They were very respectful."[81]

Leaders of Ile Ijuba note KCAII's change of emphasis from a preoccupation with personal and interior spiritual obligations and fulfillment to the social work of the Spirit. Through territorial consecrations at select locations across the nation (placing an Esu stool at each of the four corners of Trinidad, for example), and through marches for justice, days of prayer focused on national turmoil, and public healing rituals, Ile Ijuba members are assuming roles as civic priests outside the ile as much as they operate as spiritual priests inside. In territories beyond the ile, they attend to the healing of communities broken by violence and neglect and the healing of their nation.

Yet KCAII's focus on local and national societal issues should not overshadow Mother Joan's participation in international Orisa World Congresses and her bold steps to situate the Yoruba-Orisa religion as a world religion worthy of engagement from notables of other global religious traditions. Even before the turn of the twenty-first century, one of KCAII's members facilitated the visit of His Holiness the Dalai Lama, Tenzin Gyatso, to T&T. The visit included stops at Orisa sites and audiences with Orisa devotees and Yoruba religious authorities from Nigeria. The events embodied an important theme, "Harmony in Diversity." Whether devotees perceived it as such is difficult to know, but this affirmation was instructive for the wider Orisa community because the Dalai Lama's visit occurred between the 1991 incorporation of the second Orisa organization, Opa Orisha (Shango), and the formation of NCOE in 1998—a time of rapid bureaucratic growth and theological diversification among Orisa shrines and organizations. The theme also affirmed the nation's highest political aspirations of unifying a multicultural, multiracial, and multireligious citizenry.

In KCAII's official guest book, the Dalai Lama addressed the ile on September 16, 1995, with the following words: "I am very happy to be here amidst your followers in your religious faith which had originally come from Africa. I am also happy to share the opportunity of praying together with you." As spiritual diplomat of the most historic shrine in Trinidad, Mother Joan effectively placed Nigeria's globalized Yoruba religion, not to mention other Trinidadian Yoruba-Orisa authorities and herself, on a global platform with a renowned religious leader of an acknowledged world religion (see figure 4.14). Positioning her religion and her Trinidadian nation at the table of interreligious dialogue elevated the Yoruba-Orisa religion in the nation's consciousness and advanced the community's political struggle for religious rights and national recognition.

FIGURE 4.14 *Left to right:* Isaac McLeod; J. Patricia McLeod/Iya Sangowunmi; Chief Dr. Ọmọt'ṣọ Elúyẹmí, Apènà of Ifẹ̀; His Holiness the Dalai Lama, Tenzin Gyatso; and Chief Iyalode Awo Agbaye (Mother Joan Cyrus), among others, September 16, 1995. This rare photograph was taken during His Holiness the Dalai Lama's visit with Mother Joan Cyrus and members of the Kenny Cyrus Alkebulan Ile Ijuba. (Courtesy of Iya Sangowunmi, Ile Eko Sango/Osun Mil'Osa.)

Before she transitioned in 2019, Mother Joan made invaluable contributions to the wider Orisa community as a creator of devotional material currently used in Orisha worship spaces across the nation. She also reportedly initiated more than three hundred spiritual children. Among that number was Janice Patricia McLeod, the person who founded the interreligious, interethnic, and intercultural organization Harmony in Diversity (HID, 1993) that officially hosted the Dalai Lama during his visit and is described next.

CHIEF OREGI AJAGBE OBAGUNLE IYALODE SANGOWUNMI OLAKIITAN OSUNFUNMILAYO

Patricia McLeod currently answers to an eleke of titles and names such as Chief Oregi Ajagbe Obagunle Iyalode Sangowunmi Olakiitan Osunfunmilayo. By this volume's printing, her titles and names will have likely expanded to account for the depth and breadth of her leadership, and so I call her here what I have always called her since we first met in 1998: "Iya Sangowunmi" or simply "Iya."

Iya found a home, initially, at Mother Joan's Ile Ijuba long before the shrine took on its current name. Over time, she felt called to establish her own ile, and when she finally branched out, the departures she made from the standard Orisa practice put her on a path parallel to Massetungi's. However, as anthropologist Fadeke Castor was surprised to discover, Iya did not style herself within traditions emanating from the Black Power Movement, but from her pan-African consciousness.[82]

My research not only confirms this point but also illuminates how the Africana legacy of *nation-building* in Trinidad continues to flourish in Iya's unmistakable womanist blending of motherness and Pan-Africanism. Her womanist Pan-Africanism connects her to a longer heritage of spiritual mothering in Trinidad's African heritage religious traditions, not to mention analogous legacies of spiritual mothering throughout the African diaspora.[83] It also ties her to legacies of Pan-Africanism in Trinidad and throughout the Black Atlantic world. Still, according to Iya, her calling to *nation-building* began with the pulsating "sound of the drums."

Following the Sound of the Drums

Iya Sangowunmi had her first encounter with Orisa at the age of six. She was in her aunt's care while her mother was away at work. She remembers "hearing the drums beating" up the hill behind her aunt's house. While her aunt went to fetch water down the street, the young Pat snuck out back toward the outhouse, feigning the need to relieve herself. She made a dash for the top of the hill because, against her mother's previous instructions, "I decided that I wanted to go and find out what these drums [were] beating about so." Although her steps were suddenly intercepted by her aunt's voice of authority, Iya's desire to follow the sound of the drum has taken her along a path of profound involvement with the Orisa tradition.[84]

By the time Orisa entered her life, Iya had married, completed training for the nursing profession in Trinidad, studied osteopathy and physiotherapy in England, returned home to open two health spas/clinics, launched a cheese-making business, established the African Association of Trinidad and Tobago, and delivered six children into the world. She also had experienced a major physical setback when, after losing her sight, doctors discovered a brain tumor. Three surgeries later Iya is still the whirlwind she was before her illness, helping establish a new Orisa legacy in Trinidad. After several initiations into the Yoruba religion, her life purpose (ita) has long been revealed. And with the guidance of the Orisa and the ancestors, she sees clearly the path her ori has already chosen and the path of devotion she must embrace to remain faithful to her ita. It is also why one might hear her reflect on her pre-Orisa life with this insight: "you have to be careful what you say, even if you say it softly, because some day, you may have to chew on it," or "if you come here with a certain head to do something, some way it always comes out that you see it."

In the Yoruba-Orisa tradition, the physical head is the locus of the ori or the soul complex, which is also translated as "head" in English. Technically, the Yoruba soul complex conveys three distinct but related principles, which are sometimes collapsed into one (ori) or not fully explicated beyond a simplistic definition of destiny. These three principles are (1) emi or life-sustaining breath; (2) ese, which literally means "legs" and figuratively signifies the sheer effort and determination required to advance in life; and (3) ori, which in the broadest sense conveys free will, as opposed to fate or any preordained understanding of destiny. The Yoruba believe that during the moment of conception, an individual's ori chooses a particular life purpose. Ori is ultimately the spiritual principle of self-actualization.[85] It is in this sense that Iya speaks of "coming here with a certain head to do something."

As a young Pan-Africanist, for example, she was unbowed when fellow members of the African Association of Trinidad and Tobago challenged her lack of faith after years of renouncing the church. Iya now recognizes that her responses reflected a realignment with her ori, which would eventually guide her to accept what she did not understand she was inviting into her life at the time. When one associate asked if she believed in God, she replied, "'Yes I believe in God.' But not knowing that what I was saying—it was the [Yoruba/ African] tradition. I say, 'I believe in the mountains.' I say, "That is my cathedral. I believe in the sky, the sea,' I say." During a subsequent exchange with the same member and another gentleman, the subject of church attendance emerged again. Iya defended her position by critiquing the European Christian tradition as an agent of imperialism:

> I was at [____'s] house and the same lady asked me, "So you don't go to any church?" I said, "No." She said, "So you wouldn't go to any church?" I said, "You see me, all you leave me alone. Any time I decide to go back to church I going back to the church of my ancestors." I said because at that time they [Europeans] used to go and conquer people. And so, they even have the whole of the Indian Sea named after them, because that was the Egyptian Sea, I said, "So I going back to that." And I said that most casually, just being funny. And I said, "Look all you don't bother me; I ain't taking on no religion."

Iya believes that these were just two of many experiences that signaled her move toward the path her ori chose at her moment of conception. Now decades into her role as an omorisa, she is able to share with her spiritual children a central insight often overlooked in Orisa worship: "Your Ori is the most important energy after Olodumare."[86] Devotion to the Orisa begins with devotion to one's very own Ori. Developing a self-reflexive posture of interior listening and communing with her Ori, Iya Sangowunmi has made distinct contributions to her tradition's wider matricentric focus on rebirthing and repurposing ancestral traditions, devising new structures and spheres of influence, and engaging the civic public in its efforts to institutionalize the Yoruba-Orisa religion in Trinidad. Her own first step toward doing so came when she traveled to Òyó, Nigeria, in 1999 to undergo initiation into the Yoruba priesthood.

Iya Sangowunmi's Matricentric *Nation-Building* Ministries

Honoring her calling to the priesthood of Sango, the chief priest of the oldest Sàngó society in Òyó initiated Iya into the lineage of Adéyẹmọ Ajòfà and Akínṣílọlá Ìrókò. When it was determined that Osun was the Orisa of her "ancestors' lineage," she also "received Osun." She confesses that during the seclusion period of her initiation rites, she wondered out loud, "I don't know who is going to teach me this tradition when I return to Trinidad";

immediately, she heard a voice say, "We will teach you." On returning home, she remained loyal to the promises she had made to the Orisa, and ultimately to herself, during her intense period of seclusion and reflection. She began to plan for a shrine where she could institutionalize her own conception of Trinidadian Yoruba-Orisa religion as inextricably linked to a wider global practice, especially in Nigeria, other regions of West Africa, the Americas, and the Caribbean.

The shrine opened in November 1999 with a modest membership of just five women in addition to her. The initial five were all recruited from evening self-esteem classes that Iya held at her Osun Abiadama School between 1996 and 2000.[87] The women's ages ranged from thirty-three to sixty-seven, and during the first few years of the ile's launch, they gathered on two Sundays per month to study the Yoruba religion and perform rituals. In addition, Iya has continued the Yaraba nation's nineteenth-century tradition of Saraka (thanksgiving and almsgiving) services, complemented by a full suite of ceremonial events on the ile's ritual calendar to nourish her growing membership. From January to December, Ile Eko Sango/Osun Mil'Osa (IESOM) hosts Oya Day, the Obaluaye Reconnection Festival, an Ifa Retreat and Seminar, the Shrine Ebo, the Ifa Festival, the Sango/Osun Rain Festival, a River and Sea Ceremony for Osun and Water Deities that is determined by the moon's cycle, Yemoja Day, Odoun Ojo Orisa or the Festival of Lights, African History Month, Ancestors Ebo, and the Olokun Festival, all of which enhance Iya's mission of educating the Orisa community and the wider public about the richness of the Yoruba heritage in T&T.

Through her highly publicized annual rituals and celebrations, Iya has also promoted environmental sustainability, most notably during IESOM's Sango/Osun Rain Festival (see figure 4.15). First launched in the year 1999, the Rain Festival "sensitise[s] the entire nation [to] the importance and sacredness of the rain as it represents new birth, thanksgiving, cleansing, and a preparation . . . of the annual cultivation of the land and cleansing of the rivers" by "bring[ing] people together to celebrate and propitiate the deities associated with the rain cycle."[88] During the weeks prior to the Rain Festival, Iya holds press conferences and distributes informational material to encourage wide participation. She aims to cultivate awareness among all citizens of T&T of the anthropogenic consequences of their individual and corporate behaviors toward and relationships with other earth inhabitants and the natural environment. This informational material is also designed to fulfill the wider Orisa community's mission of dispelling the lingering mystery and errors about the Orisa religion.

FIGURE 4.15 Voices of Oshun performing at IESOM's Eighth Annual Sango/Osun Rain Festival in Gasparillo, Trinidad, June 8, 2007. Choir established by Sister Sylvestine Piper De Gonzalez, leader of Oshun Shrine and one of the original mothers to serve on the board of directors of NCOE. (Courtesy of Oshun Shrine.)

"Ile Eko Sango/Osun Mil'Osa" means "Teaching House of Sango and Osun our Orisa,"[89] and Iya Sangowunmi is a priest who saturates herself in the Yoruba tradition and engages the world from a Yoruba center when teaching and sharing resources with wider publics. Yet her theology cannot be categorized easily as an ethnocentric search for African authenticity. Such judgment belies her visionary leadership in founding Harmony in Diversity (HID), an organization that not only sponsored the Dalai Lama's historic visit to T&T but also explored opportunities to promote interreligious and intercultural knowledge and cooperation among HID members and the wider nation (see figures 4.16 and 4.17). Established after Iya received revelations from the Orisa Sakpanna, Harmony in Diversity has convened representatives from Orisa, Spiritual Baptist, Indigenous, Hindu, and Muslim communities to plan activities based on "respect for interfaith doctrine."[90]

A complex spiritual mother, Iya seeks to elevate her tradition through intensive training and rigorous study. Yet she cautions omorisa that "while rituals, dance, bembes and readings are fundamental to the tradition, the holistic nature of the tradition does not end at the above. There are beautiful esoteric teachings to this noble faith that are terribly neglected [and] IESOM is a vehicle to fill the gap in the teachings of religion and philosophy." At IESOM her members learn to become Yoruba, something Iya believes they must do to tend to their ruptured souls and to reverse the process of alienation from a legacy of spiritual insight and philosophical wisdom that will ultimately free them. Toward this end, IESOM sponsors classes and trainings covering "African history, theology, philosophy, [r]ites of passage (birth, puberty, marriage, eldership, initiations, and burials), self-esteem and rehabilitation of young people (ages 5–17)." However, she has never forgotten Sakpanna's

FIGURE 4.16 Iya Sangowunmi presenting Iya Melvina Rodney to His Holiness the Dalai Lama, Tenzin Gyatso, during his visit to Trinidad and Tobago, September 15, 1995. (Courtesy of J. Patricia McLeod/Iya Sangowunmi, Ile Eko Sango/Osun Mil'Osa.)

FIGURE 4.17 Iya Melvina Rodney and Iya Sangowunmi in the company of Ambassador Chandradath Singh, Head of Mission for the High Commission of the Republic of Trinidad and Tobago, New Delhi, India, and His Holiness the Dalai Lama, Tenzin Gyatso, during his visit to Trinidad and Tobago, September 15, 1995. (Courtesy of J. Patricia McLeod/Iya Sangowunmi, Ile Eko Sango/Osun Mil'Osa.)

directive to advance harmony in diversity. Promoting "comparative religions and philosophical studies/workshops, conferences, films, songs and dance" is among IESOM's seventeen stated aims and objectives.[91]

Now in her eighties, Iya feels well placed in the ~~world~~. As the governing mother of IESOM and an earnest student/teacher of Yoruba-based religious cultures, she is still authoring texts and mentoring initiates and seekers alike, at times, from classrooms on her front lawn where she teaches weekly sessions on what she calls "Yoruba metaphysics."[92] Iya Sangowunmi is a consummate priest, life coach, educator, cultural ambassador, and nation/ nation builder, and she has performed all these roles at the institutional level. She constantly gathers children around her—the omorisa who affiliate with her ile, the actual children in her immediate family, the wider Yoruba-Orisa family, and the nation at-large. She is a mother whose personal household and spiritual shrine are extensions of one another, at which spiritual seekers, clients, and family congregate for healing, sanctuary, and life skills. Iya's matricentric spiritual-domestic abode is a transnational space that stretches across diaspora landscapes because she performs healing and restorative rituals for spiritual children in other regions of the Caribbean and the Americas who cannot travel to consult with her.

Iya's mothering is not an expression of symbolic or diffused power. She exercises actual institutional power as a shrine founder, leader, and priest with wealth and resources that permit her to undertake projects that many Orisa priests in Trinidad can only dream about.[93] Her spiritual and political ministerial work contributes to the development of both the Yoruba-Orisa *nation* and the nation of T&T. But it does more: it situates Yoruba-Orisa *nation* traditions (religious culture) as accessible traditions inspiring African contributions to a national identity and, by extension, conceptions of citizenship in the Republic of Trinidad and Tobago. Under Iya's governance, the Yoruba-Orisa *nation* aims to form citizens who are noble custodians and beneficiaries of the land and natural resources; who respect their elders, ancestors, family members, and neighbors; and who contribute to wider cultural, civic, and national institutions.

If the foundations of Western societies are located in Greek and Roman civilizations, then the foundations of Iya Sangowunmi's multicultural and multireligious Trinidadian society must be found, in part, in Yoruba cultural heritage. Castor explains it well when she writes, "Iya Sangowunmi's transnational roles and links have reinforced and re-inscribed her national identity and informed a spiritual work that is aimed at healing the nation and building a decolonized national culture."[94] Matricentric traditions, I argue, underlie a shared Africana heritage that defines Iya's "transnational roles." Motherness inspires her concern not only with spiritual citizenship or Yoruba-Orisa *nation-al* citizenship but also with the very idea of national citizenship within the Republic of Trinidad and Tobago and the responsibility of the Yoruba-Orisa *nation* to participate in cultivating a conception of the nation's ideal citizen.

Admittedly, the shared understanding of *nationhood* among nineteenth-century Yoruba descendants and other African *nations* in Trinidad is no longer universally privileged among current-day Yoruba-Orisa spiritual families. Colonial processes of conscription unquestionably habituated all Trinidadians in some way to the symbols and ontologies of the imperial state, distancing most Africans in Trinidad from their *nation* identities and affiliations.[95] However, as chapter 3 argued, a decolonial black *nationalist* consciousness superseded African *nation-al* consciousness during the struggle for independence. Transforming and expanding the Yoruba-Orisa *nation*, a decolonial black *nationalist* consciousness allowed new Yoruba-Orisa leaders such as Baba Massetungi and Iya Amoye to engage postindependence T&T as a "third space" for national-*nation-al* negotiations—a third space where primordial and civic publics overlap under the gaze of a nation.[96]

Over the past twenty years, Iya Sangowunmi's influence within and beyond the Yoruba-Orisa community has helped sustain this third space of emergent conceptualizations of citizenship imparted through the interfacing of national and *nation-al* heritages. She attends to pan-Africanist and black *nationalist* preoccupations with land, particularly *homeland*, in Trinidad and the wider African diaspora through a matricentric mode of territorializing Africa. Correspondingly, the black diaspora's tendency to denominate Africa as the "Motherland," and to express deep yearnings to reconnect with its "Motherland," invites closer inspection in the context of this discussion. Unquestionably, Afro-Trinidad has demonstrated that this manner of black desire impels religious and cultural invention and even finds archival resting places in artistic productions such as Mr. Zampty's wood carving of the African continent upon which he etched: "Afrika Ile Iya Wa Maṣe Gbagbe" or "Africa Our Motherland/the Land of Our Mothers Don't Ever Forget" (see figure 3.21). Iya certainly has not forgotten. Similar to other diasporic Yoruba spiritual families, Iya Sangowunmi's current conceptualization of her headquarters performs the work of territorializing, particularly Africa's Yorùbáland, the fundament of Orisa heritage and culture in Trinidad.

When Tracey and I returned to Trinidad in 2013 after several years, innovations were evident in Iya Sangowunmi's twenty-first-century institutionalization of Yoruba sovereignty and *nationhood*, linking her mode of mothering, of *nation-building*, to the earliest preoccupations of nineteenth-century Yarabas. Matricentric pan-Africanism has led to many changes at IESOM, including its natural habitat's official denomination as "Little Oyo," signaling Iya's understanding of her shrine grounds as a microcosm of Old Ọ̀yọ́ (Nigeria/West Africa) within her nation-state of T&T. Her decision to erect a welcome sign to this effect is a gesture similar to that of Massetunji who suspends T&T's national flag next to his EOE flag and Orisa *nation* flags. The inclusion of "Trinidad" on Iya's sign is not inconsequential; it doubles as an announcement of Trinidad's incorporation of Little Oyo within its national boundaries (see figure 4.18).

Whereas citizens of Oyotunji African Village in North America establish a dividing boundary line between the political imaginary of the United States and its own Yoruba political imaginary, Iya does the opposite, declaring instead that *nation-al* belonging and national belonging are compatible and realizable in her multicultural, multiethnic, multireligious Trinidad. The IESOM members are

FIGURE 4.18 Iyalode Sangowunmi's official welcome sign indicating that Ile Eko Sango/ Osun Mil'Osa is located on the sacred grounds of Little Oyo, Trinidad. (Photo by author.)

citizens of both the spiritual *nation* of Little Oyo and the political nation-state of T&T. As the founder and spiritual head of Little Oyo, Iya's matricentric authority does not extend as far as that of the rulers of the Old Ọ̀yọ́ Empire, but it exists nonetheless in her governance of IESOM and her mothering of a growing number of spiritual children. At the same time, Iya's authority officially transgresses the boundaries of religious life, for Nigerian Yorùbá authorities have honored her with the title of Iyalode, which some in Trinidad translate as "Mother to the ~~world~~" or "~~world~~ Mother." In this capacity, Iya Sangowunmi is empowered to govern not only a religious community but also a polity—to minister to spiritual and political citizens (see figure 4.19).

The concept of "Iyalode" has been translated differently across a range of colonial and indigenous sources. However, many scholars describe the institution as a title-holding tradition that emerged in Ibadan, a city and nucleus of power whose birth coincided with the "Yorùbá wars" of the nineteenth century. Although no reliable English translation exists for the term, it was one of the many Yorùbá conventions that institutionalized the customary connections between spiritual and political jurisdictions that women-mothers who have held the title in Nigeria took for granted.[97] No one could doubt

FIGURE 4.19 (*Left to right*) Iya Eintou Pearl Springer, Joan Yuille-Williams, and Iya Sangowunmi J. Patricia McLeod at a public service in celebration of the life of Baba Erin Folami at Nelson Mandela Park, St. James, Trinidad, March 29, 2018. (Courtesy of Maria Nunes, photographer.)

that Iya Sangowunmi earned the distinction of Iyalode in Trinidad, a title increasingly being bestowed by Nigerian Yorùbá civil and religious leaders on Trinidad's accomplished mothers within the Orisa tradition.

Whether her position is defined as an office of governorship and diplomacy related to women's societies, external affairs, or public/civic authority within particular municipalities or regions, Iya Sangowunmi has exhibited leadership in all these arenas. She has counseled women and provided resources to support their holistic development. With her support, they confront the world as thinkers, knowledge bearers, and leaders who, like her, are institution builders and whose contributions sustain a third space of *nation-al*/national belonging for omorisa in T&T. She has strengthened existing and developed new Yoruba-Orisa structures and ritual traditions supporting marriage and family, education, sports, the arts, environmental awareness, ecofriendly citizenship, and civic responsibility. She was among the first cadre of priests in Trinidad to obtain a government-issued license to marry persons in the Orisa tradition, and she held Trinidad's first Orisa wedding ceremony on IESOM's grounds in 2002, just a few years after the passing of the Orisa Marriage Act (see figures 4.20 and 4.21).[98]

FIGURE 4.20 First official Orisa wedding ceremony in Trinidad, Ile Eko Sango/Osun Mil'Osa, July 2002. (Photo by author.)

FIGURE 4.21 Iya Sangowunmi, assisted by omorisa Aku Kontar, officiates Trinidad's first official Orisa wedding ceremony, Ile Eko Sango/Osun Mil'Osa, July 2002. (Photo by author.)

Iya's shrine grounds, where Yoruba prayers, powers, and protocols unite omorisa in their celebration of a young couple's marriage vows, comfortably expand into a third space where primordial and civic publics periodically bear witness to an emergent *nation-al*/national citizenship. IESOM's annual Rain Festival provides one of the most generative opportunities for the cultivation of *third-space citizens*. Throughout its solemn rites, cultural celebrations, and renewed oaths, representatives and members of the civic public enter and engage IESOM's primordial universe. No longer a counter-public determined to penetrate national and civic centers of power with demands for religious freedom, national recognition, and equal access to resources and opportunities extended to Christian, Muslim, and Hindu religious bodies in T&T, IESOM and other Yoruba-Orisa iles can and do operate as centers of merging publics and new declarations of holistic citizenship.[99]

Louis Homer, a heritage adviser from the Ministry of National Diversity and Social Integration (MNDSI) of the Republic of Trinidad and Tobago, for example, delivered opening remarks on behalf of the Honorable Clifton De Coteau, minister of NDSI, at IESOM's Fourteenth Annual Rain Festival (August 9–11, 2013)—championing the festival and, by extension, the Yoruba-Orisa tradition as a prominent symbol of national values. A compelling instance of thoughtful reflections on the relationship between primordial and civic publics—between *nation-al* and national citizens in Trinidad and Tobago—De Coteau's speech is worth discussing at length.

He began by affirming the equal importance of national holidays commemorating African emancipation from racial slavery (August 1) and independence from British colonialism (August 31) for *all* citizens of Trinidad and Tobago. Appealing to the shared sense of liberty both these events guaranteed the people of T&T, he subtly reminded the audience that custodians of minoritized religions are still vulnerable to trespasses on their civil rights. His acknowledgment of T&T's unfinished emancipation and incomplete independence was apropos for the occasion, because every person seated in the audience knew that the Orisa community, in particular, had long struggled for the "freedom to belong . . . pray . . . believe and enjoy the liberty of living" in T&T.[100]

De Coteau's ministerial obligation of fostering "ecclesiastical" diversity conveys enough about the historic privilege afforded denominational Christianity at the expense of other religious bodies. However, his remarks did more than affirm the inclusion of other religious bodies, namely Yoruba-Orisa, into the life and spiritual strivings of the nation. De Coteau acknowledged the Yoruba-Orisa *nation* as a civil religion, invoking Sango, and lauding the Rain Festival as a national festival whose promotion of nature's ecological design is a blueprint for upholding the republic's most treasured ideals of governance, citizenship, and patriotism. First, he identified "good statesmanship and governance" as one of the core ethical mandates associated with Sango:

> The Sango Rain Festival calls for the invocation of Sango, the Yoruba divinity of fire, heat, thunder, lightning and electricity; the belief in salvation from our enemies, overcoming difficulties and good statesmanship and governance. It is also an occasion to bring our community together to celebrate rebirth, commitment, understanding and responsibility in a physical and spiritual way. It is also a period of reflection, thanksgiving, cleansing and preparation. It also signals the annual cultivation of lands and the inundation of the rivers, which bring the necessary alluvial deposits to river banks and seashores. According to Yoruba teaching, it was Olodumare who made the rain to water the earth, and, therefore, this festival is held primarily to ask the blessings of the deities.

De Coteau then attached his office's mission to the ethical practice of good governance. Quoting the 1995 Copenhagen Declaration of Social Development, he described how good governance ensures "social integration" or "the process fostering societies that are stable, safe, and just and that are based on the promotion and protection of all human rights as well as on nondiscrimination, tolerance, respect for diversity, equality of opportunity, solidarity, security and participation of all people, including disadvantaged and vulnerable groups and persons." In endorsing these standards, De Coteau insisted his "ministry affirms the unity of a people," a unity made possible only when all citizens are free to exercise their rights and to participate in a just society, including the right to religious liberty:

> Such is the powerful and potent message that can take us to our desired destination. . . . So as we celebrate our freedom, our independence, we encourage the freedom of all our citizens—freedom of worship, freedom from prejudice and discrimination, freedom to believe, freedom to pray. And this is the reason for the Ministry of National Diversity and Social Integration—to enforce the inclusivity (that means everybody) of all the people in Trinidad and Tobago to rededicate ourselves based on the theme of . . . the love of liberty. . . . Sango is the embodiment of spiritual illumination. And Orisa believes that in the same way that lightning can bring light to the darkest night, so too can Sango bring instant spiritual

illumination. We call to him today as the master of strategy to illuminate our strengths and to aid in attacking our weaknesses to allow us to obtain our . . . true destiny.

After professing Sango's power to illumine a path toward collective strength and national renewal, he went on to "pay tribute to [the late] Iya Melvina Rodney," whom he called "one of the leading pioneers of this celebration." De Coteau then stunningly acclaimed the Orisa nation as the embodiment of the republic's collective will and purpose, and he recognized Sango as a national sacred symbol:

To those present here today, you are symbols of our journey towards truth, love and togetherness. You represent the ultimate goal of the search for spirituality and multiplicity. I thank you all for your courage and convictions. And the fact that you are the ones to revolutionize our independence, our patriotism, our celebration of Sango. And as we celebrate our traditions, I pray that we maintain open minds, open arms and open hearts to the power of possibility of unity in a greater purpose, one of which is divine, eternal and an embodiment of love.

Affirmed through a string of possessives—"*our* independence, *our* patriotism, *our* celebration of Sango . . . *our* traditions"— T&T's third space of new national/national citizenship, De Coteau insisted, is the Orisa community's own habitation, its revolutionary gift to the nation.

Executing his ministerial duty to promote national diversity and social integration, De Coteau's concluding remarks addressed his action plan for memorializing T&T's Orisa heritage and advancing the Orisa community's most important public-facing objective of educating the nation about its history and religious culture. "Let me give you the assurance," he said,

that all Sango sites identified in Trinidad and Tobago will be classified in the near future by the National Trust as sites of interest and later as heritage sites, all subject to your approval. . . . In addition, I want to let you know that research into Sango movement is being conducted by . . . the Ministry of National Diversity and Social Integration, and in due course a brochure will be produced with your help on the Sango movement [Yoruba-Orisa tradition] for distribution to schools and other institutions of learning.

In all my years of attending public Orisa events in Trinidad, I had never heard a speech quite like De Coteau's. I had witnessed illustrious politicians deliver opening remarks at public Orisa events, even gesturing toward civil religion in the case of former prime minister Panday.[101] However, none fused the nation's civic public with the Orisa *nation's* primordial public, signaling Orisa's transition from folk to civil religion. Certainly, other Orisa shrines, including Egbe Onisin Eledumare and Eniyan Wa, have fostered third-space citizenship ideals in and beyond the Orisa palais. That Little Oyo's Rain Festival won such praise under the leadership of an Orisa mother who is highly regarded for institutionalizing her contributions to citizen formation through educational, religious, cultural, entrepreneurial, and other missions, however, is no surprise.

Iya's womanist Pan-Africanism inspires her to harmonize rather than polarize *nation-al* and national belonging, making Little Oyo one of T&T's most pregnant third spaces of citizenship. Yet her ritual innovations and territorialization of Africa allow space for more than just a new conception and exercise of citizenship. Turning to one of the most solemn Orisa rituals ever performed in Trinidad, a ritual that epitomizes the African diasporic project of *territorial poetics*, provides an opportunity to resume discussing the nature of black religion in the African diaspora and to consider the significance of the authoritative resolve an Orisa mother such as Iya Sangowunmi exhibits in shaping Orisa theology in the twenty-first century.[102]

Mother as God: Iya Sangowunmi's Womanist ~~Worldmaking~~

Iya Sangowunmi will be remembered for many "firsts," but this "first" tops all others and invites theoretical deepening of Charles Long's conception of the nature of black religion. On January 6, 2015, Iya made history in the Yoruba-Orisa *nation* in T&T when she elevated Iya Rodney to the status of an Orisa. During our visit with her in August 2013, she had told Tracey and me of her plans to assemble the Orisa community for a celebration that would honor Iya Rodney's invisible transition from ancestor to Orisa, a clear illustration of the 400 + 1 theological principle discussed in chapter 3.

Careful reflection and meditation led Iya to call for a new phase of legacy-building at the level of localized Orisa mythography and religious memory. There was no better place to begin, she thought, than with the womanist project of literally making "Mother God." Tracey and I were observing and recording her class, "Orunmila: The First Metaphysician," and I began to reflect on how much farther Iya had moved into the terrain of Yoruba-Orisa theology, philosophy, cosmology, and ethics since my first encounter with her at the Osun Abiadama School in 1998.[103]

Orisa devotees in the diaspora, she maintains, have not sufficiently penetrated the depths of their tradition to understand its philosophical timelessness and the scientific knowledge it adumbrates. She has always wondered, for example, why perhaps the most widespread Yoruba creation narrative includes details about Obatala, the Orisa responsible for molding ~~human beings~~, descending from the abode above on a chain. Iya explained,

> To me they really put it superficially. But what is the chain they're talking about? It's the DNA chain that identifies each one of us ... to make us different but still part of. So when they say he [Obatala] came down to make ~~human beings~~ on that chain. ... We have not studied our doctrine like how they've done in the Bhagavad Gita, the Torah, the Bible, or any of the books, and I think, that is where we are lacking. This man attempted to bring something ... Maulana Karenga. ... He was one who tried to put a different spin on the Odus.

Iya was calling for a new era of formal theological reflection and historical criticism of the Ifa sacred corpus, particularly within the African diaspora:

> I have asked people, why it is that we have Ifa, we have Orisa, and we have not done any patakis [stories about the Orisa] from Trinidad or from Tobago. ... I feel we have not done anything for the tradition. We have not done anything for ourselves. Tell me why the tradition is here nearly a thousand years or more ... and we do not have an Orisa from Trinidad and Tobago. And we have survived slavery, we have emancipation. Why it is that we do not have any Orisa here in Trinidad? When you talk about the Orisa, you talk about Ogun, Osayin, and so on. Who do we have? Look at what has happened to Haiti, after Haiti did so much, after Haiti paved and carved the way for us. Who did we worship from Haiti? ... Give me one! Let me start to build on them because we call on Nigeria, and listen, don't get me wrong. I'm not saying Nigeria, Togo and so [on] [implying that she's not dismissing these African sources of Yoruba knowledge]. But you know what Baba Wándé [Abímbólá] told me? And when people talking to you, the things they not saying is the things you must listen to. I got Sango, Osun, and one hand of Ifa in Nigeria. So I said, "Baba Wándé [Abímbólá], why I had to do my initiation here?" He say, "You didn't have to do your initiation here." He say, "It's because of the road that you are walking. There would be nobody in Trinidad to do the initiation, because you had to get from Sango." He said, "But in truth and in fact, it is always better to do your initiation on your home ground because [there] you have the strength of all

your ancestors and all the people in your intimate community." You know why I stopped telling people that? Because people thought that I went to Nigeria, and I initiated and I don't want them to go to Nigeria. I say, "You could take your money and go to Nigeria, but initiate here so you get your strength from here!" Because Baba Wándé, a babalawo, the Àwíṣẹ for all them years, to tell me that, it can't just fall on deaf ears!

Iya was unequivocal: Omorisa in Trinidad were long overdue for a new god, and if Haiti's lineage of localized Lwa had not inspired others in Trinidad to take the poetic license to elevate their deserving ancestors into the ranks of the Orisa, then "the things" Baba Wándé was "not saying" were the things she would "listen to."

Scholars of African religion have noted many instances in which it seems God does not make people as much as people make God.[104] Indeed, most omorisa in the diaspora learn very early on that persons can intensify their concentrations of ashé and become Orisa. Even those unfamiliar with the verses of Ifá that address the topic have been introduced to narratives about Sango, who had lived as a person on earth before attaining divinity. A section from a poem in the Odu Okanranadasaee, for example, can be read as a suggestion that persons should aspire to become Orisa:

> Orunmila said "it is persons that become Orisa."
> I also say it is persons that become Orisa.
> They said: "That Ogun that you see, was a person who was wise and
>   very powerful;
> That is why Ogun is propitiated.
> That Oosala that you are looking at,
> Was a person who was wise and very powerful;
> That is why Oosala is propitiated."
> Therefore, persons who are wise are those that we propitiate.[105]

For two years, Tracey and I waited to see if a ~~human being~~ in Trinidad would become an Orisa. Finally, Iya Sangowunmi confirmed that the elevation festival was no longer an idea but a realized event: Iya Rodney had become another Mother God in the Yoruba-Orisa religion, launching a new chapter of womanist theological and ritual construction at Little Oyo and in T&T. Her elevation illuminates another salient aspect of Iyalode Sangowunmi's spiritual and political authority (see figure 4.22). Iyalode is sometimes translated as "mother of the homeland," a most fitting title for Iya. Her refusal to accept what has been refused to her and other African descendants

IYA GBOGBO
'Elizabeth Melvina Rodney'
Elevation Festival

Date: Tuesday 6th January 2015
Time: 1am - 6pm

Venue: I.E.S.O.M - Sacred Ground of Little Oyo, Shrines Garden, Upper Gasparillo Road, Santa Cruz, Trindad.

FIGURE 4.22 Ile Eko Sango/Osun Mil'Osa's public announcement of Iyalorisa Elizabeth Melvina Rodney's Elevation Ceremony. (Courtesy of Ile Eko Sango/Osun Mil'Osa.)

through the making of Orisa religious persons, coupled with her sacralization of Africa in denominating IESOM's headquarters the territory of Little Oyo, positions Iya Sangowunmi as a homeland mother.[106] With these and other measures, she has undertaken what Long calls the black religious task of the *second re-creation*, of reinventing creation in the midst of commodification and captivity. Her praxes of *motherness* reveal the distinct work of black religion—to disrupt the *otherness* that inheres when African descendants are naturalized as heathens, cargo, slaves, and noncitizens, while also penetrating black *otherness* to access and unfold its re-creative potentials.

Addressing the black diasporic impetus to return to the first creation—to the "motherland"—Iyalode Sangowunmi founded a homeland. Yet no homeland is ready for habitation without a homeland deity. So Iya established its connection to a Mother God whom *she* apotheosized, a young Orisa whose navel-string is buried beneath a sacred tree in Trinidad and whose thunder stones from the hidden hand of Ma Diamond, a native-born African, are also interred under the earthen floor of her historic Orisa palais.[107] Orisa Iya Rodney's subsequent manifestation at Orisa ceremonies only confirms that she is pleased with the community's efforts to intensify her concentration of ashé in the invisible domain.[108] She will likely be pleased with something else Iya Sangowunmi is pursuing. Inspired by Karenga's efforts "to put a different spin on the Odus," Iya's contributions to Trinidadian and other Yoruba-Orisa families across the Caribbean and the Americas will soon encompass the canonization of folklore from Trinidad, Jamaica, Haiti, The Bahamas, Louisiana, Georgia, South Carolina—"all over the black diaspora." Iya's perspective is that the Odu themselves are universal; however, the verses are culturally specific. Omorisa in the diaspora deserve not only native-born and bred Mother-Orisa but also sacred scriptures that reveal wisdoms and values from their local cultures. To achieve this aim, Iya is collecting diasporic orature and literature with didactic content similar to the didactic verses in the Ifa corpus. Her objective is to incorporate them into the Odu by transliterating verses born from West African contexts into diasporic alphabets, a move Long would champion given his "[interest] in other [non-Christian] forms of religion in the history of black communities—as those forms are contained in their folklore music, style of life, and so on."[109]

Iya Sangowunmi's womanist ~~worldmaking~~ —re-creating God (Orisa Iya Rodney), sacred land (Little Oyo), sacred scripture, and sacred evocations of ashé (the omorisa she is authorized to initiate)—exemplifies the role of religion in black caretaking traditions of the African diaspora. Hers is not an escapist project or an attempt to flee from the world that Afropessimists understand to be designed by humans at the expense of blacks who are always stationed within reach of its operations yet still outside it. Iya's ~~worldmaking~~ is a cooperative venture among invisible Powers and visible powers. Thus, what I am labeling the ~~world~~ is a set of emplacements established by entities, families, lineages, and *nations* with different concentrations of ashé, yet made habitable through Iya Sangowunmi's motherness. In this way, Iya's ~~worldmaking~~ is anagrammatical because motherness, as a modality, attests to the possibility of existing without the world and its organizing grammar. Motherness bears witness to the possibility of exceeding the grammar of anti-Africanness. Iya's ~~world~~, then, is a womanist anagrammatical site of care that, to quote Sharpe, "exists as an [opaque] index of violability and also potentiality."[110] Long's concept of the opaque punctuates Sharpe's insightful theorization and assumes a dual function. First, it signals the nontransparency of Iya's ~~world~~ that the Western (human) project of civilization rendered knowable and thus violable through a repertoire of obscene symbols and significations. Second, it indicates the unknowability of her ~~world's~~ concrete meaning and value whose potentiality lies in the very fact that it does not have an operative grammar within the world. Yet Iya's ~~world~~ does have a structure that poetically unfolds as an interruptive invention beside and against the world, against what Tyrone Palmer aptly terms a "metonym for colonial modernity."[111]

Another way to comprehend the effects of Iya's womanist caretaking and its potentiality is possible when we analyze how motherness testifies to modes of belonging that do not require the infrastructure of being in the world. Taking Long's interpretation of black religion to its logical beginning allows us to understand motherness as a mode of "archaic religious consciousness" beyond what Long anticipated when he identified archaic religious consciousness with black religious consciousness. Long argued that black people have had to re-create their origins and draw power from their re-creations—their new, sacred, nation-al beginnings, to refuse what has been refused to them:[112] "The meaning of the involuntary structure or the opacity of the religious symbol has within this community held together eschatological hopes and the archaic religious consciousness. In both secular and religious groups, new expressions such as Moorish Temple, Black Jews, Black Muslims retain an archaic structure in their religious consciousness and this structure is never quite settled for it is there as a datum to be deciphered in the context of their present experience."[113]

Iya's deciphering of the "datum" revolutionizes what the concept of homeland is for Trinidad's Orisa community and the wider African diaspora. No less mobilized by a desire for home than black men who have led nationalist Hebraic and Muslim movements, Iya Sangowunmi liberates the black diaspora's "homeland" from its patriarchal nation-state limitations. From Iya's standpoint, homeland is in Africa, but it is also in Trinidad. By recognizing this reality, the importance of honoring the land where the Yoruba nation repurposed its heritages and transmitted them to posterity, omorisa in Trinidad (and elsewhere) can reimagine their Orisa and themselves.[114] Fashioning a new expression of God in the image of an Orisa Mother whom the community had known intimately on earth, Iya Sangowunmi, in her role as homeland mother, introduced to Afro-Trinidadians a motherness mode of loving the Spirit, of nation-building, of motherland-ing.[115]

Iya's *motherland-ing* extends a powerful terrain from which to understand the decolonial effects of black religion and black love. Womanists and feminists across Africana contexts have affirmed the central role of love in womanist spirituality, theology, and ethics, as well as black feminist politics.[116] Layli Maparyan, in particular, takes a synthetic approach in *The Womanist Idea*. Sifting through lineages of womanist thought across three decades, she determines that a focus on love is the central unifying feature of womanism. Womanism works *affectively* rather than through oppositional politics to change hearts, minds, and worlds. Although Maparyan underscores the close kinship between womanism and black feminism, she emphasizes their differentiating approaches to social change. I appreciate and agree with much of Maparyan's analysis. However, with Alice Walker's declaration in mind that a womanist is a black feminist, I regard womanisms and black feminisms along continuums that do overlap.

The many analytical and conceptual resonances among womanist and black feminist thought are hard to ignore even across theological and secular scholarship. To take one example, Christian womanist theologian Delores Williams's excavation of a womanist tradition and biblical hermeneutic of "survival/quality of life" emerged once she decentered the black male liberation tradition that James Cone, J. Deotis Roberts, and other black male theologians expounded. As she listened to voices in deeper shades of black and in vernacular traditions from slavery to the present, she identified a long legacy of African American appropriation of the biblical character Hagar, the Egyptian woman enslaved by Abraham and Sarah. Hagar's captivity in the ancient Near Eastern world mirrored black women's captivity in "the belly of the [modern Western] world."[117] Hagar's African identity, enslavement, sexual and reproductive violation, sexual and labor surrogacy, fugitivity in the wilderness, and single motherhood, Williams observed, formed a fitting biblical narrative to guide her theological reflection on God's relationship with black women. Placing black women at the center of Christian theological construction shifted Williams's focus from the Exodus narrative, which was paradigmatic in black male liberation theology. In resurrecting Hagar's story as a salient resource for womanist God-talk, she discovered a God of survival/quality of life, rather than the God of liberation her male predecessors associated with the Exodus event.[118]

Drawing insights from Hortense Spillers's seminal theories on black flesh and black motherhood, Saidiya Hartman makes analogous moves in her scholarship. Decentering a masculinist focus on black radical politics, she poses similar black feminist/womanist questions to her interlocutors, W. E. B. Du Bois and C. L. R. James, querying, "Where does the *impossible domestic* fit into the general strike? What is the text of her insurgency and the genre of her refusal? What visions of the future world encourage her to run, or propel her flight? Or is she, as Spillers observes, a subject still awaiting her verb?" Hartman ends up where Williams does, arguing that although the black mother's "labor remains marginal or neglected in Black men's narratives of black insurgency, resistance and refusal," her love and her caretaking, specifically her "strategies of endurance and subsistence," have made black survival possible.[119] Hartman and Williams, as well as other black feminists and womanists, witness this enduring motherness tradition through varied discursive modes, but as witnesses, their testimonies evidence they are seeing and analyzing the same modes of inhabitation, of black mothers "making a way out of no way" for themselves and their entire race.[120]

The point of this example is not to efface important distinctions between womanism and black feminism. Womanism's unequivocal spiritual orientation, for instance, certainly distinguishes it from many expressions of black feminism. However, the resonances between the two perspectives are plentiful, including a long tradition of black women's commitment to what black feminist theorist Jennifer Nash calls "love politics." Expanding womanist religious thought to encompass reflection on motherness traditions in African Caribbean religious cultures exposes important overlaps between womanism and black feminism while elaborating how motherness, whether "coerced or freely given, is the black heart of [African Caribbean] social poesis, of making and relation."[121]

The motherness-inspired love politics of Iyalode Sangowunmi and other mothers in Trinidad resonates with womanism's affective and *nationalist* orientation so much that I view them as indistinguishable. Even while preferring to annotate womanism's affective work with the nongendered concept of motherness, it is important to engage womanist discourse and, for that matter, black feminist scholarship on the subject of love through the interpretive concepts they advance. A careful reflection on such concepts allows room to emphasize motherness traditions in womanism and to expand on my affective treatment of Africana religious *nationalism* in chapter 3.

Engaging what Patricia Hill Collins, Cheryl Saunders, Jennifer Nash, and others have identified as *nationalist* themes in Alice Walker's foundational womanist definition, my consideration of womanist/motherness-inspired love politics theorizes dimensions of black affect that remain unaddressed in current discussions linking black feminism and Afropessimism.[122] Yoruba-Orisa motherness-inspired love politics opens a third theoretical space beyond binary framings of racial ontologies and black liberation strategies (e.g., as either *nationalist* or universalist; identitarian *or* affective).[123] In chapter 3, I detached affective politics and identity politics (as reductively deployed in mainstream discussions) to criticize the collapsing of black religious *nationalisms* under theories of imagined communities, romantic Afrocentricity, and nostalgia. Here, I suggest pairing affective politics and identity politics (as the Combahee River Collective originally conceived it)[124] to reflect on how black religion has allowed African-descended people in the Caribbean and the Americas to observe modes of belonging that exceed the logics of whiteness.[125]

I consider how affective politics and identity politics merge to underscore something scholars often miss when conceptualizing black diasporic *nationalisms*. In response to the predicament of black involuntary presence in the Caribbean and the Americas, or what Tyrone Palmer identifies as blacks' *"felt antagonism to the World,"* black diasporic longing to *be at home* produces a powerful affect I name "heritage love."[126] Black diasporic longing resides in a complex emotional repertoire stimulated by "needs of love, belonging, joy and pride" as they relate to heritage and identity.[127] José Muñoz describes well the affective environment I privilege in my theorization of heritage love. His concept of "affective difference" references "the ways . . . various historically coherent groups 'feel' differently and navigate the material world on a different emotional register."[128] Scholars of black religion can bring theoretical substance to an interdisciplinary analysis of black emotional registers, especially because "affect theory as an academic discourse has yet to substantially account for the problematic of blackness, the particular affective dispositions that emerge in reaction to processes of racialization and racial subjugation."[129] But, to be sure, heritage love is not a departure from "the [Atlantic] hold." Nor is it a "fantasy of flight."[130] Rather, it is yet another means of refusing what has been refused, a technology of refusal housed within black religious consciousness that allows blacks to (1) orient themselves along more viable paths toward authenticity and sociality and (2) dispense with the futile project of attempting to be seen and accepted as human in a world where human identity is contingent on the white Western heritage of African/black slavemaking and the codification of black captivity and suffering. The Yorùbá commonly aver "*ọjà l'ayé*" (the world is a marketplace), a suitable adage for the world that materialized from modernity's slave markets. In these commercial spaces carnal desires brutally transubstantiated Yorùbá and other dark *nations* into both fungible commodities and producers of commodities. Whether as chattel property or indentured laborers, by virtue of their origins, they all partook in the singularity of the black slave and the fantasies white captors invented about them.

Despite centuries of the white man's burden on full display, there is no gainsaying that Christian belonging, human belonging, and world belonging have all been refused to blacks. The Christian West's sweeping racist accounts of African ethnogenesis, and the ontologically stratifying theological narratives spun from racist biblical hermeneutics, sacralized black people's racialization and racial subjugation.[131] Heritage love, one of the most prevailing affective dispositions shared across time and space among the descendants of Christian slavery in the West and its manifestation in black religious consciousness, is irrepressible. Post-Black Power Orisa families mobilized the wider Orisa community to disrupt the reproduction of citizenship through Christian conventions because of their dogged heritage love. Granted, a sense of emergency and a yearning for resolution can and often do undergird heritage love, leading to ideological rigidity and policing of blackness/Africanness. Shifting our gaze from those commonly cited missteps, however, brings into view uninvestigated phenomena in studies of Africana religious *nationalisms*.

In black religion, archaic religious consciousness engenders black expressions of heritage love. I therefore prefer to conceive of heritage love and *nation-building* politics not as reactionary but as a modality that rescues and restores the psyche and the soul as much as the material body. The terrain of heritage love, in particular, demonstrates that "emotions are not simply 'within' or 'without' [but that] emotions *do things*, and they align individuals with communities . . . through the very intensity of their attachments."[132] The feelings that issue from heritage love contend with the ubiquity of black captivity, and with the false promises that authentic redemption rests with (the colonial) Christ because the question is bound to emerge: "Redemption from what?" This nagging question has organized Africana religious responses to captivity across time and contexts, as it did for Bishop Desmond Tutu when he wrote in 1978,

> With part of himself, [the African] has been compelled to pay lip service to Christianity as understood, expressed and preached by the white man. But with an ever greater part of himself, a part he has often been ashamed to acknowledge openly and which he has struggled to repress, he has felt that his Africanness was being violated. The white man's largely cerebral religion was hardly touching the depths of his African soul; he was being

redeemed of sins he did not believe he had committed; he was given answers, and often splendid answers, to questions he had not asked.[133]

The affective terrains that Yoruba-Orisa spiritual families have established in post–Black Power Trinidad free omorisa from questions they and their ancestors had never asked. They release omorisa from ideological captivity to colonial logics and facilitate their divestment from the rewards of Christian citizenship and simultaneous investment in black opacity (i.e., new evocations of ashé).

Although the ~~worldmaking~~ powers of black religious consciousness and motherness are not necessarily directed toward dismantling what Afropessimists have incisively identified as the structural antagonism between blacks and nonblacks, they do establish a poetics of belonging that allows blacks to miraculously and uncooperatively endure the effects of that antagonism.[134] They create an *otherworld* that opens space for a landless inhabitation of homeland and establish anagrammatical religious modalities for thinking about diaspora. Through praxes of motherness, Iya Rodney, Iya Eintou Springer, Iya Molly Ahye, Iya Amoye, Mother Joan, Iya Sangowunmi, and other Yoruba-Orisa mothers in Trinidad demonstrate how the Yoruba-Orisa religion, similar to other African heritage religions, cultivates modes of dwelling that inspire devotees to focus not on *being* but on *belonging*, which involves *going*—a kind of spiritual circulation that orders creative and destructive powers and qualifies the nature of life, death, afterlife, and rebirth. *Where do I belong* and *who are my kin* are more salient questions than *who am I*, questions that inspire meditations on *becoming* rather than *being*, on *spiritual collectivity* rather than *human subjectivity*.

Orisa mothers prompt their communities to answer these two pivotal questions by accessing powers within and beyond themselves. Their praxes of motherness inspire institution-building, spiritual diplomacy, political activism, and theological and ritual innovation. They also establish habitations of going, becoming, and belonging that are ~~worldmaking~~ and motherlanding. These ~~worldmaking~~ creactivities are themselves ways of tarrying with otherworldliness not only in relation to the world but also in terms of the afterlife, the habitation where ancestral and unborn potentialities reside and become accessible to omorisa to help them uncooperatively endure the workings of an antiblack/African world.[135] During moments that arrive and depart like flashes of the spirit, tarrying with ancestral and unborn afterlife potentialities allows omorisa to exceed a different afterlife—the afterlife of slavery/colonialism.[136] Iyalode Sangowunmi, the quintessential homeland mother/founder of Little Oyo and creator of Trinidad's homeland Mother God, especially brings into focus a grounded womanist otherworldliness that my concept of motherland-ing aims to convey.

Groundings with My Mothers

Yoruba-Orisa mothers (and Spiritual Baptist mothers) have a long tradition of *grounding*,[137] of claiming spots of ground for spiritual fixation.[138] Their Orisa stools are anchored in earthen grounds; they speak of "putting orisa on the ground" when consecrating their shrines; their initiation and purification rites involve "going on the ground"; they bury thunder stones and other sacred symbols of the Orisa in the ground; and they pour libations and position many ancestral and Orisa offerings on the ground. Omorisa know there is life underground. Assemblies of ancestors, Orisa, and unborn spirits impregnate the earth with world-destroying and ~~worldmaking~~ possibilities. If "the plantation is the belly of the world[,] *Partus sequitur ventrem*—the child follows the belly," as Saidiya Hartman rightly establishes, then the terrestrial belly is the gestational habitation par excellence, the ~~world~~ of the Orisa and other unseen energies, as taught by Yoruba-Orisa mothers.[139] The child (*omorisa*) *follows this belly too.*

Among omorisa in Trinidad her intimate name is *Mama La Terre* (Mother Earth/Onile). Groundings and other sacred/territorial poetics that honor Mama La Terre and fortify creation's kinship with the primordial terrestrial belly emerge among a landless black people whose preoccupation with land invests the image of Africa "with historic and religious possibilities."[140] Black landlessness is "the afterlife of slavery." In a peculiar way, black landlessness is a haunted *place* of nonbelonging, the most fertile province of Africana religious imagination and invention in the Caribbean and the Americas. I suspect this *afterlife* is the nonnegotiable criterion that Africana womanists in the United States have in mind when they argue that womanism and feminism are essentially different theoretical perspectives with distinct ontological origins and conceptual genealogies.[141]

Addressing the black diasporic longing to be at home—the black longing for the Motherland—Iyalode Sangowunmi expands Afro-Trinidad's abiding tradition of spiritual grounding. Her ministry is a motherland-ing manifestation of heritage love. Territorializing Africa, localizing Mother Orisa, honoring the sacred ground/Mother Earth on special festival days, demythologizing colonial history through creative interpretations of Yoruba-Orisa originary narratives, and even *re-versing* the Odu with folklore from the black diaspora, prepare the ground for continued motherness innovations at Little Oyo and beyond.[142]

Tracey Hucks concluded her study of Yoruba traditions in North America by noting that "in the twentieth century, black religious *nationalism* became the space in which American social history, redefinitions of humanity, and divine meaning converged." She argued, "African Americans in North America . . . became not simply practitioners of a fixed historic Yoruba but major players in a dynamic contemporary global reorientation of orisa religious tradition," acknowledging how "in a tradition that reveres 400 + 1 orisa divinities, there is . . . room for African American improvisation and perhaps even the contribution of its own North American . . . orisa (Marie Laveau, Nina Simone, Harriet Tubman, James Baldwin, Nat Turner, and so forth) to the orisa pantheon."[143]

Iyalode Sangowunmi has certainly established such a reorienting tradition in Trinidad and Tobago, substantiating Zakiyyah Iman Jackson's argument that "black mater holds the potential to transform the terms of reality and feeling, therefore [restorying and] rewriting the conditions of possibility of the empirical."[144] Iya is a child of Sango, but she performs the motherland-ing primordial work of Obatala. The Great Orisa who suspended a long dangling chain from the abode above and slowly descended it, only to behold a watery abyss at the bottom of the chain, indeed has a counterpart in Iyalode Sangowunmi. Obatala had traveled with a snail shell filled with sand and emptied the shell into the mysterious waters, which diffused and hardened into dry ground.[145] When Iya insisted that the Yoruba-Orisa tradition needs new Odus, new Orisa, and new interpretations of received Odus, she offered the example of Obatala's chain, submitting that it was none other than the DNA chain of life's genetic code. She did not mention the ground, but perhaps a novel reading of an old Odu is forthcoming from Trinidad with diaspora verses that imagine the primordial ground as a *motherlanding* and Obatala's unfastened chain as a sign of creation's release from commodification and captivity.

5

The African Gods
Are from Tribes
and Nations

AN AFRICANA APPROACH TO RELIGIOUS
STUDIES IN THE BLACK DIASPORA

You mean Aussa. That is another nation.
There are plenty of them in Grenada.

How did cargoes become *nations* in Trinidad, Grenada, Jamaica, the United States, and everywhere else they were shipped across the Caribbean and the Americas?[1] This volume argues that Africana sacred/territorial poetics produced and continues to produce mechanisms through which commodification becomes creation. Caribbean philosopher Paget Henry elucidates the significance of Africana sacred poetics to the creative project of Africana *nation-building*. "Poetics," he explains, "usually refers to strategies of symbolic and textual production, in particular to the ways in which . . . structural components of a work of art are brought together to create new meanings. But, for many authors," Henry continues, "poetics is much more than the strategies by which meanings are produced in texts. It is also an ordering of meanings that is capable of shaping human behavior. . . . When poetically constructed systems of meaning are internalized, their rules . . .

become a grammar of human self-formation and motivation[, showing the] ... action-orienting potential of poetics."[2] The "authors" privileged in this volume are religious creatives, authors of scripts that govern their *nation-al* life. Their efforts to redesign creation demonstrate the "action-oriented potential of [Africana sacred] poetics."

In this chapter's framing epigraph, omorisa and interlocuter Margaret Buckley affirmed, during a 1939 exchange with Melville and Frances Herskovits, that Grenada's "Aussa *nation*" was one among numerous *nations*. Less than three decades before representatives of Black Power began to disclose disaffection with Trinidad's colonial heritage, African *nations* were still a fixture of Trinidadian life, and their legacies are still unfolding.[3]

This study addresses the pivotal role that religion has played in creating conditions for *nations* to breathe new life into re-created communal bodies. Religion was a foundational source of African cohesion, sociality, and spiritual stamina over centuries of trauma, and numerous African religious repertoires reaggregated in Trinidad, forging sacred plural systems of meaning and healing, including Obeah, Rada, Spiritual Baptist, and Yoruba-Orisa. During the late eighteenth and nineteenth centuries, the colonial government found Obeah and other African religious systems illegible. Custodians of African heritage religions consequently suffered brutal policing and savage violations of their bodily integrity, as when innocent African priests were punished for violating obeah laws. Obeah doctors competed fiercely with white suppliers of medicinal treatments, attracting further state scrutiny.

In the late twentieth century, as the Black Power movement waned in Trinidad, its spirit lived on in Yoruba-Orisa lineages. The palais attracted new devotees; many were middle-class artists and activists who brought black *nationalist* and pan-Africanist sensibilities to traditional Orisa families. Omorisa Burton Sankeralli describes three phases of Orisa institutional expression in Trinidad and Tobago that account for these sensibilities:

> First, in the post-emancipation 19th-century [Orisa was expressed as] worship of a defined Yoruba-based community or "nation." Second for most of the 20th century as a ritual practice—a "work"—inherent to a Trinidadian Afro-rooted religious-communal complex. Here the Orisha feast develops as the main vehicle, one that is grounded in [a] social (so-called folk) underpinning. The third phase we may term contemporary and develops from the post Black Power 1970s.[4]

Custodians of African heritage religions in Trinidad and Tobago (T&T) today enjoy hard-won rights of religious freedom and parity, civic participation, and national acknowledgment unparalleled elsewhere in the Caribbean and likely the Americas too. Milestones that have transported Orisa from the margins toward the center of public life and national recognition in T&T are rarely observed in other African diaspora regions. Orisa Acts of Incorporation, the repeal of repressive legislation censoring African religions, the inclusion of Orisa as an official religion on the national census, the Orisa Marriage Act, Orisa leaders' participation in parliamentary ceremonies, and the acquisition of government-allocated lands for Orisa ceremonies and events make T&T one of the most generative contexts for the study of Africana religious formation and sacred poetics. This aspect of Trinidad's Yoruba-Orisa tradition is what drew Tracey and me to Iya Sangowunmi's Osun Abiadama School during our first visit to Trinidad in 1998. We first learned about the Trinidadian Orisa community's accomplishments at a 1994 conference on Yoruba religion in Cuba, where Iya Molly Ahye shared the history of Orisa practice and struggle for religious rights in Trinidad. We were attracted by her regal air, but her critical intellect, satisfaction with her African heritage, and womanist leadership style and diplomacy were what most appealed to us. Hearing her lecture inspired us to investigate further the long distance between the days of Obeah proscription to those of Orisa elevation in Trinidad. Obeah would have to be considered in any history of Orisa because colonial obeah was a veil separating all children of darker Gods from worshippers of the "true" Christ and the benefits of citizenship that accrued to "authentic" Christians.

Although Spiritual Baptists fought to have the Shouters Prohibition Ordinance repealed in 1951, custodians of African heritage religions, including Spiritual Baptists, were still legally vulnerable to persecution under the 1921 Summary Offences Act (SOA), which incorporated the 1868 Obeah Prohibition Ordinance. It made sense, then, that Iya Eintou Pearl Springer would help lead and win the struggle to "remove anti-Obeah laws from the statute books" in 2000.[5] That struggle was both substantive and symbolic because the Yoruba-Orisa religious community already had some legal protections and government support for local and international Orisa activities since the incorporation of Egbe Orisa Ile Wa in 1981. However, when she spoke at the Caribbean Conference of Churches' 1994 conference on Popular Religiosity, Springer implied that Governor Picton's legacy remained influential as long as the SOA remained in the statutes:

> The Orisa religion still is not free to be practiced. There are laws on the statute books that make it mandatory for a shrine to obtain a licence

before holding an Ebo. Some of the laws have been on the statute books since the days of the Camboulay riots of the 1880s. Then there was Ordinance 6 of 1868 which prohibits the practice of obeah. [These were] incorporated into the Summary Offences Act 1921 Chapter 21 No. 17. Within the last year someone has been prosecuted under the law. I hold no brief for the spirituality of the individual, but clearly that law does not belong on our statute books.[6]

Citing Iya Melvina Rodney directly, Springer explained that Orisa devotees still face embarrassment and exploitation under the SOA when seeking licenses to "beat drums" at their ceremonies. Petitioners would find that "sometimes you don't get the paper." Springer and other omorisa did not rest until the SOA was revoked, because "the mere existence of the law is an affront to African people generally and the Orisa religion specifically." She also feared that the SOA "provides the state with a ready made [sic] lever for harassment, intimidation and manipulation of the religion and . . . individual devotees."[7]

During the October 2000 parliamentary debate on the bill to amend the SOA, Minister of Education Kamla Persad-Bissessar, later the nation's first female prime minister, celebrated Springer's tireless efforts:

When the Member made a joke out of this and said "nobody get lock up" what does that mean? Why then keep [the SOA] on the statute books if it is not being enforced? . . . I am saying firstly that just having it on the statute books is a psychological restriction and depression of people. Secondly, the fact that it is there on the statute books, they are saying that this is something wrong; do not do it. . . . Pearl Eintou Springer . . . has written reams of letters. She has done research and studies on those matters time after time over time. Nobody there paid any attention. Do you know why, Mr. Speaker? Leave it [the SOA]; nobody "ain't" getting locked up. Leave it as it stood. Leave it exactly as it was.[8]

The paths linking Obeah's fate during the slave period and Orisa's status today meet at the institutions of justice that convicted John Cooper of practicing obeah in 1871 and overturned his conviction on appeal in 1872. Cooper's (and, for that matter, Mah Nannie's) conviction and successful appeal mark overlapping periods of excessive prosecution of African religious practitioners and their attempts to defend themselves and their religions through legislative reform and judicial appeals. Cooper's experience with mistaken identity underscored the precarity of African existence after emancipation.

Mistaken first for an antisocial criminal and then for a "Yaraba," Cooper was shrouded in anonymity—his Rada religion and *nation* identity unknown in the civic public. Thus, it was fitting for Cooper, who could not read and write in any of Trinidad's colonial languages, to sign his name with an X. Yet what was supposed to be an X looks more like a deliberately placed crossroads symbol (+). I hazard Cooper left a sign from his spiritual lexicon in the colonial record to contest the reduction of his religious heritage to colonial obeah. His was an act of no small significance.

The vexing issue of Cooper's case is the through line of this two-volume study. Consider how easily Cooper was mistaken for a Yaraba. What happened to Cooper, a priest of the Rada *nation*, had to have happened to priests and devotees who *did* belong to the Yaraba *nation* (and other African *nations*), even if many of their arrests and prosecutions were never placed on record. Cooper and his brother Mah Nannie stand as the *nations'* representative victims and victors. In them we see an assemblage of African faces, their unjust punishments, and, by dint of their fortitude, the exercise of justice.

Obeah and Orisa have a linked fate in Trinidad, and Orisa devotees have long known, as have Spiritual Baptists, that they could never enjoy their full right to religious freedom without liberating African Obeah from colonial obeah's discursive, cultural, sensorial, and psychic domination.[9] Tracey and I opened this project with Babalorisa Sam Phill's definition of Obeah, for which he invoked "a very good Yoruba man" named Mr. Francis. Most people thought of Mojunta Francis as "a true Obeah man" due to his gift of using "supernatural" power. We close this project with another explanation of Obeah, a localized Obeah origin story we heard more than once during our research in Trinidad. The story was even featured in the heated House of Representatives debate that invoked Iya Eintou Pearl Springer. During her speech in defense of the SOA amendment bill, Representative Camille Robinson-Regis submitted,

> One would say that the term "obeah" has negative connotations and, really, it comes from this definition that it is "pretended assumption of supernatural powers." But if one speaks to persons who practise the Orisa tradition, they will tell you that the assumption of supernatural powers or knowledge is not a pretended assumption. . . . The term "obeah," . . . [comes from] the obi seed, which is used in their process of divination in the worship.[10]

Although some Obeah studies scholars have discovered tenable African antecedents to Obeah in the Nigerian Benin-Edo concept of *Obo-Iha* or the Igbo *dibia/abia* spiritual system of priestly knowledge and authority, this Yoruba narrative of Obeah's beginnings in Trinidad invites closer inspection.[11] Given Obeah's early eighteenth-century appearance in the transatlantic African diaspora and most Yoruba people's arrival after the 1830s, the chronology suggests that Obeah took shape in the midst of spiritual negotiations among Igbo and other West African *nations* with limited input from the Yoruba *nation*. Still, this localized account of Obeah's genesis in the Yoruba tradition of obi divination reinforces Obeah's and Orisa's interlocking histories in Trinidad for the past century and a half. Moreover, the account performs a politics of vindication, extricating African Obeah from colonial narratives of obeah. Custodians of acknowledged (if stigmatized or persecuted) African religious cultures such as Jamaican Kumina, Haitian Vodou, Brazilian Candomblé, Cuban Lucumí, and Yoruba-Ifa in the United States will have to explore their kinship with Obeah and its counterparts such as Conjure, Hoodoo, and Brujería throughout the transatlantic diaspora if they are to shift popular conceptions of their religious traditions beyond colonial imaginations.

Trinidad's African religious community has enjoyed extraordinary success in mitigating the effects of its colonial heritage compared to other diaspora contexts. Jean-Bertrand Aristide legalized Haitian Vodou in 2003. Brazil's Candomblé devotees, though legally recognized since 1890, continue to confront acts of desecration and resistance from Christian fanatics. Guyana's then-president Forbes Burnham announced but did not follow through on plans to repeal its obeah prohibition laws in 1973. Jamaican legislators are currently debating removing anti-Obeah legislation from the nation's governing statutes, and like Trinidad, Caribbean states including Anguilla (1980), Montserrat (1983), the British Virgin Islands (1997), and Barbados (1998) have amended or repealed obeah legislation.[12] The Yoruba-Orisa (and Spiritual Baptist) community's welcomed presence in T&T's civic public, however, is unparalleled in the Americas and the Caribbean. Yoruba-Orisa spiritual families enjoy the freedom to practice their faith, celebrate their Yoruba heritages in Nigeria/West Africa *and* the diaspora, and open a third space of citizenship that blends *nation-al* and national symbols and principles.

Another aim of this study has been to contribute to the burgeoning field of Africana religious studies by researching religious traditions that have received minimal scholarly attention. The methodology that guided our approach allowed us to consider the nature of religion itself by analyzing how African religious custodians confront violent realities and obscene fantasies that confine and define them. We learned from my study of Trinidad's Yoruba-Orisa legacy that one of the most salient features connecting black religions in the New World is the way they subtend mythical and historical consciousness to create authentic spaces, affects, and possibilities, as well as modes of uncooperatively enduring the antiblack/anti-African world.

In volume I, Tracey Hucks's morphology of the colonial cult of obeah fixation provides a language for theorizing the religious ecstasy Governor Picton's enforcers were feeling and the religious ethos they were producing when they whipped custodians of African spiritual traditions as if whipping a sheet of metal. Her analysis of African-descended people's gratuitous suffering and the "conflation of blackness as the ontological negation of being with Black subjects and communities" anticipated my engagement with Charles Long's theories of religion *as* desecration and the desecration *of* religion.[13] Through our study of Obeah and Orisa in Trinidad, we have reckoned with psychic registers where religion and violence coexist comfortably. Even more important, in studying a racialized black population, we have theorized the religious foundations of affective politics and identity politics for diasporaed African descendants.

We also have addressed lingering conceptual problems in the theorization of African heritage religions, especially explanatory categories such as "syncretism" and reductive treatments of black *nationalisms* as romantic expressions of identity politics and imagined communities. To circumvent these dominant theoretical tropes, I argued for an approach to theorizing African heritage religions that probes relationality and prioritizes sovereignty, kinship and family, social belonging, motherness, and *nation/nationhood*. These motifs appear throughout an array of traditions in the Caribbean and the Americas, from *nation* dances at Congo Square (New Orleans) to Pinkster sovereignty ceremonies among enslaved African descendants in eighteenth-century New Netherlands to Afro-Surinamese "Mati work" that builds networks of support among "fictive" kin through flexible motherness arrangements that privilege women's friendships, same-sex intimacy, and co-mothering responsibilities. Investigating these themes with attention to Africana religious formation in Africa and the diaspora helped dislodge assumptions about the Yoruba-Orisa religion's syncretic essence, and I suspect it will have the same impact on studies of other African heritage religions.

My suspicion that shared cultural patterns and orientations exist across diverse Africana religions is not driven by static generalizations about Africa. Rather, it emerges from engagement with scholarship on the arc of the Niger-Congo cultural imprint on African peoples across much of sub-Saharan Africa. A simple, precise example is the *Africana* coiffure of cornrows. The cultural phenomenon that birthed this hairstyle emerged up to ten thousand years ago during a period of Niger-Congo dominance in Africa, and a cornrowing culture remains rooted in the traditions of African-descended people in Bahia, Mississippi, Ilé-Ifẹ̀, Port of Spain, Bluefields, Kinshasa, Kingston, and elsewhere. The powerful institution of motherhood and the matricentric traditions and ethics—the motherness—it inspires are another *Africana* phenomenon that womanist and feminist scholars have argued crosses cultural boundaries in Africa and the African diaspora. The sacred meanings of motherhood, evident in African conventions and institutions, are far older than the cultural groups that supplied transatlantic slave ships with bleeding cargoes. A Niger-Congo cultural horizon certainly contributed to what has become "a spiritual [ana]grammar and ethic rooted in a local . . . [and] a shared pan-African matricentric heritage and value system."[14]

Motherness: A Transcontextual, Transhistorical Africana Phenomenon

Herskovits was a prominent interlocutor within social-science debates about why black mothering and black family arrangements such as Mati work tended to deviate from the idealized white patriarchal nuclear family structure in the United States and wider Americas, and he connected what other scholars deemed pathological "matriarchal" patterns in black family life to West African family and marriage systems. Herskovits provided examples of polygynous marriage and matrifocal family structures in West Africa to explain why mother–child bonds predominate among families of African descent in the Americas and the Caribbean.[15] As discussed in chapter 4, African and African diaspora feminists and womanists have expanded the research on matricentric traditions and their religious and spiritual significance. Their studies help clarify important cultural distinctions among concepts such as "women," "anatomical females," and "mothers" in Africana contexts and in some cases isolate gender and "women" as Western folk concepts that can compel idiosyncratic interpretations of Africana matricentric institutions, symbols, and rituals.[16] They also raise our awareness of motherhood's biological, social, and sacred significance in religious and cultural life.

Mothers are the cornerstone of Africana families—consanguineal and spiritual—and the reverence for mothers in Africa and the African diaspora operates alongside patriarchal and sexist conventions. In Africana social and family structures or religious institutions, patriarchy is not absolute. For example, Cheryl Townsend Gilkes suggests that African American Pentecostals repurposed West African political and familial arrangements that accommodated both matricentric and patriarchal institutions. She argues that church mothers often negotiate patriarchal power dynamics while exercising forms of culturally sanctioned authority. "These varieties of shared power or of access to authority," Gilkes maintains, "reflect the range of positions church mothers occupy. The similarities in organization of church mothers to West African social organization range from clearly articulated and established dual-sex political systems to fragments of familyhood, which modify the otherwise rigid lines of authority within episcopal style church hierarchies. These African overtones in social organization exist alongside of and in spite of a dominant cultural tradition of European sex-role organization and church politics."[17]

Studies of Islam's penetration into African societies also offer insight into the accommodations between indigenous matricentric institutions and Islamic patriarchal innovations in regions of West Africa. Michael Gomez's *African Dominion*, for example, addresses the power dynamics surrounding patriarchal, matrifocal, and matricentric negotiations in Mande political culture in medieval West Africa. Gomez reads a range of internal and external source material, including the epic of Sunjata, to access "Mande values and perspectives."[18] Examining Islam's slow, mitigated negotiations with indigenous religion, Gomez illuminates the prominence of women and mothers in Mande political ideology and intellectual culture, the result of a relationship managed through accommodation and juxtaposition between Islamic patricultural conventions and matrifocal and matricentric indigenous institutions and values.[19]

Gomez's scholarship compels me to revisit British colonial army officer Alfred Burdon Ellis's speculations about Yoruba kinship. Ellis suspected that among the peoples who came to constitute what scholars have identified as the "patrilineal" Yoruba *nation*, "acknowledgment of a father's blood-relationship to his children was brought about by the intercourse of the northern Yorubas with the Mohammedan tribes of the interior." Recognizing the "extraordinary vitality the system of descents through mothers possesses" in West Africa, Ellis appeals to an "ancient proverb" and kinship norms to support his speculation. "'The *esuo* (gazelle), claiming relationship with the *ekulu* (a large antelope), says his mother was the daughter of an *ekulu*.'" He explains, "If the male system of descents had been in vogue when this proverb was invented, the *esuo* would have been made to say that his father was the son of an *ekulu*. Moreover, in spite of the legal succession from father to sons, children by different mothers, but the same father, are by many natives still scarcely considered true blood-relations."[20]

Ellis takes a back-door approach to the Yorùbá concept *omoya*, a foundational principle through which Oyèrónké Oyěwùmí establishes her notion of *mothernity*. An "African communitarian ideology and ideal" that endowed African diaspora contexts with co-mothering institutions such as "othermothers" and "macomeres," *omoya* in English means "my mother's child or children." According to Oyěwùmí,

> The category of *omoya* transcends gender; sometimes it is used to refer to an individual, but what it encapsulates is the collectivity. It functions to locate the individual within a socially recognized grouping and underscores the significance of mother-child ties in delineating and anchoring a child's place in the family. These relationships are primary and privileged, and it is understood that they should be protected above others. *Omoya* is the primary category in the sense that it is the first and fundamental source of identification for the child in the household. To put it [succinctly], in the traditional Yoruba household, the first thing you need to know is not whether you are a boy or a girl but who are your *omoya*—[the] siblings with whom you share the same mother. Symbolically, *omoya* emblematizes unconditional love, togetherness, unity, solidarity, and loyalty.[21]

Along with many regions of the Francophone Caribbean, Trinidad sustained macomere (co-mothering) institutions, which incorporated powerful midwifery networks that continued to operate alongside and compete with the rise of a certified system of midwifery in the colony. Their African-centered approach to maternal health care was unintelligible to the medical practitioner and legislator Louis de Verteuil who, during the mid-nineteenth century, disparaged African midwives as "self-confident *commères*."[22]

Matricentric legacies exist today across the African diaspora; many of their roots extend back 3,500 years to a Bantu cultural zone and likely reflect earlier Niger-Congo institutions. Cymoune Fourshey, Rhonda Gonzales, Christine Saidi, Cheik Anta Diop, Ifi Amadiume, Laura Grillo, and others who study African motherhood have excavated its institutional import, as well as broader numinous domains of motherhood in African consciousness. Across Africana spiritual cultures in Trinidad and the wider diaspora, mothers continue to be perceived as endowments of knowledge capital. As the following story illustrates, by mastering ancestral/divine modes of communicating messages, mothers have used knowledge to enhance the *nation*—to govern, heal, teach, empower, and save lives.

In March 2012, I had an audience with Dr. Jean Herskovits in her apartment in New York City. I contacted her after reading through her father's archives at Northwestern University and her parents' archives at the Schomburg Center for Research in Black Culture, gaining access to fieldnotes and other materials on their ethnographic work in the Caribbean/Americas. Jean was a child when she traveled to Trinidad during the summer of 1939 and lived with her parents while they saturated themselves in the life and customs of the northeastern people of Toco. Her father made numerous references to her in his field notebooks, and I wondered whether she still had memories of experiences with Afro-Trinidadians. When she greeted me at the door, I perceived how fragile yet spirited she was—fragile because of her age and slight frame, spirited in her gestures, tone of voice, and defensive adoration of her parents.

To my disappointment, Jean confessed that she was only four years old when she lived in Trinidad in 1939, so she could not tell me much more than what I had gleaned from the archives. However, we talked for a while about her father's research in Trinidad, Haiti, and Brazil. She recounted her experiences in Salvador, Brazil, which she remembered more vividly than Toco in part because she suffered from a life-threatening illness in Brazil and was convinced her recovery had something to do with the spiritual intervention of a mãe-de-santo she and her parents knew well. Unprompted, she reflected on the authority and influence mothers exhibited in the Brazilian Candomblé institutions and shared an incident I had never heard or read about before meeting her.

"Have you ever wondered why there's no Brazil book," she asked? The thought had not occurred to me up to that point, but now I was eager to know. In addition to the fact that the Brazil trip was "unbearably stressful" for her dad, who struggled with health challenges, he had "lost a lot of material related to his research in Brazil." According to Jean, when she and her parents were preparing to return to the United States, one of the "Candomblé cult house mothers" ran to their residence on their scheduled day of departure and insisted that Dr. Herskovits and his family NOT board their ship.

The mother had received a warning through a dream, and she importuned them to abandon their plans to return home on the steamer waiting for them at the harbor. She also gave them a carved image of the Yoruba Orisa Oxosi "with her ax." "This was right after Pearl Harbor," Jean noted as she returned from a back room with the carving. It was beautiful, smooth, and whittled from what looked like mahogany wood. It had been immaculately preserved since 1941.

I felt a strange compulsion to gently ask if she would relinquish Oxosi to me, but I came to my senses and kept quiet, taking note of the fact that Jean had referred to Oxosi as "she." Oxosi is usually conceived of as a male Orisa in the diaspora, but Dr. Wándé Abímbọ́lá has described Ọ̀ṣọ́òsì's representation as a female Òrìṣà in Nigeria.

Her dad's response to the mother's premonition was to make flight arrangements instead. "He listened!" Jean exclaimed. Dr. Herskovits allowed their cargo to leave on the ship as planned, but he, his wife Frances, and Jean returned to the United States by plane. "The ship sank!" Jean explained. They lost their possessions on the ship, but their "lives were spared."[23]

I had been privy to many stories like Jean's in the past, if not all about sparing someone from impending death, then about other miraculous interventions that elevated spiritual mothers in the eyes of their communities and strengthened their bonds with their spiritual families and others who sought their support. When asked in a 1996 interview, "What does it mean to be a woman in this [Orisa] tradition?" Iya Molly Ahye distinguished "women" from "mothers," replying, "You had the respected mothers who had power"—a qualification that associates influence with persons who hold the title of "mother" within the Yoruba-Orisa religion.[24]

In 2019, I visited Salvador for the first time and attended Candomblé ceremonies and workshops at Nago, Angola, and Jeje *terreiros* (territories/houses). The mothers were indeed authoritative and powerful, playing central roles in their *nations*. They might not be matriarchs in a city of women, but they *are* a society of mothers.[25] Like the Trinidadian Yoruba-Orisa mothers, the US COGIC church mothers, the Jamaican Kumina mothers, and many other spiritual mothers in the diaspora, they have access to a shared yet localized Africana matricentric heritage, including the affective modality of motherness that patriarchy has not managed to conquer.

Over the years, when I revisited the transcript from my interview with Dr. Jean Herskovits, I remembered how fortunate I felt to have met her before it was too late. I had the strong intuition during our interview that her twilight years were diminishing, so much so that I would periodically enter her name into a Google search to see if she was still alive.

As I was finishing this chapter, I searched for Jean again and discovered she had transitioned on February 5, 2019. I took a moment to be silent, reflected on the power of storytelling, and wondered what ever happened to her family's Oxosi. Suddenly, I remembered that Melville Herskovits's name came up during public lectures at two of the terreiros I visited in Salvador. Even with our translator's remarkable skills, I tried to grasp as many Portuguese words as I could through my competent and proficient knowledge of Spanish and French, respectively. Perhaps I was so consumed with listening and understanding that I never thought to ask anyone about Jean's story. I wonder now if, four months after Jean Herskovits's passing, I might have unknowingly encountered in Salvador, Bahia, a descendant of the Candomblé mother who handed Oxosi to a family that needed her protection in 1941. I have developed elsewhere a theory of Africana matricentricity; however, Jean Herskovits's narrative allows me to conceptualize more pointedly *motherness* as the values and practices of care I discussed in earlier scholarship through the concept of "matricentric ethics." As in Trinidad, the institution of motherhood and the affective work of motherness in Brazil (and the wider diaspora) are essential to the salvation and efficacy of the *nation*.[26]

Africana *Nations* beyond the Caribbean

Motherness, kinship and family, sovereignty, social belonging, and *nationhood* all figure prominently in the spiritual strivings of the African diaspora and deserve additional exploration in studies of Africana religions, including theological studies. Conceptualizing theology, particularly black theology, expansively—the way my late advisor, Dr. James Cone, did in his final posthumous volume, *Said I Wasn't Gonna Tell Nobody*—the black theologian is "an interpreter of the religious imagination of [black] people."[27] Through my five central categories and others examined in this volume, I have also provided a starting point for the development of nonconfessional, nondogmatic *Africana* theologies that can launch new modes of inquiry centered on the religious imagination of African-descended peoples and *Africana sacred poetics*. With respect to one category, a foundational model for constructing comparative Africana theologies through meditations on the conceptual, cosmological, sociocultural, and spiritual underpinnings of kinship/family in African and African diasporic contexts rests between the pages of J. Deotis Roberts's prolific scholarly corpus.

Especially during the 1980s and 1990s, and concurrent with the rise of Afrocentrism, Roberts responded to the piqued curiosity of many individuals and subcultures across black communities in the United States that were exploring connections between continental Africans and diasporaed African descendants. His Africana and Afrocentric ethical frameworks accounted for African religious thought and philosophy and black *nationalist* and Pan-Africanist religious movements in the diaspora, which led him to use if not coin the term "black religious *nationalism*" decades before Tracey Hucks framed her study of African American Yoruba history through the same analytic. Across a number of articles, later collected and republished in *Black Religion, Black Theology*, and texts like *Roots of a Black Future: Family and Church* and *Africentric Christianity*, Roberts elucidates the relationship between family and faith in black Christian contexts.[28] However, twenty-first-century Africana theologies need not, indeed should not, be monopolized by a single representative religious tradition. They should, as Roberts would agree, represent the plurality of black religious cultures and their sacred poetics. This study prompts reflection on a related imperative: any Africana theology must reckon with the *nation* phenomenon as a foundational theological statement as much as it is a commentary on social and political reality. It is the *nation* structure that has allowed the sacred poetics of Africana cultural heritages to cohere and transmit meaning across generations, and even black Christian theologians can benefit from studying the histories, symbols, and indigenous hermeneutics of Africana *nations*.

As an abode for religious imagination and expression, Africana *nations* also challenge contemporary concepts of race and the overdetermination of racial blackness in African diaspora peoples' approaches to identity formation and social belonging. This study closes with one example that explores Africana *nationhood* beyond the Caribbean. In this section, I reflect on the appearance of the *nations* in North America in conversation with African American theorists who documented the concept's use among black communities and used it themselves to theorize the religious imagination and political aspirations of a landless black people. The historical role of Africana *nations* in the African diaspora uncovers an even more precise understanding of black religion as an interruptive invention of belonging—of new evocations of ashé—in an antiblack world that holds blacks captive.

Africana studies scholarship has widely documented the ubiquity of the *nations* throughout all regions of the African diasporas spawned by slavery, with the exception of the United States. Haiti's twenty-one *nasyon yo* still deserve extensive scholarly investigation. However, Cuban *naciones* and Brazilian *nações* have received significant attention when compared with Anglophone Caribbean and North American *nations*. In contrast to a number of other black diasporas produced by racial slavery, African descendants in North America have perpetually confronted the unique postslavery predicament of navigating identity in an American nation that has rendered whiteness its most treasured civil religion.[29]

In their monumental study, *Racecraft*, Karen and Barbara Fields deconstruct the Euro-derived idea of race and examine its origins (which they term "racecraft") as the foundational terrain of the American imagination and belief system. Most important for this discussion is the distinction they make between race as an ontological signifier in white discourse and race as a *nation-al* signifier in black discourse. "It was not African Americans . . . who needed a racial explanation," they maintain:

> It was not they who invented themselves as a race. Euro-Americans re- solved the contradiction between slavery and liberty by defining Afro- Americans as a race; Afro-Americans resolved the contradiction more straightforwardly by calling for the abolition of slavery. From the era of the American, French, and Haitian revolutions on, they claimed liberty as theirs by natural rights. . . . Both Afro- and Euro-Americans used the words that today denote race, but they did not understand these words the same way. Afro-Americans understood the reason for the enslavement to be, as Frederick Douglass put it, "not *color* but crime." Afro-Americans in- vented themselves, not as a race, but as a *nation*. They were not troubled, as modern scholars often are, by the use of racial vocabulary to express their sense of *nationality*. Afro-American soldiers who petitioned on behalf of "These poor *nation* of color" and "we Poore *Nation* of a Colered rast [race]" saw nothing incongruous about the language.[30]

Not only did African-descended persons in North America not see any- thing "incongruous" about investing race with a familiar understanding of their collective identity; defined by their common condition as a "poor *nation*"—a landless people—they derived their conception of *nation* from a shared Africana vocabulary that other dispersed Africans in the Americas/ Caribbean also accessed. Alexander Garden was correct when he said of en- slaved Africans, "They are as 'twere a *Nation* within a Nation. In all country settlements, they live in contiguous houses, often 2, 3, or 4 families in one house, slightly partitioned into so many apartments, so they labor together, and converse almost wholly among themselves."[31] Garden, an eighteenth- century Anglican rector in Charleston, South Carolina, penned these obser- vations in a 1740 letter to his denomination's London Office. Two centuries later, African American sociologist E. Franklin Frazier came to the same conclusion, based on substantive evidence.

Law professor Stephen Carter's twenty-first-century novel, *The Emperor of Ocean Park*, invites readers into the terrain of black *nationhood*. He uses the phrase "the darker *nation*" not only to conceptualize solidarity among black people but also to claim a space within the wider US nation. Carter discov- ered that Mary McLeod Bethune, W. E. B. Du Bois, and Alain Locke had used similar terms, connecting his coinage of the phrase to a longer intellectual lineage in the United States.[32] Legacies of the African *nations* undoubtedly sourced that intellectual lineage.

African *nations* indeed made an impact across America's landscapes of slavery, from the 1712 New York City slave revolt, in which roughly 50 percent of the participants were described as "of ye *Nations* of Coromantee & Pappa,"[33] to the peopling of Fort Mose in Spanish Florida with diverse African "*nations*" beginning in 1738.[34] Over time, and especially after Emancipation, when millions of blacks began migrating north while adopting Christianity in unprecedented numbers, African *nation* consciousness continued to shape the lives and social institutions of black Northerners and Southerners.

Ras Michael Brown's interpretive framework of African-descended people's involuntary presence in America situates slavery as a period of African *misplacement*, the postemancipation Great Migration period as African descendants' *displacement*, and the rise of black neighborhoods, towns, and homesteads as their *emplacement* in America, providing conceptual room for me to theorize the black church as a site of *nation-al* emplacement.[35] Although the emplacement offered to African descendants is not land-based, the black church—similar to the Orisa palais, the Vodou lakou, and the Candomblé terreiro—provided a *place* for belonging that nurtured African descendants' new evocation of ashé and shared sense of peoplehood—their "invent[ion of] themselves . . . as a [*nation*]."[36]

The Black Church: A *Nation-al* Structure of Belonging

As W. E. B. Du Bois theorized it, in a context where African people's movements and bodies were confined to segregated spaces, the black church in the United States was primarily a *social* institution and secondarily a religious one. Du Bois's characterization of the embryonic black church as an African phenomenon shaped by intradiasporic African spiritual customs and cultural dispositions underscores how foundational Africana *nations* were to black ecclesial formation.

Scholars of religion, particularly those studying black ecclesial institutions in the United States, have rarely explored the black church's *nation-al* roots or its historic *nation-al* role.[37] They have instead commented widely on religious phenomena that Du Bois identifies among enslaved communities: the preacher, the music, and the frenzy. Du Bois spends ample time exploring these motifs in his discussion of "Negro religion." His social theory of the black church, however, includes other elements that many scholars in religious studies have overlooked—the elements of initiation and "secret societies," sociopolitical governance, and sovereignty—which Du Bois links to an African heritage: "The Negro church of to-day is the social centre of Negro life in the United States, and the most characteristic expression of African character. Take a typical church in a small Virginia town. . . . This building is the central club-house of a community of a thousand or more Negroes. Various organizations meet here—the church proper, the Sunday-school, . . . insurance societies, women's societies, secret societies, [and others]."

Du Bois goes on to describe how large urban black churches are even better equipped to execute the institution's sociopolitical mission of *nation-building*:

> In the great city churches the same tendency is noticeable and in many respects emphasized. A great church like the Bethel of Philadelphia has over eleven hundred members . . . an annual budget of five thousand dollars, and a government consisting of a pastor with several assisting local preachers, an executive and legislative board, financial boards and tax collectors; general church meetings for making laws; sub-divided groups led by class leaders, a company of militia, and twenty-four auxiliary societies. The activity of a church like this is immense and far-reaching, and the bishops who preside over these organizations throughout the land are among the most powerful Negro rulers in the world.[38]

Du Bois's research and theoretical lens surely influenced other contemporary sociologists. During the 1930s, for instance, Benjamin Mays and Joseph Nicholson argued,

> The great importance attached to the political maneuvering at the *National Baptist Convention*, or at the General Methodist Conference, can be explained in part by the fact that the negro is largely cut off from the body politic. The local churches, associations, conventions, and conferences become the Negro's Democratic and Republican Conventions, his Legislature and his Senate and House of Representatives.[39]

E. Franklin Frazier's theorization of the black church in the United States as a "*nation* within a nation" also corresponds with the Du Boisian school of thought.[40]

Like the Trinidadian palais, whose "half religious, half civil"[41] sovereignty and governance rituals predated the arrival of Yoruba indentured laborers, black churches allowed space for an internal project of sovereignty ("negro rulers") and *nation* formation. And *nation-al* consciousness was not inconsequential to leading figures of the black church. In 1916, for instance, the president of the *National* Baptist Convention USA, Elias Camp Morris, described his institution as one that "affords an opportunity to prove to the world that the black race is capable of self-government under democratic form."[42] Our understanding of how fundamental this *nation-al* consciousness was to the identity and ecclesiology of untutored African descendants from the rural South—those likely to have had more intimate connections to African orientations than middle-class blacks—sharpens with E. Franklin Frazier's observations:

> The Negro church was not only an arena of political life for the leaders of Negroes, it had a political meaning for the masses. Although they were denied the right to vote in the American community, within their churches, especially the Methodist Churches, they could vote and [elect officers]. . . . It was the church that enlisted [their] deepest loyalties. Therefore, it was more than an amusing incident to note some years ago in a rural community in Alabama, that a Negro when asked to identify the people in the adjoining community replied: "The *nationality* there is Methodist." . . . For the Negro masses, in their social and moral isolation in American society, the Negro church community has been a *nation* within a nation.[43]

Choosing a religious affiliation—whether Methodist or another "*nationality*"—was a critical aspect of discerning and solidifying one's *social belonging* as a person, family member, and primordial citizen.[44] Black churches housed many overlapping domains of family/kinship and *nationhood* insofar as independent black congregations and denominations were none other than organized black families/polities. They were institutions of *emplacement* for misplaced and displaced African descendants navigating the afterlife of racial slavery. These connections between the black church, black kinship, black identity, and social organization were not lost on Frazier:

> The church had a political significance for Negroes in a broader meaning of the term. The development of the Negro church after Emancipation was tied up . . . largely with the Negro family. A study of Negro churches in a Black Belt county in Georgia in 1903 revealed . . . that a large proportion of the churches were "family churches." Outside the family, the church represented the only other organized social existence. The rural Negro communities in the South were named after their churches. In fact, the Negro population in the rural South has been organized in "church communities" which represented . . . the largest social groups in which

they found an identification. Moreover, since the Negro was an outsider in the American community ... the Negro church provided a refuge in a hostile white world.[45]

Frazier alludes to the fact that African descendants in the United States were not legal citizens during most of the epoch of black denominational formation. They were strangers in a foreign land, aliens within a nation whose patrimony did not extend to them until 1868. Hence, when James Weldon and John Rosamond Johnson's "Lift Every Voice and Sing" with its concluding lyrics of "true to our God, true to our native land," was released around the turn of the twentieth century, African Americans embraced it personally, communally, and institutionally. Decades after the Fourteenth Amendment had guaranteed African Americans citizenship, "Lift Every Voice and Sing" registered the long-standing custom of African American nation-building, as blacks across religious and secular arenas dubbed it the Negro National Anthem.[46]

Although his successors used the phrase, Du Bois was the first to document the negro church as "a nation within a nation." He analyzed the negro church's institutional structures and leadership traditions as data demonstrating the negro's capacity for self-governance, economic sustainability, and thus candidacy for authentic US citizenship, protection under the law, and political participation in civic life. Negroes had proven their ability to undertake under one roof the social organization essential to the efficient governance of any civil society. In fact, Mother Bethel's Black Legion, a militia of 2,500 men, materialized at the request of Philadelphia's "city fathers" during the War of 1812.[47] Du Bois's attention to this facet of Bethel's church structure prompts reflection on the ironies of nation/nation politics: What significance should one attach to white civic officials commissioning a reserve military force within a negro ecclesial institution under the direction of a negro pastor in a country where enslaved negroes were someone else's legal property and "free" negroes were not recognized as American citizens?

In this section of his commentary, Du Bois does much more than expose white America's democracy of convenience that strategically positioned Negroes to participate in its practices of empire when such participation served the nation's interests. In effect, Du Bois, Frazier, Mays, Nicholson, and other social scientists lay the groundwork for my conceptualization of the black church as a locus for Africana approaches to nation formation. However, using the modern nation state as a standard for comparison, these elite scholars generally examined the black church as an alternative space of citizenship and governance in an antiblack America. Their studies vindicated black belonging to the American nation-state and championed the politics of black churches engaged in struggles for racial justice and civil rights. Similar to Little Oyo and comparable Orisa institutions in present-day Trinidad, some black church *nationscapes* were primordial publics enacting a vision for inclusion within the civic public. At the same time, early twentieth-century studies of the black church overlooked conceptions of *nationhood* among lower-class black communities in the United States and their continuities with those of similarly situated African descendants located elsewhere. Frazier was correct when he insisted that the rural black Alabamian's idea of "*nationality*" was "more than an amusing incident," and omorisa in Trinidad understand just how unamused Frazier's Alabamian interlocutor was. Moreover, post–Black Power omorisa who today establish overlapping spaces of *nation-al* and national belonging in Trinidad are able to link two experiences of citizenship, which antiblackness has never allowed African descendants in America. Aided by their location within the deeply blended black-brown T&T nation-state, rather than polarize these forms of citizenship, omorisa currently exercise dual citizenship—the kind Du Bois and his contemporaries hoped would one day be extended to American blacks and the kind the rural Alabamian resident claimed.

Some would argue that the price black church citizens paid for their fidelity to empty promises of national inclusion was far too costly. The white American nation was invented *to* violate and *because* it violates black people's existence and citizenship "rights" with impunity. After decades of futile protest, an elder Du Bois inevitably confronted this truth and fled white nationhood by renouncing his American citizenship. He moved to Ghana, an African nation that granted him citizenship, a home, and a final resting place. Alienation from the *nationhood* that the ring shout and other African heritage spiritual traditions provided their custodians is another expensive outcome of the decorous black church's excessive preoccupation with national belonging since emancipation. African heritage religious cultures and spiritual practices qualified and existed in relationship to the primordial black church, yet their *nation* legacies were too opaque and unintelligible to the white nation and were even blasphemous and embarrassing to most upwardly mobile African Americans. They offered no currency of value to the movement for black uplift.

By contrast, and despite his involuntary presence in a nation that systemically disqualified African descendants from national belonging, indigenous hermeneutics prevailed in the social life and sacred poetics of persons like the rural black Alabamian who interpreted denominational belonging as *nation-al* belonging. Would we say that "Methodist *nationality*"—as he and presumably others in his community conceived it—was unrelated to the Yoruba *nation* in Trinidad or the Kongo *nation* in Jamaica or the Rada *nation* in Haiti or the *Nation* of Islam, and the Hip-hop *Nation* in America? I insist these *nation-al* lineages are profoundly related in ways addressed throughout this volume and in manners yet to be discovered. Africana ecclesial traditions, which Du Bois interpreted as cultural indices of the Negro's African heritage and political consciousness, were and are Africana *nations* hiding in plain sight. They are the nexus between the ring shout and the decorous black church, and while the latter often exists in ideological tension with its African religious heritage, Africana *nationhood* is what makes the decorous black church *black* in its infrastructure and/or its operation.

In chapter 1, I discussed Olabiyi Yai's position that, when African diaspora communities organized themselves into *nations*, they appropriated this Western terminology to approximate identity affiliations that mattered to them as groups linked by shared languages, customs, memories, myths, religious orientations, old-world homelands, Middle Passage experiences, and other commonalities. In Yai's summation,

> The widespread use of the word *nation* in its African acceptation testifies to its significance among Diasporan Africans. . . . In the United States for example, *nation* and its derivative *national* have become emblematic of African American identity, in fact serving as code words for "African American," as exemplified in the long-standing *National* Medical Association and the *National* Bar Association, and more recently the *National* Brotherhood of Skiers, *National* Association of Black Scuba Divers, and Hiphop *Nation*. If chance and a conspiracy theory are ruled out to account for this consistency in the use of the concept . . . , it becomes legitimate to hypothesize an explanation based on antecedents from the homeland. When an Afro-Brazilian says: "*Eu sou de nação jeje*" (I am of the Jeje *nation*), when a Cuban refers to herself as "*de nación ijecha*," or when a Haitian claims *rada nationality*, they all consciously or subliminally refer to time-honored African worldviews and practices on the continent.[48]

Yai buttresses my and his own argument with comparable cases from the Yoruba and Fon regions of West Africa, establishing a framework for interpreting the *nation* practices of African diaspora people, including black church members in the United States. He concludes, "In the Americas, Africans had to invent new institutions within which they could cultivate their

FIGURE 5.1 "Candomblé (Bahia, Brazil) Ritual Dance" depicting Brazilian Candomblé devotees performing a *nation* dance in 1962. Candomblé *nation* dances are among the many African diaspora *nation* dances performed in circular motion mirroring the directional path of the rising and setting sun. Others include Jamaican Kumina, the US African American ring shout, St. Lucian Kele, and the Big Drum *Nation* Dance in Carriacou and Grenada. Reprinted by permission from the General Secretariat of the Organization of American States. All rights reserved. (Photograph forms part of the Columbus Memorial Library Photograph Collection.)

customs and perpetuate the memory of Africa, and thus live a meaningful life. . . . Religious institutions such as Candomblé in Brazil, Santería in Cuba, Kumina in Jamaica, and the African American church in the United States are prominent instances of such invented institutions."[49]

Methodist *nationalities* and other black ecclesial *nations* are New World Africana inventions, and the ubiquity of the ring shout in the nineteenth- and early twentieth-century black church is a sign that African *nation* dances of the slave period were its most organic foundational structures (see figure 5.1).[50] *Nation* dances were the basement floors and front yards of black church edifices. The black church's eventual adoption of an ecclesial Christian identity has not severed its devotees from Africana *nation* consciousness and practices. Rather, black churches constitute one of many repertoires of a shared Africana conception of *nationhood*. And I agree with Yai: African diaspora *nations*, including the black church, "should be studied with an African[/Africana] agenda in mind, rather than anthropological [curiosity]. What, for example," Yai inquires, "were their language policies? How did they tackle the problem of the plurality of religions? What modalities of Pan-Africanism did these polities individually and collectively display?" The *Baltimore Afro-American*'s 1932 contest indicates that some African Americans were attempting to address similar questions with suggestions that the best way to "settle this business once and for all as to the best race designation" was to embrace harmony in diversity through identity labels such as "Polynational" or "Omnational."[51] These early twentieth-century concepts return us to Fields and Fields's argument that African Americans, like African Trinidadians and diasporaed Africans everywhere, "invented themselves, not as a race, but as a *nation*." Their success in doing so has been forever tethered to their *otherworld* modalities and institutional emplacements—the church, the palais, the temple, the mosque, the terreiro.

Historically, outside agitators noticed the power that the black church and other *nation* institutions had to remind their constituents that "the Occident is an accident in our millennial history." Opponents feared that power because Africana *nations* provided shelter from blacks' "*temporally homeless*" condition.[52] In nineteenth-century Trinidad, Marie Bertrand Cothonay's strategy for abolishing Afro-Creole demonstrations of sovereignty and *nation* consciousness was to "demolish the *palais*"—the structure African descendants found generative for their psychic autonomy and for nurturing their shared soul-life.[53] Deeply disturbing analogues epitomize white supremacist legacies in the North American context where, through arson, bombings, and gunfire massacres, white terrorists have attempted for centuries to demolish the black church—the most long-standing and influential institutional expression of black *nationhood* in the United States.

Despite efforts to undermine black *nationhood*, the *nations* are still here. In contesting the colonial subjugation of African descendants and equipping them with a collective sense of sovereignty and its prosocial psychic effects, the *nations*, with their structural efficacies, *are* enduring "Africanisms," demonstrating my understanding of African cultural conventions as moving continuities. I deploy Herskovits's concept deliberately here to place in bold relief the Africana sacred poetics that accounts for textured multivalent understandings of African cultures/religions against static concepts and perceptions that fossilize African and homogenize African American cultures. Paralytic approaches that treat African culture(s) as a gigantic fossil and freeze the cultural outlook and productions of African descendants in America within presentist Euro-Christian theological scripts prevent indigenous hermeneutics from playing the interpretive roles they should play in comparative assessments of African American and African cultures/religions.

The indigenous hermeneutical approach Tracey and I have advanced in this study does quite the opposite and addresses what Donald Matthews identifies as a costly oversight in black religious studies: a "methodological dualism that separates structures from meaning."[54] Our observations underscore Matthew's argument: in investigating the African heritage of the black church, we find that the field has tended to interrogate the meaning of practices rather than structures. What our study shows, however, is that Africana approaches to black religious formation must apply indigenous hermeneutics and the analytics we deem appropriate to interpret the meaning of *structures*, not solely practices or even systems. Especially in the North American context, when considering, for example, what the black church has in common with the Orisa palais, indigenous hermeneutics can help scholars attend to both seen and unseen structural imperatives that bind together these longstanding institutions, one being the *nation*.

Notwithstanding violent repression—indeed, because of it—black *nationhood* is unstoppable in the black church and its counterpart institutions across the diaspora. The Yoruba-Orisa, Kongo-Kumina, Nago-, Jeje-, and Angola-Candomblé, African Methodist Episcopal Church, National Baptist Convention, Hip-hop Nation, and Rada, Igbo, and Petro Vodou-lakou are here to stay. They declare that the Homeland blacks desire precedes and exceeds the colonial invention of Africa, and they evince also that the Africa they call the "Motherland" is and has always been *here* too, in the Americas and the Caribbean.

The Affective Turn in Africana Religious Studies

Africana religious studies and other cognate and intersecting fields will benefit tremendously from new research on affective modes of black religious consciousness. Developing a theory of black religious affect in its expression as "heritage love," this volume shows how the Africana *nation* became the mechanism that turned black refusal of what has been refused to blacks and black longing for Africa into *acts of creation*. The turn to affect also responds to James Cone's contention that the five most prominent themes in black religious experience are suffering, hope, justice, freedom, and love.[55] Moving beyond black/womanist theological assessments of Christian love to the theme of heritage love, chapters 3 and 4 analyze how omorisa in Trinidad have created new authenticating structures of belonging and home-going through the powers of the *nation*. I am not arguing that Africa remains a desideratum of all African-descended persons in the Caribbean and the Americas. Nor do I claim that all black religious traditions orient themselves toward Africa as intimately and intentionally as do Africana religious *nationalist* traditions. Rather, the affective terrain of *authentic and sacred belonging* that Africa symbolizes is what matters to black people collectively speaking. In the afterlife of slavery, black people of all religious and political persuasions confront the desire to truly belong *somewhere*. Africana *nations*, Africana religious *nationalisms*, and (per Long) Africa have appeared in deeply influential forms as places and modes of belonging. Studying what such appearances have meant for people of African descent through phenomenological rather than social-scientific or Christian theological lenses frees us from conceptual frameworks that undertheorize the nature of black religion.

Distancing this volume from identity politics and imagined communities in studies of nationalism, I have instead theorized the powerful role that affect plays in Africana *nationhood* and *nationalism* and, through engagement with womanist scholarship, the significance of spiritual mothers in nurturing and attending to black affective desire. Black feminist theorist Jennifer Nash offers a related and compelling argument for black feminist contributions to affect studies through what she calls "black feminist love politics." Her work of recovering a long genealogy of black feminist love politics uncovers a central connection between black feminism and womanism that I champion and find fruitful. However, Nash initially juxtaposed rather than harmonized this genealogy with a dominant black feminist tradition of identity politics that emerged in response to the field of (white) women's studies' appropriation and abuse of intersectionality theory.

Nash works to overcome some polarizing aspects of her initial approach in her book, *Black Feminism Reimagined after Intersectionality*. "In my earlier work," she writes, "I situated intersectionality's presumed identity politics and black feminist love-politics as wholly separate. [Here] I return to the questions I posed in previous work but answer them differently (or anew), suggesting that we need not consider love-politics and intersectionality as in opposition."[56] It is important to revisit the black feminist identitarianism, which Nash deems ultimately unproductive, to reconcile *identity* politics with *love* politics. Identity politics remains undertheorized in Nash's analysis as a defensive affect that performs work internal to the black feminist community, whereas black feminist *love* politics has the potential to address universal aims and relationality with others beyond the black community. A stratification of outward-facing love politics over inward-facing identity politics lingers in *Black Feminism Reimagined*, framing the options as choosing *either* identity politics that is intragroup focused *or* love politics that aims at intergroup affective affiliation.

In attempting to avoid oppositional framings of love and identity, however, Nash does acknowledge the importance of self-love; here is where the conclusions of this study can expand a crucial conversation that Nash initiated within black feminist studies, one that deserves no less attention within womanist and motherness studies. I realigned identity politics with affective politics in chapter 4 to underscore how questions of belonging and identity affiliation in the afterlife of slavery are aligned with heritage love (a form of self-love) in legacies of Africana religious *nationalism*.

Heritage love is important to engage in black feminist and womanist discourse because, contrary to stereotypic associations of black *nationalism* with masculinist ideologies and patriarchy, black women have ardently promoted a *womanist* tradition of heritage love across a range of Africana *nation* spaces. In Trinidad, heritage love has mobilized a spiritual politics of Africana religious *nationalism* among custodians of Yoruba-Orisa religion, many of whom are black women. Theorizing heritage love as an affective force in the religious consciousness and cultures of African descendants that spiritual mothers such as Iya Sangowunmi, Iya Eintou Springer, and Iya Amoye cultivate deepens our understanding of *motherness as a central source of womanism's love politics*.

Another rationale exists for placing this study in conversation with black feminist love politics. Treating black religion phenomenologically facilitates an apprehension of Africana religious *nationalism* as a *healing modality of going, becoming, and belonging inspired by heritage love*. This kind of love is an Africana affect cultivated in the breaches of involuntary separations from homelands and in the ontological separation that captors establish between themselves and their captives. Black people's longing for Africa and refusal to abandon this desideration also create a void between blacks and whites, many of whom are apprehensive about and vexed by black *nationalist* politics and Africana affect. Africana heritage love is unintelligible to the whites who "cast" black people "down so far," distant from the things they claim that blacks should love and desire.[57] However, this unintelligibility—black people's opacity—is their refuge, their "[ana]grammar of self-formation and motivation," and their remembrances and resemblances of Africa that invent and re-invent coveted habitations of relationality.

One of this volume's implicit arguments is that the space that heritage love creates between blacks and whites is a space of ontological pain and suffering that *whites* must enter to realize they too need a new origin story, new myths of creation, and an authentic knowing of themselves, which can only happen when they confront their long heritage of racecraft and renounce their unshakable faith in their fabricated whiteness. Without whites' descent into the abyss of negation and their initiation into a new mode of inhabitation, the ~~world~~ that lovers of justice and freedom desire will never be birthed. Exploring Yoruba-Orisa religion in Trinidad has certainly taught me that the birthing of futures beyond the world as blacks and nonblacks currently know it can only unfold consequent to the pain and suffering that trigger the reinvention of identity. I have learned too that religious studies scholarship is critical for an attentive analysis of what such futures might hold. The reinvention of *nations*, blackness, and kinship, the blending of old and new discoveries of the sacred, and the deployment of both the memory and symbol of Africa in Africana sacred poetics, as I have tracked these phenomena in the context of Trinidad across several centuries, serve to remind us that the reinvention of identity is an ongoing dynamic in personal, social, and political life everywhere we find blacks and nonblacks on this planet. Processes of reinvention assume a sacred valence not only because myths of origin and orientation necessarily come into play, but also because the reinvention of identity is simultaneously the reinvention of relationality. When carefully scrutinized, we see that relationality reveals lived religion and authentic religious devotion, and this argument is indeed the strongest theoretical intervention tightly binding together both volumes of this study.

Connections can and should be made across global cultures with respect to the reinvention of identity, but there are explicit connections that must be made among people of African descent, particularly diaspora*ed* Africans, which is what Tracey and I have privileged throughout our chapters. By pondering how bleeding cargoes became *nations* in the African diaspora, this two-volume study shows how the sacred/territorial poetics of black religious consciousness create inestimable habitations of black sociality in an antiblack world. Profoundly affected by omorisa of Trinidad and their modes of inhabitation, Tracey and I believe that they and other custodians of Africana religious *nationalism* possess the Soul-force needed to *have guts like calabash* and to *make a way out of no way*.[58] In the afterlife of John Cooper's cat-o'-nine tails whipping and of Yala's and Youba's severed ears, omorisa have taught us that re-creating cargoes as *nations* is a religious experience in itself—an interruptive invention of belonging, and a new evocation of ashé—that harbors potentials for exceeding this world of ontological terror.[59]

Afterword

ORISA VIGOYANA FROM GUYANA

Koro masa goro,
Vigoyana Samedona

Iya Sangowunmi was correct in only one sense when she said Trinidad's Orisa community had not made a local contribution to its inherited family of West African Orisa—the way Haiti had done with its Vodou family of Lwa. At some time and place, omorisa in Trinidad had welcomed into its family of invisible powers a Guyanese power named Vigoyana.[1] An aggressive deity whom some consider to be a forest Power or shrine surveyor, he answers to sobriquets such as "Guyanese buck" or simply "buck." I am not sure Iya would have been impressed if I had reminded her about Vigoyana, who most certainly is not found among the Powers of any other diasporic Orisa community. Most likely Iya had in mind an African personality who would represent some time period, significant event, or noble virtues deserving of apotheosis, as her elevation of Iya Rodney suggests. Fair enough, given the achievements of the Orisa community in Trinidad and especially given Trinidad's reputation as an originary site of African spiritual heritage for many eastern Caribbean religious custodians who share entangled histories with Orisa shrines and Spiritual Baptist houses of worship.

But Vigoyana intrigues me. His songs and drum rhythms are as West African in ritual language and syncopation as the Orisa who traveled to Trinidad through the Extended

Middle Passage. Vigoyana might be unruly, but he ultimately obeys the protocols of the Yoruba-Orisa palais. In his ritual invocation, recorded for an album titled Songs of the Orisha Palais, Vigoyana takes his place among a cadre of Yoruba deities, namely, Shakpanna (Soponna), Erinle, Osayin, Oya, and Shango.[2] The chants for each Orisa slide one into another, and Vigoyana's is no different. He introduces no disruption of the Yoruba-Orisa tradition's African ritual aesthetic and protocols. His adoption into the Yoruba-Orisa family is unquestionable.

At the same time, the Orisa Vigoyana exemplifies the principle of "cognitive openness" that Kọ́lá Abímbọ́lá has emphasized in his scholarship and teaching. Abímbọ́lá locates that principle in the Ifá sacred corpus and uses the example of Ifá's encouragement of adherence to Islam as the appropriate path for some Yoruba devotees. So, why does Ifá permit its followers such theological/ritual openness and exploration? "This is because Yorùbá Religion has a practical purpose," says Abímbọ́lá. "It is not merely concerned with faith and the afterlife, but also with practical guidelines on how to live together in a diverse, multi-cultural, global, and cosmopolitan world."[3]

Because of its rich multicultural, multiethnic, multiracial, multi-nation-al, and multireligious heritage, Trinidad and Tobago is a geography teeming with origin, migration, repatriation, and re-creation stories. T&T's postindependence struggle to construct a national story inclusive of all its heritages, though fraught with competition and contestation, has allowed room for the Orisa community to put Ifá's "practical guidelines" to work and to make opportunities out of its multicultural heritage. Certainly a nation that could adopt Vigoyana would have the social intelligence to capitalize on its shared pluralistic heritage with fellow citizens of South Asian descent, many of whom are Hindu or Muslim and have organized to preserve their religious and cultural liberties since the nineteenth century.[4] Without a doubt, the colony-turned-nation has been home to a distinct ethno-racial-religious dynamic in the African diaspora that has allowed Trinidad to exist as a unique postindependence space of black national belonging, especially in the wake of Orisa and Spiritual Baptist demands for religious freedom and civic inclusion.[5]

The nineteenth-century Baptist missionary Reverend William H. Gamble, who served in the southern coastal city of San Fernando, offered a colorful portrait of the colony's ethno-racial-religo-nation-al design at a dynamic moment in Trinidad's history. Roughly thirty years postslavery, the ethnic and religious diversity that increasingly characterized postemancipation Trinidad had yet to be considered an imperial treasure. For this reason, religious pluralism did nothing to alter the privileges reserved for churchgoing Christians. It did force, however, a sober assessment of Trinidad's mission field as a particularly challenging terrain to conquer for Christ, as Gamble confessed in "Progress in Trinidad" in the 1867 issue of The Missionary Herald. Setting aside for the moment his ethnocentric depictions of Asians and the African nations, the details of the region's diverse populations are striking:

You will be pleased to know that the kingdom of Christ is making some progress among the people of Trinidad. . . . Our work is comparatively easy in the American villages, but most difficult in San Fernando. In this small town of some five to six thousand inhabitants, we have many creeds and many tongues, and much confusion. The creoles may be regarded as Romanists, and they perhaps form half the population; the other half consists of a handful of Episcopalians, a sprinkling of Wesleyans, a score of Presbyterians, a dozen Baptists, and a couple of Free-Churchmen, besides the idolatrous and Mahommedan Coolies, and Chinese. The different forms of face and dress, the variety of sounds you will hear, are perplexing. The Chinese, with their high cheekbones, and small oval eyes, long tail and monosyllabic speech; the jet black African Yarraba, or Congoe, with his flat nose and thick lips, and sturdy limbs, walking side by side wih the gracefully, slightly-formed Asiatic, his features of the Caucasian mould. These, with here and there a Frenchman or an Englishman, with endless mixtures, and varieties of the whole, make up the people that buy and sell in our stores, and walk in our streets. To reach all these, one would need the gift of tongues. Consider their different languages, religions, customs, opinions, colours, prejudices, and how hopeless the task of trying to blend all these diversities into one harmonious whole. And yet such is the force and influence of climate and long residence, that these very different peoples would in a short period be shaken together, and made one by the all-levelling hand of time, were it not that we are constantly importing fresh Coolies, new Chinese, and other Africans. What the influence of the Gospel would be, I know not; but to bring all these people under the sound of the truth, would require a very large and very learned staff of men.[6]

Gamble's prejudiced observations provide, if nothing else, a window into the social composition of postemancipation Trinidad and the impossible project of "bring[ing]" such a diverse population "under the [Christian] sound of truth." In this context, religious "truth," circulated through many languages, and linguistic diversity further complicated racial, ethnic, and cultural distinctions across the colony's manifold social enclaves. In the 1860s, for example, one readily encountered racially black populations—from the ex-enslaved and West India Regiment soldiers to the African American Loyalist and liberated African indentured settlers—who spoke French Creole, English, Yoruba, Kikongo, Mandingo, and other African languages. Missionaries with the requisite "gift of tongues" whom Gamble desired were hardly forthcoming, a circumstance his predecessor, George Cowen knew all too well. "Send us a French and Spanish scholar," Cowen desperately wrote in his 1843 Baptist Magazine report, "if you can procure such, who will spend and be spent in this dark land."[7]

Still, the prospect of uniting Trinidadians under the catholic canopy of Christian faith was bleak during the mid-nineteenth century and, despite tremendous progress, has remained an ambitious objective up to the present century. A perusal of T&T's national holidays illustrates how salient Hindu, Muslim, and African religious ceremonies are across the country.[8] Despite their personal religious convictions, prominent government officials regularly appear at public events linked to significant Hindu, Muslim, and Orisa celebrations (as discussed in chapter 4). In addition, census figures for 2011 indicate that religious pluralism continues to define Trinidad's national identity: approximately 25 percent of the population identified their official religion as Hinduism, Islam, or Orisa.[9]

African religions in Trinidad are experiencing their best days since the Middle Passage. Observing the nation's flag suspended alongside Orisa nation flags, procuring government-donated land (the Orisa Village Site in Maloney) for nation-al events and initiatives, viewing Orisa priests offering official prayers at the opening of Parliament, hearing elected officials deliver remarks at Orisa events, and reading the transcribed reports of members of Parliament defending Obeah as a legitimate African spiritual system of belief and practice, one can only conclude that the Yoruba-Orisa community in Trinidad is actually transforming its nation-state through a harmonized vision of citizenship, one that bridges Africana nation-al belonging and national belonging. Omorisa in Trinidad are "Polynational" and "Omnational," to quote the Baltimore Afro-American contestants who devised these twin categories that actually precede and exceed racial designations.[10]

The heavy footprints of Pan-Africanism, Black Power, and Africana religious nationalism are unmistakable in Orisa devotees' struggle for religious freedom and national inclusion in Trinidad, throwing into sharp relief what has been a clash of ideologies, loyalties, and identities when we examine the fate of Pan-Africanism, Black Power, and Africana religious nationalism under the crushing weight of state power in the United States of America.[11] African descendants in Trinidad and the United States share historical moments of migration, settlement, and enhancing one another's welfare. African American soldiers settled in Trinidad's company villages during the early nineteenth century and contributed distinct patterns of worship to the Spiritual Baptist heritage. African Americans such as Anna Julia Cooper, Anna Jones, and W. E. B. Du Bois, and Trinidadians such as Henry Sylvester Williams and Richard Emmanuel Phipps collaborated, delivered speeches, and served on leadership committees at the first Pan-African Conference in 1900. And Trinidad's native son Stokely Carmichael (aka Kwame Toure) studied at Howard University and became a prominent voice in the Student Nonviolent Coordinating Committee and a pioneering theoretician of Black Power.[12] Trinidad's Black Power leaders, organizations, and enthusiasts were profoundly inspired by Carmichael's political vision and organizational skills and by other leading Black Power figures such as Kathleen Cleaver (see figure Aft.1).[13]

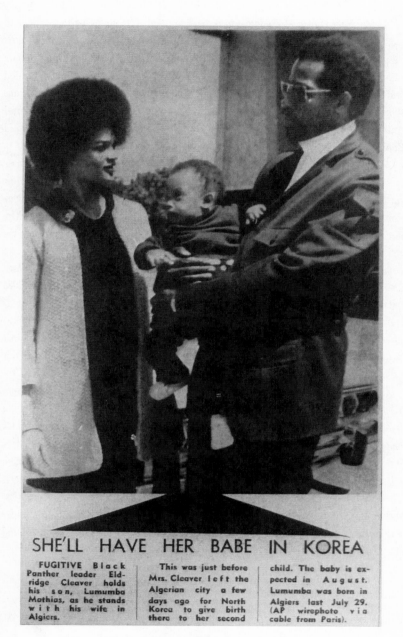

SHE'LL HAVE HER BABE IN KOREA

FUGITIVE Black Panther leader Eldridge Cleaver holds his son, Lumumba Mathias, as he stands with his wife in Algiers.

This was just before Mrs. Cleaver left the Algerian city a few days ago for North Korea to give birth there to her second

child. The baby is expected in August. Lumumba was born in Algiers last July 29. (AP wirephoto via cable from Paris).

FIGURE AFT.1 Kathleen Cleaver with Eldridge Cleaver and Lumumba Mathias Cleaver in Algiers, Algeria. Black Power activists in Trinidad followed the events and political engagements of Black Nationalist comrades such as Kathleen Cleaver, her husband, and other US advocates of Black Power. (*Evening News*, June 9, 1970. Courtesy of Guardian Media Limited.)

Today, Egbe Onisin Eledumare and Little Oyo collaborate with Oyotunji Village to plan and execute transnational Yoruba-Orisa ceremonies and events. But their sociopolitical positionalities vis-à-vis the nation-state could not be more dissimilar. Omorisa who embody nationalist principles take pride in singing the national anthem of Trinidad and Tobago, "Forged from the Love of Liberty," at Orisa events.[14] African Americans have shown much more patriotic singularity when occasions arise to sing the Negro National Anthem, "Lift Every Voice and Sing," than when prompted to sing "The Star-Spangled Banner."

What is unfolding now in Trinidad seems unthinkable in the Anglo-Protestant American ethos that Yoruba-Ifa communities and other devotees of African-heritage religions currently experience, despite the United States' rhetoric of extending democratic participation and religious freedom to all "Americans." In the current US political climate where national leaders and politicians have weaponized white power in ways unseen since the 1960s, I expect that omorisa in the United States are more likely to view the national flag as "a thin veil to cover up crimes which would disgrace a nation of savages."[15] In which America might we witness a counter-public such as Oyotunji African Village assembled with elected US officials at an Orisa event creating a third space of citizenship that subtends nation-al and national belonging?[16] Whereas Yoruba-Orisa post–Black Power communities are now creating coextensive or collaborative publics in T&T, Oyotunji and other Yoruba devotional families in the United States still contend with a deep-seated double exclusion from national belonging based on race and religion.

The 2020 US Census tells America how less white it is today than it was ten years ago. Yet the browning of America through a rise in the Latinx population will mean nothing if America's antiblack and anti-African structures remain comfortably in place. Black belonging in the United States is a "hope unborn [that] died."[17] But the "interruptive invention" that can set us all free resides in the afterlife of that hope.[18] The omorisa who offered a dwelling place to Vigoyana from Guyana perhaps know this better than most. They are well positioned to draw from their powerful motherness-inspired love politics, their kinship ethic of inclusion, and their legacy of cooperative creactivity to help organize local and trans-nation-al responses to the challenges of citizenship, nationhood, and the nation-state in the twenty-first-century African diaspora.[19]

Abbreviations Used in Notes

EN	*Evening News*
MFH Papers	Melville Herskovits, "Trinidad Field Trip-Diary," Melville J. & Frances S. Herskovits Papers, Schomburg Center for Research in Black Culture, The New York Public Library, New York
MH Papers	"Memorandum for Andrew Carr/Some Research Problems among African Derived Groups in Trinidad," Melville Herskovits Papers, Box 55, Folder 21, Series 35/6, Northwestern University Archives, Evanston, Illinois
MS-AC	Alexander Garden to London Office, May 5, 1740, Box 20 from Lambeth Palace Library, vol. 941, no. 72, Manuscripts of the Archbishop of Canterbury.
NA-DS	National Archives, U.S. Department of State, Record Group 59, College Park, Maryland
NCOE Papers	National Council of Orisa Elders Papers, Port of Spain, Trinidad
POSG	*Port of Spain Gazette*
TC	*Trinidad Chronicle*
TE	*Trinidad Express*
TTG	*The Trinidad Guardian*
T&TG	*Trinidad and Tobago Guardian*
T&TN	*Trinidad and Tobago Newsday*

Notes

Preface

1 Layli Maparyan discusses "harmonizing and coordinating" as an important component of womanist methodology in *The Womanist Idea*, 56–57.

2 Vansina, *Paths in the Rainforests*, 258.

3 Long, *Significations*.

4 "Within the discipline of religion, David D. Hall and Robert Orsi have for close to two decades been at the forefront in pioneering 'a history of practice' in American religious history through the heuristic rubric of 'lived religion.' Inspired from the French concept *la religion vécue*, Hall and Orsi sought to encourage new innovations in 'cultural and ethnographical approaches to the study of religion and American religious history' by 'enlisting perspectives' that privilege human practice as an important lens for determining how humans 'live with and work through multiple realms of meaning.' Through examining 'modalities of practice' over and against normative theologies, doctrines, or elite orthodoxies, lived religion sought to recast the disciplinary representation of religion into a more flexible, 'complex and multifaceted phenomenon.' Lived religion expanded the interpretive gaze of American religious history to include not only practice as a crucial site for engaging religious meaning but also the inclusion of non-elite popular communities as significant actors in religious production." Quoted in Hucks, "Perspectives in Lived History," 3.

5 Long, *Significations*, 6.

6 Fields and Fields, *Racecraft*, 5.

7 Olúpọ̀nà, *City of 201 Gods*, esp. 1–5.

8 JanMohammed, *The Death-Bound-Subject*.

9 Scholars such as Tweed, *Crossing and Dwelling*; Tandberg, *Relational Religion*; Mwale, *Relationality in Theological Anthropology*; Harris et al., "Womanist

Theology"; and Krech, "Relational Religion," have proposed the need for developing relational theories of religion and theology. Our approach to relationality is distinct from these perspectives in that it takes its point of departure from a Longian conception of orientation.

10 Italics mine. James, *Varieties*, 31–32. On "soul-life," see chapter 3, n. 65 of this volume.

11 See James, *Varieties*.

Introduction

1 *Nation, nationhood,* and related word compounds are italicized in this study to indicate Africana constructions of sociocultural networks and institutions that include governing offices and micropolitical activities but are not political state structures. For more information, see n. 3 of Hucks's "Introduction" in *Obeah, Orisa, and Religious Identity in Trinidad.*

2 On concepts of primordial and civic publics, see Ekeh, "Colonialism."

3 Trinidadian term for elders. Here it references elders in the Orisa religion, especially those who grew up socialized in the tradition before the rise of the Black Power Movement and black consciousness.

4 At this writing, only Castor's *Spiritual Citizenship* has offered a book-length treatment of Orisa religious formation since the 1960s.

5 León, *La Llorona's Children*, 5.

6 The Spiritual Baptist tradition is the other conspicuous, influential African religious complex that overlaps Orisa religion in Trinidad. Whether the Spiritual Baptist repertoire is considered an African-*heritage* religion might be debatable. Although I think it certainly is, in this context I refer to the religious heritages transplanted in Trinidad by the African *nations* during and immediately after slavery.

7 I invoke Tracey Hucks's concept of "diasporaed" to emphasize the fact that, when discussing the African captives of the transatlantic slave trade and slavery in the Western Hemisphere, which led to the formation of an African diaspora, central to our analysis should be the fact that the "diaspora" *happened* to those African captives who found themselves involuntarily exiled from their African homelands and enslaved or indentured in the Caribbean and the Americas. See n. 24 in Hucks's "Introduction" in *Obeah, Orisa, and Religious Identity in Trinidad* for her concept of "diasporaed."

8 Grillo, *An Intimate Rebuke.*

9 Fernheimer, *Stepping into Zion*, 4.

10 I borrow Saidiya Hartman's term "afterlife" throughout this text, perceiving its double meaning as apt for a religious studies investigation such as this that attends to conceptualizations of afterlife (postdeath). See "Venus in Two Acts," 13.

One. I Believe He Is a Yaraba, a Tribe of Africans Here

1 TC, April 9, 1872 (title quotation also from same source). John Cooper was
   arrested on November 25, 1871. See Hucks, *Obeah, Orisa, and Religious Identity*,
   for more on Cooper's case. I depart from Orlando Patterson's argument that
   the slave/diasporaed African only has a past but not a heritage. No matter
   how alienating slavery as social death was for African-descended people,
   commodification could not deprive them of cultural memory, knowledge, or
   all structures and mechanisms for reproducing aspects of their intangible heritage, especially when considering African conceptions of blood and blood
   ties in the transmission of cultural knowledge and ways of life. Examples
   of significance to a study such as this pertain to the role of altered states of
   consciousness in the transmission of heritage. As I discuss in this volume,
   dreams and manifestation (aka possession trance) are conduits for the transmission of heritage, often through the intention/agency of blood ancestors
   in Yoruba and other African heritage religious cultures. See Patterson, *Slavery
   and Social Death*, 5. See also Rucker, *Gold Coast Diasporas* for his concept of "social resurrection," which complicates and resists the demarcation Patterson
   draws between "the past" and "heritage."
2 Cooper likely learned the "little French" he knew through interactions with
   French-speaking Creoles in Trinidad, who outnumbered English speakers
   at the time of his arrest. French Creole remained Trinidad's predominant
   language throughout most of the late nineteenth century, especially among
   commoners. See Warner-Lewis, *Trinidad Yoruba*, 51; Wood, *Trinidad in Transition*; Brereton, *Race Relations in Colonial Trinidad*, 165–66.
3 Roughly nine thousand Africans entered Trinidad after emancipation, mostly
   as liberated captives from slave ships; Yorubas comprised a significant
   percentage. For more, see Hucks, *Obeah, Orisa, and Religious Identity*; Adderley, *"New Negroes from Africa"*; Trotman, "Reflections on the Children," 215.
   On Cooper's ethnic/cultural heritage, see Brereton, *Race Relations in Colonial
   Trinidad*, 154–55. For helpful demographics on the settlement of liberated
   Africans throughout the wider Caribbean/Americas, see Cwik, "End of the
   British Atlantic Slave Trade."
4 On the censuring of African culture, see Trotman, "Reflections on the
   Children," 222–27; Brereton, *Race Relations in Colonial Trinidad*, esp. 152–75;
   Springer, "Orisa and the Spiritual Baptist Religion," 85–107.
5 See introduction, n. 2.
6 Africana assertions of *nation* identities and productions of *nation* mechanisms were a widespread phenomenon among enslaved and indentured laborers in every corner of the European slaveholding and colonial world. For
   more on these institutions and their religious frameworks see Yai, "African

Diasporan Concepts"; Carneiro, *Candomblés da Bahia*; "Structure of African Cults in Bahia"; Dantas, *Vovó Nagô e Papai Branco*.

7 Decolonial scholars have introduced conceptually rich theories of sovereignty that cohere with my understanding of sovereignty exceeding state formations. Modes of sovereignty addressed in this chapter accord with what David Treuer describes as sovereignty's "social dimension" in *Heartbeat of Wounded Knee*, 388–89. According to Treuer, "sovereignty isn't only a legal attitude or a political reality; it has a social dimension as well. The idea and practice of sovereignty carries with it a kind of dignity—a way of relating to the self, to others, to the past, and to the future that is dimensionally distinct. . . . To believe in sovereignty, to let it inform and define not only one's political and legal existence but also one's community, to move through the world imbued with the dignity of that reality, is to resolve one of the major contradictions of modern Indian life: it is to find a way to be Indian and modern simultaneously." Azoulay's concept of "worldly sovereignty" in *Potential History*, 388, is also conversant with Treuer's theorizations.

8 TTG, July 10, 1919, 7. This case is also discussed in Eastman, *Fight for Dignity*, 106–7. The town of Carenage is in northwest Trinidad near Port of Spain.

9 A Rada religious rite was described without reference to Obeah in at least one 1872 newspaper report (see n. 139). See Warner-Lewis, *Guinea's Other Suns*, 52, for her reflections on the scarcity of sources about nineteenth-century liberated Africans of Yoruba heritage.

10 TTG, September 7, 1929.

11 TTG, September 11, 1929. This must be the same editorial Herskovits read while briefly in Trinidad in 1929. To access Herskovits's discussion of the complaint, see Herskovits, *Trinidad Village*, v.

12 TTG, September 12, 1929. The author's handling of religion and culture intersects a long-standing debate in the comparative study of African religions and provides a basis for revisiting the position that "religion" is nothing more than a Western folk construct and a scholarly classificatory device with no bearing on studies of African societies and spiritual traditions. I use the term "religion" as a conceptual tool and an explanatory mechanism for scholarly thinking about persons' and communities' imagination, orientation, and behavior vis-à-vis the visible/invisible world(s).

13 Trotman, "Reflections on the Children," 217–18.

14 Smith, *Imagining Religion*; Smith, *Map Is Not Territory*; Braun and McCutcheon, *Introducing Religion*.

15 Trotman, "Reflections on the Children," 215.

16 For an important analysis of changing West African and diasporic ethnonymic interpretations of "Nago" identity as a "Yoruba" designation in the eighteenth and nineteenth centuries, see Law, "Ethnicity and the Slave Trade," 205–19.

17 T.71/501: 1813, Slave Register, Trinidad Plantation Slaves. Silveste's 1815 death is recorded in a column marked "Corrections." This Register includes information for each enslaved person under the following headings: Names, Surnames, Colour, Employment, Age, Stature, Marks, Country, Relations, and Corrections.

18 Higman, *Slave Populations of the British Caribbean*; John, *Plantation Slaves of Trinidad*. Exceptions might include St. Hillaire Begorrat (1759–1851). According to De Verteuil, *History of Diego Martin*, 58, the slaveholder imported 100 Yoruba and Congo captives to labor on his properties in Diego Martin and allowed "each tribal group . . . to live in [its] own 'village.'" "The Congoes . . . lived in Congo Village and the Yorubas in St. Mary's Village." See chapter 2 of Hucks, *Obeah, Orisa, and Religious Identity*, for more information about Begorrat. De Verteuil does not provide sources to support the claim that the 100 Africans captives were "Congoes" and "Yorubas." See also Besson, *Book of Trinidad*.

19 Trotman, "Reflections on the Children," 222.

20 Warner-Lewis, *Guinea's Other Suns*.

21 Trotman, *Crime in Trinidad*; Warner-Lewis, *Guinea's Other Suns*, 34, 78, 119; *Trinidad Yoruba*, 37.

22 Wood, *Trinidad in Transition*, 39.

23 Warner-Lewis's research indicates that nineteenth-century "Africans termed their tribal groupings 'nations.'" Elder's scholarship and Herskovits's fieldnotes make clear that "nation" identities were still salient among liberated African descendants in the twentieth century not only in Trinidad but also in neighboring countries such as Grenada. See Warner-Lewis, *Guinea's Other Suns*, 15; Elder, "Yoruba Ancestor Cult in Gasparillo," 7.

24 I acknowledge the term as an etic scholarly analytic employed to frame my analysis of Yoruba-Orisa ritual and culture across a period (nineteenth century to the present) when perhaps a significant percentage of Orisa custodians in Trinidad and elsewhere would find the rubric of "religion" an unsuitable classification for their tradition.

25 Yai, "African Diaspora Concepts," 245–46. Primary documents from the slave trade era reveal that sixteenth- and seventeenth-century European handlers (missionaries, merchants, etc.) introduced what was for them an ethnolinguistic category, "nation" (*nacion*), to delineate captive Africans. Across various European tongues, the term "nation" and its cognates can be found in records of sale, transport, inventory, and desertion. The shared realities that defined diasporaed African "nations" were shifting, often revolving around spoken languages, bodily scarification patterns, and other mechanisms of cultural belonging.

26 I use the concept "pre-Yoruba" to avoid imposing a "Yoruba" meta-identity on people-groups that had not yet unified as Yoruba peoples before the mid- to late nineteenth century. Some scholars even question whether Yoruba is a

cultural or ethnic concept. Kólá Abímbólá resists standard interpretations of the Yoruba designation as an ethnic identifier. Similar to the Jewish identity, he argues "Yoruba" is a religious identity. See Abímbólá, "Yorùbá Diaspora," 317–26.

27 Thornton, *Africa and Africans*, 220, 322 (italics mine).

28 Caron, "'Of a Nation,'" 113–16.

29 Warner-Lewis, *Guinea's Other Suns*, 15–24; Chambers, "Ethnicity in the Diaspora"; Gomes, "'Atlantic Nations' and the Origins of Africans."

30 Matory writes of African heritage religions in the diaspora that "these are religions of spirit possession, divination, and healing that also define peoplehoods called 'nations,' which link them with specific places in Africa." See his *Black Atlantic Religion*, 5. For a sound treatment of this topic in the Brazilian context, see Parés, "The 'Nagôization' Process." Parés analyzes how the Candomblé religious structure solidified multiple *nations* in Bahia.

31 Byrd, "Eboe, Country, Nation," and Equiano, *Interesting Narrative*," 145–46; Sweet, "Quiet Violence of Ethnogenesis."

32 See Warner and Lunt, *Social Life of a Modern Community*, for the first instance of the term "ethnicity" in US American literature. See also Lachenicht, "Ethnicity." Lovejoy's treatment of "ethnicity" and "nation" in the West and Africa is a textured sociohistorical analysis of both terms, satisfying to many. Yet it leaves me wondering whether ethnicity carries too much baggage, especially in the United States, to be salvaged as a synonym for Africana *nationhood*. See Lovejoy, "Identifying Enslaved Africans," 8–13.

33 Emphasis in original. Michael Jackson, *As Wide as the World Is Wise*, 15.

34 See Carneiro, *Candomblés da Bahia*; "Structure of African Cults"; Dantas, *Vovó Nagô e Papai Branco*; *Nagô Grandma and White Papa*; Matory, *Black Atlantic Religion*; Taylor, *Nation Dance*, 1–13; Daniel, *Dancing Wisdom*.

35 This study complements the findings of Castor's research on post-Black Power Orisa communities in Trinidad not just during the late twentieth and early twenty-first centuries (cf. chapters 4 and 5 in this volume) but also during the nineteenth and early twentieth centuries. See Castor's *Spiritual Citizenship*.

36 Yai, "African Diasporan Concepts," 244.

37 Warren, "Black Care," 46.

38 Warren, "Black Care," 41. See also Daniel, *Dancing Wisdom*, 4. Daniel's comparative study of African heritage religions in three diaspora contexts explores the spiritual, cultural, micropolitical, and affective dimensions of *nation-building* through the structures of Haitian Vodou, Cuban Yoruba, and Brazilian Candomblé; it affirms, for African-descended groups, that "expressing nationhood in the Americas was dependent on several characteristics, religion being one." When referring to "nations," Daniel explains, "I do not mean geopolitical nations. I am referring to continental loyalties and legacies

based on heritage, marriage, adoption, and allegiances that were understood in Africa as 'ethnic group identity.' I also include those congregations . . . created by the experience of enslavement—that is, those who were captured and dispersed in the Americas and who, as a result, were named by their captors or named themselves" (48–49). Daniel brings into focus some of the material and existential conditions of transatlantic enslavement that precipitated *nation*-based groupings among many diasporaed Africans.

39 Yai, "African Diasporan Concepts," 254.

40 See Peel, *Religious Encounter*; Matory, "English Professors of Brazil," esp. 82–88, 96–97; *Black Atlantic Religion*. Peel's and Matory's conclusions should be balanced against Olatunji Ojo's argument that custodians of Orisa worship and practice in the homeland also played a significant role in the "birth of Yoruba ethnicity," which could be why Abímbólá considers Yoruba a "religious" identity. See Ojo, "'Heepa' (Hail) Òrìṣà," 9. See also n. 33.

41 Peel, *Religious Encounter*, 284.

42 Peel, *Religious Encounter*. Italics mine.

43 Equiano's use of the terms *nation* and *country* in his eighteenth-century memoir is analogous. Both concepts are multivalent designations, inclusive of diverse structures of social and political organization. See *Interesting Narrative*. See also Byrd, "Eboe, Country, Nation."

44 Pre-Yorùbá groups were likely more similar to one another than they were to most other cultural groupings. An important exception is the Rada *nation*.

45 Warner-Lewis devotes a chapter of *Guinea's Other Suns* to unpacking the relationship between political and historical events in pre-Yorùbáland and Yoruba *nation* songs, expressions, and memories in Trinidad. See esp. 1–5.

46 Warner-Lewis, *Guinea's Other Suns*, 93. The original Yoruba verses are

> Ẹrú Ọlọ́fà!
> Orín nàá ń jágbọ́n erí ọmọ o
> Ẹrú Ọlọ́fà!
> Ayá ń kí lọ́mọ Yorùbá

47 Onipede and Adegbite, "Igbon, Iresa, and Ikoyi," 27.

48 Warner-Lewis, *Guinea's Other Suns*, 93. The original Yoruba verses are

> A màá rèlémará wa
> Yorùbá ti kó
> Ká lọ ìwò.

49 Warner-Lewis, *Trinidad Yoruba*, 44. Scholars have written about analogous nineteenth-century "native courts" or indigenous adjudicatory systems among enslaved and emancipated/liberated African descendants across the Caribbean and the Americas. See R. Stewart, *Religion and Society*, 130–32.

50 Warner-Lewis, *Guinea's Other Suns*, 30–31, 54, 65. See also Herskovits's note on pp. 273–74 of *Trinidad Village* concerning Margaret Buckley and her description of "Egungun" in Trinidad.

51 Warner-Lewis, *Trinidad Yoruba*, 43–44; *Guinea's Other Suns*, 118; POSG, June 19, 1912, 1.

52 For example, Warner-Lewis interviewed Mrs. Evelyn Bonaparte in 1971 when Bonaparte was eighty-five years old. Her family stories reached back to her paternal grandmother, Josephine, who "had come to Trinidad in her late teens and died in 1899, when Evelyn was twelve." See *Guinea's Other Suns*, 61.

53 Warner-Lewis, *Guinea's Other Suns*, 125–40.

54 At least twenty-two public notices to this effect were published between 1907 and 1914. Most involve the properties of Tom, Jack, Eloi, and John Yaraba. The April 28, 1909, POSG, on p. 5, carried an article, "The Caroni Local Board Inquiry," that mentions "Xerxes and Yaraba roads."

55 See POSG stories on Obeah, "Voodoo," and other analogous phenomena in the following countries: Demerara (August 6, 1911); Jamaica (March 9, 1908); Montserrat (December 19, 1908); Haiti (August 24, 1911; June 2, 1912); Cuba (January 22, 1913; January 10, 1914) and United States (March 15, 1912). Other reports about Obeah in Trinidad were published also.

56 Anonymous writer, "A Bush Doctor's Bath," POSG, January 19, 1911.

57 POSG, June 26, 1910. Compare with Warner-Lewis's description of annual "African dances" Yoruba *nation* members "held earlier in this [twentieth] century at Tunapuna." Some Yorubas were also members of the Societies of St. Peter and St John. They "celebrated their annual anniversaries by attending Mass and then inviting the priest to bless the food for the feast. The occasion continued with drumming and dancing." *Guinea's Other Suns*, 119.

58 Herskovits, *Trinidad Village*, 327–31.

59 The scholarly assumption or assertion that Catholic elements were incorporated into Trinidad's Yoruba-Orisa religion during the nineteenth century is widespread. However, I have yet to see scholars provide evidence to corroborate this belief. Perhaps the data exist in newspaper accounts, colonial records, and oral memory. If scholars have access to such evidence, they have not cited sources to this effect.

60 Herskovits, *Trinidad Village*, 321.

61 Herskovits, Trinidad Field Trip-Diary, 112, box 15, folder 83A, MFH Papers, Schomburg Center for Research in Black Culture, The New York Public Library, New York.

62 Herskovits, *Trinidad Village*, 324.

63 Herskovits, Trinidad Field Trip-Diary, 112, MFH Papers.

64 Glazier, "Wither Sango," 239.

65 Trotman, "Reflections on the Children," 216–17. For figures concerning the 20,656 slaves turned apprentices who were fully emancipated on August 1,

1838, see *Reports from Committees, 1847–8: Supplement No.1 to the Eighth Report from the Select Committee on Sugar and Coffee Planting* (Ordered by the House of Commons to be printed 29 May 1848), 66.

66 Glazier, "Wither Sango," 242. Mọgbà is often spelled *mongba* in the literature on Trinidadian Orisa. In Ọ̀yọ́, the mọgbà were the senior priests of Ṣàngó at the royal shrine at Kòso. See Pemberton and Afọláyan, *Yorùbá Sacred Kinship,* 152.

67 See n. 2. Britain invaded Trinidad in 1797 and established governorship; however, Spain formally ceded the territory to Britain in 1802.

68 Cothonay, *Trinidad,* 61–66. Original translation with the assistance of Dali Cintras Bathares.

69 Cothonay, *Trinidad,* 290–91.

70 Piersen, *Black Yankees,* 117–42; Kerr-Ritchie, *Rites of August First;* Southern, *Music of Black Americans;* Dewulf, *Pinkster King.*

71 For documentation of parallel traditions among African descendants in Spain, Portugal, and Latin America, see Peabody, "'Dangerous Zeal,'" 79–80. Peabody notes that similar celebrations among French natives occasioned the "reversal of social roles, with apprentices acting as kings and wives ruling their husbands."

72 Trotman, "Reflections on the Children," 217.

73 "*Kábíyèsí*" translated means "No-one-dare-challenge-or-question-your-authority." See Akínyẹmí, "Place of Ṣàngó," 26. Traditions, interpretations, and translations of "Ṣàngó/Sango" as an Orisa and historical figure are legion and complicated in scholarly and devotional contexts. See https://www.diannemstewart.com/books for Kọ́lá Abímbọ́lá's assessment of "five different Ṣàngó" in which he disaggregates and typologizes major interpretive traditions regarding this prominent Òrìṣà.

74 Cocoa production and trade exploded during the late 1870s and lasted until 1920 when oil production increased. See Trotman, "Reflections on the Children," 222–23.

75 Warner-Lewis, *Guinea's Other Suns,* 42, 117, 123 n. 10. As far as I know, the earliest written reference to an Orisa "palais" is from an apparently unpublished paper by Charles S. Espinet. Espinet sent the paper, "Manifestation of Wêrê in Trinidad Shango," to Herskovits with a cover letter dated November 29, 1945. He writes, "Wêrê mediums . . . break 'palais' conventions," and explains "palais" is "the name given to the bamboo and thatched roof 'tent' in which the dancing takes place." In two of the earliest scholarly studies of African heritage religious cultures in Trinidad, Herskovits and Carr both identify the ritual spaces reserved for worship as inclusive of a "tent" and "chapelle." Their descriptions of the tent are consistent with Espinet's definition of the palais and with later anthropological studies of the Yoruba-Orisa palais.

76 Warner-Lewis, *Guinea's Other Suns*, 49–50.

77 Viscount Goderich, "Dispatch from Viscount Goderich to Major-General Sir Lewis Grant," 31. *Papers Relative to the Legislative Council in Trinidad* 353. *Accounts and Papers of the House of Commons. United Kingdom: Ordered to Be Printed, 1832.*

78 Original translation. Cothonay, *Trinidad*, 303–5.

79 Glazier, "Wither Sango," 234.

80 By the mid-1930s Trinidadian calypsonians began recording songs about the Yoruba religion, including Gerald Clark and the Keskidee Trio's "Shango" (1935), Tiger's "Yaraba Shango" (1936), Cobra's "Shango Song" (1937), and Lord Caresser's "Shango" (1938). Roaring Lion's "Shango Dance" (1940), released the year following Herskovits's research trip to Trinidad, expanded this repertoire, and other calypsos addressing Trinidad's Yoruba-based religious complex as "Shango" appeared in the following decades. RCA/Rounder Records was the first to record most early calypsos about "Shango" between 1934 and 1940. For more on the history of Calypso in Trinidad, see Rohlehr, *Calypso and Society*, and Hill's compendium volume, *Calypso Calaloo*, 252–55. See also Trotman, "Reflections on the Children," 226–27, for an analysis of the "self-denigrating agenda" that many early calypsonians promoted in Trinidadian popular culture through demeaning lyrics about Yoruba-Orisa religion.

81 Branding is both a psychological and physical ritual process. It is unclear how widespread was the physical practice of branding captive Africans with hot irons. Roger Hepburn, "Branding," 67, observes that "many . . . European governments, slave traders and trading companies, and African monarchs branded the Africans to ensure others were aware to whom the slaves belonged." Other sources suggest that the Portuguese, Dutch, French and British all engaged in the practice, as did individual slave owners.

82 Warner-Lewis, *Guinea's Other Suns*, 7–15, 28–29, 52.

83 Brereton, *Race Relations in Colonial Trinidad*, 135.

84 See https://www.diannemstewart.com/books for additional information on the relationship between "Yé! Ekún ara wa la mí sun" and the Odù Ogbèatè.

85 Aiyejina, Gibbons, and Phills, "Context and Meaning," 129. See tracks 15, "Yé! Ekún ara wa la mí sun," and 16, "Explanation of Yé! Ekún ara wa la mí sun," on *Peter Was a Fisherman: The 1939 Trinidad Field Recordings of Melville and Frances Herskovits*, Vol. 1 (Rounder Records, CD 1114, 1939).

86 Trotman, "Reflections on the Children," 218–19, proposes that the Orisa, Shango, became emblematic of Yoruba-Orisa religion in Trinidad for two reasons. First, he "provide[d] [a] . . . unifying symbol for the original heterogeneous Yoruba imperial rule and serve[d] as a mechanism of cultural integration in the empire. In a strange, [new] land," Trotman writes, "various subethnic Yoruba groups may have sought to transcend intraregional

animosities and rivalries by emphasising the common symbol of Shango." Second, "the preeminence of Shango may have also been the result of the numerical dominance of arrivals from Oyo or people from . . . areas where Shango was already the pre-eminent deity in the pantheon." On sovereignty, see n. 7.

87 In "Ambivalent Representations of Ṣàngó," 187, Akínyẹmí translates "Ṣàngó pípè" as "intoning Ṣàngó" and describes this collection of stories and information about Ṣàngó as "praise poetry." In "Religious Politics," 95, Ìṣọlá notes that some scholars prefer the classification "descriptive poetry" because, as a prime example of the oriki genre, the Ṣàngó pípè "tells the whole story of its subject, including all the unpleasant details . . . oriki is not all praise."

88 Ìṣọlá, "Religious Politics," 94.

89 According to Kọ́lá Abímbọ́lá, telephone communication with author, February 22, 2022, "A contemptuous aláàfin had to commit suicide once the calabash was presented. That was the law because the calabash is presented by the Oyo Mesi (the aláàfin's Executive Council), who were all associated with important Orisa, and were all regarded as the voice of the people. Bearing in mind that the tenure of an aláàfin's reign is for life, 'suicide' here is not really suicide; it is 'regicide' in the British sense of the word. . . . It is the judicial execution of a monarch after a 'trial' and 'legal sentence' of death has been passed. By this I mean that the Oyo Mesi would have conferred with their constituents and would have held meetings in which they would have come to a unanimous agreement that it was time for the reign of that Alaafin to come to an end. Abdication was not a possibility then. There can't be two living individuals with the ceremonies of aláàfin conferred on them. This is one of those things that indicate that the Yorùbá political structure was not really a 'monarchy.' It was a representative democracy." I use the third person plural pronoun as a gender-neutral option. Some scholars have noted that not all precolonial rulers of the territories that would become Yorùbáland were male. For example, Aláàfin, Ọba Ọ̀rọ̀pọ̀tọ̀ Iyùn (also Ọba Ọ̀rọ̀pọ̀tọọyùn or Ọba Ọ̀rọ̀pọ̀tọníyùn), was a woman. See Oyěwùmí, Invention of Women, 80–120.

90 According to Law, "Early Yoruba Historiography," 73, this "Fourth Reading Book" was likely prepared by Agbebi and Ọkẹ but includes substantial portions of Hethersett's history of Ọ̀yọ́. See Iwe Kika Ẹkẹrin Li Ede Yoruba (Lagos, Nigeria: C.M.S. Bookshop; Exeter: James Townsend and Sons [Printers], 1944 [1911]). I have not been able to locate what Law describes as Hethersett's "history of Ọyọ" (73). Although Law also mentions "historical texts by A. L. Hethersett" (77), he does not provide any official title or titles of Hethersett's corpus, leading me to believe it might be inaccessible today or have had limited circulation as an unpublished manuscript. Law's bibliography offers more details about the materials in the Fourth Reading

Book: "*Iwe Kika Ẹkẹrin li Ede Yoruba*. Lagos: C.M.S. Bookshop, 1911. Contains material on the history of Ọyọ by A.L. Hethersett, of Ijaye by E.H. Ọkẹ, and of Abeokuta by Rev. E.W. George (pp. 49–78, 120–29, 165–86)." Hethersett, who was of Yorùbá descent, had worked for British agents in the region, serving as the chief clerk and interpreter in the Governor's Office at Lagos; he might have had strong motives for planting a disparaging narrative about Ṣàngó in the minds of his audiences.

91 Ìṣòlá, "Religious Politics," 96.

92 Akínyẹmí, "Ambivalent Representations of Ṣàngó," 209.

93 Akínyẹmí, "Ambivalent Representations of Ṣàngó," 208.

94 Hethersett died in 1896. Thus it is probable his account of Ṣàngó served as an ur-text for Ellis's and Johnson's texts.

95 Warner-Lewis, *Guinea's Other Suns*, 79, 83, 133.

96 Herskovits, *Trinidad Village*, 330–31. Yorùbá-speaking people from the Aradagun area of Badagry in contemporary Lagos State might have introduced the Orisa Dada (or Dadda) to Trinidad. See McKenzie, *Hail Orisha!*, 291.

97 See Henry, *Reclaiming African Religions*, 22, 25.

98 Olawaiye, *Yoruba Religious and Social Traditions*, 125. Father Isaac had to have been Orisa priest Isaac "Sheppy" Lindsay who was widely respected for his spiritual expertise during the 1970s and 1980s. His name rolled off the tongues of many devotees, who honored him as a renowned custodian of the Orisa religion during my fieldwork in Trinidad in the early 2000s.

99 Abímbọ́lá, email message to author, December 17, 2017.

100 Aremu, "Saving Sungbo's Eredo," 70; "Archaeological and Historical Significance," 31; "Enclosures of Old Oyo," 145–52.

101 Herskovits, *Trinidad Village*, 330–31; Osterman Mischel, "Shango Religious Group," 94; "African 'Powers' in Trinidad," 55.

102 Warner-Lewis, *Guinea's Other Suns*, 63–64, 82–83, 101, 133, 136 n. 7. See also her *Trinidad Yoruba*, 90.

103 Abímbọ́lá, email message to author, December 21, 2017, translates the chant Warner-Lewis transcribed as follows:

Ẹ má bú Ṣàngó mi (Do not abuse my Ṣàngó)
Ọba kò so (Monarch from/of Kòso)

Abímbọ́lá believes the transcription of the words "kò so" is incorrect and should be "Kòso." Warner-Lewis does not acknowledge the use of translators in *Guinea's Other Suns*. However, in *Trinidad Yoruba*, p. x, she acknowledges the translational assistance of two Nigerians while she taught at the University of Ifẹ̀ (currently Ọbáfẹ́mi Awólọ́wọ̀ University) between 1974 and 1975. "This visit enabled translation of field texts by Tele Nadi and Tokumbo (Shyllon) Adetunji," writes Warner-Lewis. The materials that her translators worked on must have included data she collected in 1968 and 1970 for *Guinea's*

Other Suns. Even more significant, in *Trinidad Yoruba*, Warner-Lewis provides a list of names and honorifics for the various "deities" worshipped within the Orisa tradition. The list is presented in two columns: the left indicating the "*Names of Divinities in Trinidad*" and the right indicating corresponding "*Mainland Yoruba Sources*" that offer interpretations for the same or cognate words. The entry for the words "Obakoso/Ọbakuso/Abakoso/Abakuso" translates them as "honorific of Shango" under the column that lists Trinidadian interpretations. Under the column that lists Nigerian Yorùbá interpretations directly to the right of this explanation, Warner-Lewis writes, "Ọbakòsó: king did not hang; honorific of Shango." See *Trinidad Yoruba*, 88–90. In *Guinea's Other Suns*, whenever she attributes translations of Oba Koso/Obakoso to her interlocutors, the translation is always "king of Koso" or "king of Koso town" (see pp. 83, 101, 133). In contrast, the one instance when she translates "ọba kò so" (or ọba Kòso) as "king did not hang," she states it matter-of-factly and does not attribute the meaning to any specific person or source, which arguably signals that her Nigerian translators are the interpreters in this case (see p. 82). In note 7 on p. 136, she also includes the phrase "he did not hang" to provide additional information about the place where Sango was believed to have been "transported heavenwards." However, she does not connect the phrase to the Trinidadian sources she mentions in the same endnote indicating that "Shango died at a ward of Old Ọyọ city called Ajagban."

In Nigeria, the popular perception of Ṣàngó as the "king" who "did not hang" was reinforced by playwright Dúró Ládipọ̀, whose internationally acclaimed play, *Ọba Kò So*, dramatized the Christian fabrication of Ṣàngó's suicidal death by hanging beginning in 1964. During the 1970s, when Warner-Lewis was teaching in Nigeria, the play was extremely popular and was staged across Nigeria. In 1974, the year Warner-Lewis taught in Nigeria, *Ọba Kò So* toured the United States and "was reportedly performed some 2,000 times in at least 15 countries before the playwright's death in 1978," including those of the Caribbean and South America. Ozoluah Uhakheme, "Sango Returns in Oba Koso," April 1, 2012, https://yeyeolade.wordpress .com/2012/01/08/oba-koso-returns-sango-ti-de-live-yoruba-theatre-in-lagos -from-the-nation-newspaper/.

104 According to Houk, *Spirit, Blood, and Drums*, 159, 189, OYCO was founded in 1985. See esp. Houk's charts on pp. 148–49 and 185.

105 Houk, in particular, notes the many different St. Johns connected with Shango. See *Spirits, Blood, and Drums*, 185–86.

106 All quoted phrases directly before and including the block quotation are from Abímbọ́lá, email message to author, December 17, 2017. In the same message, Abímbọ́lá corrected the improper spelling of the words *Baálẹ̀*, *gbà*, and *wá*, originally transcribed in Houk's text without important diacritical marks.

107 The spelling of the words (ọba Kòso) belies the translation "King who did not hang" (ọba ko so).

108 See Ìṣọ̀lá, "Religious Politics," and Akínyẹmí, "Ambivalent Representations of Ṣàngó."

109 Although published details about Hethersett's life are scant, he and Samuel Johnson were pupils of German CMS missionary Gottlieb Friedrich Bühler in 1863. For more on Hethersett's CMS training, see Olabimtan, "Bühler, Gottlieb Friederick."

110 Historically grounded comparative Yoruba diaspora studies will prove helpful to this kind of investigation. In the only documentation I have found of *obacouçu* (Oba Koso) in Brazilian Candomblé's nineteenth-century ritual vocabulary, the term is defined as "a name for Xangô [Sango]." See, for example, Parés, *Formation of Candomblé*, 109. In *El Monte*, 10, 253, 580, Cuban ethnographer Cabrera acknowledges one of her interlocutors as "José de Calazán Herrera Bangoché, alias el Moro, son of Oba Koso." She also cites invocations of Changó (Sango) that refer to him as "Oba Koso." Finally, she includes two photos of statues depicting Changó as "Obákoso" and "Oggoddó ma Kulenkue." In the photo where Changó is described as "Obákoso," the statue is adorned with regal elegance, suggesting the deity's status as monarch of Koso. These examples from Brazil and Cuba support the argument that Oba Koso was not related to narratives about Ṣàngó's purported suicide by hanging for nineteenth-century custodians of Yoruba religious cultures in the Caribbean/Americas.

111 Caron, "'Of a Nation,'" 98.

112 Lovejoy cites the work of Thornton to make a similar point: "When John Thornton reveals the influence of the Kongo civil wars on the revolution in St. Domingue, he is not only addressing issues of agency in the Americas but also uncovering new material on the Kongo civil wars themselves." See Lovejoy, "Identifying Enslaved Africans," 9.

113 See Olupona, *Kingship, Religion, and Rituals*, for a definitive treatment of Yoruba indigenous religion as civil religion. See also Ajala and Nolte, "Ambivalence and Transgression."

114 For more on Carriacou's Big Drum/Nation Dance, see McDaniel, *The Big Drum Ritual*, and Taylor, *Nation Dance*. For more on Jamaica's Myal Dance traditions, see Stewart, *Three Eyes for the Journey*.

115 Chambers, "'My Own Nation,'" 1; Byrd, "Eboe, Country, Nation," 128.

116 Italics mine. See Eastman, *Fight for Dignity*, 43, for his important discussion of how "Shango" emerged as a commonly accepted title for the Orisa religion in Trinidad. Other early appellatives include "Ebo," "Orisa work," or "Yaraba work." See Osterman Mischel, "Shango Religious Group," v, 87, 89. See also Warner-Lewis, *Guinea's Other Suns*, 49, 171.

117 The appellation "Shango" might have become popularized during the nineteenth century as Yoruba devotees sought to explain and translate the

essence of their religious tradition to colonial officials. It would have been reasonable to identify their practice as focused through worship of a central deity, Shango. Such a classification or naming of the tradition could have signaled the practice of something more legitimate than the sorcery automatically associated with obeah to Christian outsiders who also worshipped a central deity.

118 Henry, "Frances Henry Recalls," 61.

119 Surviving songs and oral data suggest that the term "Orisa" was as much an internal identifier for the tradition as was "Shango." See Warner-Lewis, "Yoruba Religion in Trinidad," 26; Guinea's Other Suns, 140; Mischel and Mischel, "Psychological Aspects of Spirit Possession," 259.

120 Herskovits, Trinidad Field Trip-Diary, 96, MFH Papers. Margaret Buckley is the same person who performed the Emancipation dirge "Yé! Ekún ara wa la mí sun," for the Herskovitses in 1939 (see n. 85). I coined the term christianisms as a theoretical category for explaining what some have conceptualized as the process of "syncretism" and religious formation in African heritage religions in the diaspora. See Stewart, Three Eyes for the Journey, 120–31, 162, 213–31.

121 Herskovits, Trinidad Field Trip-Diary, 96; 98–99, MFH Papers. Perhaps "Aussa" is a reference to the Hausa nation.

122 Herskovits, Trinidad Village, 29.

123 Warner-Lewis, Trinidad Yoruba, 24.

124 Adderley provides one of the most nuanced treatments of identity formation and affiliation among liberated Africans in Trinidad to date. See her "New Negroes from Africa."

125 Another newspaper article used the term "creole Yarabas" in 1872, signaling that second- and third-generation Yoruba descendants were culturally connected to their Yoruba heritage. See n. 139.

126 While conducting field research for his book Trinidad Village in 1939, Herskovits met an "elderly woman" (likely Margaret Buckley) in Toco who "identified herself primarily with things African. She called herself 'Yarriba,' and recorded a considerable number of songs in the Yoruban language, which she said she could also speak." This encounter took place twenty years after the report about the "Yaraba Creoles" was published in the POSG.

127 Warner-Lewis, Trinidad Yoruba, 73–74.

128 Warner-Lewis, Trinidad Yoruba, 47–48; Trotman, "Reflections on the Children," 221.

129 Gomez, Exchanging Our Country Marks, 10, theorizes the "life-styles" of enslaved US African Americans as "polycultural rather than syncretic."

130 Newman's point that "virtually everywhere on the continent, group boundaries, even religious ones, were flexible and permeable" is worth keeping in mind in this discussion. See his The Peopling of Africa, 6. Cited in Caron, "'Of a Nation,'" 102.

131 Carr, "A Rada Community in Trinidad," 47–48.

132 John Cooper arrived in Trinidad under the liberated African resettlement program in 1860 and died in 1877. See Brereton, *Race Relations*, 154. In Hucks, *Obeah, Orisa, and Religious Identity*, she discusses Mah Nannie's ordeals with the colonial justice system that criminalized his religion and prosecuted him for violating the OPO.

133 "Memorandum for Andrew Carr/Some Research Problems among African Derived Groups in Trinidad," 2, box 55, folder 21, series 35/6, MH Papers, Northwestern University Archives, Evanston, IL. Herskovits sent the "Memorandum" to Carr in response to Carr's July 25, 1952, request that Herskovits critique his article, "Some Research Problems among African Derived Groups in Trinidad." In an August 18, 1952, reply to Herskovits, Carr indicates he received Herskovits's "Memorandum" on the same day.

134 Espinet, "Manifestation of Wêrê," 5, Herskovits Papers. Espinet mailed his article manuscript to Herskovits on November 29, 1945.

135 Espinet, "Manifestation of Wêrê," 5.

136 Espinet, "Manifestation of Wêrê," 1, 5, 7. It is possible that Afro-Brazilians influenced Trinidadian Orisa's Wêrê phenomenon directly because some established new roots in Trinidad during the liberated African settlement period. See Hucks, *Obeah, Orisa, and Religious Identity*.

137 TC, January 16, 1872. See Carr, "Rada Community," 39, for information about the two Rada compounds in Belmont.

138 The connection between Sakpata and Shoponna/Sopona/Ṣọpọna remains unresolved in terms of origins and borrowings. See Bay, *Wives of the Leopard*, 111.

139 The smallpox epidemic broke out in November 1871 and subsided in January 1872, leaving more than 12,500 persons (approximately 10% of the total population) infected, of whom 2,449 died. Among the dead were Yoruba- and other African Trinidadians, including a girl from "'a fine family of what we call creole Yarabas.'" See "Country News—Mayaro," TC, n.s., no. 245, January 2, 1872.

140 Gang disputes were rampant between 1875 and 1899. See Trotman, *Crime in Trinidad*, 167–69; 179–82.

141 Carr, "Rada Community," 36.

142 Asiwaju, "Aja-Speaking Peoples of Nigeria"; Newbury, *Western Slave Coast*; Akinjogbin, *Dahomey and Its Neighbours*.

143 Even if largely undetected by eighteenth- and nineteenth-century writers, it is highly likely that many devotees of Vodun/Vodou were among those enslaved Africans who moved from Saint-Domingue/Haiti to Trinidad with their owners during the late eighteenth century. One contemporary, colonial officer A. R. Gray (discussed in volume I), suggested that Trinidad's

Dahomean descendants created a distinct community in the wake of emancipation separate from that of the Radas, who entered the colony as liberated Africans. Settlements comprising Ewe-Fon families were indeed known to exist in several areas of the colony, including Sangre Grande, Freeport, Toco, and, most notably, Port of Spain's Belmont-Laventille area.

144 According to Warner-Lewis, information gathered from interlocutors indicate "the Rada and Yoruba would give mutual invitations to their feasts" during the nineteenth and early twentieth century. See Warner-Lewis, *Guinea's Other Suns*, 118. See also 117.

145 Adédìran, *Frontier States of Western Yorùbáland*; Akinjogbin, *Dahomey and Its Neighbours*; Asiwaju, "Aja-Speaking Peoples of Nigeria;" Newbury, *Western Slave Coast*; Schuler, "Alas, Alas, Kongo"; Warner-Lewis, *Guinea's Other Suns*; Adderley, "*New Negroes from Africa*"; "Orisha Worship and 'Jesus Time.'"

146 Yai, "African Diasporan Concepts," 244–55, esp. 246–48.

147 See preface, n. 4.

148 Warner-Lewis, *Guinea's Other Suns*, 63, 127, 137. See also Reis and Mamigonian's discussion of a similar case in Brazil: "Nagô and Mina," 83. See Falola, *African Diaspora*, 122–23, for more on the wide distances that Yoruba traders, both male and female, were known to travel.

149 Maldonado Torres, "Topology of Being," 39.

150 Adderley points out that the courts at Havana provided the most comprehensive information about liberated Africans who were processed under the wider jurisdiction of the international antislavery Mixed Commission courts. In addition to Havana, Cuba, these courts adjudicated cases at Freetown, Sierra Leone; Boa Vista and Rio de Janeiro, Brazil; and Luanda, Angola. See Adderley, "*New Negroes from Africa*," 95–97, 103–5.

151 Byrd, "Eboe, Country, Nation," 130.

152 See also Chambers's discussion of Igbo identity and presence in the Americas/Caribbean in "Tracing Igbo into the African Diaspora," 55–71.

153 Byrd, "Eboe, Country, Nation," 145.

154 Caron, "'Of a Nation'"; Hall, *Slavery and African Ethnicities*; Thornton, *Africa and Africans*; Parés, "'Nagôization' Process"; Gomes, "'Atlantic Nations.'"

155 Chambers, "Ethnicity in the Diaspora," 27.

156 See Sidbury and Cañizares-Esguerra, "Mapping Ethnogenesis," for processes of ethnogenesis shaping Amerindian, Euro-American, and African Caribbean/American peoples.

157 Chambers, "Ethnicity in the Diaspora," 31.

158 Ojo, "'Heepa' (Hail) Òrìṣà," 32.

159 Byrd, "Eboe, Country, Nation," 147.

160 I think it is neither coincidental nor insignificant that the most common vernacular designation for the "Orisa" in Trinidad is "Power."

Two. I Had a Family That Belonged to All Kinds of Things

1   Some Yoruba descendants in Trinidad have understood "Aba Koso" as
    another name for Sango. This chapter's title is attributed to Iya Molly Ahye,
    interview by author and Tracey Hucks, tape recording, Petit Valley, Trinidad,
    July 29, 2002. Iya Ahye was the distinguished priestess of a prominent shrine,
    Opa Orisa Shango, whom Tracey and I first met in Cuba in 1994.
2   South Asian and South American deities include Samedona, Bogoyana, and
    Vigoyana (Vigoyanna).
3   Jackson, Thin Description, 13.
4   Van der Leeuw, Religion in Essence and Manifestation, 674–75.
5   Smart, Dimensions of the Sacred, 2–4.
6   See, for example, Klieman, "Pygmies Were Our Compass," 66–94; Ehret, Civiliza-
    tions of Africa; Herskovits, "Peoples and Cultures," 17, 19–20. Scholars date the
    Niger-Congo language family as far back as 10,000 years ago. For more on
    the emergence of Niger-Congo peoples, see Clark and Brandt, From Hunters to
    Farmers, 20–30, and Manning, African Diaspora, 45–50.
7   MacGaffey, "Cultural Tradition of the African Forest," 20, 22. Like MacGaffey,
    I explore African "cosmologies" not in the strict philosophical or scientific
    sense but in the way comparative religions scholars explain people's concep-
    tions of time, space, location, reality, nature, relationships, and containment.
8   Stewart Diakité and Hucks, "Africana Religious Studies," 64.
9   Rawle Gibbons, interview by author and Tracey Hucks, tape recording,
    St. Augustine, Trinidad, June 29, 2001.
10 For social-scientific studies of kinship and family, see Malinowski, Sexual Life
    of Savages; "Kinship."
11 Ojo, "'Heepa' (Hail) Òrìṣà," 35–37. See also Roberts, "Yoruba Family, Gender,
    and Kinship," 252.
12 Ojo, "'Heepa' (Hail) Òrìṣà," 49. Ojo points out, for example, that Ile-Ife was
    already commonly "recognized as the Yoruba ritual Mecca" by the 1830s.
13 Although Yoruba-Orisa theology and sacred literature seemingly idealize
    heteronormative family arrangements, scholars have documented homosocial
    institutions and rituals that accommodate same-sex and same-gender intima-
    cies among the Yoruba and other African societies. See, for example, Matory,
    Sex and the Empire; Black Atlantic Religion. See also n. 16 in this volume's chapter 5.
14 Abímbọ́lá, Ifa Will Mend Our Broken World, 15.
15 Persuaded by Afropessimist and black nihilist assessments that blacks are
    excluded from the category of "being" in modernity, I employ the term
    "relational poetics" as a translational placeholder that can convey the African
    spiritual and social concept that to be is to be relational: I am because we—
    visible and invisible entities—are. I expand upon this framing in chapter 3
    where I conceptualize "ashé" as "a primordial poetics of relation." Similarly,

spiritual collectivity is a translational placeholder for the shared nature of entities and presences that coinhabit the universe.

16 As George Brandon notes in *Santeria*, 75, 135–36, 148–49, terms of kinship are employed to qualify the spiritual relationships devotees develop with special Orisa.

17 Kọ́lá Abímbọ́lá rendered this translation. See also translations in Abímbọ́lá, *Ifá Divination Poetry*; *Ijinle Ohun Enu Ifa*.

18 Earlier studies mention Shango's consanguineal ties to Dada and Aba Koso, whereas later research tends to note only Shango's younger brother Dada (the patron Orisa of children). In some sources Oba koso/Obakoso is one of Shango's titles. See chapter 1 for a more extensive discussion and relevant sources. See also Warner-Lewis, *Guinea's Other Suns*, 4; *Trinidad Yoruba*, 88; Houk, *Spirits, Blood and Drums*, 185–86.

19 Ìdòwú, *Olódùmarè*, 91–92.

20 Ìdòwú, *Olódùmarè*, 75–76.

21 Ìdòwú, *Olódùmarè*, 75.

22 Edwards and Mason, *Black Gods*, 32, 85, 77. Edwards and Mason offer slightly different diacritical markings for "Yẹmọja" than the standard Nigerian spelling "Yemọja."

23 Warner-Lewis, *Trinidad Yoruba*, 90–91. Warner-Lewis, *Guinea's Other Suns*, 140, n. 51, includes an alternative version of the poem identifying a male sibling accompanying Ogere.

24 Sangowunmi, *Esu*, 13, 32. The title of "iyalode" recognizes women-mothers as spiritual and political leaders. See chapter 4 for more information.

25 Alvarado, *Voodoo Hoodoo Spellbook*, 34–35.

26 Hunter, "'Oro Pataki Aganjú,'" 216.

27 Ìdòwú, *Olódùmarè*, 93.

28 See the following: Odù: Èjì Ogbè for poems on friendship; Ìwòrì Méjì for poems on loyalty; and Òdí Méjì and Òyẹ̀kú Méjì for poems on spousal responsibility and bonding.

29 Clarke, *Description of the Manners*, 153–54. See Hucks, *Obeah, Orisa, and Religious Identity*, chapter 4.

30 As far as I am aware Orí-àṣẹ is my original coinage.

31 Abímbọ́lá, *Yorùbá Culture*, 50–51.

32 Scott, *Conscripts of Modernity*, 106–7.

33 This construct, *consciousness of belonging*, references what might be conceived as "insider/outsider consciousness" vis-à-vis institutional structures and the cultural and psychological significance attached to social belonging in Yorùbá society. I am not arguing, however, that they are uniquely Yorùbá. I suspect that any number of Niger-Congo-descended African societies might embrace similar precepts and meanings.

34 Asad, *Genealogies of Religion*, 27–54.

35 Henry, *He Had the Power*, 205.

36 In chapter 4, Frances Henry indicates Pa Neezer is wearing implements connected to the Oddfellows lodge. Henry, *He Had the Power*, 73.

37 Henry, *He Had the Power*, 61–96.

38 Henry, *He Had the Power*, 74–75.

39 Fadipẹ, *Sociology of the Yoruba*, 243–60.

40 Van Gennep, *Rites of Passage*.

41 Lloyd, "Craft Organization in Yoruba Towns," 37.

42 Lloyd, "Craft Organization," 43. Lloyd's research suggests that only males were lineage elders. Oyèrónkẹ́ Oyěwùmí's research challenges the essentialist gender bias in Yorùbá studies that automatically situates masculinity as a category of seniority or eldership. See Oyěwùmí, *Invention of Women*.

43 To reinforce my argument about the salience of *nationhood* as a category of group identity to Africana peoples, I take creative license to italicize *nation* in Agwuele's remarks. Agwuele, "Popular Culture of Yoruba Kinship Practices," 44. Agwuele's outline aligns with many of the detailed remarks that Alfred Ellis published about Yoruba kinship and family structure. See "Laws Related to Kinship and Inheritance" from chapter 11, "Laws and Customs," *Yoruba-Speaking*, 174–82.

44 Schwab, "Kinship and Lineage," 356.

45 Fadipẹ, *Sociology of the Yoruba*, 129. For a corroborating overview of Yoruba cosmology, social organization, and neighborly relations, see Akinjogbin, "Specificities and Dynamics," 57–70.

46 Oyěwùmí, *Invention of Women*, 40.

47 Agwuele, "Popular Culture," 48.

48 Oyěwùmí, *Invention of Women*, 40–64. See also Bascom, "Principle of Seniority," 37–46.

49 Oyěwùmí, *Invention of Women*, 44–45. See also Agwuele, "Popular Culture," 45–49.

50 Brooks Higginbotham, *Righteous Discontent*, 186–87.

51 See also Scher, "Unveiling the Orisha," 320.

52 Cothonay, *Trinidad*, 66.

53 See Mahmood, *Politics of Piety*.

54 Hays, "Structure and Agency," 57–59.

55 Italics mine. I replace Hays's term "agency" with my preferred coinage *creactivity*. I use creactivity as a concept for black creativity and black activity that "make a way out of way" in an antiblack world. The concept aligns better than Hays's "agency" with the argument this book makes about Africana sacred poetics while taking into consideration disputes about black agency in Afropessimism and philosophy. At this writing, I am less interested in debating whether blacks have agency and more interested in exploring how blacks are *creactive*, namely, how they engage in creative activity or activities that make a way

out of no way. Additional word forms related to the stem creactive include *creactivate*, *creactivities*, *creactivism(s)*, and *creaction(s)*. See Hays, "Structure and Agency," 70–71; "Constructing the Centrality of Culture?"; Wang, "Agency."

56 The Ifá corpus is composed of 16 major Odù and 240 minor Odù. Each Odù constitutes a volume or "book" of sacred literature. After casting the ọ̀pẹ̀lẹ̀ divination chain, the Ifá diviner reads the pattern or sign of the convex and concave oval plates along the chain and chants from the Odù represented by that sign. Other instruments are also used during Ifá divination sessions, and seniority is very important in the divination process when attending to clients' questions. For more on the subject, see Abímbọ́lá, *Ifá*.

57 See Ìdòwú, *Olódùmarè*, 165.

58 Roberts, "Yoruba Family," 253, says it well when he writes, "The debate is no longer about 'agency,' 'stability,' or even 'survival' but rather the innovative manner in which Yoruba and their descendants used New World institutions to further their own. . . . Using institutions such as the Roman Catholic Church to further their aim of emphasizing their 'Yoruba-ness' . . . the Yoruba succeeded in establishing a New World version of Yoruba culture."

59 Osterman Mischel, "Shango Religious Group," 51.

60 Osterman Mischel, "Shango Religious Group," 2–3.

61 Brereton, *Race Relations in Colonial Trinidad*, 152–75. See p. 158 for quoted passages.

62 Eastman, *Fight for Dignity*, 103. For more on masquerading as an interpretive analytic in the study of African heritage religions, see Stewart, *Three Eyes*.

63 Harvey, "'Life Is War,'" 146–47.

64 Brandon, *Santeria*, 155.

65 Brandon, *Santeria*, 155. Tracey Hucks maintains that the same logic of revelation and concealment holds true for the commercial space of the botanica.

66 Brandon, *Santeria*, 155. See p. 121 for a 1930 photograph of an analogous altar arrangement at a Santero's home in Matanzas, Cuba.

67 Brandon, *Santeria*, 155. Assigning ultimate power, value, and respect to native African spiritual and health experts and spiritual/medicinal materials is a widespread theme throughout the diaspora. For additional sources, see Carneiro, "Structure of African Cults," 278; Chireau, *Black Magic*, 35–58; Barcia, *Seeds of Insurrection*, 41–48.

68 Italics mine. Vélez, *Drumming for the Gods*, 141.

69 Stephen Glazier observes that the incorporation of symbols from more than one African diaspora religion does not always indicate the workings of syncretism; it can reflect instead a process of juxtaposition in ritual life and religious thought. See Glazier, "Syncretism and Separation," 49–62.

70 Italics in original. Ìdòwú, *Olódùmarè*, 66.

71 Ninian Smart, Benson Saler, and Peter Byrne, for example, have adapted Ludwig Wittgenstein's linguistic framework of "family resemblances" to suit

their theoretical approaches to the study of religion. For a critical discussion of their approaches and a refutation of the family resemblances model in religious studies, see Fitzgerald, *Ideology of Religious Studies*, 25–26, 57–58, 72–97.

72 Friedson, *Remains of Ritual*, 34.

73 Hurston, *The Sanctified Church*, 103.

74 Fakuade, "Yoruba Personal Naming System," 251–71.

75 Roberts, "Yoruba Family," 256.

76 Original translation and emphasis mine. Cothonay, *Trinidad*, 303–5.

77 Cothonay, *Trinidad*, 303–5.

78 Italics mine. Vélez, *Drumming for the Gods*, 139.

79 Roberts, "Yoruba Family," 250. Vélez, *Drumming for the Gods*, esp. 3. Villamil's heritage also speaks to *inter-nation-alism* in Cuba. His mother's lineage connected him to a Yoruba grandfather and his fathers to a Kongo grandfather.

80 Edison Carneiro was among the early Brazilian scholars to document this kind of *inter-nation-al* cross-fertilization in the Bahian Candomblés. He even documents dual *nation-al* belonging among some of the 1930s and 1940s Candomblé cults. See "Structure of African Cults," 271–72. See also Roberts's discussion of enslaved Yorubas in Brazil, "many [of whom] apparently joined the Angolan sodalities and therefore appropriated the ascendant identity of 'Angolan' in spite of their real ethnic background," in "Yoruba Family," 253.

81 See preface, n. 2.

82 Osterman Mischel, "Shango Religious Group," v, 87, notes that devotees of the Yoruba-Orisa religion popularly called "Shango" also referred to themselves as "Orisha workers," a title "they prefer[ed] to be called," when she conducted research in Trinidad in 1956. See also Simpson, "Shango Cult," 1215; and Burton Sankeralli's analysis of the second stage of Orisa devotion in Trinidad in this volume's chapter 5.

83 See Yai's discussion of Orisha/Vodun spiritual lineages in "African Diaspora Concepts," 248; Carneiro, "Structure of African Cults," 272.

84 Peel, *Religious Encounter*, 102. Lakijena is a local lineage Òrìṣà.

85 See "Research Materials, Trinidad Field Trip," 31, MFH Papers.

86 Sweet, *Domingos Álvares*, 33. See also pp. 23–24. Gbe-languages include Ewe, Adja, Fon, Phla-Pherá (Xwla-Xwéla), and Gen, languages spoken today in Ghana, Togo, Benin, and Nigeria.

87 Italics mine. Ogbonmwan, "Reflections on African Traditional Value Systems," 3.

88 Sweet, *Domingos Álvares*, 33. Sociologist Muniz Sodré, *O Terreiro e a Cidade*, also argues that the African concept of kinship within Brazilian Candomblé measures wealth, power, and prestige by the strength of one's familial connections and relationships.

89 De Verteuil, *Trinidad*, 175.

Three. "We Smashed Those Statues or Painted Them Black"

1 Winer, *Dictionary of the English*, 6. This chapter's title is attributed to Eintou Pearl Springer, "Black Power, Religion, and Spirituality" (unpublished paper, Heritage Library, Port of Spain, Trinidad, no date), 1.

2 To support her third definition of "African," Winer cites Simpson's 1970 publication, *Religious Cults of the Caribbean*.

3 For a discussion of the discursive, social, cultural, political, and historical conventions that facilitated an Afro-Creole identity during the nineteenth century, see Cudjoe, *Beyond Boundaries*.

4 In chapter 4, I revisit "identity politics" based on Barbara Smith's/the Combahee River Collective's original definition and argue for ways to bridge identity and affective politics in Africana religious imagination/traditions. See "(1977) The Combahee River Collective Statement," BlackPast, https://www.blackpast.org/african-american-history/combahee-river-collective-statement-1977, accessed May 26, 2021.

5 See Paton, *Cultural Politics of Obeah*, 153–54, for several examples of defendants charged under obeah laws who were Yoruba-Orisa devotees.

6 Paton, *Cultural Politics of Obeah*, 162.

7 Paton, *Cultural Politics of Obeah*, 153–54.

8 Jacobs, *Joy Comes in the Morning*; Stevens, *Spiritual Baptist Church*. See also Paton, "Teacher Bailey, Trinidad, 1918." This scholarly website includes a wealth of information on the legal persecution of African Caribbean religions since the colonial period; see Paton, *Cultural Politics of Obeah*, 151–52, for more information on statutes and context.

9 Many devotees of the African-inspired Spiritual Baptist religion today insist that "Shouters" is a colonial misnomer employed to disparage their tradition. See also Paton, *Cultural Politics of Obeah*, 150–51.

10 Paton, *Cultural Politics of Obeah*, 164. The figure of five hundred does not represent the number of cases but the number of individuals prosecuted across the twenty-nine cases found between 1917 and 1939.

11 Laitinen (aka Forde) offers a synthesis of the varied roots of the Spiritual Baptist heritage in T&T in "Marching to Zion," 39–43. Laitinen also notes that the first wave of American Negro soldiers settled in Trinidad's Naparima area in 1803 after the American Revolutionary War.

12 Influenced by Trinidad's Spiritual Baptist heritage, Barbados also has many Spiritual Baptists.

13 The TTG, July 10, 1919, 7.

14 The TTG reports "Mr. E. M'zumbo Lazare" as Samuel's legal counsel. Lazare, a prominent pan-Africanist, was known to accept such cases. See also Sherwood, *Origins of Pan-Africanism*, 9–10; 227. Sherwood also discusses the

pan-Africanist Edgar Maresse-Smith, another solicitor who "worked for all strata of society including the poor."

15 Wilderson, *Red, White, and Black*, esp. 9.

16 Data exist to support my numenymic reading of the "Shouter" designation. Numenyms and numenymic phrases and inferences are legion in Africa and the African diaspora. For example, colonial Jamaica played a large role in shaping the "obeah" numenym during slavery. However, in the postemancipation period, the "pocomania" numenym was invented to classify a Jamaican religious tradition analogous to Spiritual Baptist practice in the southern Caribbean.

17 See "Shouter in Court," POSG, January 9, 1918, cited from Paton, "Teacher Bailey, Trinidad, 1918."

18 Phills, interview by author and Tracey E. Hucks, tape recording, Port of Spain, May 8, 2001.

19 See Paton's point in *Cultural Politics of Obeah*, 164, n.10, that even if the closing of Spiritual Baptist churches and actual prison sentences were a rare or unseen result of the SPO, many defendants had to contend with prohibitive fines.

20 Phills, interview.

21 Phills, interview.

22 All elders interviewed for this volume shared similar narratives of learning quite early about the scorn and rebuke directed by the general public at Yoruba-Orisa practitioners.

23 Franklin, *After Many Days*, 22.

24 Brereton, "Social Organisation and Class," 36; Ryan, *Race and Nationalism*, 19–20.

25 Brereton, *History of Modern Trinidad*, 96–103.

26 Knippers Black et al., *Area Handbook*, 64–68. See p. 66 for direct citation of Cipriani.

27 Bolland, *On the March*, 86.

28 Paton, *Cultural Politics of Obeah*, 264.

29 Reddock, "Women Workers' Struggles," 19–40; Kiely, *Politics of Labour*, 82–84.

30 Kiely, *Politics of Labour*, 72–75, 82–86; MacDonald, *Trinidad and Tobago*, 160–67.

31 MacDonald, *Trinidad and Tobago*, 105–11; Ryan, *Race and Nationalism*, 128–82. See also "Trinidad and Tobago General Election Results." After independence, it took fourteen years for T&T to adopt a constitution and establish itself as a republic on August 1, 1976.

32 Valley, *Black Power Revolution*.

33 Shah, "Reflections on the Mutiny," 513.

34 Of the 374 directors representing 355 organizations that met the study's criteria, 233 participated. Camejo, "Racial Discrimination," 309–10. For data on Chinese presence in Trinidad, see Millett, *Chinese in Trinidad and Tobago*, 4.

35 Teelucksingh, "Black Power Movement in Trinidad and Tobago," 160–61.

36 Fryer, *Staying Power*, 279–87. See p. 280 for direct citation of Williams. See also Sherwood, *Origins of Pan-Africanism*, 110.

37 See James, *George Padmore and Decolonization*, 10. On James's childhood relationship with Padmore, see Cripps, *C. L. R. James*, 21. For Williams's, Padmore's, and James's contributions to Pan-Africanism see Sherwood, *Origins of Pan-Africanism*; James, *George Padmore and Decolonization*; Worcester, *C. L. R. James*; Henry and Buhle, *C. L. R. James's Caribbean*; Cudjoe and Cain, *C. L. R. James*.

38 Worcester, *C. L. R. James*, 200.

39 Martin, *Pan-African Connection*, 12–13.

40 Martin, *Race First*, 16; Teelucksingh, *Ideology, Politics, and Radicalism*, 12–26.

41 Meeks, "Caribbean Black Power," 268.

42 In fact, C. L. R. James would remain influential through his active role in Trinidadian politics, his critique of neocolonial politics, and his commitment to improving the material conditions of the poor and working classes. See Jerome Teelucksingh, "Good, the Bad, and the Ugly."

43 Ryan, "Struggle for Black Power in the Caribbean."

44 See Aiyejina and Gibbons, "Orisa (Orisha) Tradition in Trinidad," 49.

45 Sutton, *Forged from the Love of Liberty*, 203.

46 For unemployment data, see MacDonald, *Trinidad and Tobago*, 145–60, esp. 156; Craig, "Background to the 1970 Confrontation," 398. For information on strikes and labor unrest, see Millette, "Towards the Black Power Revolt," 64.

47 Millette, "Towards the Black Power Revolt," 60, 64. See also Nunez, "Trade Unionist Recalls 1970," 261–71. For extensive unemployment figures and a comprehensive historical analysis of political and economic developments of the period, see MacDonald, *Trinidad and Tobago*, 98–189. According to Ryan, "Struggle for Black Power," 40, "by 1970, most of the [Caribbean] islands had approximately 25 percent of their work-force unemployed even though official sources gave figures ranging from 13 percent to 18 percent."

48 MacDonald, *Trinidad and Tobago*, 164.

49 See William Christensen's correspondence in U.S. Mission, Port of Spain, to U.S. Department of State, November 24, 1961, Central Decimal File, Trinidad, NA-DS, box 1671, folder 741F.00/11-161.

50 Williams's remarks to the nation on March 23, 1970. See Meeks, "1970 Revolution," 159. See also Teelucksingh, "Black Power Movement," 167 and Ryan, *Race and Nationalism*, 369–70, 457–60.

51 Hurston's character Lucy Pearson phrases it this way in *Jonah's Gourd*: "You can't clean yo'self wid yo' tongue lakuh cat," 129.

52 Meeks, "Caribbean Black Power," 266–67; Teelucksingh, "Black Power Movement."

53 Shah, "Reflections on the Mutiny and Trial," 515.

54 Meeks, "1970 Revolution," 88.

55 Teelucksingh, "Black Power Movement," 179.

56 See Ryan and Stewart, *Black Power Revolution 1970*, for accounts of the range and significance of demonstrations and marches.

57 John "Gerard" King, interview by author and Tracey Hucks, digital recording, St. James, Port of Spain, Trinidad, August 19, 2013.

58 King, interview, August 19, 2013.

59 King, interview, August 19, 2013.

60 Ibeji are twin deities, and ori is the head (spiritual and physical) in Yoruba theology. Ori is also every individual's personal deity.

61 Castor draws a similar conclusion in her monograph, *Spiritual Citizenship*, and renders a sustained theorization of this motif in current-day Orisa/Ifa religious culture. See also her article, "Shifting Multicultural Citizenship."

62 King, interview, August 19, 2013.

63 Oloye Ogundare Ife Olakela Massetungi, interview by author and Tracey Hucks, tape recording, Petit Valley, Trinidad, May 9, 2001.

64 Massetungi, interview, May 9, 2001.

65 Du Bois, *The Souls of Black Folk*, esp. 49, 116, and 122.

66 Modern, "Evangelical Secularism," 806.

67 Here, I borrow language from Haitian American novelist Edwidge Danticat's poignant phrase about African reincarnation theology in Haitian Vodou and familial culture. On seeing her great-granddaughter for the first time, Ife, one of the main characters in *Breath, Eyes, Memory*, 105, exclaims, "Isn't it a miracle that we can visit with all our kin, simply by looking into this face?"

68 For a more extensive discussion of Carnival's significance in Trinidad, see volume I of this study.

69 See James Scott, *Domination and the Arts of Resistance*.

70 King, interview. Carnival took place from February 9–10, 1970. King's reference is to Chancellor Williams, *Destruction of Black Civilization*.

71 Kambon, "Black Power in Trinidad & Tobago," 220. References are to contemporary politicians John Enoch Powell, the longtime conservative British member of Parliament whose April 20, 1968, "Rivers of Blood" speech expressed anti-immigration sentiments directed toward African, South Asian, and Caribbean immigrants from Commonwealth countries, and Balthazar Johannes (John) Vorster, South Africa's far-right nationalist prime minister from 1966–78, who subsequently served as president for one year.

72 See Memmi, *Colonizer and the Colonized*.

73 The April 21–November 20, 1970, state of emergency aimed to squash Black Power and labor demonstrations through a daily curfew from dusk to dawn. For more on this topic, see Kiely, *Politics of Labour*, 127–31.

74 Nelson Island was a port of entry and departure for many indentured immigrant laborers during the nineteenth century.

75 Mutope acknowledges there were "one or two fellows who were a bit aggres-sive" among the group that entered the cathedral, including one young man who can be seen, in journalistic photos that covered the event, posing in an elaborate throne "that the archbishop would normally sit in when he was in that church." Apoesho Mutope, interview by author, digital recording, Port of Spain, August 21, 2013. Other narratives of the event indicate that demon-strators did drape the Catholic statues in black cloth. See, for example, Raoul Pantin's January 29, 2011, recounting in his TE article, "Black Power Storms the Cathedral."

76 Demonstrators targeted Canadian interests out of solidarity with Trinidadian students involved in antiracist protests at Sir George Williams University in Montreal. See Valley, *Black Power Revolution.*

77 Mutope, interview.

78 Mutope interview.

79 Shah, "People Have Absolved," 471.

80 Aiyejina and Gibbons, "Orisa Tradition," 49; Houk, *Spirits, Blood, and Drums,* 188–90; Castor, *Spiritual Citizenship.*

81 This phrase is attributed to former *Washington Post* editor and publisher Philip Graham, who used it in two public addresses in 1953 and 1963. In recent years, it has come to light that journalist Alan Barth used the phrase in a 1943 book review published in *New Republic.* See Shafer, "Who Said It First?"

82 After reviewing every issue of Trinidad's leading newspapers during the criti-cal three-month period of black nationalist protest, I only found two articles that mention "Shango."

83 According to Mutope (Mutope, interview), "1970 brought the terminology 'African' into effect" among the collective Afro-Trinidadian population. Winer's definition of the term as discussed in this chapter (see n. 1) affirms Mutope's position. On the likelihood of Black Power-influenced spiritual seekers attaching themselves in large numbers to other African religious traditions, see n. 90.

84 Mutope, interview.

85 See Granovetter, "Strength of Weak Ties," 201–33.

86 Springer, "Black Power, Religion and Spirituality."

87 Lartey, *Postcolonializing God.*

88 The COVID-19 pandemic delayed T&T's plans to conduct a national census for the year 2020, and at this writing, the most recent available figures are from the 2011 census.

89 Castor, *Spiritual Citizenship.*

90 By the early 1970s, Orisa was most attractive for Black Power sympathizers in search of African spiritual communities of belonging. Rada worship had dwindled to a limited genealogical family circle, making it not nearly as

accessible as Orisa. The Rastafari tradition became a noticeable presence in Trinidad only during the mid-1970s. For more on Rastafari in Trinidad, see Van Dijk, "Chanting down Babylon Outernational," 191–92.

91 Massetungi, interview, June 8, 2001. Massetungi recalls that the article "Black Power in Disguise" was either published in the *Mirror* or the TE. My search for the article has proven unsuccessful.

92 Massetungi, interview, Trinidad, May 8, 2001.

93 Massetungi, interview, May 9, 2001.

94 Massetungi, interview by author and Tracey Hucks, tape recording, Port of Spain, June 28, 2001. See Harricharan, *Catholic Church in Trinidad*, 29–30, for additional information on La Divina Pastora. Lord Hanuman is a Hindu god worshipped in Trinidad as the most noble among the warrior gods.

95 Massetungi, interview, June 28, 2001.

96 Massetungi, interview, June 28, 2001.

97 Yemaya/Yemoja/Yemanjá is the Orisa associated with the seven seas or ocean waters, particularly the top layers of the ocean.

98 I agree with Maurice Halbwachs and other sociologists who argue that collective memory is constructed memory. See Halbwachs, *On Collective Memory*.

99 Olokun can be conceived as male or female depending on the regional context.

100 "Orisa Festival Starts This Weekend," accessed October 29, 2016, http://news .anotao.com/link/tt/www.guardian.co.tt/lifestyle/2016-10-06/orisa-festival -starts-weekend.

101 The other Carnival band was delayed by one year. Iya Sangowunmi Patricia McLeod's shrine, Ile Eko Sango/Osun Mil'Osa, launched its *Faces of Osun* in T&T's 2002 Carnival.

102 Massetungi, interview, June 8, 2001. See also Hucks and Stewart, "Authenticity and Authority."

103 See Henry, *Reclaiming African Religions*, 185–90, for a discussion of EOE's Carnival performances across the three-day event.

104 Massetungi, interview, June 8, 2001.

105 See chapter 1 for an extended discussion of this topic.

106 Massetungi, interview, June 8, 2001. See also Frances Henry, *Reclaiming African Religions*, 187.

107 Henry, *Reclaiming African Religions*, 187.

108 Pilgrimage as used here indexes elements of "ritual, organized travel, objects of veneration, the constitution of temporary 'communities' at special sites, sacrifice of time and effort, and requests and offerings directed towards sacred figures." See Rahkala's working definition in "In the Sphere of the Holy," 75. For the quotation, see her article "What is Ritual Theatre," accessed

November 28, 2016, https://ritualtheatre.wordpress.com/2011/12/01/what-is
-ritual-theatre.

109 Forty is an approximate figure. See Henry, *Reclaiming African Religions*, 188.

110 Although Frazier appears to have been the first scholar to use the phrase "a nation within a nation," Du Bois's theorization of the negro church as a nation preceded Frazier's research and likely influenced it. See Du Bois, *Souls of Black Folk*, 213–14.

111 Hucks, *Yoruba Traditions*, 167–68.

112 Oya is a prominent female Orisa whom devotees associate with winds and storms.

113 David Goldberg's argument that the modern Western nation state is founded conceptually, philosophically, and materially on the concept of race offers insight into white American nationhood and African American responses to it. See Goldberg, *Racial State*.

114 The Nation of Islam relaxed these restrictions during the 2008 and 2012 presidential election races when Barack Obama, an African American, ran for and won the office of president.

115 I cherished the rare opportunity to come face to face with a mode of spirit manifestation I had never before witnessed. "A sensation of personal and professional satisfaction settled inside," I recorded that night in my field-notes. Personal notes from field notebook, November 9, 2000.

116 One year later, early general elections were held after the UNC lost its majority in the House of Representatives. The People's National Movement assumed leadership after President A. N. R. Robinson nominated the party's leader, Patrick Manning, for the office of prime minister. Robinson's intervention resulted in a tied number of eighteen seats for each party, despite the fact that the UNC won a larger amount of votes. See also Castor, *Spiritual Citizenship*, 62–68, for an insightful analysis of Panday's relationship with the Orisa community.

117 *Ïère* might also be a corruption of the Arawak term *caeri*, which means "island." See Winer, *Dictionary of the English/Creole*, 445.

118 Massetungi, telephone communication with author, January 27, 2017.

119 McNeal, *Trance and Modernity*, 259–310, examines the influence of Black Power politics ("the first of four main chapters in TT's postcolonial multiculturalism," 287) on African and Indian religious movements during the 1970s. McNeal's analysis complements my discussion of the BPM and treatment of EOE's Africana religious nationalism.

120 Anderson's *Imagined Communities* has inspired much of this theorizing in black studies and other diaspora studies scholarship.

121 Long, *Significations*; Noel, *Black Religion*.

122 Noel, *Black Religion*, 39–40. Otto used the term "wholly other" or "numinous" to rescue the idea of "the holy" from its more derivative and obscurant

cultural connotations. Noel's use of "Holy Other" in this context is perhaps a deliberate attempt to reinforce Otto's point. See Otto, *Idea of the Holy*, 5–7.

123 Noel, *Black Religion*, 39–40; Otto, *Idea of the Holy*, 5–7.

124 Black imaginings of the first creation can bridge mythical and historical consciousness through interpretations of the image of Africa. Long's argument about black religion, *Significations*, 171–98, I argue, corresponds with this point.

125 Long's theory of the modern European project of the making of the black slave can be summarized as the "commodification of creation" in *Significations*; Calvin Warren, "Black Nihilism," 237.

126 Fields and Fields, *Racecraft*. I posit "new evocations of ashé" as a fitting conceptualization for ~~being~~. With Afropessimist and black nihilist criticisms of Western metaphysics and this text's focus on Yoruba thought and religious culture in mind, I develop the concept "new evocations of ashé" as an emically grounded Africana rendering of ~~being~~ that invalidates exactly what the strikethrough feature nullifies—Western formulations and enactments of being that exclude blacks.

127 Spillers, "Mama's Baby, Papa's Maybe," 70.

128 Calvin Warren, "Black Nihilism," 237.

129 Fanon, *Black Skin, White Masks*, 229; Wynter, "Unsettling the Coloniality."

130 Fernheimer, *Stepping into Zion*, 4.

131 Long, *Significations*, 181, 184.

132 Glissant's *Poetics of Relation* advances arguments that both dovetail with and depart from my use of the same concept in this context.

133 Brar Anansi, Brer Rabbit, and High John the Conqueror are Africana mythic heroes that abound in Afro-Caribbean and American orature. See Tanna, *Jamaican Folk Tales*; Abrahams, *African American Folktales*; Beaulieu Herder and Herder, *Best Loved Negro Spirituals*.

134 Washington, *Up from Slavery*, 34.

135 Washington, *Up from Slavery*, 34.

136 Hildebrand, *Times Were Strange and Stirring*, xvii.

137 See Turner, *Islam in the African-American Experience*, esp. 1–4, 45, 71–108.

138 Coates, *Between the World and Me*. James Baldwin originally penned the phrase in an April 1984 *Essence Magazine* essay, "On Being White," 180.

139 Long, *Significations*, 184. See also Long, *Ellipsis*, 136–39, 179, 274, 334.

140 Wynter, "Unsettling the Coloniality," 268. Judy's reading of black folk culture complements Wynter's and Long's perspectives. See esp. "Thinking with Blackness"; and *Sentient Flesh*. David Marriott's reading of Frantz Fanon addresses "invention" in a manner that seems decisive for Afropessimist thinking about how to efficaciously contend with the antiblack world. See his *Whither Fanon?* With this backdrop in mind, I would emphasize that religion makes space for impetus to invent.

141 Long, *Significations*, 183.

142 Long, *Significations*, 184.

143 Rosaldo, *Culture and Truth*, 88.

144 I borrow from Elaine Penagos's conceptualization of the Orisa as "concentrations of aché" in "Santería Poetics," 22, and extend it to encompass all carriers of ashé; that is to say, all entities and life forces, including animals, plants, minerals, and ~~human beings~~, each of which has different concentrations of ashé, but have ashé nonetheless. In n. 126 I explain that I introduce the concept "evocations of ashe" to convey an Africana understanding of ~~being~~. In tandem with this formulation and building from Penagos's rich conceptualization, I experiment here with the concept "concentrations of ashé" as an emically grounded Africana rendering of the *infrastructure* of ~~being~~. Aché (Spanish-language spelling) or "the power to make things happen" has the following cognates: àṣẹ (Yorùbá), ashé (English), and *axé* (Portuguese).

145 Long, *Significations*, 190.

146 See Hucks, *Yoruba Traditions*, 173, for her concept of "territorialization."

147 Jennifer Nash's theoretical approach to affect in black feminist activism informs my perspective. See her "Practicing Love." For a comparable perspective on the Candomblé *terreiro* as a symbol of the African landmass, see Sodré, *O Terreiro*. See also Harding, *Refuge in Thunder*, 150–51.

148 Massetungi, interview, June 28, 2001.

149 Daniel, *Dancing Wisdom*.

150 Diop, *Towards the African Renaissance*.

151 My phenomenological analysis of EOE's significance is not based on the group's numerical size but on its conspicuous commitment to re-creating black ~~being~~ and identity and its heavy reliance of Yoruba religion to do so. At the time of this writing, EOE is a small organization with a spiritual family network of thirty-five initiates. When Massetungi provided this figure, he estimated that EOE has initiated around 120 persons into the Orisa tradition since its founding in 1971.

152 Henry, "Religion and Ideology," 63.

153 In conversation with Frances Henry on Shango's resurgence, McNeal, *Trance and Modernity*, 287–95, examines these and other social and political elements.

154 Otto, *Idea of the Holy*, 25–30.

155 Abímbọ́lá, *Yoruba Culture*, 50. Some traditions exist that number the Orisa as 800 + 1 and 600 + 1.

156 Abímbọ́lá, *Yoruba Culture*, 50–51.

157 Egungun was an established institution among earlier generations of liberated Yorubas in Trinidad before waning and being reestablished during the post–Black Power period. Custodians of Egungun have learned about its

protocols, responsibilities, and masquerading performances through visions and dreams as well as Nigerian experts.

158 Other powerful ceremonial traditions of ancestral remembrance abound across the African diaspora in connection with the oceanic deities Yemaya and Olokun. See Pittman Walke, "Mother of the Movement.'"

159 Coopan, "Memory's Future," 71.

160 For studies of how affective landscapes can source violent nationalist and colonial regimes, see Maksic *Ethnic Mobilization*; Ahmed, *Cultural Politics of Affect*. For an insightful study of affect and material religion, see Scheper Hughes, "Cradling the Sacred."

161 See Stewart, *Black Women, Black Love*, 59–105, esp. 87; Nixon, *Slow Violence*, for more on the concepts of swift violence and slow violence.

162 Massetungi, interview, May 8, 2001.

163 Phills, interview. These comments seem to gesture toward what some scholars are describing as "Otherwise worlds." See chapter 4 in this volume for a more extensive discussion of this subject.

164 Settles, "Flesh and Blood," 61.

165 A gesture of genuflection, usually bending to the ground on both knees, conveying honor and deference.

Four. You Had the Respected Mothers Who Had Power!

1 Warner-Lewis, *Guinea's Other Suns*. This chapter's title is attributed to Molly Ahye, interview with *Gayelle Television*, accessed March 10, 2017, https://www.youtube.com/watch?v=5A26IM5Iihw. The interview took place during Trinidad and Tobago's first Oshun Festival at Salybia in August 1990.

2 Pasley, "The Black Power Movement in Trinidad"; Alexander, "Not Just (Any) Body Can Be a Citizen," esp. 14.

3 Elekes are sacred beaded necklaces that omorisa wear symbolizing their consecration to or spiritual relationship with the Orisa.

4 Iya Eintou Pearl Springer, interview by author and Tracey Hucks, tape recording, Port of Spain, Trinidad, July 22, 2002.

5 Aiyejina and Gibbons, "Orisa Tradition in Trinidad," 44.

6 Sister Sylvestine Piper De Gonzalez, the leader of Oshun Shrine, is a good example. "Sister," as she is affectionately called, is no less a mother than those discussed later in this chapter.

7 I am grateful to Isabelle Ensass for encouraging me to conceptualize the caretaking culture and practices of mothers I describe with the term "motherness."

8 Phillips, *Womanist Reader*, xix–xxxvi.

9 For more on these concepts, see n. 14.

10 Sharpe, *In the Wake*.

11 Fourshey, Gonzales, and Saidi, *Bantu Africa*; Klieman, "*Pygmies Were Our Compass*"; Ehret, *Civilizations of Africa*; Diop, *Cultural Unity of Black Africa*; Manning, *African Diaspora*.

12 Oyĕwùmí, *What Gender Is Motherhood?* 68.

13 Grillo, *Intimate Rebuke*, 44.

14 Amadiume, *Re-Inventing Africa*; Oyĕwùmí, *African Women and Feminism*; Acholonu, *Motherism*; Kolawole, *Womanism and African Consciousness*, 43–71. See also Maparyan, *Womanist Idea*.

15 See Stewart Diakité, "'Matricentric' Foundations."

16 Smith, *West Indian Family Structure*.

17 Warner-Lewis, *Trinidad Yoruba*, 46–47. In 1949, American anthropologist Joseph Moore, "Religion of Jamaican Negroes," 24, noted similar arrangements in his study on Afro-Jamaican religions.

18 Over years of collecting oral data in Trinidad, numerous interlocutors emphasized how pivotal a spiritual mother was in their journey to and within the Orisa religion and/or Spiritual Baptist tradition.

19 Phills, interview, 2001.

20 Maparyan, *Womanist Idea*, 62, addresses these qualities and principles under the subheading "Mothering: Love and Leadership."

21 My understanding of an Africana womanist perspective sympathizes with some concerns Clenora Hudson Weems raised when she coined the term "Africana womanism," but it is still a distinct concept developing out of a dialogical and harmonizing womanist vision that perceives connections and overlapping preoccupations between womanisms and black feminisms. See also n. 141 for additional remarks on Weems's project.

22 Gibbons, interview. Most omorisa call NCOE the "Council of Orisa Elders" or "the Council."

23 See chapter 3 for my coinage and theorization of *numenym* and related terms.

24 This is no minor point. Guyana was moving toward legalizing Obeah during the 1970s under Forbes Burnham's government, but no official amendments or new statutes were recorded. Despite Brazil's 1890 decree, Candomblé devotees still experience extreme forms of social and bureaucratic repression. See Johnson, "Law, Religion, and 'Public Health,'" for additional information on freedom of religion and Candomblé. See also chapter 5 of this volume for information on other Caribbean nations.

25 See "Act for the Incorporation of the Orisa Movement of Trinidad and Tobago. Egbe Orisa Ile Wa," Act 35 of 1981, Fifth Session, First Parliament, September 17, 1981, 790.

26 See "Act for the Incorporation of Opa Orisha (Shango) of Trinidad and Tobago," Act 27 of 1991, Fifth Session, Third Parliament, August 29, 1991, 206.

27 For Peter Ray Blood's article on the Ọ̀ọ̀ni visit to T&T and accompanying photographs, see https://www.diannemstewart.com/books. Despite some contest-

ing opinions, most in the Orisa community concur that Iya Melvina Rodney was indeed chosen as the spiritual head during Ọ̀ọ̀ni Ṣíjúwadé Olúbùṣe II's 1988 visit. I studied in Nigeria during the fall 1988 semester and had the privilege of visiting Ọ̀ọ̀ni Ṣíjúwadé Olúbùṣe's palace. During my group's audience with him, I mentioned my natal Jamaican origins, and the Ọ̀ọ̀ni responded with a comment about how impressed he was that blacks in the Caribbean and the Americas have preserved much of their African cultural and religious heritage. He went on to recount his recent visit to Trinidad and Tobago. He also blessed me with the Yoruba name, Àdùnní, and told me that it references the concept of pricelessness, sweetness, something "good as gold." This experience is even more meaningful today since I am now aware of the many Nigerian (including Yorùbá) ancestors in my maternal and paternal lineages. I never imagined then that I would end up learning about the Ọ̀ọ̀ni's visit to T&T ten years after my encounter with him at his palace in Ifẹ̀.

28 Local experts estimated there were roughly eighty active shrines in Trinidad in the late 1980s.

29 Gibbons, interview.

30 Gibbons, interview. Gibbons explained how stealthily Iya Rodney approached the process of selecting the other elder directors: "She . . . went around and essentially surveyed. She wouldn't tell them that was what she was doing. She would invite them to join the Council. But she'd be doing her own spiritual check, because a lot of people she may not have known; she had only heard of. She was in her eighties, and she went with us. . . . We'd let the people know before, so they could be prepared, and she would place the invocation on the table, she would be allowed to check the shrine and so on. So she did that for everyone and in the end, the six we now have are the persons who came up out of it."

31 NCOE of Trinidad and Tobago, "Resolutions before the General Meeting mandated by the Convention 2000 to Consider the Constitution and Election of Officers," December 3, 2000, NCOE Papers.

32 Gibbons, interview.

33 With regard to the first rule on this list, NCOE was fighting at the time to repeal anti-Obeah statutes and would not have expected omorisa to comply with such unjust laws. NCOE, "Rules and Regulations: General," December 3, 2000, 11, NCOE Papers.

34 NCOE, "Rules and Regulations: General," 12, NCOE Papers.

35 Babalorisa Sam Phills, NCOE of Trinidad and Tobago, "We Are Still 'Other'" (Communiqué, Private Collection of Sam Phills, May 24, 2000).

36 Babalorisa Sam Phills, NCOE of Trinidad and Tobago, "Members of the Public Are Advised" (Communiqué, Private Collection of Sam Phills, May 24, 2000).

37 In the 2011 census, 0.9 percent of respondents identified as Orisha devotees (roughly 11,952), whereas 5.7 percent identified as Baptist and 21.6 percent

identified as Roman Catholic. The total population of T&T was 1,328,019. Of these, 36.3 percent were Afro-Trinidadian; 37.6 percent Indo-Trinidadian; and 22.8 percent of mixed ethnicity made up of 8,669 whites, 1,062 Middle Easterners, and 4,003 Chinese. A total of 3,149 children under the age of fifteen are included in the Orisa religious population, indicating roughly 8,803 persons make up the adult Orisa community (15–80+ years old). When re-creating census tables for publication, it was noted there are some statistically negligible variances between totals reported for religious traditions per age group and the actual totals of the numbers provided. To retain fidelity to the official 2011 report, tables 4.1 and 4.2 reproduced all reported data from the original tables.

38 Gibbons, interview.

39 Oyěwùmí, *Invention of Women*.

40 I discuss some of their achievements in greater detail later in this chapter. See also Barnes, *Africa's Ogun*; Henry, *Reclaiming African Religions*; McNeal, *Trance and Modernity*; Hucks, "I Smoothed the Way."

41 Iya Eintou Springer, interview; Hucks, "I Smoothed the Way."

42 Ahye, interview; McNeal, *Trance and Modernity*, 273.

43 Ahye, interview.

44 All quotations regarding this conversation were accessed through Tracey Hucks's personal cassette tapes of the First World Congress of Orisha Tradition and Culture, Ilé-Ifè, Nigeria, June 1981. Aiyejina, Gibbons, and Phills offer a complementary perspective in "Context and Meaning," 135.

45 Sankeralli, "Remembering Iya L'Orisha Molly Ahye."

46 Long, *Significations*.

47 Ahye, interview with *Gayelle Television*.

48 On creactivity, see chapter 2, n. 55.

49 Iyalode Awo Agbaye Ifakemi Aworeni (Iya Amoye), interview by author and Tracey Hucks, digital recording, Tableland, Trinidad, August 18, 2013.

50 Melville Herskovits's and Maureen Warner-Lewis's ethnographic interviews with elder Yoruba descendants during the 1930s, 1960s, and 1970s include discussion about Egungun (ancestor) institutions among nineteenth-century liberated Yoruba indentured laborers and their early twentieth-century descendants. See chapter 1 for citations of relevant sources.

51 Iyalode Awo Agbaye Ifakemi Aworeni (Iya Amoye), interview by author and Tracey Hucks, digital recording, Tableland, Trinidad, August 18, 2013.

52 Asunta Serrano was a Puerto Rican Yoruba priestess in the Cuban Lucumí tradition. Serrano became well known for initiating many early African American devotees into the Yoruba religion.

53 Iya Amoye, interview.

54 Iya Amoye, interview.

55 Iya Amoye, interview.

56 Obaluaye, Orisa of the earth, infectious diseases, and healing, is also known as Sakpata/Sagbata (Orisa of smallpox) among the Rada and as Shakpanna among earlier generations of Yoruba-Orisa custodians in Trinidad. See chapter 1 for discussion of a Rada ceremony for Sakpata during the nineteenth century in Trinidad (aka Ṣọpọna in Nigeria).

57 Iya Amoye, interview.

58 As discussed extensively in chapter 3, Long's theory that Africa is the most potent religious symbol for African diaspora communities undergirds my interpretation.

59 Iya Amoye, interview.

60 Iya Amoye's sermon has been posted at several internet sites including Eniyan Wa's Facebook page.

61 Iya Amoye, interview. Iya Amoye is also the first woman to deliver Orisa prayers at the opening of Parliament.

62 EOE, "Eniyan Wa's 15th Annual Egungun Festival 2013 a Success," accessed March 13, 2015, https://yorubasacredsciencecentre.wordpress.com/tag /eniyan-wa.

63 Iya Amoye, interview.

64 Iya Amoye, interview.

65 Doris, *Vigilant Things*, 70.

66 Beaubrun, *Nan Domi*, 71.

67 Iya Amoye, interview.

68 Iya Amoye, interview.

69 Afro-Jamaicans evidence a similar understanding about dreams that feature ancestors. The agency behind the dream always rests with the invisible family member or Power who appears in the dream; "Mama dream mi lahs night" (my mother dreamt me last night) is the African Jamaican way of saying in the West, "I dreamt about my mother last night."

70 When describing how Eniyan Wa came to celebrate Gelede, Iya Amoye discussed how the ancestors gave precise instructions. "And we were told to get a special vessel and the manifestation came and told us to prepare it in a special way. That's what I tell people about Spirit guidance. People don't believe it; they don't understand it." Iya Amoye, interview.

71 Beliso-De Jesús, *Electric Santería*.

72 For her compelling theorization of sacred objects as "ritual participants," see Daniels, "Ritual," 403.

73 García-Peña, *The Borders of Dominicanidad*, 84; see also 82–96.

74 Alexander's *Pedagogies of Crossing*, esp. 311–322; Janzen, "African Religion and Healing," 13–16.

75 Mother Joan transitioned April 1, 2019, at age seventy.

76 Phills, interview.

77 Mother Joan Cyrus (Chief Ifakorede Oyayemi Aworeni), interview by author and Tracey Hucks, digital recording, Enterprise, Trinidad, August 18, 2013.

78 See chapter 1 for my discussion of this subject.

79 Mother Joan is the only person I encountered who referred to Ebenezer Elliott as "Papa" rather than "Pa" Neezer, signaling a greater degree of intimacy with him than most had in the Orisa community.

80 Baba Sam Phills described Mr. Francis as an Orisa expert who was known as an "Obeah man."

81 Mother Joan, interview. Located in East Port of Spain, Laventille began as a colonial settlement. Legend has it that enslaved Africans often chose the hills of Laventille when they fled captivity. Laventille gave birth to the steel pan and has been home to Trinidadians of lower socioeconomic classes. Locals often refer to neighborhoods throughout eastern Port of Spain as part of "Laventille."

82 Castor, *Spiritual Citizenship*, 89–90.

83 Stewart Diakité, "'Matricentric' Foundations."

84 This quotation is from a December 16, 1998, meeting, the first of many sessions Tracey Hucks and I spent recording Iya Sangowunmi's oral history. Iya Sangowunmi's quotations throughout the remainder of the chapter are from the interview cited here and four subsequent interviews we conducted in 2001, 2002, 2005, and 2013.

85 Abímbọ́lá, *Yorùbá Culture*, 70–74; "Yoruba Diaspora."

86 I use the uppercase for "Ori" here because Iya Sangowunmi appears to be referencing the concept of Ori as one's personal Orisa.

87 Iya founded Osun Abiadama School in April 1996 to provide a rigorous and progressive academic setting for primary through secondary school education. When Tracey and I returned to Trinidad in 2013, the school was "in transition" after Iya devised plans to "build a new school at Gasparillo, Santa Cruz." During its operative years, however, the school was not restricted to Orisa members, but parents were informed of the curricular emphasis on African heritage and Orisa theological and philosophical principles.

88 Aku Kontar, Ile Sango/Osun Mil'Osa, "Rain Festival," 1.

89 "Ile Eko Sango/Osun Mil'Osa (IESOM) History," (Unpublished Manuscript, Private Collection of Iyalode Sangowunmi/Patricia McLeod), 3.

90 "IESOM History," 1.

91 "IESOM History," 4, 7.

92 Iya understands "metaphysics" as a translational term for spiritual knowledge, discipline, and power.

93 Iya Sangowunmi's late husband Isaac T. McLeod was a successful real estate entrepreneur with holdings and businesses throughout the nation.

94 Castor, *Spiritual Citizenship*, 98.

95 When Rada priest and elder Sedley Cadet Johnson Antoine passed away in 2001, the funeral program included sympathies expressed on behalf of the "Yoruba Community" and the "West African Rada Community." If Antoine had died a century earlier, sympathies would have been offered by the Yoruba (Yaraba) *Nation* and the West African Rada *Nation*. See chapter 3 for a discussion of Antoine's funeral.

96 Using national media outlets to extend a public invitation to *all* citizens of T&T to attend EOE's Olokun Festival and delivering a keynote address before Parliament that educates the nation about Yoruba ethics and its relevance for political ethics and good governance are just two examples of Yoruba-Orisa devotees' efforts to shape national belonging and citizenship through their rich *nation-al* inheritance. I employ the term "gaze" here to invoke its prosaic meanings rather than any critical theoretical, psychoanalytical, or other academic meanings. Similarly, my concept of "third space" is distinguished from the term's conceptual genesis and genealogy in postcolonial studies.

97 Adéèkó, *Arts of Being Yorùbá*. For more on women's traditional and contemporary political and spiritual leadership roles in Nigeria, see Olasupo, "Women's Associational Life"; "Women and Religion in Nigeria."

98 Her marriage rite was apparently the first to be used in an official Orisa wedding ceremony after the passage of the Orisa Marriage Act in 1999. See "Orisa Marriage Act," Act 22 of 1999, Fourth Session, Fifth Parliament, August 16, 1999, http://www.ttparliament.org/legislations/a1999-22.pdf.

99 I speak here of a merging that often takes place when Orisa custodians enter and participate in the affairs of the civic public, especially those involving bureaucratic matters, legislative decisions, court proceedings, and parliamentary ceremonies. For a compelling treatment of the counter-public in an Africana context, see Terrence Johnson's engagement of Evelyn Brooks Higginbotham's concept of the black church as a counter-public in "Exploring Race, Religion, and Slavery."

100 I attended the Rain Festival and witnessed many affirmative gestures from audience members. They expressed audible signs of agreement, words of affirmation, and, toward the end of the speech, a cheerful collective expression of ululation. Louis Homer, on behalf of the Honorable Clifton De Coteau, Ministry of National Diversity and Social Integration, "Opening Remarks," Sango/Osun Rain Festival, Ile Eko Sango/Osun Mil'Osa (Little Oyo), August 9, 2013. I digitally recorded these and other remarks quoted from Mr. Homer's speech.

101 Basdeo Panday often defended a place for Orisa in T&T's multicultural and multireligious society. See also Castor, *Spiritual Citizenship*, especially 54–70.

102 See chapter 3 for my discussion of territorialization in relation to EOE's understanding and employment of the symbol of Africa.

103 Iya uses the term "metaphysician" as a translational term to describe Orun-mila as the owner of knowledge about the world/universe, including seem-ingly inscrutable processes and invisible reality.

104 A classic study that develops this idea is Karin Barber, "How Man Makes God." See also Springer, "Orisa and the Spiritual Baptist Religion," 86.

105 Toyin Falola translates this poem differently than I do here (with the as-sistance of Kọ́lá Abímbọ́lá). See *African Diaspora*, 209, for Falola's translation and the original Yoruba stanza. I chose to insert the personal names "Ogun" (line 4) and "Osala" (line 7) rather than attempt to translate the nongendered pronoun into the English gendered pronoun "he." "Persons" should not be interpreted as limited to human beings. Rather, the term signifies all entities with agency, obligations, duties, privileges, and entitlements, including flora and fauna.

106 Harney and Moten, *Undercommons*, 8, describes this kind of refusal as "a game-changing kind of refusal . . . that signals the refusal of the choices as offered."

107 When Henry, *Reclaiming African Religions*, 19, asked Iya Rodney about her rela-tionship with her famed spiritual father, Pa Neezer, she relayed how "lucky" she was to have received "de same thunder stone dat he [Pa Neezer] say he got . . . from Ma Diamond . . . and he hand meh a good bit." Pa Neezer also had consecrated Iya Rodney's shrine, placing thunder stones at the four cor-ners and center of her "chapel." Iya Rodney's "luck," it would seem, came not just because of Ma Diamond's priestly reputation and expertise in Trinidad but especially because of Ma Diamond's natal tie to Africa.

108 During the first week of each new year IESOM organizes annual rituals to "renew" and augment Iya Rodney's elevation. Iyalode Sangowunmi Olakiitan Osunfunmilayo (Patricia McLeod), telephone communication with author and Tracey Hucks, December 9, 2020.

109 Iya Sangowunmi, telephone communication with author and Tracey Hucks, February 11, 2022; Long, *Significations*, 7.

110 Sharpe, *In the Wake*, 75. Several essays in King, Navarro, and Smith, *Otherwise Worlds* explore concepts similar to my concepts of ~~world~~ and ~~worldmaking~~.

111 Long, *Significations*, 89–123; Palmer, "Otherwise Than Blackness," 253.

112 A student of Mircea Eliade, Long deployed his conception of "archaic" religious consciousness to theorize the nature of black religion, not to reify stereotypes about traditional societies. For more on Eliade's concept of the archaic religious worldview, see *Myth of the Eternal Return*. See also Brown, "Eliade on Archaic Religion," 429–49, for a summary of arguments challeng-ing Mircea Eliade's conception of archaic societies. On refusal, see n. 106.

113 Italics mine. Long, *Significations*, 193.

114 On "heritage," see chapter 1, n. 1.

115 Among IESOM's approximately twenty Rain Festivals across the years, many were designed to address matricentric womanist themes of relevance to the entire Orisa community in Trinidad, including "We and Our Environment Are One" (June 27–30, 2008) and "Women—The Holders of Tradition, Initiating Balance" (August 5–7, 2016).

116 Maparyan, *Womanist Idea*. See also Sandoval, *Methodology of the Oppressed*, for her pioneering conceptualization of decolonial love.

117 Hartman, "Belly of the World."

118 Williams, *Sisters in the Wilderness*.

119 Hartman, "Belly of the World," 171.

120 Delores Williams and other Christian womanist theologians often cite this popular African American expression in their scholarship.

121 Hartman, "Belly of the World," 171.

122 Hill Collins, "What's in a Name?"

123 The early school of black liberation theology debated whether political aims and desires were either too particular (black/*nationalist*) or too universalist (white/integrationist). For a summary of this debate, see Hucks and Stewart, "African American Religion." See also Nash, "Practicing Love," for her framing of identitarian politics versus affective politics.

124 I use the term "identity politics" here as Barbara Smith and her sister comrades in the Combahee River Collective coined and used it in 1977—"that Black women have a right to determine our own political agendas." See Amy Goodman's interview with Barbara Smith, "Feminist Scholar Barbara Smith on Identity Politics and Why She Supports Bernie Sanders for President," *Democracy Now!*, February 12, 2020. https://www.democracynow.org/2020/2/12/barbara_smith_identity_politics_bernie_sanders. See also BlackPast, "(1977) The Combahee River Collective Statement," https://www.blackpast.org/african-american-history/combahee-river-collective-statement-1977.

125 I gesture here toward Christina Sharpe's insights about the "anagrammatical" and black care sites of habitation that exceed the logics of "the hold." See Sharpe, *In the Wake*.

126 Palmer, "Otherwise than Blackness," 258.

127 Holm, "Analyses of Longing," esp. 624.

128 Muñoz, "Feeling Brown," 70.

129 Palmer, "'What Feels More than Feeling?'" 35. Palmer's article, "Otherwise than Blackness," raises questions about the kind of conceptual moves I make in my discussion of affect. However, with ~~worldmaking~~, "otherworldliness," and alternative related terms, I am attempting to attend to the anagrammatical site of black care that Christina Sharpe explores. Consequently, my work on affect accounts for the kind of nonrelational affect vis-à-vis "the World" Palmer delineates in his theorization of black affect.

130 Wilderson, *Red, White, and Black*, xi, 132, 279; Harney and Moten, *Undercommons* 12, 87–99.

131 Gerbner, *Christian Slavery*.

132 Ahmed, "Affective Economies," 120."

133 Tutu, "Whither African Theology," 366.

134 If Calvin Warren and Christina Sharpe's contention that "the antiblack world is irredeemable"—that "the only certainty is the weather that produces a pervasive climate of antiblackness"—is true, then I would hazard that black religious consciousness is the throne of that "dynamic enduring power of the spirit" Warren insists we must now attempt to apprehend. See Warren, *Ontological Terror*, 171; Sharpe, *In the Wake*, 106.

135 On creactivities, see chapter 2, n. 55.

136 The limitations of this project do not allow me to elaborate the resources available in Yoruba-Orisa and other African-heritage religions for thinking productively with Afropessimist thinkers and conversation partners about otherworldliness. The resonances are significant and deserve attention from scholars in religious studies and black studies. Moten, "Blackness and Nothingness," 744, 776, and Crawley, "Stayed | Freedom | Hallelujah," 28–9, are two pivotal thinkers whose reflections on otherworldliness offer important starting points for such explorations.

137 This subheading is a spin on Walter Rodney's foundational text *Groundings*.

138 Duncan, *Spot of Ground*.

139 Hartman, "Belly of the World," 166.

140 "Black landlessness" is an outcome of African-descended people's involuntary presence in Trinidad spawned by the transatlantic slave trade. See Long, *Significations*, 190–94.

141 Clenora Hudson Weems made this point in her text *Africana Womanism*, even maintaining that black feminism and Africana womanism are incompatible. Although Layli Maparyan acknowledges Weems as a foundational womanist foremother, she distinguishes black feminism from womanism based on other criteria, including the two traditions' approaches to critical thought and social change, and she discusses at length how intimately related black feminism and womanism are. I am sympathetic to some of the criticisms and observations Weems makes about white feminisms, especially her suspicion of a dominant Western intellectual horizon and the lingering effects of white feminisms on some forms of black feminism. It is impossible to ponder Jennifer Nash's analysis of the white liberal academy and women's studies programs' racist treatment of black feminisms without sympathizing with Weems on these points. However, I differ with both Weems and Maparyan in conceiving womanism's relationship to black feminism. There are repertoires of womanism and repertoires of black

feminism so similar as to be indistinguishable. For Nash's most comprehensive assessment of the liberal American university and women's studies programs, see *Black Feminism Reimagined*. African womanists have also criticized Western feminisms as ill fitted for African contexts and instead articulate visions of womanisms they argue are transcontextual and transcultural across diverse settings within Africa. See, for example, Ogunyemi, *Africa Wo/Man Palava*; Acholonu, *Motherism*; and Kolawole, *Womanism and African Consciousness*.

142 *Re-versing* is my shorthand for Iya's latest hermeneutical innovation of substituting verses from African Caribbean and African American orature for some West African Yorùbá Odù-Ifá verses.

143 Italics mine. Hucks, *Yoruba Traditions*, 312–13.

144 Jackson, *Becoming Human*, 39.

145 Variants of this creation story feature Olorun or Ifa as Orisa who descended from the abode above on a long chain.

Five. The African Gods Are from Tribes and Nations

1 This chapter's title is attributed to a Central African descendant and Kumina devotee in St. Thomas, Jamaica who was speaking to Joseph Moore, "Religion of Jamaican Negroes," 27. The epigraph's source is Herskovits, Trinidad Field Trip-Diary, 96, MFH Papers.

2 Henry, *Caliban's Reason*, 104. In light of Sharpe's concept of the "anagrammatical," I prefer to describe what Henry calls a "grammar" as an "anagrammar."

3 J. D. Elder's documentation of nation consciousness and nation groupings among Africans in twentieth-century Trinidad is critical for historicizing nationhood. See Elder, "Yoruba Ancestor Cult."

4 Burton Sankeralli, "Trinidad Orisa—Legitimacy or Agency?" (unpublished paper, October 19, 2012), 1.

5 Iya Eintou Springer, interview, July 22, 2002. The Miscellaneous Laws Act of 2000 amended the Summary Offences Act to remove all discriminatory language pertaining to obeah. Spiritual Baptists were instrumental in the fight to remove anti-Obeah language from the laws of T&T; Senator Barbara Burke was foremost among them.

6 Springer, "Orisa and the Spiritual Baptist Religion," 93. During Parliamentary debates concerning the bill to amend the SOA, the Honorable Ramesh Maharaj reminded his colleagues that "in 1994 somebody from the Orisa faith was arrested, under these [SOA] laws." See House of Representatives, Miscellaneous Laws Bill, Wednesday, October 11, 2000, 72.

7 Springer, "Orisa and the Spiritual Baptist Religion," 96.

8 In other words, there was no need to revise what was supposedly a defunct law. However, as Springer made clear the demeaning law was still available,

no matter how infrequently it was being deployed. See House of Representatives, Miscellaneous Laws Bill, Wednesday, October 11, 2000, 44, 46.

9 Although I use the term "linked fate" with unintended reference to Michael Dawson's theory of "linked fate," there are some resonances with Dawson's explanation of it as the sentiment that an individual's prospects for success or failure are inextricably tied to their racial group's fate. Orisa devotees and other custodians of African heritage religions in Trinidad have pursued their civil right to religious freedom with some sense of linked fate based on a shared Africana spiritual heritage, inclusive of plural, blended, and dynamic religious traditions. See Dawson, *Behind the Mule*.

10 See House of Representatives, Miscellaneous Laws Bill, Wednesday, October 11, 2000, 35. See also the Reverend Hazel-Ann Gibbs-De Peza's remark: "You can use the obi for a number of ailments. So, there is a lot of mystery surrounding it and because of that, people associate the term obeah coming from use of the obi." Corey Connelly, "Obeah, They Wukking Obeah," T&TN, October 14, 2018, https://newsday.co.tt/2018/10/14/obeah-they-wukking-obeah/. Gibbs-De Peza, a prominent ordained Spiritual Baptist minister, is also an author and assistant professor who has served as chairperson of the National Congress of Incorporated Baptist Organisations of T&T.

11 Usuanlele, "Tracing the African Origins"; Handler and Bilby, "Early Use and Origin."

12 Paton, "Obeah Acts," 5.

13 Sharpe, *In the Wake*, 14. See volume I for Hucks's discussion of Governor Picton's policing of African populations in colonial Trinidad.

14 Stewart Diakité, "'Matricentric' Foundations." See also Diop, *Cultural Unity*; Amadiume, *Re-Inventing Africa*; *Male Daughters, Female Husbands*; Oyěwùmí, *Invention of Women*; *African Women and Feminism*; Grillo, *Intimate Rebuke*; Saidi, *Women's Authority and Society*; Collins, *Black Feminist Thought*; Acholonu, *Motherism*.

15 Herskovits also acknowledged that the socioeconomic conditions of slavery reinforced African matrifocal family structures and polygynous marital/mating arrangements. See Herskovits, *Myth of the Negro Past*, 167–86; "Negro in Bahia."

16 Extensive study is still required to understand indigenous African concepts of biology and anatomy before we can close the discussion on terms such as "anatomical female" and "woman." However, gender may be an ill-fitting or inadequate category for theorizing social constructions of anatomical females and anatomical males in many precolonial African contexts. A place to begin might be with sociolinguistic and semantic studies on the term *gender* in the West and cognate or approximate terms in African languages. Interventions of LGBTQI theorists who raise questions about gender-nonconforming, nonbinary, and intersex persons are important to consider and might lead to new knowledge production in African religious studies

because persons now described as LGBTQI were associated with the spirit world or with anomalous spiritual gifts and roles in some African cultures. See Somé, *Spirit of Intimacy*; Conner and Sparks, *Queering Creole Spiritual Traditions*; Murray and Roscoe, *Boy-Wives and Female Husbands*.

17 Gilkes, *If It Wasn't for the Women*, 72–73.

18 Gomez, *African Dominion*, 63.

19 Gomez, *African Dominion*, 61–91.

20 Ellis, *Yoruba-Speaking Peoples*, 176.

21 Oyĕwùmí, *African Women and Feminism*, 12.

22 De Verteuil, *Trinidad*, 166.

23 Jean Herskovits, interview by author, digital recording, New York, NY, March 24, 2012.

24 Molly Ahye, *Gayelle* interview, https://www.youtube.com/watch?v=5A26IM5Iihw.

25 See Matory, *Black Atlantic Religion*, 188–223, for his argument against Ruth Landes's thesis that, because of its African heritage, Candomblé is a matriarchal space where men are marginal and compelled to accommodate feminine modes of spiritual belonging. See also Landes, *City of Women*.

26 Stewart Diakité, "'Matricentric' Foundations." See also Hucks, "I Smoothed the Way."

27 Cone, *Said I Wasn't Gonna Tell Nobody*, 151.

28 See Roberts, *Black Religion*; *Roots*; *Africentric Christianity*. See also Hucks, *Yoruba Traditions*, 41.

29 Long, "African American Religion," 17.

30 Fields and Fields, *Racecraft*, 141–42. I have italicized "nation" and "nationality" throughout this chapter to align with my conceptualization of Africana *nations*. The other italicized term "color" is original. For evidence supporting Fields and Fields's argument, see Weisenfeld, *New World A-Coming*, and Johnson, "Rise of Black Ethnics," 125–63. Both scholars make compelling cases for African American religious movements that rejected the Euro-Western concept of race. I would add to Johnson's focus on ethnicity that Nation of Islam leaders replaced the concept of race with an Africana concept of *nation* that extended a new ethnogenesis to the "Tribe of Shabazz." As Weisenfeld clarifies in *New World*, 59, "Fard and Muhammad's teaching emphasized that the time-bound creation of whites made them a *race*, and as such they would die out. In contrast, the original black people were a *nation*, which has no beginning or end." Du Bois's theorization of the black church as a *nation*/government complicates race, nation, and ethnicity for a people who, Johnson argues, were never permitted to have ethnicity. Father Divine's movement precedes postmodern efforts to deconstruct race as a social category. Father Divine and his disciples claimed to belong to the "human" race and refused to designate social identity based on flawed, imagined racial categories.

31 Alexander Garden to London Office, May 5, 1740, Box 20 from Lambeth Palace Library, vol. 941, no. 72, MS-AC. See also Creel, "A Peculiar People," 81.

32 Stephen Carter, "Author Interview: Stephen Carter," interview by Robert Birnbaum, Identity Theory, July 14, 2002, http://www.identitytheory.com /stephen-carter/.

33 Dewulf, The Pinkster King, 147; Rucker, River Flows On, 27–58.

34 Landers, Black Society in Spanish Florida, 29–30, 50–51, 158.

35 Brown, "Place and Culture in African American History," unpublished manuscript, May 4, 2019.

36 See n. 30.

37 Glaude's Exodus! is a noteworthy exception that explores the motifs of nation and nationalism in connection with prominent nineteenth-century African American Christian appropriations of the Exodus narrative in the Bible. My Africana approach differs in that it grounds black nationhood, including my interpretation of the black church as nation, in legacies of African nations in North America and the wider diaspora. These legacies predated, and I would argue even opaquely permeated, nineteenth-century African American figural strategies of biblical interpretation.

38 Du Bois, Souls of Black Folk, 213–14.

39 See Mays and Nicholson, Negro's Church, 9.

40 See Frazier and Lincoln, Negro Church/Black Church, 35–51.

41 Nineteenth-century Dominican missionary Cothonay described the palais as a space where the Afro-Creole population staged their "half religious" and "half civil" activities.

42 National Baptist Convention, Journal of the Thirty-sixth Annual Convention, 40. Cited by Brooks Higginbotham, Righteous Discontent, 270. Elias C. Morris served as the convention's president between 1895 and 1922.

43 Frazier and Lincoln, Negro Church/Black Church, 49. Frazier identified black nation-al consciousness with rural southern negro communities, whose cultural outlook would have been redolent of African heritage thought systems and customs. John Thornton's proposal that "in North America, the churches helped supplant the nation in a creolizing population" (italics mine), privileges the theory that nation allegiances were forged and sustained through shared African languages. I propose that the black church extended and reconfigured antecedent Africana nation-al aspirations, which encompassed more than the preservation of African languages and other cultural practices and heritage symbols. The black church also addressed political ideas and customs that have inspired expressions of Africana nationhood at least since the sixteenth century, as Thornton documents in places such as Mexico, Brazil, the United States, Antigua, and Jamaica. See his Africa and Africans, esp. 331.

44 I use "primordial citizen" in this context because it signals black belonging to a nation that the (white) American nation does recognize.

45 Frazier and Lincoln, *Negro Church/Black Church*, 49–50.

46 NAACP History Explained, "Lift Every Voice and Sing," accessed January 21, 2019, https://www.naacp.org/naacp-history-lift-evry-voice-and-sing.

47 Newman, *Freedom's Prophet*, 191–94. According to several sources, Richard Allen, Absalom Jones, and James Forten raised the militia for "the defense of Philadelphia during the War of 1812. Asked by the mayor [and the Philadelphia Vigilance Committee] to form a black regiment, the preaching pair mustered 2,500 troops. . . . They saw no action in the war, however." See Independence Hall Association in Philadelphia, "Mother Bethel A.M.E. Church," USHistory.org, accessed March 10, 2013, http://www.ushistory.org /tour/mother-bethel.htm; Johnson, *African American Soldiers*.

48 Yai, "African Diasporan Concepts," 245–46.

49 Yai, "African Diasporan Concepts," 248.

50 Stuckey's *Slave Culture* offers convincing evidence for my argument. He even notes that the ring shout was not a local or brief practice among African descendants in North America. Rather, it became a national phenomenon in the black church. See esp. 36, 62–63, 93–97.

51 *Baltimore Afro-American*, March 26, 1932. Cited in Weisenfeld, *New World A-Coming*, 14–15.

52 Warren, "Black Time, 61.

53 Du Bois, *Souls of Black Folk*.

54 Matthews, *Honoring the Ancestors*, esp. 11–14; Stewart-Diakité and Hucks, "Africana Religious Studies," 48–49. Resonant with Tracey's and my comparative approach, and not surprisingly so, one of Matthews's central categories for comparing African American and African cultural thought and meaning is family.

55 Cone, *Martin and Malcolm and America*.

56 Nash, *Black Feminism Reimagined*, 115. See also Nash, "Practicing Love," for her earlier perspective on black feminist affect.

57 Baldwin, *Fire Next Time*, 26.

58 Barrett, *Soul-Force*. See also my translation of Soul-force as Orí-àṣẹ (Ori-ashé) in chapter 3.

59 Warren, *Ontological Terror*. See also, Spillers, "Mama's Baby, Papa's Maybe," 70. See Hucks, volume I, for more information on Cooper's, Yala's, and Yobua's traumatic experiences with colonial policing and punishment.

Afterword

1 Alternatively spelled "Vigoyanna." Aiyejina, Gibbons, and Phills suggest Central Africa as another possible homeland. In "Context and Meaning," they write, "Vigoyana (considered by some as the surveyor of the shrine and by others as a forest essence, likely of Kongo origin)," 133. I wonder if Vigoy-

ana's homeland might be in South Asia given the name and large numbers of South Asian Guyanese nationals who either have traveled back and forth between Guyana and Trinidad or have permanently settled in Trinidad. To date I have been unable to confirm my conjecture.

2 "Soponna, Erinle, Vigoyana, Oya, Shango," track 8 on Gibbons et al., *Songs of the Orisa Palais: Trinidad and Tobago: Learning the Way*, SANCH Electronix, 2005, compact disc 2.

3 Abímbọ́lá, "Yorùbá Diaspora," 324.

4 For a detailed discussion of the Hindu organization Sanatan Dharma Maha Saba's celebration of Ganesh, which they invited the Orisa community to attend, see Mitchell, "Crucial Issues in Caribbean Religions," 193, and Henry, *Reclaiming African Religions*, 86–89.

5 Another salient example of a third space that merged Trinidad's primordial and civic publics was the June 2011 public treeplanting ceremony that had a dual function: to honor two prominent Orisa ancestors who had recently passed away, Baba Clarence Forde and Iya Melvina Rodney, and to "mark the official opening of the Orisa Village Site at Maloney." See "Orisa Devotees Count Blessings with Tree-planting," T&TG, June 28, 2011, http://www .guardian.co.tt/article-6.2.445378.13d2117e80.

6 *The Missionary Herald: Containing Intelligence, at Large, of the Proceedings and Operations of the Baptist Missionary Society* (London: G. Wightman, 1867), 122.

7 One year later, Cowen claimed with satisfaction, "our circulation last year amounted to 1999 copies of the Scriptures in English, French, Spanish, Portuguese, Chinese, and the various languages spoken by emigrants from the East." Cowen was the first Baptist missionary to work in Trinidad. He began evangelization efforts among African American Loyalist settlers as an agent of the Lady Mico Charity in 1836 and around 1843 began working as a member of the Baptist Missionary Society until his death in 1852. *The Baptist Magazine for 1843, Volume XXXV (Series IV.VOL.VI)* (London: Houlston and Stoneman, 1843), 498.

8 At this writing, Trinidad has seven public holidays in recognition of African and Indian religio-cultural and political traditions: Carnival, Carnival/Shrove Tuesday, Spiritual Baptist Liberation Day (March 30); Indian Arrival Day (May 30), Emancipation Day (August 1), Eid-al-Fitr, and Diwali/Deepavali.

9 Reported figures are as follows: Hindus (18.2 percent), Spiritual Baptists (5.7 percent), Muslims (5 percent), and Orisa (0.9 percent). It is highly likely the percentage of Orisa practitioners is underrepresented in this census report because negative stigmas associated with Orisa religious culture still exist. Orisa practitioners are undoubtedly represented among Spiritual Baptist adherents, given that many Spiritual Baptists are active in both traditions and might not disclose their connections to Orisa in official or public registers.

10 See chapter 5, n. 51.

11 Sylvester Johnson narrates this protracted and troubling story of African American colonial experience in *African American Religions*.

12 I refer here to the intellectual articulation of Black Power in Carmichael and Hamilton, *Black Power*.

13 EN, June 9, 1970, 9. When I shared this image with Kathleen Cleaver, she was surprised to learn I had found it in the newspaper collection at the National Archives of Trinidad and Tobago.

14 A moment I witnessed many times throughout my field research in Trinidad.

15 Frederick Douglass, "What to the Slave Is the Fourth of July," July 5, 1852, Michael Harriot ed., *The Root*, July 4, 2019, https://www.theroot.com/what-to-the-slave-is-the-fourth-of-july-1836083536.

16 See Johnson, "Exploring Race, Religion, and Slavery."

17 See chapter 5, n. 46.

18 See introduction, n. 10.

19 On creactivity, see chapter 2, n. 55.

Bibliography

Abímbọ́lá, Kọ́lá. "Yorùbá Diaspora." In *Encyclopedia of Diasporas: Immigrant and Refugee Cultures around the World*, edited by Melvin Ember, Carol Ember, and Ian Skoggard, 317–26. New York: Kluwer Academic, 2004.

Abímbọ́lá, Kọ́lá. *Yorùbá Culture: A Philosophical Account*. Birmingham, UK: Iroko Academic, 2006.

Abímbọ́lá, Wándé. *Ifá Divination Poetry*. Lagos: NOK Publishers, 1977.

Abímbọ́lá, Wándé. *Ifá: An Exposition of Ifá Literary Corpus*. New York: Athelia Henrietta Press, 1997.

Abímbọ́lá, Wándé. *Ifa Will Mend Our Broken World: Thoughts on Yoruba Religion and Culture in Africa and the African Diaspora*. Roxbury, MA: AIM Books, 1997.

Abímbọ́lá, Wándé. *Ijinle Ohun Enu Ifa: Apa Kin-in-Ni*. Ibadan, Nigeria: University Press PLC, 2006.

Abrahams, Roger. *African American Folktales: Stories from Black Traditions in the New World*. New York: Pantheon Books, 1985.

Acholonu, Catherine. *Motherism: The Afrocentric Alternative*. Abuja, Nigeria: Afa Publications, 1995.

Adderley, Rosanne M. *"New Negroes from Africa": Slave Trade Abolition and Free African Settlement in the Nineteenth-Century Caribbean*. Bloomington: Indiana University Press, 2006.

Adderley, Rosanne M. "Orisha Worship and 'Jesus Time': Rethinking African Religious Conversion in the Nineteenth-Century Caribbean." *Pennsylvania History* 64 (July 1997): 183–206.

Adédìran, Bíódún. *The Frontier States of Western Yorùbáland: Circa 1600–1889: State Formation and Political Growth in an Ethnic Frontier Zone*. Ibadan, Nigeria: IFRA, 1994.

Adéẹ̀kọ́, Adélékè. *Arts of Being Yorùbá: Divination, Allegory, Tragedy, Proverb, Panegyric*. Bloomington: Indiana University Press, 2017.

Agwuele, Augustine. "Popular Culture of Yoruba Kinship Practices." In *Africans and the Politics of Popular Culture*, edited by Toyin Falola and Augustine Agwuele, 41–63. Rochester, NY: University of Rochester Press, 2009.

Ahmed, Sara. "Affective Economies." *Social Text* 72, no. 2 (Summer 2004): 117–39.

Ahmed, Sara. *The Cultural Politics of Affect*. New York: Routledge, 2004.

Aiyejina, Funso, and Rawle Gibbons. "Orisa (Orisha) Tradition in Trinidad." *Caribbean Quarterly* 45, no. 4 (December 1999): 35–50.

Aiyejina, Funso, Rawle Gibbons, and Baba Sam Phills. "Context and Meaning in Trinidad Yoruba Songs: *Peter Was a Fisherman* and *Songs of the Orisha Palais*." *Research in African Literatures* 40, no. 1 (Spring 2009): 127–36.

Ajala, Aderemi, and Insa Nolte. "Ambivalence and Transgression in the Practice of Ṣàngó." In *Beyond Religious Tolerance: Muslim, Christian & Traditionalist Encounters in an African Town*, edited by Insa Nolte, Olukoya Ogen, and Rebecca Jones, 53–73. Rochester, NY: James Currey, 2017.

Akinjogbin, I. A. *Dahomey and Its Neighbours, 1708–1818*. Cambridge: Cambridge University Press, 1967.

Akinjogbin, I. A. "The Specificities and Dynamics of African Negro Cultures: The Yoruba Area." In *Distinctive Characteristics and Common Features of African Cultural Areas South of the Sahara*, edited by UNESCO, 57–70. Colchester, UK: Spottiswoode Ballantyne, 1985.

Akínyẹmí, Akíntúnde. "The Ambivalent Representations of Ṣàngó in Yorùbá Literature." In *Ṣàngó in Africa and the African Diaspora*, edited by Joel Tishken, Toyin Falola, and Akíntúnde Akínyẹmí, 23–43. Bloomington: Indiana University Press, 2009.

Akínyẹmí, Akíntúnde. "The Place of Ṣàngó in the Yorùbá Pantheon." In Tishken, Falola, and Akínyẹmí, *Ṣàngó in Africa and the African Diaspora*, 187–200.

Alexander, M. Jacqui. "Not Just (Any) Body Can Be a Citizen: The Politics of Law, Sexuality and Postcoloniality in Trinidad and Tobago and the Bahamas." *Feminist Review* 48 (Autumn 1994): 5–23.

Alexander, M. Jacqui. *Pedagogies of Crossing: Meditations on Feminism, Sexual Politics, Memory, and the Sacred*. Durham, NC: Duke University Press, 2005.

Alvarado, Denise. *Voodoo Hoodoo Spellbook*. San Francisco, CA: Weiser Books, 2011.

Amadiume, Ifi. *Male Daughters, Female Husbands: Gender and Sex in an African Society*. London: Zed Books, 1987.

Amadiume, Ifi. *Re-Inventing Africa: Matriarchy, Religion and Culture*. London: Zed Books, 1997.

Anderson, Benedict. *Imagined Communities: Reflections on the Origin and Spread of Nationalism*. New York: Verso, 1983.

Aremu, David. "Archaeological and Historical Significance of Koso Wall in Old Oyo National Park." *West African Journal of Archaeology* 34, nos. 1 & 2 (2004): 20–35.

Aremu, David. "Enclosures of the Old Oyo Empire, Nigeria." In *African Indigenous Knowledge and the Sciences: Journeys into the Past and Present*, edited by Gloria Emeagwali and Edward Shizha, 145–51. Rotterdam: Sense Publishers, 2016.

Aremu, David. "Saving Sungbo's Eredo: A Challenge to Nigerian Archaeologists." *West African Journal of Archaeology* 32, no. 2 (2002): 63–73.

Asad, Talal. *Genealogies of Religion: Discipline and Reasons of Power in Christianity and Islam*. Baltimore: Johns Hopkins University Press, 1993.

Asiegbu, Johnson. *Slavery and the Politics of Liberation, 1787–1861*. London: Longman, 1969.

Asiwaju, Anthony I. "The Aja-Speaking Peoples of Nigeria: A Note on Their Origins, Settlement and Cultural Adaptation up to 1945." *Africa: Journal of the International African Institute* 49, no. 1 (January 1979): 15–28.

Azoulay, Ariella. *Potential History: Unlearning Imperialism*. Brooklyn, NY: Verso, 2019.

Baldwin, James. *The Fire Next Time*. New York: Knopf Doubleday, 2013.

Baldwin, James. "On Being White . . . and Other Lies." In *Black on White: Black Writers on What It Means to Be White*, edited by David Roediger, 177–80. New York: Schocken Books, 1998.

The Baptist Magazine for 1843, Volume XXXV (Series IV.VOL.VI). London: Houlston and Stoneman,1843.

The Baptist Magazine for 1866. London: Elliot Stock, 1866. https://www.google.com/books/edition/The_baptist_Magazine/nVYEAAAAQAAJ?hl=en&gbpv=1&dq=our+circulation+last+year+amounted+to+1999+copies+of+the+Scriptures+in+English,+French,+Spanish,+Portuguese,+Chinese,+and+the+various+languages+spoken+by+emigrants+from+the+East&pg=PA665&printsec=frontcover.

Baptist Missionary Society. *The Baptist Magazine*. London: J. Burditt and W. Button, 1849. https://www.google.com/books/edition/The_baptist_Magazine/-lMEAAAAQAAJ?hl=en&gbpv=1&dq=would+do+much+to+break+down+the+barbarous+customs+that+prevail+throughout+the+interior&pg=PA661&printsec=frontcover.

Barber, Karin. "How Man Makes God in West Africa: Yoruba Attitudes towards the 'Orisa.'" *Africa: Journal of the International African Institute* 51, no. 3 (1981): 724–45.

Barcia, Manuel. *Seeds of Insurrection: Domination and Resistance on Western Cuban Plantations, 1808–1848*. Baton Rouge: Louisiana State University Press, 2008.

Barnes, Sandra T., ed. *Africa's Ogun: Old World and New*. 2nd ed. Bloomington: Indiana University Press, 1997.

Barrett, Leonard. *Soul-Force: African Heritage in Afro-American Religion*. New York: Doubleday, 1974.

Bascom, William. "The Principle of Seniority in the Social Structure of the Yoruba." *American Anthropologist* 44, no. 1 (1942): 37–46.

Bay, Edna G. *Wives of the Leopard: Gender, Politics, and Culture in the Kingdom of Dahomey*. Charlottesville: University of Virginia Press, 1998.

Beaubrun, Mimerose. *Nan Domi: An Initiate's Journey into Haitian Vodou*. Translated by D. J. Walker. San Francisco: City Lights Books, 2013.

Beaulieu Herder, Nicole, and Ronald Herder, eds. *Best Loved Negro Spirituals: Complete Lyrics to 178 Songs of Faith*. Mineola, NY: Dover Publications, 2001.

Beliso-De Jesús, Aisha. *Electric Santería: Racial and Sexual Assemblages of Transnational Religion*. New York: Columbia University Press, 2015.

Besson, Gerard. *The Book of Trinidad*. Port of Spain, Trinidad: Paria Publishing 2010.

Besson, Jean. "Women's Use of ROSCAs in the Caribbean: Reassessing the Literature." In *Money-Go-Rounds*, edited by Shirley Ardener and Sandra Burman, 1–19. Oxford: Berg, 1985.

Bolland, Nigel. *On the March: Labour Rebellions in the British Caribbean, 1934–39*. Kingston, Jamaica: Ian Randle, 1995.

Brandon, George. *Santeria from Africa to the New World: The Dead Sell Memories*. Bloomington: Indiana University Press, 1993.

Braun, Willi, and Russell T. McCutcheon. *Introducing Religion: Essays in Honor of Jonathan Z. Smith*. London: Equinox Publishing, 2008.

Brereton, Bridget. *A History of Modern Trinidad 1783–1962*. Kingston, Jamaica: Heinemann Publishers, 1982.

Brereton, Bridget. *Race Relations in Colonial Trinidad: 1870–1900*. Cambridge: Cambridge University Press, 1979.

Brereton, Bridget. "Social Organisation and Class, Racial and Cultural Conflict in 19th Century Trinidad." In *Trinidad Ethnicity*, edited by Kevin Yelvington, 33–55. Knoxville: University of Tennessee Press, 1993.

Brooks Higginbotham, Evelyn. *Righteous Discontent: The Women's Movement in the Black Baptist Church, 1880–1920*. Cambridge, MA: Harvard University Press, 1994.

Brown, Robert. "Eliade on Archaic Religion: Some Old and New Criticisms." *Studies in Religion* 10, no. 4 (1981): 429–49.

Buhle, Paul. *C. L. R. James: The Artist as Revolutionary*. New York: Verso, 1989.

Byrd, Alexander. "Eboe, Country, Nation, and Gustavus Vassa's Interesting Narrative." *William and Mary Quarterly* 63, no. 1 (January 2006): 123–48.

Cabrera, Lydia. *El Monte*. Miami: Ediciones Universal, 1983.

Camejo, Acton. "Racial Discrimination in Trinidad and Tobago: A Study of the Business Élite and the Social Structure." *Social and Economic Studies* 20, no. 3 (September 1971): 294–318.

Carmichael, Stokely, and Charles Hamilton. *Black Power: The Politics of Liberation*. New York: Random House, 1967.

Carneiro, Edison. *Candomblés da Bahia*. Bahia, Brazil: Secretaria de Edicação e Saúde, 1948.

Carneiro, Edison. "The Structure of African Cults in Bahia." *Journal of American Folklore* 53, no. 210 (October–December 1940): 271–78.

Caron, Peter. "'Of a Nation Which the Others Do Not Understand': Bambara Slaves and African Ethnicity in Colonial Louisiana, 1718–60." *Slavery and Abolition* 18, no. 1 (1997): 98–121.

Carr, Andrew T. "A Rada Community in Trinidad." *Caribbean Quarterly* 3, no. 1 (1953): 35–41.

Carter, Stephen. *The Emperor of Ocean Park.* New York: Knopf, 2002.

Castor, Fadeke. "Shifting Multicultural Citizenship: Trinidad Orisha Opens the Roads." *Cultural Anthropology*, 28, no. 3 (2013): 475–89.

Castor, N. Fadeke. *Spiritual Citizenship: Transnational Pathways from Black Power to Ifa in Trinidad.* Durham, NC: Duke University Press, 2017.

Chambers, Douglas. "Ethnicity in the Diaspora: The Slave-Trade and the Creation of African 'Nations' in the Americas." *Slavery and Abolition* 22, no. 3 (December 2001): 25–39.

Chambers, Douglas. "'My Own Nation': Igbo Exiles in the Diaspora." *Slavery and Abolition* 18, no. 1 (1997): 72–97.

Chambers, Douglas. "Tracing Igbo into the African Diaspora." In *Identity in the Shadow of Slavery*, edited by Paul Lovejoy, 55–71. London: Continuum, 2000.

Chireau, Yvonne. *Black Magic: Religion and the African American Conjuring Tradition.* Berkeley: University of California Press, 2003.

Clark, J. Desmond, and Stephen Brandt, eds. *From Hunters to Farmers: The Causes and Consequences of Food Production in Africa.* Berkeley: University of California Press, 1985.

Clarke, Robert. *Sierra Leone: A Description of the Manners and Customs of the Liberated Africans; with Observations Upon the Natural History of the Colony, and a Notice of the Native Tribes.* London: J Ridgway, 1843.

Coates, Ta-Nehisi. *Between the World and Me.* New York: Spiegel & Grau, 2015.

Cone, James. *Martin and Malcolm and America: A Dream or a Nightmare.* Maryknoll, NY: Orbis Books, 1991.

Cone, James. *Said I Wasn't Gonna Tell Nobody: The Making of a Black Theologian.* Maryknoll, NY: Orbis Books, 2018.

Conner, Randy, and David Sparks. *Queering Creole Spiritual Traditions: Lesbian, Gay, Bisexual, and Transgender Participation in African-Inspired Traditions in the Americas.* Binghamton, NY: Haworth Press, 2004.

Coopan, Vilashini. "Memory's Future: Affect, History, and New Narrative in South Africa." *Concentric Literary and Cultural Studies* 35, no. 1 (March 2009): 51–75.

Cothonay, Marie Bertrand. *Trinidad: journal d'un missionnaire dominicain des Antilles anglaises.* Paris: V. Retaux et fils, 1893.

Craig, Susan. "Background to the 1970 Confrontation in Trinidad and Tobago." In *Contemporary Caribbean: A Sociological Reader*, Vol. 2, edited by Susan Craig, 385–423. St. Augustine, Trinidad: Unknown Binding, 1982.

Crawley, Ashon. "Stayed | Freedom | Hallelujah." In *Otherwise Worlds: Against Settler Colonialism and Anti-Blackness*, edited by Tiffany Lethabo King, Jenell Navarro, and Andrea Smith Andrea Smith, 27–37. Durham, NC: Duke University Press, 2020.

Creel, Margaret Washington. *"A Peculiar People": Slave Religion and Community-Culture among the Gullahs*. New York: New York University Press, 1988.

Cripps, Louise. *C. L. R. James: Memories and Commentaries*. Cranbury, NJ: Cornwall Books, 1997.

Cudjoe, Selwyn. *Beyond Boundaries: The Intellectual Tradition of Trinidad and Tobago in the Nineteenth Century*. Wellesley, MA: Calaloux Publications, 2003.

Cudjoe, Selwyn, and William Cain, eds. *C. L. R. James: His Intellectual Legacies*. Amherst: University of Massachusetts Press, 1995.

Cwik, Chris. "The End of the British Atlantic Slave Trade or the Beginning of the Big Slave Robbery." In *The Second Slavery: Mass Slaveries and Modernity in the Americas and the Atlantic Basin*, edited by Javier Lavina and Michael Zeuske, 19–37. Berlin: Lit Verlag, 2014.

Daniel, Yvonne. *Dancing Wisdom: Embodied Knowledge in Haitian Vodou, Cuban Yoruba, and Bahian Candomblé*. Champaign: University of Illinois Press, 2005.

Daniels, Kyrah. "Ritual." In *The Encyclopedia of Aesthetics*, edited by Michael Kelly, 400–4. New York: Oxford University Press, 2014.

Dantas, Beatriz Góis. *Nagô Grandma and White Papa: Candomblé and the Creation of Afro-Brazilian Identity*. Translated by Stephen Berg. Chapel Hill: University of North Carolina Press, 2009. Originally published as *Vovó Nagô e Papai Branco*.

Dantas, Beatriz Góis. *Vovó Nagô e Papai Branco, Usos e abusos da África no Brasil*. Rio de Janeiro: Edições Graal, 1988.

Danticat, Edwidge. *Breath, Eyes, Memory*. New York: Random House, 1998.

Dawson, Michael. *Behind the Mule: Race and Class in African-American Politics*. Princeton, NJ: Princeton University Press, 1994.

De Verteuil, Anthony. *A History of Diego Martin: Begorrat-Bruntun, 1784–1884*. Port of Spain, Trinidad: Paria Publishers, 1987.

De Verteuil, Louis Antoine Aimé Gaston. *Trinidad: Its Geography, Natural Resources, Administration, Present Condition, and Prospect*. London: Ward and Lock, 1858.

Dewulf, Jeroen. *The Pinkster King and the King of Congo: The Forgotten History of America's Dutch-Owned Slaves*. Jackson: University Press of Mississippi, 2017.

Diop, Cheikh Anta. *The Cultural Unity of Black Africa: The Domains of Matriarchy and Patriarchy in Classical Antiquity*. London: Karnak House, 1989.

Diop, Cheikh Anta. *Towards the African Renaissance: Essays in Culture and Development, 1946–1960*. Trenton, NJ: Red Sea Press, 2000.

Doris, David. *Vigilant Things: On Thieves, Yoruba Anti-Aesthetics, and the Strange Fates of Ordinary Objects in Nigeria*. Seattle: University of Washington Press, 2011.

Douglass, Frederick. "What to the Slave Is the Fourth of July: Read the Full Text of Frederick Douglass' Iconic Speech." July 5, 1852. Edited by Michael Harriot. *The Root*, July 4, 2019. https://www.theroot.com/what-to-the-slave-is-the -fourth-of-july-1836083536.

Du Bois, W. E. B. *The Souls of Black Folk*. Mineola, NY: Dover Publications, 1994.

Du Bois, W. E. B. *The Souls of Black Folk: 100th Anniversary Edition*. New York: Signet Classics, 1995.

Duncan, Carol. *This Spot of Ground: Spiritual Baptists in Toronto*. Waterloo, Ontario, Canada: Wilfrid Laurier University Press, 2008.

Eastman, Rudolph. *The Fight for Dignity and Cultural Space: African Survivals and Adaptations in Trinidad: A Study of Orisa*. Bloomington, IN: Xlibris Corporation, 2009.

Edwards, Gary, and John Mason. *Black Gods: Orisa Studies in the New World*. New York: Yorùbá Theological Archministry, 1998.

Ehret, Christopher. *The Civilizations of Africa: A History to 1800*. Charlottesville: University Press of Virginia, 2002.

Ekeh, Peter. "Colonialism and the Two Publics in Africa: A Theoretical Statement." *Comparative Studies in Society and History* 17, no. 1 (January 1975): 91–112.

Elder, Jacob. "The Yoruba Ancestor Cult in Gasparillo: (Its Structure, Organization, and Social Function in Community Life)." *Caribbean Quarterly* 16, no. 3 (1970): 5–20.

Ẹlẹbuìbọn, Ifáyẹmí. *Adventures of Ọbàtálá, Part 2: Orikis by the Awìsẹ of Osogbo*. Lynwood, CA: Ara Ifa Publishing, 1998.

Eliade, Mircea. *The Myth of the Eternal Return*. Princeton, NJ: Princeton University Press, 2018.

Ellis, Alfred Burdon. *The Yoruba-Speaking Peoples of the Slave Coast of West Africa*. London: Chapman and Hall, 1894.

Equiano, Olaudah. *The Interesting Narrative of the Life of Olaudah Equiano, or Gustavus Vassa, the African: Written by Himself*. Edited by Shelly Eversley. New York: Random House, 2004.

Fadipẹ, Nathaniel. *The Sociology of the Yoruba*. Ibadan, Nigeria: Ibadan University Press, 1970.

Fakuade, Gbenga, Joseph Friday-Otun, and Hezekiah Adeosun. "Yoruba Personal Naming System: Traditions, Patterns and Practices." *Sociolinguistic Studies* 13, no. 2–4 (2019): 251–71.

Falola, Toyin. *The African Diaspora: Slavery, Modernity, and Globalization*. Rochester, NY: University of Rochester Press, 2013.

Fanon, Frantz. *Black Skin, White Masks*. Translated by Charles Lam Markmann. New York: Grove Press, 1967.

Fernheimer, Janice. *Stepping into Zion: Hatzaad Harishon, Black Jews, and the Remaking of Jewish Identity*. Tuscaloosa: University of Alabama Press, 2014.

Fields, Karen, and Barbara Fields. *Racecraft: The Soul of Inequality in American Life*. New York: Verso Books, 2014.

Finnegan, Ruth H. *The Oral and Beyond: Doing Things with Words in Africa*. Chicago: University of Chicago Press, 2007.

Fitzgerald, Timothy. *The Ideology of Religious Studies*. New York: Oxford University Press, 2000.

Forde, Maarit. "The Moral Economy of Spiritual Work: Money and Rituals in Trinidad and Tobago." In *Obeah and Other Powers: The Politics of Caribbean Religion and Healing*, edited by Diana Paton and Maarit Forde, 198–219. Durham, NC: Duke University Press, 2012.

Fourshey, Cymoune, Rhonda Gonzales, and Christine Saidi. *Bantu Africa: 35000 BCE to Present*. New York: Oxford University Press, 2017.

Franklin, C. B. *After Many Days: A Memoir, Being a Sketch of the Life and Labours of Rev. Alexander Kennedy, First Presbyterian Missionary to Trinidad, Founder of Greyfriars Church . . .* Port of Spain, Trinidad: Franklin's Electric Printery, 1910.

Frazier, Edward Franklin, and Charles Eric Lincoln. *The Negro Church in America/The Black Church since Frazier*. New York: Schocken Books, 1974.

Friedson, Steven M. *Remains of Ritual: Northern Gods in a Southern Land*. Chicago: University of Chicago Press, 2009.

Fryer, Peter. *Staying Power: The History of Black People in Britain*. London: Pluto Press, 1984.

García-Peña, Lorgia. *The Borders of Dominicanidad: Race, Nation, and Archives of Contradiction*. Durham, NC: Duke University Press, 2016.

Gerbner, Katharine. *Christian Slavery: Conversion and Race in the Protestant Atlantic World*. Philadelphia: University of Pennsylvania Press, 2018.

Geurts, Kathryn Linn. *Culture and the Senses: Bodily Ways of Knowing in an African Community*. Oakland: University of California Press, 2002.

Gibbons, Rawle. "Syncretism and Secretism in the Manifestation of African Spirituality: The Restitution of the Spirit." In *At the Crossroads: African Caribbean Religion & Christianity*, edited by Burton Sankeralli, 67–84. St. Augustine, Trinidad: Caribbean Conference of Churches, 1995.

Gilkes, Cheryl Townsend. *If It Wasn't for the Women: Black Women's Experience and Womanist Culture in Church and Community*. Maryknoll, NY: Orbis Books, 2001.

Glaude, Eddie. *Exodus! Religion, Race and Nation in Early Nineteenth-Century Black America*. Chicago: University of Chicago Press, 2000.

Glazier, Stephen D. "Syncretism and Separation: Ritual Change in an Afro-Caribbean Faith." *Journal of American Folklore* 98, no. 387 (January 1985): 49–62.

Glazier, Stephen D. "Wither Sango, An Inquiry into Sango's Authenticity and Prominence in the Caribbean," In Tishken, Falola, and Akínyẹmí, Ṣàngó *in Africa and the African Diaspora* (Bloomington: Indian University Press, 2009), 233–47.

Glissant, Édouard. *Poetics of Relation*. Translated by Betsy Wing. Ann Arbor: University of Michigan Press, 1997.

Goldberg, David. *The Racial State*. Malden, MA: Blackwell, 2002.

Gomes, Flávio. "'Atlantic Nations' and the Origins of Africans in Late-Colonial Rio de Janeiro: New Evidence." *Colonial Latin American Review* 20, no. 2 (August 2011): 213–31.

Gomez, Michael. *African Dominion: A New History of Empire in Early and Medieval West Africa*. Princeton, NJ: Princeton University Press, 2018.

Gomez, Michael. *Exchanging Our Country Marks: The Transformation of African Identities in the Colonial and Antebellum South.* Chapel Hill: University of North Carolina Press, 1998.

Granovetter, Mark. "The Strength of Weak Ties: A Network Theory Revisited." *Sociological Theory* 1 (1983): 201–33.

Grillo, Laura. *An Intimate Rebuke: Female Genital Power in Ritual and Politics in West Africa.* Durham, NC: Duke University Press, 2018.

Halbwachs, Maurice. *On Collective Memory.* Translated and edited by Lewis Coser. Chicago: University of Chicago Press, 1992.

Hall, David, and Robert Orsi, eds. *Lived Religion in America: Towards a History of Practice.* Princeton, NJ: Princeton University Press, 1997.

Hall, Gwendolyn. *Slavery and African Ethnicities in the Americas: Restoring Links.* Chapel Hill: University of North Carolina Press, 2005.

Handler, Jerome, and Kenneth Bilby. "On the Early Use and Origin of the Term 'Obeah' in Barbados and the Anglophone Caribbean." *Slavery and Abolition* 22, no. 2 (August 2001): 87–100.

Harding, Rachel. *A Refuge in Thunder: Candomblé and Alternative Spaces of Blackness.* Bloomington: Indiana University Press, 2003.

Harney, Stefano, and Fred Moten. *The Undercommons: Fugitive Planning and Black Study.* New York: Minor Compositions, 2013.

Harricharan, John. *The Catholic Church in Trinidad, 1498–1852.* Port of Spain, Trinidad: Imprint Caribbean, 1983.

Harris, Janée, Natoya Haskins, Janise Paker, and Aiesha Lee. "Womanist Theology and Relational Cultural Theory: Counseling Religious Black Women." *Journal of Creativity in Mental Health* (2021): 1–19. 10.1080/15401383.2021.1999359.

Hartman, Saidiya. "The Belly of the World: A Note on Black Women's Labors." *Souls* 18, no 1. (January–March 2016): 166–73.

Hartman, Saidiya. "Venus in Two Acts." *Small Axe* 12, no. 2 (2008): 1–14.

Harvey, Marcus. "'Life Is War:' African Grammars of Knowing and the Interpretation of Black Religious Experience." PhD diss., Emory University, 2012.

Hays, Sharon. "Constructing the Centrality of Culture—and Deconstructing Sociology?" *Contemporary Sociology* 29, no. 4 (July 2000): 594–602.

Hays, Sharon. "Structure and Agency and the Sticky Problem of Culture." *Sociological Theory* 12, no. 1 (March 1994): 57–72.

Henry, Frances. *He Had the Power: Pa Neezer, the Orisha King of Trinidad: A Personal Memoir.* Port of Spain, Trinidad: Lexicon Trinidad, 2008.

Henry, Frances. *Reclaiming African Religions in Trinidad: The Socio-Political Legitimation of the Orisha and Spiritual Baptist Faiths.* Mona, Jamaica: University of the West Indies Press, 2003.

Henry, Frances. "Religion and Ideology in Trinidad: The Resurgence of the Shango Religion." *Caribbean Quarterly* 29, no. 3/4 (September–December 1983): 63–69.

Henry, Frances. "Social Stratification in an Afro-American Cult." *Anthropological Quarterly* 38, no. 2 (April 1965): 72–78.

Henry, Paget. *Caliban's Reason: Introducing Afro-Caribbean Philosophy*. New York: Routledge, 2000.

Henry, Paget, and Paul Buhle, eds. *C. L. R. James's Caribbean*. Durham, NC: Duke University Press, 1992.

Herskovits, Melville. *The Myth of the Negro Past*. Boston: Beacon Press, 1990.

Herskovits, Melville. "The Negro in Bahia, Brazil: A Problem in Method." *American Sociological Review* 8, no. 4 (August 1943): 394–404.

Herskovits, Melville. "Peoples and Cultures of Sub-Saharan Africa." *Annals of the American Academy of Political and Social Science* 298, no. 1 (March 1955): 11–20.

Herskovits, Melville. *Trinidad Village*. New York: Knopf, 1947.

Higman, Barry. *Slave Populations of the British Caribbean 1807–1833*. Cambridge: Cambridge University Press, 1976.

Hildebrand, Reginald. *The Times Were Strange and Stirring: Methodist Preachers and the Crisis of Emancipation*. Durham, NC: Duke University Press, 1995.

Hill, Donald. *Calypso Calaloo: Early Carnival Music in Trinidad*. Gainesville: University Press of Florida, 1993.

Hill Collins, Patricia. *Black Feminist Thought: Knowledge, Consciousness, and the Politics of Empowerment*. New York: Routledge, 2000.

Hill Collins, Patricia. "What's in a Name? Womanism, Black Feminism, and Beyond." *Black Scholar* 26, no.1 (Winter/Spring 1996): 9–17.

Holm, Olle. "Analyses of Longing: Origins, Levels, and Dimensions." *Journal of Psychology* 133, no. 5 (November 1999): 621–30.

Hørsjberg, Christian. *C. L. R. James in Imperial Britain*. Durham, NC: Duke University Press, 2014.

Houk, James. *Spirit, Blood, and Drums: The Orisha Religion in Trinidad*. Philadelphia: Temple University Press, 1995.

Hucks, Tracey E. "I Smoothed the Way, I Opened the Doors: Women in the Yoruba-Orisha Tradition of Trinidad." In *Women and Religion in the African Diaspora: Knowledge, Power, and Performance*, edited by R. Marie Griffith and Barbara Savage, 19–36. Baltimore: Johns Hopkins University Press, 2006.

Hucks, Tracey E. *Obeah, Orisa, and Religious Identity in Trinidad: Africans in the White Colonial Imagination-Obeah: Volume I*. Durham, NC: Duke University Press, 2022.

Hucks, Tracey E. "Perspectives in Lived History: Religion, Ethnography, and the Study of African Diasporic Religions." *Practical Matters* 3 (Spring 2010): 1–17.

Hucks, Tracey E. *Yoruba Traditions and African American Religious Nationalism*. Albuquerque: University of New Mexico Press, 2012.

Hucks, Tracey, and Dianne Stewart. "African American Religion: History of Study." In *Encyclopedia of Religion*, Vol. 1, 2nd ed., edited by Lindsay Jones, 73–83. Detroit: Macmillan References, 2005.

Hucks, Tracey, and Dianne Stewart. "Authenticity and Authority in the Shaping of Trinidad Orisha Identity: Toward an African-Derived Religious Theory." *Western Journal of Black Studies* 27, no. 3 (Fall 2003): 176–85.

Hunter, Jo Anna. "'Oro Pataki Aganjú:' A Cross Cultural Approach towards the Understanding of the Fundamentos of the Orisa Aganjú in Nigeria and Cuba." In *ORISA: Yoruba Gods and Spiritual Identity in Africa and the Diaspora*, edited by Toyin Falola and Ann Genova, 209–223. Trenton, NJ: Africa World Press, 2006.

Hurston, Zora Neale. *Jonah's Gourd Vine*. New York: Harper Perennial, 1990.

Hurston, Zora Neale. *The Sanctified Church*. New York: Marlowe & Company, 1997.

Ìdòwú, E. Bólájí. *Olódùmarè: God in Yoruba Belief*. London: Longmans, Green and Co., 1962.

Ìṣòlá, Akínwùmí. "Religious Politics and the Myth of Ṣango." In *African Traditional Religions in Contemporary Society*, edited by Jacob Olupona, 93–99. St. Paul, MN: Paragon House, 1991.

Iwe Kika Ẹkẹrin Li Ede Yoruba. Lagos, Nigeria: C.M.S. Bookshop; Exeter: James Townsend and Sons (Printers), 1944 (1911).

Jackson, John. *Thin Description: Ethnography and the African Hebrew Israelites of Jerusalem*. Cambridge, MA: Harvard University Press, 2013.

Jackson, Michael. *As Wide as the World Is Wise: Reinventing Philosophical Anthropology*. New York: Columbia University Press, 2016.

Jackson, Zakiyyah. *Becoming Human: Matter and Meaning in an Antiblack World*. New York: New York University Press, 2020.

Jacobs, C. M. *Joy Comes in the Morning: Elton George Griffith and the Shouter Baptists*. Port of Spain, Trinidad: Caribbean Historical Society, 1996.

James, Leslie. *George Padmore and Decolonization from Below: Pan-Africanism, the Cold War, and the End of Empire*. New York: Palgrave Macmillan, 2015.

James, William. *The Varieties of Religious Experience*. 2nd ed. New York, NY: Longmans, Green and Co., 1902.

JanMohammed, Abdul. *The Death-Bound-Subject: Richard Wright's Archaeology of Death*. Durham, NC: Duke University Press, 2005.

Janzen, John. "African Religion and Healing in the Atlantic Diaspora." In *Oxford Research Encyclopedia of African History*. July 27, 2017. Accessed March 26, 2022. https://oxfordre.com/africanhistory/view/10.1093/acrefore/9780190277734.001.0001/acrefore-9780190277734-e-54.

John, A. Meredith. *The Plantation Slaves of Trinidad, 1783–1816*. Cambridge: Cambridge University Press, 1988.

Johnson, Jr., Charles. *African American Soldiers in the National Guard: Recruitment and Deployment during Peacetime and War*. Westport, CT: Greenwood Press, 1992.

Johnson, Paul. "Law, Religion, and 'Public Health' in the Republic of Brazil." *Law and Social Inquiry* 26, no. 1 (Winter, 2001): 9–33.

Johnson, Samuel. *The History of the Yorubas: From the Earliest Times to the Beginning of the British Protectorate*. Cambridge: Cambridge University Press [1921] 1966.

Johnson, Sylvester. *African American Religions, 1500–2000: Colonialism, Democracy, and Freedom.* New York: Cambridge University Press, 2015.

Johnson, Sylvester. "The Rise of Black Ethnics: The Ethnic Turn in African-American Religions, 1916–45." *Religion and American Culture: A Journal of Interpretation* 20, no. 2 (Summer 2010): 125–63.

Johnson, Terrence. "Exploring Race, Religion, and Slavery at the Museum of the Bible." In *The Museum of the Bible: A Critical Introduction,* edited by Jill Hicks-Keeton and Cavan Concannon, 37–46. Lanham, MD: Lexington Books, 2019.

Judy, R. A. *Sentient Flesh: Thinking in Disorder, Poiesis in Black.* Durham, NC: Duke University Press, 2020.

Judy, R. A. "Thinking with Blackness, Thinking with the Human: An Interview with RA Judy." Being Human Podcast, University of Pittsburgh, November 9, 2020, https://soundcloud.com/being-human-pgh/thinking-with-blackness -thinking-with-the-human-an-interview-with-ra-judy.

Kambon, Khafra. "Black Power in Trinidad & Tobago: February 26-April 21, 1970." In *The Black Power Revolution 1970,* edited by Selwin Ryan and Taimoon Stewart, 215–42. St. Augustine, Trinidad: ISER, 1995.

Kerr-Ritchie, Jeffrey R. *Rites of August First: Emancipation Day in the Black Atlantic World.* Baton Rouge: Louisiana State University Press, 2007.

Kiely, Ray. *The Politics of Labour and Development in Trinidad.* Kingston, Jamaica: University of the West Indies Press, 1996.

King, Tiffany Lethabo, Jenell Navarro, and Andrea Smith, eds. *Otherwise Worlds: Against Settler Colonialism and Anti-Blackness.* Durham, NC: Duke University Press, 2020.

Klieman, Karin. *"The Pygmies Were Our Compass:" Bantu and Batwa in the History of West Central Africa, Early Times to c. 1900 C.E.* Portsmouth, NH: Heinemann, 2003.

Knippers Black, Jan, et al. *Area Handbook for Trinidad and Tobago.* Washington, DC: Foreign Area Studies of the American University, 1976.

KnowledgeWalk Institute. "Trinidad and Tobago General Election Results—24 September 1956," http://www.caribbeanelections.com/tt/elections/tt_results _1956.asp.

Kolawole, Mary. *Womanism and African Consciousness.* Trenton, NJ: Africa World Press, 1997.

Krech, Volkhard. "Relational Religion: Manifesto for a Synthesis in the Study of Religion." *Religion* 50, no. 1 (2020): 97–105.

Lachenicht, Susanne. "Ethnicity," *Oxford Bibliographies.* http://www .oxfordbibliographies.com/view/document/obo-9780199730414/obo -9780199730414-0022.xml.

Laitinen, Maarit. "Marching to Zion: Creolisation in Spiritual Baptist Rituals and Cosmology." PhD diss., University of Helsinki, 2002.

Landers, Jane. *Black Society in Spanish Florida.* Champaign: University of Illinois Press, 1999.

Landes, Ruth. *The City of Women*. Albuquerque: University of New Mexico Press, 1947.

Lartey, Emmanuel Y. *Postcolonializing God: An African Practical Theology*. London: SCM Press, 2013.

Law, Robin. "Early Yoruba Historiography." *History in Africa* 3 (1976): 69–89.

Law, Robin. "Ethnicity and the Slave Trade: 'Lucumi' and 'Nago' as Ethnonyms in West Africa." *History in Africa* 24 (January 1997): 205–19.

Law, Robin. *The Oyo Empire c. 1600–c. 1836: A West African Imperialism in the Era of the Atlantic Slave Trade*. New York: Oxford University Press, 1977.

León, Luis. *La Llorona's Children: Religion, Life, and Death in the U.S.–Mexican Borderlands*. Berkeley: University of California Press, 2004.

Lloyd, Peter. "Craft Organization in Yoruba Towns." *Africa: Journal of the International African Institute* 23, no. 1 (January 1953): 30–44.

Long, Charles. "African American Religion in the United States of America: An Interpretive Essay." *Nova Religio: The Journal of Alternative and Emergent Religions* 7, no. 1 (July 2003): 11–27.

Long, Charles. *The Collected Writings of Charles H. Long: Ellipsis*. London: Bloomsbury Publishing, 2018.

Long, Charles. *Significations: Signs, Symbols, and Images in the Interpretation of Religion*. Aurora, CO: Davies Group, 1995.

Lovejoy, Paul. "Identifying Enslaved Africans in the African Diaspora." In *Identity in the Shadow of Slavery*, edited by Paul Lovejoy, 1–29. London: Continuum, 2000.

MacDonald, Scott. *Trinidad and Tobago: Democracy and Development in the Caribbean*. New York: Praeger, 1986.

MacGaffey, Wyatt. "The Cultural Tradition of the African Forest." In *Insight and Artistry in African Divination*, edited by John Pemberton, 13–24. Washington, DC: Smithsonian Institution Press, 2000.

Mahmood, Saba. *Politics of Piety: The Islamic Revival and the Feminist Subject*. Princeton, NJ: Princeton University Press, 2004.

Maksic, Adis. *Ethnic Mobilization, Violence, and the Politics of Affect: The Serb Democratic Party and the Bosnian War*. New York: Palgrave Macmillan, 2017.

Maldonado Torres, Nelson. "The Topology of Being and the Geopolitics of Knowledge." *City* 8, no. 1 (April 2004): 29–56.

Malegapuru, William Makgoba, ed. *African Renaissance*. Cape Town, SA: Tafelberg Publishers, 1999.

Malinowski, Bronislaw. "Kinship." *Man*, 30 (February 1930): 19–29.

Malinowski, Bronislaw. *The Sexual Life of Savages in North Western Melanesia*. London: Routledge and Kegan Paul, 1929.

Manning, Patrick. *The African Diaspora: A History through Culture*. New York: Columbia University Press, 2010.

Maparyan, Layli. *The Womanist Idea*. New York: Routledge, 2012.

Marriott, David. *Whither Fanon? Studies in the Blackness of Being*. Stanford, CA: Stanford University Press, 2018.

Martin, Tony. *The Pan-African Connection: From Slavery to Garvey and Beyond*. Dover, MA: Majority Press, 1984.

Martin, Tony. *Race First: The Ideological and Organizational Struggles of Marcus Garvey and the United Negro Improvement Association*. Dover, MA: Majority Press, 1976.

Matory, J. Lorand. *Black Atlantic Religion*. Princeton, NJ: Princeton University Press, 2005.

Matory, J. Lorand. "The English Professors of Brazil: On the Diasporic Roots of the Yorùbá Nation." *Comparative Studies in Society and History* 41, no. 1 (January 1999): 72–103.

Matory, J. Lorand. *Sex and the Empire That Is No More: Gender and the Politics of Metaphor in Oyo Yoruba Religion*. New York: Berghahn Books, 1995.

Matthews, Donald. *Honoring the Ancestors: An African Cultural Interpretation of Black Religion and Literature*. New York: Oxford University Press, 1998.

Mays, Benjamin, and Joseph Nicholson. *The Negro's Church*. Stratford, NH: Ayer Co., 1969.

Mbeki, Thabo. "Address by Executive Deputy President Thabo Mbeki, to Corporate Council on Africa's 'Attracting Capital to Africa' Summit," April 19–22, 1997. Chantilly Virginia, USA." http://www.dirco.gov.za/docs/speeches/1997/mbeko419.htm.

McDaniel, Lorna. *The Big Drum Ritual of Carriacou: Praisesongs in Rememory of Flight*. Gainesville: University Press of Florida, 1998.

McKenzie, Peter. *Hail Orisha! A Phenomenology of a West African Religion in the Mid-Nineteenth Century*. Leiden: Brill, 1997.

McNeal, Keith. *Trance and Modernity in the Southern Caribbean: African and Hindu Popular Religions in Trinidad and Tobago*. Gainesville: University Press of Florida, 2011.

Meeks, Brian. "Caribbean Black Power." In *The Encyclopedia of the African Diaspora: Origins, Experiences, and Culture*, Vol. 1, edited by Carol Boyce Davies, 265–68. Santa Barbara: ABC-CLIO, 2008.

Meeks, Brian. "The 1970 Revolution: Chronology and Documentation." In Ryan and Stewart, *Black Power Revolution*, 135–77.

Memmi, Albert. *The Colonizer and the Colonized*. Translated by Howard Greenfeld. Lexington, MA: Plunkett Lake Press, 2013.

Millett, Trevor. *The Chinese in Trinidad and Tobago*. Port of Spain, Trinidad: Imprint Caribbean, 1993.

Millette, James. "Towards the Black Power Revolt of 1970." In Ryan and Stewart, *Black Power Revolution*, 59–95.

Mischel, Walter, and Frances Osterman Mischel. "Psychological Aspects of Spirit Possession." *American Anthropologist* 60, no. 2 (1958): 249–60.

The Missionary Herald: Containing Intelligence, at Large, of the Proceedings and Operations of the Baptist Missionary Society. London: G. Wightman, 1867.

Mitchell, Mozella. *Crucial Issues in Caribbean Religions.* New York: Peter Lang, 2006.

Modern, John. "Evangelical Secularism and the Measure of Leviathan." *Church History: Studies in Christianity and Culture* 77, no. 4 (December 2008): 801–76.

Moore, Joseph. "The Religion of Jamaican Negroes: A Study of Afro-American Acculturation." PhD diss., Northwestern University, 1953.

Moten, Fred. "Blackness and Nothingness (Mysticism in the Flesh)." *South Atlantic Quarterly* 112, no. 4 (Fall 2013): 737–80.

Muñoz, José. "Feeling Brown: Ethnicity and Affect in Ricardo Bracho's 'The Sweetest Hangover (and Other STDs).'" *Theatre Journal* 52, no. 1 (March 2000): 67–79.

Murray, Stephen, and Will Roscoe. *Boy-Wives and Female Husbands: Studies of African Homosexualities.* New York: Palgrave Macmillan, 1998.

Mwale, Jones. *Relationality in Theological Anthropology: An African Perspective.* Sunnyvale, CA: Lambert Academic Publishing, 2013.

Nash, Jennifer. *Black Feminism Reimagined after Intersectionality.* Durham, NC: Duke University Press, 2019.

Nash, Jennifer. "Practicing Love: Black Feminism, Love–Politics, and Post-Intersectionality." *Meridians* 11, no. 2 (2011): 1–24.

National Baptist Convention. *Journal of the Thirty-sixth Annual Convention of the National Baptist Convention and the Sixteenth Annual Session of the Women's Convention Held in Savannah, Georgia, September 6–11, 1916.* Nashville: Sunday School Publishing Board, 1916.

Newbury, Colin W. *The Western Slave Coast and Its Rulers: European Trade and Administration among the Yoruba and Adja-Speaking Peoples of South-Western Nigeria, Southern Dahomey and Togo.* Oxford: Clarendon Press, 1961.

Newman, James. *The Peopling of Africa: A Geographic Interpretation.* New Haven, CT: Yale University Press, 1995.

Newman, Richard S. *Freedom's Prophet: Bishop Richard Allen, the AME Church, and the Black Founding Fathers.* New York: New York University Press, 2008.

Noel, James. *Black Religion and the Imagination of Matter in the Atlantic World.* New York: Palgrave Macmillan, 2009.

Nunez, Clive. "A Trade Unionist Recalls 1970." In Ryan and Stewart, *Black Power Revolution*, 261–71.

Ogbonmwan, Stephen. "Reflections on African Traditional Value Systems and the Challenges in Sustaining and Preserving These in the Diaspora." Paper presented at the Edo Community Cultural Weekend, Vienna, Austria, August 29–31, 2008. https://ihuanedo.ning.com/profiles/blogs/reflections-on-african-traditional-value-systems.

Ogunyemi, Chikwenye. *Africa Wo/Man Palava: The Nigerian Novel by Women.* Chicago: University of Chicago Press, 1995.

Ojo, Olatunji. "'Heepa' (Hail) Òrìṣà: The Òrìṣà Factor in the Birth of Yoruba Identity." *Journal of Religion in Africa* 39, no. 1 (February 2009): 30–59.

Olabimtan, Kehinde. "Bühler, Gottlieb Friederick: 1829–1865." *Dictionary of African Christian Biography*, 2011. https://dacb.org/stories/nigeria/buhler-gottlieb/.

Olasupo, Fatai. "Women and Religion in Nigeria." *Journal of Traditions & Belief* 2, art. 10 (2016): 1–18. https://engagedscholarship.csuohio.edu/jtb/vol2/iss1/10.

Olasupo, Fatai. "Women's Associational Life within Traditional Institutions in Yorùbá States." In *Contesting the Nigerian State*, edited by Mojúbàolú Okome, 173–98. New York: Palgrave Macmillan, 2013.

Olawaiye, James Adeyinka. *Yoruba Religious and Social Traditions in Ekiti, Nigeria and Three Caribbean Countries: Trinidad-Tobago, Guyana, and Belize*. PhD diss., University of Missouri, 1980.

Olúpònà, Jacob. *City of 201 Gods: Ilé-Ifẹ in Time, Space, and the Imagination*. Berkeley: University of California Press, 2011.

Olupona, Jacob. *Kingship, Religion, and Rituals in a Nigerian Community: A Phenomenological Study of Ondo Yoruba Festivals*. Stockholm: Almqvist and Wiksell International, 1991.

Onipede, Kayode, and Folaranmi Adegbite. "Igbon, Iresa, and Ikoyi: A Pre-Historic Relationship till Present Time." *Historical Research Letter* 15 (2014): 24–28.

Osterman Mischel, Frances. "African 'Powers' in Trinidad: The Shango Cult." *Anthropological Quarterly* 30, no. 2 (April 1957): 49–59.

Osterman Mischel, Frances. "A Shango Religious Group and the Problem of Prestige in Trinidadian Society." PhD diss., Ohio State University, 1958.

Otto, Rudolf. *The Idea of the Holy*. 2nd ed. Translated by John W. Harvey. New York: Oxford University Press, 1958.

Oyěwùmí, Oyèrónk,. *African Women and Feminism: Reflecting on the Politics of Sisterhood*. Trenton, NJ: Africa World Press, 2003.

Oyěwùmí, Oyèrónké. *The Invention of Women: Making an African Sense of Western Gender Discourses*. Minneapolis: University of Minnesota Press, 1997.

Oyěwùmí, Oyèrónké. *What Gender Is Motherhood?* New York: Palgrave Macmillan, 2015.

Palmer, Tyrone. "Otherwise than Blackness: Feeling, World, Sublimation." *Qui Parle: Critical Humanities and Social Sciences* 29, no. 2 (December 2020): 247–83.

Palmer, Tyrone. "'What Feels More than Feeling?': Theorizing the Unthinkability of Black Affect." *Critical Ethnic Studies* 3, no. 2 (Fall 2017): 31–56.

Parés, Luis Nicolau. *The Formation of Candomblé: Vodun History and Ritual in Brazil*. Translated by Richard Vernon in collaboration with Luis Nicolau Parés. Chapel Hill: University of North Carolina Press, 2013.

Parés, Luis Nicolau. "The 'Nagôization' Process in Bahian Candomblé." In *The Yoruba Diaspora in the Atlantic World*, edited by Toyin Falola and Matt Childs, 185–208. Bloomington: Indiana University Press, 2004.

Pasley, Victoria. "The Black Power Movement in Trinidad: An Exploration of Gender and Cultural Changes and the Development of a Feminist Consciousness." *Journal of International Women's Studies* 3, no. 1 (November 2001): 24–40.

Paton, Diana. *The Cultural Politics of Obeah: Religion, Colonialism and Modernity in the Caribbean.* Cambridge: Cambridge University Press, 2015.

Paton, Diana. "Obeah Acts: Producing and Policing the Boundaries of Religion in the Caribbean." *Small Axe* 13, no. 1 (March 2009): 1–18.

Paton, Diana. "Teacher Bailey, Trinidad, 1918." *Obeah Histories: Researching Prosecution of Religious Practice in the Caribbean.* https://obeahhistories.org/.

Patterson, Orlando. *Slavery and Social Death: A Comparative Study.* Cambridge, MA: Harvard University Press, 1985.

Peabody, Sue. "'A Dangerous Zeal': Catholic Missions to Slaves in the French Antilles, 1635–1800." *French Historical Studies* 25, no. 1 (Winter 2002): 53–90.

Peel, J. D. Y. *Religious Encounter and the Making of the Yoruba.* Bloomington: Indiana University Press, 2003.

Pemberton, John, and Fúnṣọ́ Afọláyan. *Yorùbá Sacred Kinship: "A Power like That of the Gods."* Washington, DC: Smithsonian Institute Press, 1996.

Penagos, Elaine. "Santería Poetics: Africana Continuity through Afro-Cuban Religious Narratives." PhD diss, Emory University, 2022.

Phillips, Layli. *The Womanist Reader.* New York: Routledge, 2006.

Piersen, William. *Black Yankees: The Development of an Afro-American Subculture in Eighteenth-Century New England.* Amherst: University of Massachusetts Press, 1988.

Pittman Walke, Chadra. "Mother of the Movement: Remembering Bambara and the 'African Bones in the Briny Deep.'" *The feminist wire,* November 17, 2014. http://www.thefeministwire.com/2014/11/african-bones-in-the-briny-deep/.

Rahkala, Mari Johanna. "In the Sphere of the Holy: Pilgrimage to a Contemporary Greek Convent." In *Pilgrims and Travellers in Search of the Holy,* edited by René Gothóni, 69–96. Bern: Peter Lang, 2010.

Reddock, Rhoda. "Women Workers' Struggles." In *Revisiting Caribbean Labour: Essays in Honor of O. Nigel Bolland,* edited by Constance Sutton, 19–40. Kingston, Jamaica: Ian Randle, 2005.

Reis, João José, and Beatriz Gallotti Mamigonian. "Nagô and Mina: The Yoruba Diaspora in Brazil." In *The Yoruba Diaspora in the Atlantic World,* edited by Toyin Falola and Matt Childs, 77–110. Bloomington: Indiana University Press, 2004.

Roberts, J. Deotis. *Africentric Christianity.* Prussia, PA: Judson Press, 2000.

Roberts, J. Deotis. *Black Religion, Black Theology: The Collected Essays of J. Deotis Roberts.* Edited by David Goatley. Edinburgh, Scotland: Bloomsbury T&T Clark, 2003.

Roberts, J. Deotis. *Roots of a Black Future: Family and Church.* Largo, MD: Strebor Books, 2002.

Roberts, Kevin. "Yoruba Family, Gender, and Kinship Roles in New World Slavery." In Falola and Childs, *Yoruba Diaspora*, 248–59.

Robeson, Paul. *Paul Robeson Speaks*. Edited by Philip Foner. New York: Citadel Press, 1978.

Rodney, Walter. *The Groundings with My Brothers*. London: Bogle-L'Ouverture Publications, 1975.

Roger Hepburn, Sharon A. "Branding." In *Encyclopedia of the Middle Passage*, edited by Toyin Falola and Amanda Warnock, 67–68. Westport, CT: Greenwood Publishing, 2007.

Rohlehr, Gordon. *Calypso and Society in Pre-Independence Trinidad*. Port of Spain, Trinidad: Rohlehr, 1990.

Rosaldo, Renato. *Culture and Truth: The Remaking of Social Analysis*. Boston, MA: Beacon Press, 1993.

Rucker, Walker. *Gold Coast Diasporas: Identity, Culture, and Power*. Bloomington: University of Indiana Press, 2015.

Rucker, Walker. *The River Flows On: Black Resistance, Culture, and Identity Formation in Early America*. Baton Rouge: Louisiana State University Press, 2006.

Ryan, Selwyn. *Race and Nationalism in Trinidad and Tobago: A Study of Decolonization in a Multiracial Society*. Toronto: University of Toronto Press, 1974.

Ryan, Selwyn. "The Struggle for Black Power in the Caribbean." In Ryan and Stewart, *Black Power Revolution*, 25–57.

Ryan, Selwyn, and Taimoon Stewart. *Black Power Revolution*. Trinidad and Tobago: ISER, University of the West Indies, 1995.

Saidi, Christine. *Women's Authority and Society in East-Central Africa*. Rochester, NY: University of Rochester Press, 2010.

Sandoval, Chela, *Methodology of the Oppressed*. Minneapolis: University of Minnesota Press, 2000.

Sangowunmi, Iyalode. *Esu: Personifications of Essences*. Santa Cruz, Trinidad: Sangowunmi Publishers, 2011.

Sankeralli, Burton. "Remembering Iya L'Orisha Molly Ahye." *National Workers Union: Workers of the World Unite*, April 24, 2018. http://www.workersunion.org.tt/where-we-stand/nwu-news/rememberingiyalorishamollyahyebyburtonsankeralli.

Scheper Hughes, Jennifer. "Cradling the Sacred: Image, Ritual, and Affect in Mexican and Mesoamerican Material Religion." *History of Religions* 56, no. 1 (August 2016): 55–107.

Scher, Philip. "Unveiling the Orisha." In *Africa's Ogun: Old World and New*, edited by Sandra Barnes, 315–31. Bloomington: Indiana University Press, 1997.

Schrader, Claire. "What is Ritual Theatre." https://ritualtheatre.wordpress.com/2011/12/01/what-is-ritual-theatre/, accessed November 28, 2016.

Schuler, Monica. "*Alas, Alas, Kongo*:" *A Social History of Indentured African Immigration into Jamaica, 1841–1865*. Baltimore: Johns Hopkins University Press, 1980.

Schwab, William. "Kinship and Lineage among the Yoruba." *Africa: Journal of the International African Institute* 25, no. 4 (October 1955): 352–74.

Scott, David. *Conscripts of Modernity: The Tragedy of Colonial Enlightenment.* Durham, NC: Duke University Press, 2004.

Scott, James. *Domination and the Arts of Resistance: Hidden Transcripts.* New Haven, CT: Yale University Press, 1990.

Settles, Shani. "Flesh and Blood, Breath and Spirit: African Diaspora Religions and Womanist Discourses of Wholeness." PhD diss., Emory University, 2014.

Shafer, Jack. "Who Said It First? Journalism is the 'First Rough Draft of History.'" *Slate*, August 30, 2010. https://slate.com/news-and-politics/2010/08/on-the-trail-of-the-question-who-first-said-or-wrote-that-journalism-is-the-first-rough-draft-of-history.html.

Shah, Raffique. "The People Have Absolved Me." In Ryan and Stewart, *Black Power Revolution*, 441–508.

Shah, Raffique. "Reflections on the Mutiny and Trial." In Ryan and Stewart, *Black Power Revolution*, 509–22.

Sharpe, Christina. *In the Wake: On Blackness and Being.* Durham, NC: Duke University Press, 2016.

Sherwood, Marika. *Origins of Pan-Africanism: Henry Sylvester Williams, Africa, and the African Diaspora.* New York: Routledge, 2011.

Sidbury, James, and Jorge Cañizares-Esguerra. "Mapping Ethnogenesis in the Early Modern Atlantic." *William and Mary Quarterly* 68, no. 2 (April 2011): 181–208.

Simpson, George Eaton. "The Acculturative Process in Trinidadian Shango." *Anthropological Quarterly* 37, no. 1 (1964): 16–27.

Simpson, George Eaton. *Religious Cults of the Caribbean: Trinidad, Jamaica, and Haiti.* Buenos Aires: Institute of Caribbean Studies, 1970.

Simpson, George Eaton. "The Shango Cult in Nigeria and in Trinidad." *American Anthropologist* 64, no. 6 (1962): 1204–19.

Smart, Ninian. *Dimensions of the Sacred: An Anatomy of the World's Beliefs.* Berkeley: University of California Press, 1996.

Smith, Jonathan Z. *Imagining Religion: From Babylon to Jonestown.* Chicago: University of Chicago Press, 1988.

Smith, Jonathan Z. *Map Is Not Territory: Studies in the History of Religions.* Chicago: University of Chicago Press, 1978.

Smith, Michael. *West Indian Family Structure.* Seattle: University of Washington Press, 1962.

Sodré, Muniz. *O Terreiro e a Cidade: A Forma Social Negra-Brasileira.* Salvador, Brazil: Secretaria da Cultura e Turismo/Imago, 2002.

Somé, Sobonfu. *The Spirit of Intimacy: Ancient African Teaching in the Ways of Relationships.* New York: HarperCollins, 2002.

Southern, Eileen. *The Music of Black Americans: A History*. New York: W. W. Norton, 1997.

Spillers, Hortense. "Mama's Baby, Papa's Maybe: An American Grammar Book." *Diacritics* 17, no. 2 (Summer 1987): 65–81.

Springer, Pearl Eintou. "Orisa and the Spiritual Baptist Religion in Trinidad and Tobago." In Sankeralli, *At the Crossroads*, 85–107.

Stevens, Patricia. *The Spiritual Baptist Church: African New World Religious History, Identity & Testimony*. London: Karnak House, 1999.

Stewart, Dianne M. *Black Women, Black Love: America's War on African American Marriage*. New York: Seal Press, 2020.

Stewart, Dianne M. *Three Eyes for the Journey: African Dimensions of the Jamaican Religious Experience*. New York: Oxford University Press, 2005.

Stewart, Dianne M. "Weapons of the Spirit: Distilling the Science of Obeah and Other Powers of Engagement." Unpublished manuscript, last modified June 19, 2016.

Stewart Diakité, Dianne "'Matricentric' Foundations of Africana Women's Religious Practices of Peacebuilding, Sustainability and Social Change." *Bulletin of Ecumenical Theology* 25 (2013): 61–79.

Stewart Diakité, Dianne, and Tracey Hucks. "Africana Religious Studies: Toward a Transdisciplinary Agenda in an Emerging Field." *Journal of Africana Religions* 1, no. 1 (2013): 28–77.

Stewart, Robert. *Religion and Society in Post-Emancipation Jamaica*. Knoxville: University of Tennessee Press, 1992.

Stuckey, Sterling. *Slave Culture: Nationalist Theory and the Foundations of Black America*. New York: Oxford University Press, 1987.

Sutton, Paul. *Forged from the Love of Liberty: Selected Speeches of Dr. Eric Williams*. New York: Longman, 1981.

Sweet, James. *Domingos Álvares, African Healing, and the Intellectual History of the Atlantic World*. Chapel Hill: University of North Carolina Press, 2011.

Sweet, James. "The Quiet Violence of Ethnogenesis." *William and Mary Quarterly* 68, no. 2 (April 2011): 209–14.

Tandberg, Håkon. *Relational Religion: Fires as Confidants in Parsi Zoroastrianism*. Göttingen, Germany: Vandenhoeck & Ruprecht, 2019.

Tanna, Laura. *Jamaican Folk Tales and Oral Histories*. Corona, CA: DLT Associates Inc., 2000.

Taylor, Patrick. *Nation Dance: Religion, Identity, and Cultural Difference in the Caribbean*. Bloomington: Indiana University Press, 2001.

Teelucksingh, Jerome. "The Black Power Movement in Trinidad and Tobago." *Black Diaspora Review* 4, no. 2 (Winter 2014): 160–61.

Teelucksingh, Jerome. "The Good, the Bad, and the Ugly: Eric Williams and the Labor Movement in Trinidad and Tobago, 1955–1981." In *The Legacy of Eric Williams: Into the Postcolonial Moment*, edited by Tanya Shields, 126–48. Jackson: University Press of Mississippi, 2015.

Teelucksingh, Jerome. *Ideology, Politics, and Radicalism of the Afro-Caribbean*. New York: Palgrave Macmillan, 2016.

Thornton, John. *Africa and Africans in the Making of the Atlantic World: 1400–1800*. Cambridge: Cambridge University Press, 1998.

Treuer, David. *The Heartbeat of Wounded Knee: Native America from 1890 to the Present*. New York: River Head Books, 2019.

Trinidad and Tobago Election Centre. "Trinidad and Tobago General Election Results—24 September 1956." Caribbean Elections. Updated August 5, 2021. http://www.caribbeanelections.com/tt/elections/tt_results_1956.asp.

Trotman, David. *Crime in Trinidad: Conflict and Control in a Plantation Society, 1838–1900*. Knoxville: University of Tennessee Press, 1986.

Trotman, David. "Reflections on the Children of Shango: An Essay on a History of Orisa Worship in Trinidad." *Slavery and Abolition* 28, no. 2 (August 2007): 211–34.

Turner, Richard Brent. *Islam in the African-American Experience*. Bloomington: Indiana University Press, 2003.

Tutu, Desmond. "Whither African Theology." In *Christianity in Independent Africa*, edited by E. Fasholé-Luke, R. Gray, A. Hastings, and G. Tasie, 364–69. London: Rex Collings, 1978.

Tweed, Thomas. *Crossing and Dwelling: A Theory of Religion*. Cambridge, MA: Harvard University Press, 2006.

Usuanlele, Uyilawa. "Tracing the African Origins of Obeah (Obia): Some Conjectures and Inferences from the History of Benin Kingdom." *West Bohemian Historical Review* 6, no. 2 (2016): 165–84.

Valley, Joseph, dir. *Black Power Revolution: Trinidad and Tobago 1970—Let the Truth Be Told*. DVD. Trinidad and Tobago: J'Angelo Productions, 2012.

Van der Leeuw, Gerardus. *Religion in Essence and Manifestation*. Translated by J. E. Turner. Princeton, NJ: Princeton University Press, 1986.

Van Dijk, Frank Jan. "Chanting down Babylon Outernational: The Rise of Rastafari in Europe, the Caribbean, and the Pacific." In *Chanting down Babylon: The Rastafari Reader*, edited by Nathaniel Samuel Murrell, William David Spencer, and Adrian Anthony McFarlane, 178–98. Philadelphia: Temple University Press, 1998.

Van Gennep, Arnold. *The Rites of Passage*. Hove, UK: Psychology Press, 2004.

Vansina, Jan. *Paths in the Rainforests*. Madison: University of Wisconsin Press, 1991.

Vélez, María. *Drumming for the Gods: The Life and Times of Felipe García Villamil, Santero, Palero, and Abakuá*. Philadelphia: Temple University Press, 2000.

Wang, Yong. "Agency: The Internal Split of Structure." *Sociological Forum* 23, no. 3 (September 2008): 481–502.

Warner, W. Lloyd, and Paul S. Lunt. *The Social Life of a Modern Community*. New Haven, CT: Yale University Press, 1941.

Warner-Lewis, Maureen. *Guinea's Other Suns: The African Dynamic in Trinidad Culture*. Fitchburg: Majority Press, 1991.

Warner-Lewis, Maureen. *Trinidad Yoruba: From Mother-Tongue to Memory*. Tuscaloosa: University of Alabama Press, 2009.

Warner-Lewis, Maureen. "Yoruba Religion in Trinidad—Transfer and Reinterpretation." *Caribbean Quarterly* 24, no. 3/4 (1978): 18–32.

Warren, Calvin. "Black Care." *Liquid Blackness: Black Ontology and the Love of Blackness* 3, no. 6 (December 2016): 36–47.

Warren, Calvin. "Black Nihilism and the Politics of Hope." *CR: The New Centennial Review* 15, no. 1 (2015): 215–48.

Warren, Calvin. "Black Time: Slavery, Metaphysics, and the Logic of Wellness." In *The Psychic Hold of Slavery: Legacies in American Expressive Culture*, edited by Soyica Diggs Colbert, Robert Patterson, and Aida Levy-Hussen, 55–68. New Brunswick, NJ: Rutgers University Press, 2016.

Warren, Calvin. *Ontological Terror: Blackness, Nihilism, and Emancipation*. Durham, NC: Duke University Press, 2018.

Washington, Booker T. *Up from Slavery: An Autobiography*. New York: Doubleday, Page & Company, 1907.

Weems, Clenora Hudson. *Africana Womanism: Reclaiming Ourselves*. New York: Routledge, 2020.

Weisenfeld, Judith. *New World A-Coming: Black Religion and Racial Identity during the Great Migration*. New York: New York University Press, 2016.

Wilderson, Frank. *Red, White, and Black: Cinema and the Structure of US Antagonisms*. Durham, NC: Duke University Press, 2010.

Williams, Chancellor. *The Destruction of Black Civilization: Great Issues of a Race from 4500 B.C. to 2000 A.D.* Chicago: Third World Press, 1987.

Williams, Delores. *Sisters in the Wilderness: The Challenge of Womanist God-Talk*. Maryknoll, NY: Orbis Books, 1993.

Wilson, Peter. "Reputation and Respectability: A Suggestion for Caribbean Ethnology." *Man* 4, no. 1 (1969): 70–84.

Winer, Lise, ed. *Dictionary of the English/Creole of Trinidad & Tobago: On Historical Principles*. Montreal: McGill-Queen's University Press, 2008.

Wood, Donald. *Trinidad in Transition: The Years after Slavery*. New York: Oxford University Press, 1986.

Worcester, Kent. *C. L. R. James: A Political Biography*. Albany, NY: State University of New York Press, 1995.

Wynter, Sylvia. "Unsettling the Coloniality of Being/Power/Truth/Freedom: Towards the Human, after Man, Its Overrepresentation—An Argument." *CR: The New Centennial Review* 3, no. 3 (Fall 2003): 257–337.

Yai, Olabiyi. "African Diasporan Concepts and Practice of the Nation and Their Implications in the Modern World." In *African Roots/American Cultures: Africa in the Creation of the Americas*, edited by Sheila S. Walker, 244–65. Lanham, MD: Rowman & Littlefield, 2001.

Index

Du Bois, W. E. B., 128, 215, 236–37, 239–41, 285n110, 300n30
Duennes (spirits), 45–46

East Indians in Trinidad, 96–98, 102
Eastman, Baba Rudolph, 72–74, 149
economic conditions: Trinidad labor movement and, 96–97, 102–4
ecumenicalism in Trinidad and Tobago, 171–72
Edwards, Gary, 60
Ẹ́rìndínlógún orature-literature, 61–62
Egbe Onisin Eledumare (EOE) spiritual organization and shrine, 6; African identity and, 84–85, 185; Black Power and, 106–7; Carnival and, 123–28; commodified creation in Black religion and, 135–41, 287n151; nation building and, 128–34; Orisa Olokun festival and, 121–23; Orisa tradition and, 118–28, 208, 287n151; Plus I Yoruba diaspora theology and, 141–45
Egbe Orisa Ile Wa (EOIW), 153–55, 223
Egungun masquerade, 143, 178–82, 185, 287n157, 291n50
Èjì Ogbè (Odù narrative), 59
Elder, J. D., 72, 298n3
elekes (sacred beaded necklaces), 147, 288n3
Eliade, Mircea, 297n112
Elliott, Ebenezer (Pa Neezer), 6, 41, 64, 66, 152, 155, 189–90, 293n79, 295n107
Ellis, Alfred Burdon, 35, 39, 229–30, 276n43
El Segundo Encuentro Internacional Yoruba, xiii
Ẹ̀mí (Orisa deity), 58–59
The Emperor of Ocean Park (Carter), 235
Eniyan Wa shrine, 177–88, 208, 292n70
environmental sustainability: Iya Sangowunmi's promotion of, 196
Equiano, Olaudah, 41, 49–50, 263n43
Espinet, Charles Sydney, 45, 265n75
Esu Odara (Orisa deity), 60, 127–28, 181. *See also* Osetura (Esu) (Pataki deity)
"Esu Wielder of Protocol" (Iyalode Sangowunmi [Patricia McLeod]), 60–61
ethnicity: Western concepts of, 262n32; Yoruba concept of, 19–26, 50–51

Ewe Vodu, 77
Excelent, Diligent, 15
Exodus! (Glaude), 301n37

Fadipẹ, Nathaniel, 65, 67
family. *See* kinship/family
Fanon, Frantz, 136
Falola, Toyin, 295n105
February Revolution of 1970 (Trinidad), 103–4
Fernheimer, Janice, 136
Fields, Barbara, 234–35, 243, 300n30
Fields, Karen, 234–35, 243, 300n30
Forde, Clarence, 157, 177, 181
Forten, James, 302n47
401 Meets 2001 Carnival band, 143
Fourshey, Cymoune, 230
Francis, Mojunta, 190, 225
Frazier, Edward Franklin, xiv, 128, 235, 238–40, 285n110, 301n43
free Africans in Trinidad: class structure and, 96; kinship/family structures of, 81; pre-Yoruba identity among, 42–43, 261n26, 263n45; transnational identities among, 48–51, 261n23; Yoruba links to, 28–33, 259n2
Friedson, Steven, 77

García Peña, Lorgia, 188
Garden, Alexander, 235
Garvey, Marcus, 101–2
Gelede festival, 181, 188, 292n70
gender: African concepts of, 299n16
genealogy: in Yoruba-Orisa tradition, 55, 57–62
Ghana: Asante culture in, 46
Gibbons, Rawle, 55–56, 149, 156, 290n30
Gilkes, Cheryl Townsend, 228–29
Gimmey, Magdelaine, 15
Gimmey, Pierre, 15
Gimmey, Silveste, 15
Gimmey, Marie, 15
Glaude, Eddie, 301n37
Glazier, Steven, 26, 27, 31, 41, 277n69
Gois Dantas, Beatriz, 20
Gomez, Michael, 229
Gonzales, Rhonda, 230
Gozen ceremony (Rada culture), 45

Mandingo identity: of Trinidad Africans, 49

"Manifestation of Wêrê in Trinidad Shango" (Espinet), 265n75

Manning, Patrick, 285n116

Maparyan, Layli, 149, 152, 214, 297n141

Maraj, Bhadase Sagan, 97

marriage customs: Iya Sangowunmi's rite for, 203–8, 294n98; motherness and, 228–33; Yoruba-Orisa kinship structure and, 67–68

Martin, Tony, 101

mas bands: Black Power movement and launching of, 108–10; Carnival and, 124–28

Mason, John, 60

Massetungi, Oloye Ogundare Ife Olakela (Oludari): African religious nationalism and, 132, 134; on Black Power, 106–7; on Carnival, 144–46; on Egbe Onisin Eledumare, 118–21, 123–28, 130; on healing and healthcare, 140; nationhood and, 200–201; Orisa practices and, 193

Mati structures, 228

Matory, J. Lorand, 20–21, 262n30, 263n40

Matthews, Donald, 244, 302n54

Mays, Benjamin, 237, 239

Mbeki, Thabo, 140

McLeod, Isaac T., 293n93

McLeod, Patricia. See Iyalode Sangowunmi (Patricia McLeod)

McNeal, Keith, 38, 141

micronation (micro-nation) heritage: Yoruba identity and, 19–26, 56–57, 64–65

Millette, James, 103

Miscellaneous Laws Act 2000 (Trinidad and Tobago), 298n5

Mischel, Frances (aka Henry), 36–38, 70

missionaries: severance from Orisa by, 34; Yoruba nationhood in diaries of, 21, 25–28

Monseque, Arthur, 157

Morris, Elias Camp, 237–38

Mother Bethel's Black Legion, 88, 239, 302n47

motherness. See also Yemoja (motherhood): grounding in, 219–20; heritage

love and, 214–19; Iya Sangowunmi's nation-building ministries as, 195–208; legacy-building and, 171–93, 228; NCOE composition and structure and, 161–71; salvation story and, 231–33; seniority and ruling under, 153–71; transcontextual, transhistorical aspects of, 228–33; womanism of Iya Sangowunmi and, 208–13; in Yoruba-Orisa tradition, 4, 6–7, 145–46, 149–52

multicultural, multinational, multi-nation-al, and multireligious heritages: Africana religions and, 43–51, 222–28; syncretism in Yoruba-Orisa tradition and, 52–57

Muñoz, José, 216

Mutope, Apoesho, 111–12, 114–15, 283n75, 283n83

Nago culture: African interpretations of, 260n16; in Brazil, 22; Candomblé and, 232; slaves identified as, 15

Nash, Jennifer, 215, 245–46, 297n141

National Council of Orisa Elders (NCOE), 7, 290n33; founding of, 191; Inter-Religious Organization and, 172; seniority and ruling order in, 153, 155–71, 290n30

nation-al identity (nation, nationhood, nation-al): African constructions of, xvi–xvii, 8, 17–18, 258n1, 259n6, 261n23, 276n43; African heritage religions and, 40, 128–34, 222–28, 262n30, 262n38; Black Power movement and, 115–22; definitions of African identity and, 83–84; ethnicity as separate from, 6, 19–26; European terminology for, 20; kinship/family and, 77–82; matricentric tradition and, 7; multicultural, multinational, multi-nation-al, and multireligious identities and, 43–51; Olokun (Ase Odun Olokun) festival and, 121–23; Orisa power and Black Power and, 105–18; religious nationalism and, 128–34; of Sangowunmi, 193–208; Western concepts of, 262n32; women as keepers of, 147–52, 185–88; Yoruba-Orisa tradition and, 4, 6, 10, 16–17, 19–26

Orisa tradition. *See also* Yoruba-Orisa
tradition: Black Power movement
and, 106–18, 283n90; campaigns for
official recognition of, 14; Carnival
and, 125–28; census of Trinidad/To-
bago practitioners, 160–71, 290n37,
303nn8–9; colonial persecution of,
91–95; community of Powers in, 37–40,
52, 57–62; in Cuba, 61; custom labeling of, 14; early research on, 15–18;
Egbe Onisin Eledumare (EOE) and,
118–28; evolution in Trinidad of, 1–8,
10, 271n119; grounding in, 219–20;
kinship/family and social belonging in,
4, 6, 55–62; matricentric tradition and
legacy in, 7; Nigerian roots of, 4, 36–40,
45, 155–56, 173–74; Obeah link to, 4,
11–12, 223–28; past, present and future
of, 145–46; repression of, 223–28; seniority and rules in, 153–71; sovereignty
rituals in, 31–33; statistics on devotees
of, 118; transitions in, 145–46; women
in, xvi–xviii, 147–52
Orisa World Congress, 153, 173, 178, 191
Orisa Youths Cultural Organization
(OYCO), 37, 39
Òrokò (Orisa deity), 60
Orsi, Robert, 257n4
orthography and terminology, xi–xii
Orunmila (Orisa deity), 60, 295n103
Osetura (Esu) (Patakí deity), 61
Oshitólá, Babaláwo Kóláwolé, 186
Oshun shrine, 175, 288n6
Osogbo Yorùbá kinship system, 67
Òsóòsì (hunter), 60, 181
Òsun (river), 60, 175–77, 184, 195–96
Osun Abiadama School, 196, 208, 223,
293n87
Òsùpá (moon), 60
Otherworldliness, 218–19, 296n129,
297n136
Ouga Attehah (market of the dead), 62
Oxosi (Yoruba Orisa), 231–33
Oya (winds), 60, 181, 184, 285n112
Oyeku Meji (Carnival Queen), 127–28
Oyěwùmí, Oyèrónke, 67–68, 151, 230,
276n42
Òyó Empire, collapse of, 56–57

Òyó culture, Iya Sangowunmi's concept
of, 201; Yoruba nationhood and, 21,
31–33, 36–40
Òyó Mèsì (advisory board), 33
Oyotunji African Village (Sheldon, South
Carolina), 131–34, 140, 180, 182, 201–2

Padmore, George (Malcolm Ivan Meredith
Nurse), 100–101
palais structure: religious syncretism in,
75; as Yoruba nationhood symbol, 27–33,
265n75
Palmer, Tyrone, 216, 296n129
Pan-African Conference, 100
Pan-Africanism: Black Power Move-
ment and, 100–104, 108–18; Egbe
Onisin Eledumare (EOE) and, 118–28;
Sangowunmi and, 193–95, 201–8; in
Trinidad, 88–89, 100–101; Yoruba-Orisa
culture and, 45
Panday, Basdeo, 132, 134
Patakí, sacred narrative of, 61–62
Paton, Diana, 86
patriarchal leadership structures: African
motherness and, 229; Yoruba-Orisa
motherness as alternative to, 171
patrilocal residences in Trinidad: kinship/
family ties and, 66–67
Patterson, Orlando, 101, 259n1
Paul, Emil, 80
Peel, J. D. Y., 21, 263n40
Penagos, Elaine, 287n144
People's Democratic Party (PDP), 97
People's National Movement (PNM), 97,
103, 285n116
performativity: of Carnival, 125–28; in
Yoruba-Orisa tradition, 175
Persad-Bissessar, Kamla, 224
Phills, Baba Sam, 3, 91, 94–95, 145–46,
152, 157, 189, 225
Picton, Thomas (Sir), 89–90, 227
pluralism in Trinidad: of postemancipa-
tion community, 13–14
plurination, nationhood and, 19
Plus I Yoruba diaspora theology, 141–45
politics: Africana nation-building and,
131–34, 223–28; motherness and, 150;
Trinidad labor movement and, 96–104

Port-of-Spain Coloured Association, 101
Port of Spain Gazette, 23, 43, 86–88
Portuguese Madeirans in Trinidad, 96, 98
Powell, John Enoch, 282n71
power: coloniality of, 139–41; community of Powers, in Orisa tradition, 37–40, 52, 57–62; motherness and dynamics of, 229; Orisa as term for, 273n160; Orisa seniority and rule procedures and, 155–71; Yoruba-Orisa Powers in Black Power Movement, 104–18
pre-Yoruba groups: colonial and missionary framing of, 21–22; Dahomey links with, 47–48; micronation heritages of, 56–57; *nation* identity of, 17–18, 27, 42–43, 261n26
Protestantism: kinship, seniority and belonging in Yoruba-Orisa culture and, 63–71

race and racism: Africana *nation-building* and, 131–34, 285n113; black theology and, 234–36; ethnicity and nationhood and, 19–26; Trinidad class structure and, 96–99
Racecraft (Fields), 234–35
"A Rada Community in Trinidad" (Carr), 45
Rada culture: Black Power movement and, 283n90; Carnival and, 125–28; Gozen ceremony in, 45; Herskovits's research on, 26; in Trinidad, 9, 11, 43, 260n9, 272n143; Yoruba-Orisa and influence of, 45–51, 225, 294n95
Rawlings, Baba Neal Ryan, 172
"Reflections on the Children of Shango: An Essay on a History of Orisa Worship in Trinidad" (Trotman), 14–15
Register of Trinidad Plantation Slaves, St. Magdelaine plantation, 15–16
relational poetics, 175; kinship/family structures and, 58, 274n15
relation politics: Africana religious studies and, 222–28, 257n9
religious imagination: African Caribbean, 150; of African descendants, 233, black, xvi, xvii, 7, 8, 233, Orisa, 42, 55
religious freedom: labor campaign for, 97
ring shout, 242, 302n50

Roberts, J. Deotis, 214, 233–34
Roberts, Kevin, 78, 277n58
Robinson, A. N. R., 285n116
Robinson, Carol, 178
Rodney, Ijoye Elizabeth Melvina: Elliott (Pa Neezer) as spiritual father of, 295n107; National Council of Religious Elders and, 153–71, 290n30; as Orisa spiritual leader, 147, 149, 190, 199, 224, 289n27; womanist ministry of, 208, 210–13, 218
Rodney, Walter, 101
Roots of a Black Future: Family and Church and Africentric Christianity (Roberts), 234

sacred poetics/sacred narrative: Africana nation-building and, 221–22; genealogical and social details in, 61–62; North American Africa diaspora and, 233–36; Plus I Yoruba diaspora theology and, 143–45; seniority and kinship in, 4, 6, 55–57, 62–71; syncretism in, 53–57; Yoruba-Orisa tradition and, 5, 41–51, 57–62
Saidi, Christine, 230
Said I Wasn't Gonna Tell Nobody (Cone), 233
saints, cult of: kinship, seniority and belonging in Yoruba-Orisa culture and, 63–71, 73–77
Sakpata (Sagbata) (Rada deity), 47, 197–99, 272n138, 292n56
Salvador, Candomblé in, 232
Sampson, Arthur, 44
Samuel, Paulina, 10–12, 41, 85, 88–89
Ṣàngó (thunder and lightning), 30–40, 60, 184, 205–8, 265n66, 265n73, 268n103, 271n1
Sango/Osun Rain Festival, 196–97, 294n100, 296n115
Ṣàngó pípè (oral praise poetry), 33, 267n87
Sangowunmi Olakiitan Osunfunmilayo, Oregi Ajagbe Obagunle (Iyalode) (Patricia McLeod), 7, 60, 152, 193–213, 275n24; love politics of, 215, 218–19; nation-building of, 195–208; spiritual grounding in ministry of, 219–20; womanist activism of, 208–13

Sankeralli, Burton, 173, 175, 222–23
Santería tradition, 74–75, 277nn65–67
Saraka (thanksgiving and almsgiving) services, 196
Saunders, Cheryl, 215
Saunders, Francis, 189
Schön, James, 21
Schwab, William, 67
Scott, David, 63
secret societies, in Yoruba-Orisa culture, 64–66
seniority: in kinship/family lineages, 63–71; Orisa privilege and status determined by, 155–61, 171
Serrano, Assunta, 178, 291n52
Shah, Raffique, 98, 104, 114
"A Shango Religious Group and the Problem of Prestige in Trinidadian Society" (Mischel), 70–71
"'Shango' Is Not a Religion" (*Trinidad Guardian* letter), 12–13
Shango tradition: Black Power movement and, 115–18; Brereton's analysis of, 72; decline in Trinidad Yoruba-Orisa culture of, 41; defense of, 12–13; historical references to, 24–26; newspaper accounts of, 12–13; origins of, 33–40; Orisa religion and, 6; priestesses in, 178; religious persecution and, 86, 91–95; seniority and social belonging in, 70–71, 275n18, 278n82; in Trinidad, 2–3, 5, 35–36, 266n86; 270nn116–17; womanist scholarship on, xiii–xiv; Yoruba *nation-al* sovereignty and, 27–33
Sharpe, Christina, 296n129, 297n134
Shoponna (Yoruba deity), 47, 272n138
Shouters Prohibition Ordinance, 86–91, 97, 223–24, 280n17
Sierra Leone: Akoos in, 62; Yoruba subgroups in, 21
Simpson, George Eaton, xiii, 31, 72
situational ethics: in African religions, 90–91
slavery: branding and, 32, 266n81; commodification of creation and, 135–41; cultural memory and, 259n1; ethnicity and *nationhood* and, 20–26, 261n25; kinship, seniority and belonging in

Yoruba-Orisa culture and, 63–71; motherness and, 151–52; *nation* identity and, 259n6; North American African diaspora and, 234–36; registries of, 15–16; womanist heritage love and, 215–19; Yoruba-Orisa tradition and, 15–18
smallpox epidemic (Trinidad), 46–47, 272n139
Smith, Barbara, 296n124
social belonging: Black church and, 236–44; decolonization politics and, 106; interruptive invention of, 136–41; kinship/family and, 4, 6, 52–82; *nationhood* and, 77–82; seniority and kinship and, 62–71; womanist heritage love politics and, 217–19; Yoruba-Orisa tradition and, 4, 6, 55–57
social hierarchy in Trinidad, 96
Societies of St. Peter and St. John, 264n57
soul complex, in Yoruba-Orisa tradition, 194
"The Souls of Black Folk" (Brereton), 72
Southern Liberation Movement (SLM), 103
sovereignty: African religious *nationalism* and, 131–34; Black church and, 237–38; decolonial scholarship on, 260n7; Iya Sangowunmi's concept of, 201; Yoruba-Orisa tradition and, 4, 6, 10, 21–22; Yoruba rituals of, 27–33
Spillers, Hortense, 214–15
Spiritual Baptist tradition: emergence in Trinidad of, 72, 74, 76, 171–72, 258n6; 279n9; grounding in, 219; religious persecution of, 88–91, 223–25, 280n19
Springer, Eintou Pearl, 117, 147, 171–73, 218, 223–25
St. James United (SJU), 108–10
St. John the Baptist: Shango associated with, 25, 37–40
suffrage campaign in Trinidad, 96–97
sugar industry: decline in Trinidad of, 96–97
suicide: disputed status in Yoruba culture of, 33–37, 267n89
Summary Offences Act (SOA, 1921), 223–24, 298n5
Sunjata, epic of, 229

Weems, Clenora Hudson, 289n21, 297n141
Weldon Johnson, James, 239
Wèrè (spiritual experience), 45–46
West Africa: free Africans from, 42–43; kinship/family structures in, 81; Rada-Yoruba exchange in, 45; Vodun in, 47–51; Yoruba nationhood evolution in, 22
Western Enlightenment: Black religion and, 137–38
West India Regiment, 96
West India Royal Commission (WIRC), 97
Williams, Delores, 214–15
Williams, Eric, 97, 102–4, 107–8
Williams, Henry Sylvester, 100–101
"Wither Sango? An Inquiry into Sango's 'Authenticity' and Prominence in the Caribbean" (Glazier), 27
womanist activism: Africana religion and, xiii–xviii, 7–8; black affect and heritage love and, 214–19; motherness and, 6–7, 145–46; of Sangowunmi, 208–13, 193?; terminology of, 289n21; Yoruba-Orisa tradition and, 147–52
The Womanist Idea (Maparyan), 214
The Womanist Reader (Maparyan), 149
Wong Ka (Chinese deity), 52
Wood, Donald, 16
Wynter, Sylvia, 139

Yai, Olabiyi, 17, 80, 241–43
Yaraba identity: colonial construction of Yoruba as, 9–11, 24–25, 41–42, 224–25; Yaraba Creoles and, 43–44; creole Yarabas and, 271n125
"Yé! Ekún ara wa la mí sun" (Yoruban dirge), 32–33
Yẹmọja (motherhood), 60, 181, 184, 275n22
Yomi Yomi, 178
Yoruba-Ifa: in United States, 226
Yorùbá language: orthography and terminology, xi–xii

Yoruba-Orisa tradition. See also Orisa tradition: Africana elements in sovereignty of, 27–33; African nation-building and, 20–26; African religious persecution and, 85–95; African Trinidadian awareness of, 12–13; Black Power Movement and, 2–6, 37, 39–40, 81–82, 102–18, 262n35; Christian and Catholic elements in, 3–8, 33–40, 264n57, 264n59; colonial misidentification of, 9–12, 14–16; cultural memory in, 33–40; Dahomean culture and, 25–26, 45–51; demographic categories on Trinidad census and, 160–71, 290n37, 303nn8–9; diaspora theology, 141–45; drazon litanies in, 48; early research on, 15–18, 25–26; Egbe Onisin Eledumare and, 118–28; ethnicity and nationhood in, 19–26, 263n40; familial logics and symbol management and use in, 71–77; heritages and legacies of, 41–51, 262n30; kinship/family in, 4, 6, 55–57, 62–71; legitimation campaign in Trinidad for, 155–71; motherness love politics in, 216–19; mothers rule and seniority in, 153–71; orthography and terminology, xi–xii, 261n26; past, present and future of, 145–46; in postemancipation community, 13–15; prereflexive norms of, 10; public acceptance in Trinidad of, 226–28; Rada culture and, 45–51; religious persecution and, 85–95; sacred narrative in, 33–40, 57–62; songs in, 266n80, 268n103; sovereignty and nationhood in, 6; suicide in, 33; syncretism in, 52–57; transitions in, 145–46; in Trinidad and Tobago, xiii, xvii–xviii, 1–8, 10; women and, 147–52
Yoruba paradigm: African vs. American-Caribbean variants, 120–23
The Yoruba-Speaking Peoples of the Slave Coast of West Africa (Ellis), 35
Young Men's Coloured Association, 101